The Right Women

The Right Women

Republican Party Activists, Candidates, and Legislators

Malliga Och and Shauna L. Shames, Editors

Gender Matters in U.S. Politics
Juliet A. Williams, Series Editor

BLOOMSBURY ACADEMIC
NEW YORK • LONDON • OXFORD • NEW DELHI • SYDNEY

BLOOMSBURY ACADEMIC
Bloomsbury Publishing Inc
1385 Broadway, New York, NY 10018, USA
50 Bedford Square, London, WC1B 3DP, UK
29 Earlsfort Terrace, Dublin 2, Ireland

BLOOMSBURY, BLOOMSBURY ACADEMIC and the Diana logo
are trademarks of Bloomsbury Publishing Plc

First published in the United States of America by ABC-CLIO 2018
Paperback edition published by Bloomsbury Academic 2024

Cover photo: American Republican elephant vector. (Skunkeye/Shutterstock)
Jacket design by Silverander Communications

Library of Congress Cataloging-in-Publication Data
Names: Och, Malliga, editor. | Shames, Shauna Lani, editor.
Title: The right women : Republican party activists, candidates, and legislators /
Malliga Och and Shauna L. Shames, editors.
Description: Santa Barbara, California : Praeger, an Imprint of ABC-CLIO, LLC, [2018] |
Series: Gender matters in U.S. politics | Includes bibliographical references and index.
Identifiers: LCCN 2017041540 (print) | LCCN 2017054332 (ebook) |
ISBN 9781440851636 (eBook) | ISBN 9781440851629 (hardcopy : alk. paper)
Subjects: LCSH: Women—Political activity—United States—History. |
Women legislators—United States—History. | Republican Party (U.S. : 1854-)—History. |
Conservatism—United States—History.
Classification: LCC HQ1236.5.U6 (ebook) | LCC HQ1236.5.U6 R54 2018 (print) |
DDC 305.42—dc23
LC record available at https://lccn.loc.gov/2017041540

ISBN: HB: 978-1-4408-5162-9
PB: 979-8-7651-3447-4
ePDF: 978-1-4408-5163-6
eBook: 979-8-2161-3984-3

Series: Gender Matters in U.S. Politics

To find out more about our authors and books visit www.bloomsbury.com
and sign up for our newsletters.

To all the women of both major U.S. parties
who step up to make our communities
a better place for future generations

Contents

Series Foreword

From the nearly century-long campaign for women's suffrage, to ongoing contestation over reproductive rights, to 2012 presidential candidate Mitt Romney's meme-worthy claim of having "binders full of women," politics has been a central staging ground in the United States for debates about gender. The 2016 presidential campaign was no exception. For the first time in the nation's history, a woman received a major party nomination to head the ticket as candidate for president. As it happens, the Republican Party nominee also served as a lightning rod for discussions of gender issues, particularly in the days following revelations of his vulgar boasting about the sexual assault of women. The eventual outcome of the 2016 presidential election took many experts by surprise, revealing that many observers had badly misjudged how women would cast their votes. In the end, the 2016 campaign season confirmed not just the ongoing centrality of gender in U.S. politics, but that we still have a long way to go in understanding *how* gender matters—to each of us as individuals and as members of a shared polity.

The *Gender Matters in U.S. Politics* series pushes the boundaries of existing research on gender and politics. Traditionally, political scientists have engaged the subject of gender primarily by looking at differences in the way men and women behave—as voters, candidates, leaders, policy makers, activists, and citizens. Today, there is growing recognition—within the field of political science and beyond—of the critical need to think more broadly and more deeply about gender. Across the social sciences, researchers now recognize that gender is not only an individual attribute but a "socially constructed stratification system" that plays a central role in determining an individual's place in the social order."[1] At the same time, scholars are bringing a more intersectional perspective to the study of gender in recognition of the influence of race, sexuality, and other axes of social difference on gender identity and gender politics.[2] These new ways of conceptualizing gender have far-reaching implications for political scientists with interests in topics ranging from electoral behavior, to social movement mobilization, to media and politics.

The books in this series address a wide array of topics—from conservative women pundits to political cartoons—to demonstrate the far-reaching, and sometimes quite unexpected, ways that gender is mobilized in contemporary political discourse. Some authors bring new insight to the study of gender in familiar settings, such as grassroots political campaigning. Others take a closer look at gender politics in less well-studied contexts, such as media coverage of political sex scandals—thereby reminding us that that politics doesn't stay neatly within the boundaries of official institutions. And while some books in this series highlight the persistence of gender inequalities, others draw attention to the distinctive ways women's political roles have changed in the wake of second-wave political activism and legal reforms as well as technological advances that have given new forms of voice and visibility to historically marginalized groups.

Finally, while the terms "women and politics" and "gender and politics" have in the past sometimes been used synonymously, the authors in this series emphasize that gender impacts the lives of women *and* men. The books presented in this series are intended to inform, engage, and inspire readers to think in new ways about issues of deep importance to all of us. In making clearly written, empirically grounded, and thoughtfully argued research available to interested audiences, this series aims to spark conversation and produce new understanding.

—Juliet A. Williams
Department of Gender Studies, UCLA

NOTES

1. Barbara Risman, "Gender as a Social Structure: Theory Wrestling with Activism," *Gender & Society* 18 (2004): 429–450.

2. See, for example, Leslie McCall, "The Complexity of Intersectionality," *Signs* 30 (2005): 1771–1800.

Acknowledgments

We would like to first and foremost thank Political Parity and Swanee Hunt Alternatives, especially Swanee Hunt, Marni Allen, and Melissa Luna, as well as Sarah Lenti, for the initial Political Parity report "Primary Hurdles," out of which this book project grew. We also want to thank the original research team behind the "Primary Hurdles" report (Marni Allen, Stephen Eisele, Nadia Farjood, Bob Carpenter, Nicole McClesky, and several of the academic researchers whose work is published in this volume) for their initial work and research. Thank you to Dr. Shames's research assistants (alphabetically: Ian Biluck, Chelsea Coccia, Chakera Hightower, Annalisa Klein, and Daniel Wallsten) for their indispensable help in the past two years as this was being produced. We want to thank Jessica Gribble at Praeger, our fearless editor, and her team for making this volume a reality. Finally, we extend our deepest gratitude to the countless Republican activists, legislators, candidates, and officeholders who lent their expertise, insight, and time to the chapters in this volume.

Introduction

Kira Sanbonmatsu

The 2016 presidential election was one for the history books. As the election unfolded, one of the main narratives concerned the voting intentions of women. Women were not the only voting bloc under discussion; the voting intentions of Latinos, African Americans, and working-class whites, among other groups, were subjects of much analysis. And attention often focused on Republican women specifically. Would Republican women support Donald Trump? Or would they defect to Hillary Clinton?

The category of gender was unusually salient in the 2016 election. Hillary Clinton made history as the first female major party presidential nominee. But Donald Trump's campaign was also historic with respect to gender, albeit in some unintended ways. Trump's *Access Hollywood* audiotape, alleged sexual assault, and misogynist comments led to questions about the Republican Party's ability to compete for women voters.

The controversies surrounding Trump were unexpected and violated contemporary norms about gender. They were also surprising in light of contemporary Republican Party politics. In the postmortem to Mitt Romney's defeat in the 2012 presidential election, the Republican National Committee and Chairman Reince Priebus committed the party to more diverse outreach, including bolstering the party's standing with minority and female voters. Attracting diverse candidates, and not just voters, was part of this strategy. Addressing the continuing challenges the Republican Party faces with minority and female voters was to be the first step in readying the party for the next presidential election.

Republican women officeholders welcomed this opportunity to add to their numbers and forward a more positive message about their party. As officeholder data from the Center for American Women and Politics (CAWP) make plain, Democratic women maintain a significant edge over Republican women. As of 2017, Republican women constitute 25 percent of all female members of Congress and 38 percent of all female major party state legislators. Women are just under 10 percent of all Republican members of Congress and about 17 percent of Republican state legislators. A gender gap persists in the electorate in which women voters are more likely than men to prefer Democratic over Republican candidates.

Republican women have been taking steps to expand their ranks. With efforts such as Project GROW, View PAC, and She PAC, the Republican Party has sought to overcome its deficit of women candidates.[1] And Republican women have been eager to combat the Democratic Party's allegation that there is a "Republican War against Women." Although this slogan stems from policy differences between the two parties on reproductive rights issues, it reflects a larger competition between them around the question of which party is best able to represent women as a group. Insensitive comments about rape in the 2012 elections by Republican male candidates further fueled this image problem and were thought to undermine the Republican Party's ability to capture the U.S. Senate. During the 2016 election, Republican women often found themselves in the awkward position of once again defending their party in light of the sexism of a male candidate from their party.

As the Trump administration continues to unfold, Republican women are at a crossroads. The visibility of Republican women candidates and officeholders remains the most powerful challenge to the notion that the party is unresponsive or insensitive to women. Yet, Trump selected few women or minorities for his cabinet. Meanwhile, the Women's March on Washington brought hundreds of thousands of protesters to the district the day following Trump's inauguration, outnumbering the inauguration attendees the day before.[2] Marches across the country, and the world, united women in opposition to the new Republican president.

Scholars are at a crossroads as well. More than ever before, researchers are turning to the study of Republican women in politics. The case of Republican women offers an important area of investigation. First, scholarly attention to Republican women, and conservative women more generally, complicates core concepts and theories in the study of women and politics.[3] A large body of scholarship has sought to understand the consequences, if any, of having women in elective office, asking whether the presence of women legislators leads to the substantive representation of women. The underrepresentation of women in elective office prompts scholars to ask whether women officeholders feel a special responsibility to represent women voters and those issues that are of disproportionate concern to women. These inquiries pose a host of challenges to researchers because of the many ways that women's lives differ from each other, including by party. And whether a set of policies exists that can be labeled "women's issues" is made less clear when party and ideological differences among women are taken into account.

Second, just as attention to the intersectionality of race/ethnicity and gender brings a more complete and nuanced understanding of the category of gender, so too can attention to the ways that gender intersects with the category of political party. Scholars have shown the shortfalls of treating gender in isolation from other categories and called for more complex treatments of how gender intersects with race/ethnicity and other identities.[4]

Today's environment of party polarization (see Glossary) makes a party analysis of women's political activities increasingly necessary. As Democratic and Republican voters and officeholders become more distinct in their political views, party has become a more pronounced division among women as well. At the same time, studies show that gender persists as a significant category within legislative institutions even in a heightened era of party discipline.[5] How women from the Republican and Democratic Parties interact, and whether and when they find common ground as women, is an enduring question for the study of women's representation (see "Representation of Women," Glossary).[6]

Attention to the interaction and intersection of categories can reveal additional complexity within the category of Republican women. Ideological, religious, racial/ethnic, generational, and other factors operate within the sizable group of "Republican women." Scholars have analyzed what divides Democratic women from Republican women, and Republican women from Republican men, but they have also identified meaningful demarcations within Republican women as a group.[7]

Third, investigation of Republican women is inevitable simply because such a large proportion of American women identify with and support the Republican Party. As the authors of this volume explore, women are more Democratic than Republican. Exit polls from the 2016 election showed that more women than men supported Hillary Clinton, with an 11-point gender gap. Yet, while 54 percent of all women voted for Hillary Clinton for president, 42 percent of women voted for Donald Trump.[8]

Finally, although Democratic women constitute the majority of elected women officials and may attract more attention due to their numbers, the activities of Republican women elites are also significant. With the

Republican Party in control of the presidency and both chambers of Congress, as well as most state legislatures and governors' mansions, understanding how women operate within the Republican Party and with what effect becomes even more pressing for understanding contemporary American politics.

It surprises many that the Republican Party, historically, was strongly supportive of women's rights; support for women's suffrage and the Equal Rights Amendment (see Glossary) was more forthcoming from the Republican Party than the Democratic Party.[9] For most of the 20th century, Republican women state legislators outpaced Democratic women as a share of their party's officeholders.[10] It was a Republican woman, Senator Margaret Chase Smith of Maine (see Glossary), who in 1964 became the first woman to be considered for the presidency at a major party convention. Women were always active in Republican Party politics, even before they had the right to vote.[11]

As both party coalitions shifted over the first half of the 20th century and the second wave of the women's movement took shape, this correspondence between women's rights and party would change. The feminist activists who emerged in the 1960s and 1970s did so largely from the Democratic coalition, and their most vocal opponents—conservative women—had their home in the Republican Party. Over time, feminist activists within the Republican Party would find it increasingly difficult to wield influence at their party's conventions.[12] The parties' platforms of 1972, barely distinguishable from each other on women's rights, would become increasingly distinct in many ways in subsequent years. Today's party platforms, in which the two parties offer distinct positions on abortion and other women's rights issues, are surprising in light of the platforms' similarities in the early 1970s.[13]

The parties' positions on women's rights issues have consequences for women's access to elective office.[14] The Democratic Party boasts political action committees (PACs; see Glossary), such as EMILY's List, and a stronger ideological commitment to electing more women to public office.[15] Political parties can create candidates by encouraging women to run who might not otherwise have emerged.[16]

Early studies of the election of women to office did not focus on party differences among women. Instead, the emphasis was on factors that affected women's candidacies and levels of representation overall. And an implicit assumption of many studies was that gains for women were inevitable.[17]

Yet, stagnation in women's election to office at the state legislative and executive offices over the past two decades has led to a reconsideration of officeholding patterns.[18] Overall, data from the Center for American Women and Politics reveal that women are 19.4 percent of all members of Congress and 24.9 percent of all state legislators; just six women serve as governors.[19] As many of the coming essays discuss, party differences are apparent in these time trends; while women have stagnated as a share of Republican officeholders, women's share of Democratic officeholders has ticked upward. For example, the pattern in the U.S. House of Representatives reveals that Democratic women have grown as a percentage of all Democratic members, whereas the same is not true for Republican women within their conference (see Figure I.1).

These party differences take shape at the candidacy stage. As Figure I.2 shows, more Democratic women than Republican women have entered primaries for the U.S. House of Representatives and secured the nomination. Together, the data show that Republican women lag behind Democratic women in running for and holding office. It is not clear whether the situation of Republican women will improve in the future.

The chapters in this volume offer compelling, diverse, and timely perspectives on Republican women in politics. With rigorous and creative means, the authors address the roots of Republican women's

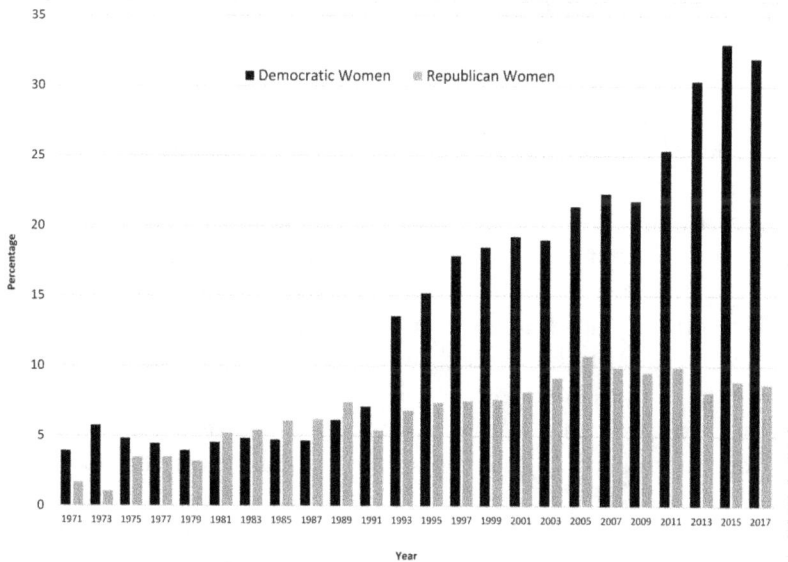

Figure I.1   Democratic Women Outpace Republican Women as a Percentage of Their Party's Caucus in the U.S. House of Representatives

Source: Center for American Women and Politics.

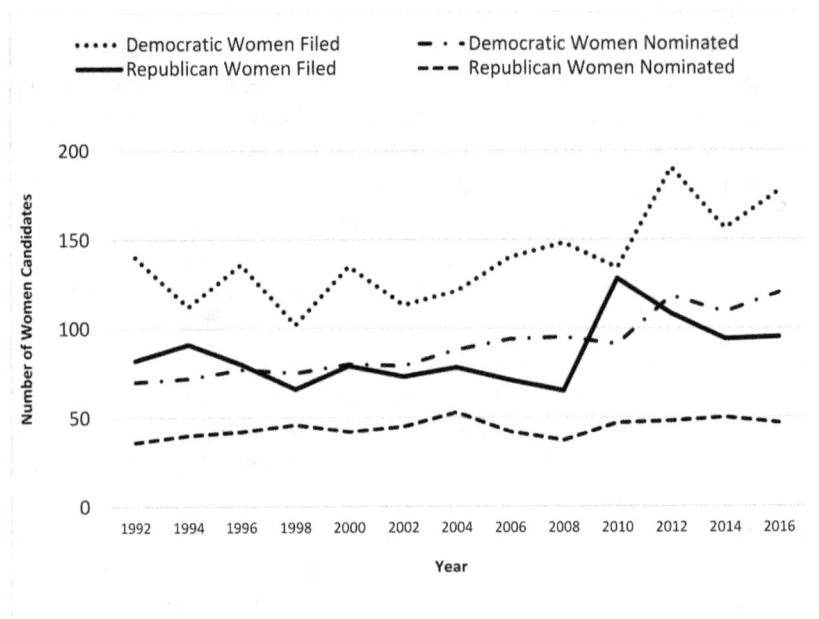

Figure I.2 Democratic Women Outnumber Republican Women as Candidates for the U.S. House of Representatives

Source: Center for American Women and Politics.

underrepresentation in elective office, the ideas and motivations that drive their activism and political behavior, and their connection to larger trends in American politics. In doing so, the authors pave the way for further analysis of how gender operates politically.

Malliga Och situates the study of Republican women within a comparative perspective and shows that conservative parties' efforts to win women voters is certainly not limited to the United States. Och asks whether the Republican Party has embarked on a process of "feminization" and whether the party's efforts are symbolic or substantive.

As women participate in the life of the Republican Party, they navigate Republican Party culture and are influenced by it. But as Catherine Wineinger's chapter on Congress indicates, Republican women are also putting their imprint on the party and striving for leadership positions. Wineinger's research shows us that Republican women engage in a form of identity politics as they campaign and legislate.

Melissa Deckman turns to the grassroots and the relationship between Tea Party women and the Republican Party. Her research provides a window into the activism of conservative women on the ground while also drawing on survey data to compare the policy attitudes of Tea Party and non–Tea Party women. Importantly, her analysis tackles Republican women's views on Trump and immigration.

Danielle M. Thomsen takes up changes in the ideology of congressional candidates over time. As her analysis makes plain, one consequence of polarization is the more difficult path to office facing moderates. Thomsen shows that men and women candidates of both parties have become more polarized.

The puzzle of why Republican women are outnumbered by both Republican men and Democratic women is taken up in the next set of chapters. Shauna L. Shames identifies primary elections as the most significant hurdle to increasing the presence of Republican women, emphasizing infrastructure and fund-raising challenges.

This theme continues in the contribution by Rosalyn Cooperman and Melody Crowder-Meyer. With original survey data of donors, they offer a unique analysis of one of the key differences dividing women by party: access to funding from women's PACs. Early funds are especially lacking for Republican women.

Turning to the most recent election cycle, Kelly Dittmar assesses Republican women's 2016 candidacies, including Carly Fiorina's presidential campaign. Finding that Republican women's officeholding declined after the election, Dittmar's analysis provides a sobering assessment of how women are faring in the Trump era.

While Republican women lag Democratic women in state legislative officeholding, the picture for Republican women varies across the United States. Among other implications, Laurel Elder's research points to the significance of ideology and region in shaping Republican women's access to office in the states. The state legislative arena is also the focus of H. Abbie Erler, who investigates the career patterns of women by party. Her comparison of women state representatives reveals the limited opportunities that Republican women face for higher office.

Once in office, Republican women navigate a complex environment that includes legislative institutions, their party conference, and various actors, such as interest groups and the media. As Michele L. Swers shows, party divisions within Congress are readily apparent on women's issues, including in the actions of women members on abortion and reproductive issues. Christina Xydias also considers women in Congress and analyzes the extent to which Republican women conform, or not, to the language used in their party's platform.

Finally, Ronnee Schreiber concludes the volume with a thematic assessment of the chapters and suggests directions for future research.

NOTES

1. Laurel Elder, "Contrasting Party Dynamics: A Three Decade Analysis of the Representation of Democratic versus Republican Women State Legislators" (paper presented at the American Political Science Association, Washington, DC, 2014).

2. Luz Lazo, "Women's March Helps Set Record for Public Transit across the Region," *Washington Post*, January 24, 2017, www.washingtonpost.com/news /dr-gridlock/wp/2017/01/24/womens-march-helps-set-record-for-public-transit -across-the-region.

3. Susan. J. Carroll, "Representing Women: Congresswomen's Perceptions of Their Representational Roles," in *Women Transforming Congress*, ed. Cindy. S. Rosenthal (Norman: University of Oklahoma Press, 2002), 50–68; Karen Beckwith, "Plotting the Path from One to the Other: Women's Interests and Political Representation," in *Representation: The Case of Women*, eds. Maria. C. Taylor-Robinson and Michelle M. Escobar-Lemmon (New York: Oxford University Press, 2014), 19–40; Karen Celis and Sarah Childs, *Gender, Conservatism and Political Representation* (Colchester, UK: ECPR Press, 2014).

4. Kimberlé Crenshaw, "Demarginalizing the Intersection of Race and Sex: A Black Feminist Critique of Antidiscrimination Doctrine, Feminist Theory and Antiracist Politics," *University of Chicago Legal Forum* 140 (1989): 139–167; Jane Junn and Nadia Brown, "What Revolution? Incorporating Intersectionality in Women and Politics," in *Political Women and American Democracy*, eds. Christina Wolbrecht, Karen Beckwith, and Lisa Baldez (New York: Cambridge University Press, 2008), 64–78.

5. Tracy L. Osborn, *How Women Represent Women: Political Parties, Gender, and Representation in the State Legislatures* (New York: Oxford University Press, 2012); Michele L. Swers, *Women in the Club: Gender and Policy Making in the Senate* (Chicago: University of Chicago Press, 2013); Kelly Dittmar, Kira Sanbonmatsu, and Susan J. Carroll, "The Challenges of Being a Woman in the 114th Congress" (paper presented at the American Political Science Association, Philadelphia, PA, September 1–4, 2016).

6. Michele L. Swers, *The Difference Women Make: The Policy Impact of Women in Congress* (Chicago: University of Chicago Press, 2002); Irwin N. Gertzog, *Women and Power on Capitol Hill: Reconstructing the Congressional Women's Caucus* (Boulder, CO: Lynne Rienner Publishers, 2004); Debra L. Dodson, *The Impact of Women in Congress* (Oxford: Oxford University Press, 2006).

7. Rebecca Klatch, *Women of the New Right* (Philadelphia: Temple University Press, 1987); Ronnee Schreiber, *Righting Feminism: Conservative Women and American Politics* (Oxford: Oxford University Press, 2008); Melissa Deckman, *Tea Party Women: Mama Grizzlies, Grassroots Leaders, and the Changing Face of the American Right* (New York: New York University Press, 2016); Tiffany Barnes and Erin Cassese, "American Party Women: A Look at the Gender Gap within Parties," *Political Research Quarterly* 70, no. 1 (2017): 127–141.

8. Center for American Women and Politics (CAWP), "Historic Gender Gap Isn't Enough to Propel Clinton to Victory in 2016 Presidential Race" (Center for American Women and Politics, Eagleton Institute of Politics, Rutgers University, New Brunswick, NJ, November 9, 2016).

9. Jo Freeman, "Whom You Know versus Whom You Represent: Feminist Influence in the Democratic and Republican Parties," in *The Women's Movements of the United States and Western Europe: Consciousness, Political Opportunity, and Public Policy*, eds. Mary Fainsod Katzenstein and Carol McClurg Mueller, (Philadelphia: Temple University Press, 1987), 215–244; Jo Freeman, *A Room at a Time: How Women Entered Party Politics* (Lanham, MD: Rowman & Littlefield, 2000); Christina Wolbrecht, *The Politics of Women's Rights: Parties, Positions, and Change* (Princeton, NJ: Princeton University Press, 2000); Kira Sanbonmatsu, *Democrats, Republicans, and the Politics of Women's Place* (Ann Arbor: University of Michigan Press, 2002); Corrine M. McConnaughy, *The Woman Suffrage Movement in America: A Reassessment* (New York: Cambridge University Press, 2013).

10. Elizabeth M. Cox, *Women State and Territorial Legislators, 1895–1995: A State-by-State Analysis, with Rosters of 6,000 Women* (Jefferson, NC: McFarland and Company, 1996).

11. Melanie Susan Gustafson, *Women and the Republican Party, 1854–1924* (Urbana: University of Illinois Press, 2001).

12. Freeman, "Whom You Know versus Whom You Represent."

13. Susan B. Hansen, *The Politics of Sex: Public Opinion, Parties and Presidential Elections* (New York: Routledge, 2014).

14. Susan. J. Carroll and Kira Sanbonmatsu, *More Women Can Run: Gender and Pathways to the State Legislatures* (New York: Oxford University Press, 2013).

15. Schreiber, *Righting Feminism*; Barbara C. Burrell, *Gender in Campaigns for the U.S. House of Representatives* (Ann Arbor: University of Michigan Press, 2014).

16. David Niven, "Party Elites and Women Candidates: The Shape of Bias," *Women and Politics* 19, no. 2 (1998): 57–80; Kira Sanbonmatsu, *Where Women Run: Gender and Party in the American States* (Ann Arbor: University of Michigan Press, 2006); Richard L. Fox and Jennifer Lawless, "If Only They'd Ask: Gender, Recruitment, and Political Ambition," *Journal of Politics* 72, no. 2 (2010): 310–326.

17. Carroll and Sanbonmatsu, *More Women Can Run*.

18. Laurel Elder, "Whither Republican Women: The Growing Partisan Gap among Women in Congress," *Forum* 6, no. 1 (2008); Carroll and Sanbonmatsu, *More Women Can Run*.

19. Center for American Women and Politics (CAWP), "Women in Elective Office 2017" (Center for American Women and Politics, National Information Bank on Women in Public Office, Eagleton Institute of Politics, Rutgers University, New Brunswick, NJ, 2017).

PART 1

Activists and Ideology

The role of political parties in a democracy is twofold. In elections, parties present voters with a menu of policy programs and directions for the country, giving voters a meaningful choice between candidates and political parties. In governing, especially legislating, parties help create the coalitions necessary to write, debate, and enact policy. Neither function necessitates an ideological basis for parties, but this has historically been the dividing line between parties, both in the United States and in other democracies. Parties generally espouse positions and publish policy platforms based on ideological positions that can usually be categorized as leftist, conservative, or centrist—although what is "leftist" (or "liberal" in the U.S. context) versus what is "conservative" can change over time. Such changes may derive from the actions of ambitious office seekers or officeholders, from the work of behind-the-scenes party leaders, or from the efforts of activists to push their party in a certain direction.

In this section, four authors provide their takes on how activism and ideology have shaped the current U.S. political climate for Republican women. In chapter 1, Malliga Och examines the 2014 congressional elections and evaluates the extent to which GOP leadership attempted to "feminize" their party to attract more women voters. Ultimately, she finds, there was such an attempt, but it was more symbolic than practical in its support for women as candidates. In chapter 2, Catherine Wineinger looks at the historical evolution of Republican Party culture to trace a pattern of gendered change over time, much of which constrains rather than helps women as candidates within the party. In chapter 3, Melissa Deckman examines Tea Party women by comparing the goals, activism, and rhetorical strategies of this subgroup of

Republican women with those more in the mainstream of the Republican Party. And, finally, in chapter 4, Danielle M. Thomsen measures candidates' ideological scores for both parties over time, finding that since the 1990s Republicans have become more conservative and Democrats more leftist.

CHAPTER 1

The Grand Old Party of 2016: No Longer a Party of Old White Men?

Malliga Och

The 2012 presidential election seemed to confirm what many had said all along: the GOP had a women problem. Women have favored the Democratic Party since 1980, and the 2012 gap was the biggest in history.[1] With the major blunders by Todd Akin (that "legitimate rape" rarely leads to pregnancy[2]) and Richard Mourdock (that every pregnancy from rape is something "God intended"[3]) when discussing women's issues, the GOP increasingly seemed to fall out of favor with women voters. This experience, however, is not limited to the Republican Party; conservative parties in other countries have faced similar challenges. For example, the Conservative Party in the United Kingdom has faced accusations of sexism,[4] and in Germany, the Christian Democratic Union has had difficulty attracting young and female voters.[5] Thus, it is not surprising that, for a long time, conservative parties have been considered unlikely places for women's representation.

Left-leaning parties typically have more women in their party caucuses,[6] have closer ties to the women's movement, ideologically support the inclusion of marginalized groups,[7] and have most likely adopted some form of voluntary party quotas to ensure the representation of women in politics.[8] This is certainly also true for the United States and the Democratic Party. While the Democratic Party has not adopted any kind of electoral gender quotas, it has a history of actively recruiting and supporting women candidates.[9] Specifically, Democrats receive the backing of many women's organizations, such as EMILY's List, Emerge America, and the National Organization for Women (NOW), who actively work or train Democratic women to run for office. Further, the Democratic Party has elected far more women to Congress than the Republican Party, and the partisan gender gap has been particularly pronounced since 1992.[10] As a result, the study of women's representation as it relates to conservative parties has been neglected.

Yet, more recently, conservative parties have improved both the descriptive (numerical) and substantive (inclusion of women's interests in party platforms) representation of women. In the United Kingdom, the Conservative Party doubled its number of female representatives in the 2010 election, and the number continued to rise in the 2015 election; in South Korea, conservative Park Geun-hye became the first female president in 2013; and in Germany, Angela Merkel of the Christian Democratic Union (CDU) has governed as the first female chancellor since 2005. Likewise, we have seen conservative governments advance such feminist policies as equitable parental leave policies (see "Parental Leave, Equitable," Glossary) in Germany and corporate board quotas in Kenya, and conservative prime minister Shinzo Abe in Japan even made *womenomics* (see Glossary) a central pillar of his economic recovery strategy to build a society where all women can shine. As a result, studies have attempted to broaden the theoretical and analytical focus to include conservative parties to explain why conservative parties have increasingly put in significant effort to propose women-friendly policies and elect more women to parliament.[11] Recent studies of conservative parties in Europe illustrate that conservative parties embark on a process of *feminization* when they realize that winning back the women's vote represents the key to staying or returning to power.

The process of feminization[12] has three distinct dimensions: the feminization of descriptive representation (i.e., increasing the number of women in the conservative party); the feminization of substantive representation (i.e., proposing policies reflective of women's interests); and the feminization of symbolic representation (i.e., making female representatives more visible in public).[8] Accordingly, conservative parties will recruit more women and advocate for women-friendly policies based on electoral calculation. Not too long ago, women tended to vote for conservative parties because they shared the religious attachment and traditional family values that conservative parties supported.[13] This phenomenon is referred to as the *traditional gender gap*, but the direction of the gender gap started to change in the 1980s. Women's increased participation in the workforce, greater educational attainment, the breakdown of the traditional family,

the emergence of new gender roles, and the women's liberation movement changed women's political views and opinions. A new gender gap—
the *modern gender gap*—emerged when women started to align themselves
more closely with parties on the left that supported women's equality and
progressive roles for women and men. As a result, conservative parties lost
the women's vote and, with it, their ability to win elections.

Feminization literature argues that once the conservative parties realize
that women and young voters represent the keys to returning to power,
they will try to reform their images. Conservative parties hope to improve
their electoral fortunes by recruiting more women into their ranks and by
incorporating women's issues (see Glossary) into their party platforms.[14]
Winning back the women's vote becomes a crucial strategy in returning to
political power. Electoral calculation is thus the main driving factor that
explains why conservative parties recruit more female candidates and pay
greater attention to women's issues.

Drawing on these insights from the comparative literature, this chapter
will apply the feminization process approach to the case of the Republican Party and its response to the "war on women." It seems that the GOP
embarked on a process of feminization after the 2012 election: the party
leadership emphasized the need for a new approach to candidate recruitment and voter engagement and started to rethink its strategies for the
upcoming 2014 election. This resulted in many great firsts for Republican
women: Mia Love (Utah) became the first Republican African American elected to the House of Representatives. Elise Stefanik (New York)
is the youngest member to ever serve in Congress. Joni Ernst (Iowa) is
the Republican Party's new face in the Senate, and Barbara Comstock
(Virginia), Mimi Walters (California), and Martha McSally (Arizona)
have joined Love and Stefanik as newly elected Republican women in
the House.[15] Comstock and Ernst became the first women elected to the
U.S. Senate from their respective home states.

This chapter will show that, for the Republican Party, the feminization process, while actively pursued, remained largely symbolic. Paying
special attention to Project GROW (Growing Republican Opportunities for Women), a program by the National Republican Congressional
Committee (NRCC), this chapter shows that the greatest effort has gone
into changing the image of the party by modifying its communication and
outreach strategies to the female electorate and by countering the war on
women narrative with the help of prominent female candidates and well-
developed TV ads. In contrast, the GOP did not attempt any feminization
in regard to the substantive representation of women. The Republican

Party did not reach out to women voters by embracing policies that are favored by them. Quite to the contrary, the party still opposed paid family leave and equal pay legislation. Likewise, attempts to recruit more women have also remained largely symbolic. While the Women on the Right UNITE initiative and Project GROW received much media attention and were greatly supported by major Republican actors, they remained largely symbolic commitments.

This chapter will proceed as follows: First, I will show that the Republican outreach to women and active responses to the war against women rhetoric were clearly motivated by efforts to win over women voters and close the gender gap in voting. Second, I will analyze the attempts made by the GOP to recruit more women to political office, specifically Project GROW, established in 2013 by the NRCC. Third, I will discuss the way in which the Republican Party tried to counteract the war against women rhetoric by drawing heavily on its female party members to project a women-friendly image. I conclude that while the efforts remained largely symbolic, they still show that the Republican Party is aware of its women problem and had actively engaged in rectifying the issue in 2014.

FEMALE VOTER OUTREACH AFTER THE 2012 ELECTION

The significant gender gap in voting in the 2012 election did not go unnoticed by the GOP party leadership. An internal GOP report titled "Republicans and Women Voters: Huge Challenges, Real Opportunities" confirmed the dire state of the GOP with female voters. On almost all issues, the GOP trails the Democratic Party significantly. The report found that women considered the Democratic Party to be the party looking out for women by a 40-point margin.[16] Further, a report by the Growth and Opportunity Project describes that former Republican members now see the GOP as "scary, narrow minded . . . [and] a party of stuffy old men"[17] and identified the large gender gap as one of the reasons that contributed to the loss of the 2012 election.[13]

Accordingly, the report outlines several recommendations to reverse this impression by "improving its efforts to include female voters and promote women to leadership ranks within the [Republican National Committee, RNC]"[18] because "when developing [the GOP's] message, women need to be part of this process to represent some of the unique concerns that female voters may have."[19] Specifically, it tasks the RNC with implementing training programs for Republican candidates that focus on how to reach out to women voters through better communication and messaging strategies, featuring more Republican women across media platforms, developing a strategy to combat the Democratic "war on women" rhetoric, and improving its recruiting mechanism for female candidates.

Thus, all the lessons drawn from the 2012 election stressed the need to feminize the Republican Party to win back women voters and counter the war against women narrative at the same time. Feminization in the context of the Republican Party meant increasing the spotlight on female Republican candidates, recruiting more women to run, and incorporating women's concerns in the party's messages to voters. The rest of the chapter will discuss how the GOP translated its own advice into tangible action by feminizing the symbolic representation of women, by highlighting the presence of women in the Republican Party, and by tailoring messages directly to women voters.

THE DESCRIPTIVE REPRESENTATION OF REPUBLICAN WOMEN

When it comes to the descriptive representation of women within the Republican Party, there is much room to grow. In comparison to the Democratic Party, the number of women in the Republican Party in Congress has not increased significantly. The Democratic caucus will soon be gender balanced, but the percentage of women in the Republican Party has not yet reached critical mass, or 30 percent of the Republican caucus (see Figure I.1 in the introduction). One of the reasons that we do not see the same growth in terms of women's representation within the Republican caucus is because the Republican Party itself has not prioritized recruiting women and is openly critical of, if not opposed to, identity politics.[20] Thus, the party has made fewer efforts to actively recruit women candidates, as one female Republican leader put it, "We haven't spent time developing a farm team. The Democrats have done a better job encouraging women to run for municipal and state office, and it puts them in a position to run in congressional seats."[21]

Republican women also lack a broad and well-developed fund-raising network that could rival the efforts on the Democratic side, especially EMILY's List, or a broad network of women's organizations that support female Republican candidates (see chapter 6). The efforts by the few Republican political action committees (PACs) who work on electing more conservative women to office are disjointed and have a small footprint. Only 10 percent of Republican donors are aware of the work by Susan B. Anthony List, VIEW PAC, ShePAC, or Maggie's List compared to 93 percent of Democratic donors who are familiar with EMILY's List.[22] And conservative donors rarely know about Project GROW, a program established to increase the number of conservative women in the House.[23] As a female Republican party leader explained,

> [Democrats] have more women running in general. I think it is because the Democratic Party has very strong women's organizations that support their women candidates from the outside. Emily's List, NARAL, Planned Parenthood. All these organizations are dedicated to getting women elected [and] spend time and resources training women to be candidates, activists. They have amazing fundraising ability.[24]

As a result, Republican women have been lagging behind Democratic women for more than a decade. Although the parties had roughly the same number of women in their respective congressional caucuses for most of the last decade, this drastically changed with the establishment of EMILY's List in 1985 by Ellen Malcolm.[25] At the same time, the galvanization of women across the country during the Anita Hill hearings led to the Year of the Woman (see Glossary) and the emergence of a partisan gender gap between the two parties that became more pronounced as the years went by. Today, the Democratic caucus has almost three times as many women as the Republican caucus. Percentagewise, this means that women in the Democratic caucus now make up over a third of their caucus, while Republican women remain at less than 10 percent of their caucus.

The same gender gap persists among the pool of female candidates for each party. Democratic women run in greater numbers in primaries than Republican women.[26] Further, Democratic women have a better chance of winning the general election than Republican women.[27] In 2014, 62 percent of all women who filed as primary candidates in congressional House races were Democrats, and 69 percent of the women who won their primary races were Democrats.[28] As Figure 1.1 shows, three-quarters of female candidates who managed to win their general elections were Democrats.[29] In contrast, the Senate primaries were more even, with 15 Democratic and 16 Republican women running.[30] Although Democratic candidates won their primaries more often than Republican senatorial primary candidates (66% win rate for Democrats, 31% win rate for Republican women), Republican women clearly outperformed their Democratic counterparts in the general election. Three Republican senatorial candidates, or 60 percent, won their elections compared to just one Democratic candidate, or 10 percent.[31] (See chapter 5.)

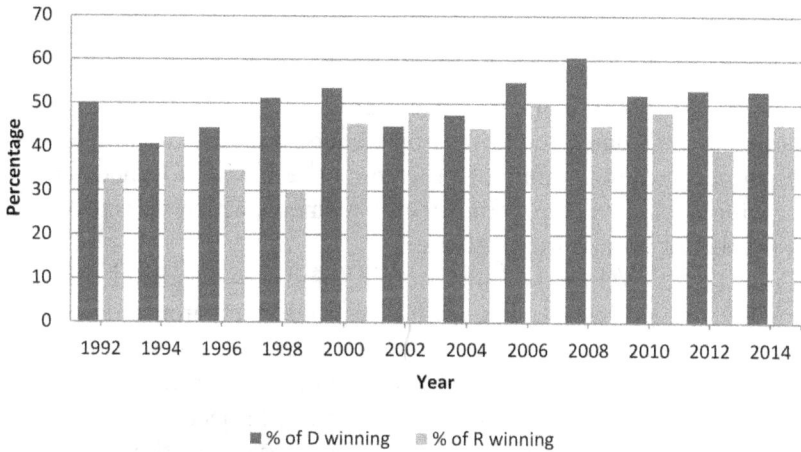

Figure 1.1 Percentage of Women Winning General Election by Party (Senate and U.S. House Combined)

Source: Center for American Women and Politics, 2014, "Elections," accessed January 5, 2015, http://www.cawp.rutgers.edu/facts/elections/past_candidates#e2014.

If we look at trends for Republican women over time, we can see that Republican female candidates who ran in the general election won at a greater rate than the year before.[32] In total, Republican women increased their presence in the Senate from 4 female senators to 6 and from 19 representatives in the House to 21 for a total increase in both chambers of 4 women.

Feminization and the Descriptive Representation of Women

Following the recommendation outlined in the Growth and Opportunity Project report, the Republican Party did attempt to recruit more women to run for office. Unfortunately, these strategies had not been structured in a way that substantially increased the number of Republican women elected to Congress.

First, in June 2013, the RNC announced a new initiative in cooperation with six major Republican committees called Women on the Right Unite,[33] which aims to recruit and support Republican women candidates overall.[34] At the launch of the initiative, Sharon Day (RNC cochair) stated that the GOP needed to recruit more women, arguing that women are not adequately represented in politics and that both parties need to make sure that women are part of the party leadership.[35] She emphasized the need for more concrete efforts to recruit more women, such as the Ready to Run Initiative by the RNC, which helps women understand how to set up a campaign as well as providing mentoring, training, and resources. While the Women on the Right Unite initiative aims to facilitate the rise of women to elected and leadership positions at all levels of the party, the most prominent program is the NRCC's Project GROW (Growing Republican Opportunities for Women), which seeks to increase the number of women in the House.[36]

Project GROW launched in June 2013 and was spearheaded by Rep. Ann Wagner (Missouri). The initiative provides mentoring and advice to female candidates. However, Project GROW is not a pure recruitment tool for Republican women, as it also includes messaging training for male candidates. Before the 2014 election, Project GROW released a list of 13 Republican woman candidates whose races they had prioritized[37] (see Table 1.1) and who would receive training in campaigning and fund-raising.[38]

Project GROW served as a signal to the public that the RNCC is recognizing the importance of female candidates. The results of Project GROW have been mixed: 5 out of the 13 candidates prioritized by the project were elected, and 3 candidates lost their general elections because they ran in difficult districts that either leaned Democratic or were toss-up districts. Further, all of them ran as challengers to incumbents, which made victory even less likely as incumbency remains one of the greatest obstacles to elected office in the United States.[39] The remaining 5 women, however, never made it past the primary stage, even though 4 of them were running in an open seat election in Republican districts. Past research has shown that early support, especially in terms of fund-raising, is crucial to signal that women are viable contenders and thus increasing their chances of winning primaries.

Providing the necessary training, fund-raising, and mentoring in the primary stage significantly increases the chances of women advancing to the general election, particularly if women are running in safe or open districts. For example, four of the five successful candidates ran in open seat contests in Republican-leaning or toss-up districts. This fact indicates that if the five women had made it out of the primary, they should have been able to win the general election, increasing the number of Republican women even further. The question we need to ask is why did candidates not clear the primary hurdle despite being supported by Project GROW?

The short answer is that the Republican Party overall and Project GROW specifically cultivate a hands-off approach to primaries.[40] A study commissioned by Political Parity found that the leadership of the

Table 1.1 Project GROW Short List

District	Candidate	Outcome	Margin	Type of Seat	Ideological Profile of District
AZ 2	Martha McSally	Won	0	Incumbent	R+15
NY 21	Elise Stefanik	Won	+21.7	Open seat	Even
UT 4	Mia Love	Won	+3.2	Open seat	R+16
VA 10	Barbara Comstock	Won	+16.2	Open seat	R+2
CA 45	Mimi Walters	Won	+30.4	Open seat	R+7
IL 11	Darlene Senger	Lost	−6.4	Challenger	D+8
IA 2	Mariannette Miller-Meeks	Lost	−5	Challenger	D+4
NY 18	Nan Hayworth	Lost	−1.6	Challenger	Even
MN 6	Rhonda Sivarajah	Lost primary	−46.6	Open seat	R+10
WV 2	Charlotte Lane	Lost primary	−17.9	Open seat	R+11
GA 10	Donna Sheldon	Lost primary	−18.2	Open seat	R+14
CA 7	Elizabeth Emken	Lost primary	−40	Challenger	Even
GA 11	Tricia Pridemore	Lost primary	−19.5	Open seat	R+19

Source: Sharon Johnson, "13 Female House Challengers Carry the GOP Banner," Women's eNews, January 22, 2014, accessed July 13, 2016, http://womensenews.org/2014/01/13-female-house-challengers-carry-the-gop-banner.

Republican Party emphasizes the importance of primaries as producing the best possible candidate, whether that candidate is female or male. As a male party leader explained, "Again, I think to try to elect and recruit female candidates because they're female is a disservice to females. Having quality candidates is a priority. But, it is important [to have more women running for office]."[41] This is one of the reasons why Project GROW did not offer primary support to female candidates. As Rep. Ann Wagner, who headed Project GROW, stated, "At the end of the day, you've got to run your own campaign, and we can't be there on the ground doing it for them"[42]

However, women need training and help early on because women struggle with early fund-raising to get their message out, according to Sharon Day, the cochair of the RNC.[43] Further, money is not everything. Women tend to perform better when the party offers campaign training and the candidates have campaign teams that are staffed with the most talented people to run them.[44] Unfortunately, Project GROW did not offer fund-raising help nor campaign training to its women candidates. As Representative Wagner stated, "I want a GOP win first and a GOP woman second. If I can get both, it's a two-fer. . . . I'm willing to play in primaries, but at the end of the day, what I'm providing to these women candidates, [along with] people like Diane Black and many others working through Project GROW, is advice.[45]

As the election outcomes for Republican women demonstrate, mentorship alone is not enough to push Republican women over the finish line (especially in the primary stage). Bob Carpenter, the founder and president of Chesapeake Bay Consulting, speaking about the Republican Party more generally, said that the 2014 election could have seen significantly more women elected if Republican women would have received early help from Republican committees throughout the primaries and the full campaign process.[46] Without financial and logistic resources for Republican women early in the election cycle, the NRCC was unable to secure a greater number of Republican women advancing to and winning the general election.[47]

While the hands-off approach to primaries mostly held for House candidates, there were notable exceptions in Senate races. The National Republican Senatorial Committee (NRSC) was involved in primary races for three female candidates: Monica Wehby (Oregon), Joni Ernst (Iowa), and Shelly Moore Capito (West Virginia).[48] This should not be surprising, as all three races played crucial roles in winning back the Senate majority. By far, Joni Ernst received the most attention among these three candidates, with major Republican figures campaigning for her in the primary. For example, Mitt Romney, Sarah Palin, and Republican leadership PACs directed more than $700,000 toward her primary contest.[49] Monica Wehby had the backing of Mitt Romney and Rick Santorum, and Senate Minority Leader McConnell and Senators Ayotte, McCain, Collins, and Chambliss donated to her primary bid.[50] Jerry Moran, the NRSC chairman, also supported her early on, and the NRSC helped her manage a scandal involving stalking accusations by her ex-boyfriend.[51] Because Wehby is a physician and an early critic of the Patient Protection and Affordable Care Act (or "Obamacare") as well as a socially moderate Republican (she is pro-choice), Republicans were hoping that she could win the Oregon Senate race. In the same manner, Jerry Moran also supported Shelly Moore Capito during the primary process.[52] These three examples show that the Republican Party is willing to actively support female candidates under the right circumstances; yet, these cases are atypical.

Another element typical in Republican Party recruitment is the value it places on gender-neutral recruitment.[53] This emphasis—while not discriminatory—makes it harder for women to be successful.[54] As former Massachusetts lieutenant governor Kerry Healey points out, "the

GOP has traditionally been gender neutral regarding candidate recruitment and support. . . . Many in the party are now taking a second look at how this choice has impacted electability and growth."[55] Likewise, one Republican congresswoman argues, "When we have a quality leader running, there needs to be a commitment to get her through the primary. We've always adopted a hands-off approach to primaries. That changed in 2014. . . . There's a growing recognition that we can't sit out primaries. We need to get the right person elected.[56]

Gender-neutral recruitment strategies also mean that electoral races with Republican women are not prioritized simply because a woman is running, but only when the race is crucial to the overall electoral strategy of the party. In fact, the former strategy is typically dismissed as identity politics, something that the Republican Party is highly critical of. A case in point is Nan Hayworth, who fell short of winning back her congressional seat by a mere 1.6 percent, which she lost to her Democratic opponent in 2012 when the latest redistricting occurred.[57] Her loss might have simply been a case of bad electoral luck. She ran against a well-placed incumbent, a Bill Clinton protégée for whom Hillary Clinton campaigned. However, the district is considered a toss-up district, and the election of the Democratic incumbent was not guaranteed. After all, Elise Stefanik won her election in the same state and in a similarly composed district. So why did the RNC not spend more money on Hayworth's race? A likely explanation is that the race was not a high priority for the RNC because the focus was on securing a Republican majority in the Senate; the House majority was never in question.[58] Thus, Nan Hayworth did not receive additional support by the RNC to push her over the finish line, which resulted in fewer women in Congress than could have been possible based on the competitiveness of races alone.

In 2016, Republican women did not fare much better. In fact, their numbers in Congress declined (for an in-depth analysis, see chapter 7). And with rampant sexism playing out in the 2016 presidential campaign, the focus on individual Republican women receded to the background. Project GROW was active in 2016, but it was less active than in the previous election. For once, Project GROW had limited room to expand: in 2016, the Republican Party was only competitive in 4 open seat races, compared to 12 in 2012.[59] Further, the program continued to emphasize mentoring over active campaign help, such as staffing or fund-raising,[60] and ideology remained more important than supporting women in primaries.[61]

A case in point is Rep. Renee Ellmers, who was very active with Project GROW in the previous election cycle. She faced a primary challenge from her own party and ended up losing against the male challenger, who was supported by Susan B. Anthony List.[62] This clearly shows that ideology still trumps identity or diversity in the Republican Party.

Finally, it seems likely that Project GROW will be merged with the Young Guns program, a candidate and recruitment program of the NRCC.[63] However, this merger will not bode well for increasing the number of Republican women in Congress: fewer than 20 percent of Young Guns are female.[64]

When it comes to the descriptive representation of women, the GOP clearly acknowledges the need to increase the number of Republican women in Congress. However, diversity and gender identity remain second to other considerations, most importantly ideological commitment to the GOP brand of conservatism as well as gender-neutral recruitment within primaries as the only means to ensure that the best candidate wins. Together, this makes an active feminization strategy almost impossible, as feminization is predicated on active support of female candidates to ensure their election.

SUBSTANTIVE REPRESENTATION OF REPUBLICAN WOMEN

Party platforms are an important sign of both the values a political party espouses and the types of policy proposals it commits to realizing. As such, the writing of the GOP platform in 2016 is an ideal place to signal to women voters that the Republican Party cares about women's issues and has changed some of its policy positions to appeal to more women voters. In this section, I will compare the 2012 GOP platform with the 2016 GOP platform to understand whether changes have occurred in terms of women's issues. The key question is whether there was any movement toward a more women-friendly platform in 2016, which could be a sign of the party's feminization. Unfortunately, this was not the case. Instead, the 2016 platform moved the party further to the right and used harsher and more condemnatory language on issues important to women voters, such as reproductive rights and Title IX.[65]

The 2012 GOP platform emphasized traditional conservative family values,[66] such as a commitment to traditional marriage—defined as between a man and a woman—as the ideal family form; reaffirmed its pro-life status, antiabortion stances, particularly on late-term abortion, and opposition to using public funds for abortions; rejected the ratification of the Convention on the Elimination of All Forms of Discrimination against Women (CEDAW), a UN treaty that promotes gender equality and nondiscrimination in national laws and practices; and supported abstinence-only sex education in schools. Further, the platform did not touch upon (paid) parental leave or equal pay. This should not be surprising, as the Republican Party has continuously stood up for traditional family values and opposed state interference into business, which paid leave or equal pay mandates would require.

The 2016 platform restates the commitment to protect the life of the unborn child, including opposition to abortion. In contrast to 2012, however, the 2016 section is more detailed and extensive. To put it in perspective, the 2012 platform dedicated 410 words to the issue, and there are 742 words on the subject in the 2016 platform. Further, the Republican Party added a full paragraph on the party's opposition to fetal-harvesting practices, which the 2012 platform only mentioned in passing. The 2016 platform also includes the party's support for the Born-Alive Abortion Survivors Protection Act, which criminalizes abortion providers who "fail to provide treatment and care to an infant who survives an abortion, including early induction delivery whether the death of the infant is intended."[67] Further, the 2016 platform directly calls out the Democratic Party as "extreme on abortion."[68] The GOP platform also reiterates the party's opposition to public funding of abortion providers, the coverage of abortion under Obamacare, and the morning-after pill. In addition, the platform reaffirms its commitment to abstinence-only programs and rejects federal funds for any school clinics or programs that teach about abortion and contraception in their sex education classes.

New to the 2016 platform is a section on Title IX that reaffirms the GOP's commitment to ending discrimination based on sex. However, the platform then voices its opposition to including sexual orientation under this protection and criticizes the management of Title IX on college campuses, calling it micromanagement.[69] Further, the GOP continues to reject women's participation in combat and the ratification of the UN women's rights treaty (CEDAW), and it does not touch upon equal pay legislation or paid/parental leave. Thus, the 2016 platform does not propose any specific policies on how to combat sex-based discrimination or, in some cases, ignores the subject entirely (parental leave and equal pay). Finally, the platform's language is much less forgiving and detailed when it comes to lesbian, gay, bisexual, and transgender (LGBT) rights. Again, the platform reinstates the party's support for traditional marriage, but it also calls for overturning the *Obergefell v. Hodges* Supreme Court decision, protecting businesses and individuals who oppose same-sex marriage and LGBT rights, and appointing conservative judges that respect traditional family values both on LGBT and reproductive rights.

To summarize, it seems that the Republican Party did not heed the advice set out in the Growth and Opportunity Project after the 2012 election, as it failed to incorporate women's issues and language that could have been appealing to women voters in the 2016 platform. Thus, in terms of the integration of women's issues in its party program, we do not see a feminization process at work when it comes to the substantive representation of women.

SYMBOLIC REPRESENTATION OF REPUBLICAN WOMEN

When it comes to the symbolic representation of women, the GOP has made great strides to highlight emerging female leaders within the party. Most notably, the response to the State of the Union has been given by women in three consecutive years: Rep. Cathy McMorris Rodgers (Washington) in 2014, Sen. Joni Ernst (Iowa) in 2015, and Gov. Nikki Haley (South Carolina) in 2016.[70] This represents a significant change from the earlier years of Obama's presidency, when emerging male leaders, such as Marco Rubio (2013) and Bobby Jindal (2009), were recruited to give the response to the State of the Union. When Bill Clinton was in office, only one woman was tapped to give a response alone (Gov. Christine Todd Whitman (New Jersey) in 1995); in 1999 and 2000, the responses were given by a pair of male and female Republican congress members. It is unlikely that the decision to have women give the response to the State of the Union in three consecutive years is a coincidence. Rather, it points to an effort on behalf of the GOP to showcase its diversity.

Further, the GOP leadership and GOP candidates tried to counteract the "war on women" rhetoric by emphasizing their gender identity during campaigns and by offering training in how to talk and engage with women voters. Prominent female candidates strategically emphasized their gender to counter the accusation that the Republican Party is waging a war on women. For example, Karen Handel tried to play up the fact that she is a woman in the primary to demonstrate to voters that she would be the best choice to take on Michelle Nunn, the Democratic candidate, in Georgia's Senate race. For example, by stating, "I would really love to see Michelle Nunn drop the war on women on me,"[71] she essentially implied that by becoming the GOP nominee for the Senate race, she could neutralize any Democratic attempts to accuse the GOP of undermining women's rights. In another example, Terri Lynn Land—a GOP hopeful for the Senate in Michigan—ran a TV ad in which she opens with the following line: "Congressman Gary Peters and his buddies want you to believe I'm waging a war on women. Really? Think about this for a moment." Then she pauses and takes a long sip out of a mug before continuing, "I'm Terri Lynn Land, and I approve this message because, as a woman, I might know a little bit more about women than Gary Peters."[72] These are just two examples of Republican women candidates actively playing up their gender to counter any war on women accusations.

What is more, several media outlets reported that the NRCC had instituted training to teach Republican staff and male candidates how to talk about women, women's issues, and the best ways to reach out to women voters, especially when running against a female opponent.[73] Speaker of the House John Boehner himself admitted in 2013 that the party needs to do a better job of communicating with women. These training sessions were meant to avoid gaffes similar to those committed by Todd Akin's infamous "legitimate rape" remarks. Instead, the party leadership advised male candidates to connect with women through their roles as fathers and husbands. For example, Stewart Mills—the Republican candidate for Minnesota's 8th district—emphasized his strong commitment to fighting domestic violence by showcasing his participation in the Walk a Mile in Her Shoes event, a fund-raiser for victims of domestic violence.[74] Other TV ads showed Republican male candidates as caring people concerned with traditional "women's concerns," such as military sexual assault and health issues, and as champions for families and children.[75] According to a Republican consultant, male candidates were also encouraged to hold women's forums in their districts to reach out to women voters and to show that they took women seriously.[76] Taken together, there have been many serious efforts to reach out to female voters by improving the messaging of candidates and highlighting the presence of Republican women in the party.

During the 2016 election, the issue of the symbolic representation of women played little role. It seems that the GOP was playing defense most of the time to counteract the blatant sexism by its presidential nominee. And with Hillary Clinton as the first female presidential candidate, little attention was paid to the down-ballot races and female candidates and elected officials. It remains to be seen whether this will change. Cooperman and Deckman argue that the Republican Party will rely heavily on its female members to articulate its "A Better Way" vision and GOP party messages generally during the 115th Congress because women are well suited for articulating why such GOP policies as tax reform or reducing the national debt are good for American families.[77] The Trump administration has also experienced pressure to ensure a gender-balanced cabinet. The president has appointed four women so far, but they all preside over cabinet portfolios that are less influential.[78] Taken together, the GOP will probably continue to highlight conservative women in its party image and messages. However, the Republicans won both the presidency and the majority in both chambers of Congress, despite a 13 percent gender gap in the 2016 election.[79] That could add weight to the argument that identity politics are not important for winning elections, rolling back any feminization strategies.

CONCLUSION

As the above discussion has shown, the attempts of the GOP to feminize the party have been largely symbolic. The greatest effort has gone into changing the image of the party by changing its communication and outreach strategies to the female electorate and by countering the "war on women" narrative with the help of prominent female candidates and well-developed TV ads. Further, the GOP did not attempt any feminization in regard to the substantive representation of women. The Republican Party did not reach out to women voters by embracing policies that are favored by them. Quite to the contrary, the party still opposed paid family leave and equal pay legislation. Republican Party platforms across the nation continued to emphasize the right to life, including the reversal of Roe v. Wade; support for abortion restrictions; and opposition to gay marriage.[80] Thus, feminizing the policy priorities either in rhetoric or in action has not been a priority of the party.

Attempts to recruit more women have also remained largely symbolic. The Women on the Right UNITE initiative and Project GROW received much media attention and were greatly supported by major Republican actors, but they remained rhetorical commitments. The fact that Project GROW is not solely focused on recruiting women but includes messaging and male candidate training limits the resources that it has to improve the descriptive representation of women within the party. Further, because Project GROW did not provide any tangible help to women candidates, such as fund-raising and campaign training during the primary stages, it is fair to say that is serves more as window dressing than an actual effort to see more women being elected. In the end, Project GROW will only succeed in increasing the number of Republican women in the House if it challenges the gender-neutral approach of the GOP to candidate recruitment as well as its hands-off approach in primaries. Anything short of that and Project GROW will remain a program without real teeth.

Nevertheless, the situation for aspiring Republican women is not as dire as one would think. A highly successful model of female candidate recruitment at the state level is the Right Women, Right Now initiative launched by the Republican State Leadership Committee (RSLC). In the months leading up to the 2014 midterm elections, the committee assembled an advisory board, cochaired by Lt. Gov. Rebecca Kleefisch (Wisconsin), Speaker of the House Beth Harwell (Tennessee), and Secretary of State Kim Wyman (Washington),[81] and recruited 558 women to run for seats in the state legislatures across the nation.[82] The gravitas of the board allowed the initiative to raise enough money to support these candidates through training, mentoring, and financial support; in total, the initiative raised $6 million in support of these female candidates.[83] In the end, 138 women won their elections, considerably boosting the number of Republican women at the state level.[84] In 2016, the program built on its success by electing 165 candidates to statewide offices.[85]

Thus, if the GOP is truly serious about feminizing the party by recruiting more women, they already have a successful model to replicate on the federal level. But unless the party is willing to play in the primaries, abandon its gender-neutral recruitment efforts, and invest early money in these women candidates, the Republican Party's efforts will remain symbolic, and we will continue to see only modest or even stagnant growth of Republican women in Congress.

NOTES

1. Jeffrey Jones, "Gender Gap in 2012 Vote Is Largest in Gallup's History," Gallup, November 9, 2012, accessed July 13, 2016, http://www.gallup.com /poll/158588/gender-gap-2012-vote-largest-gallup-history.aspx.

2. Jones, "Gender Gap in 2012 Vote."

3. Lucy Madison, "Richard Mourdock: Even Pregnancy from Rape Something 'God Intended,'" CBS News, October 24, 2012, accessed July 13, 2016, http://www.cbsnews.com/news/richard-mourdock-even-pregnancy-from-rape -something-god-intended.

4. Dina Rickman, "Women and the Conservative Party: Where Is the Love?," *Huffington Post United Kingdom*, September 19, 2011, accessed October 12, 2016, http://www.huffingtonpost.co.uk/2011/09/19/women-and-the-conservative -party_n_970466.html.

5. Frank Decker, "Wahlergebnisse und Wählerschaft der CDU," Bundeszentrale für politische Bildung, May 3, 2016, accessed December 16, 2016, https:// www.bpb.de/politik/grundfragen/parteien-in-deutschland/42068/wahlergebnisse -und-waehlerschaft.

6. Miki Caul, "Political Parties and the Adoption of Candidate Gender Quotas: A Cross-National Analysis," *Journal of Politics* 63, no. 4 (November 2001): 1214–1229; L. Kenworthy and M. Malami, "Gender Inequality in Political Representation: A Worldwide Comparative Analysis," *Social Forces* 78, no. 1

(September 1, 1999): 235–268; Pippa Norris, "Gender and Contemporary British Politics," in *British Politics Today*, ed. Colin Hay (Cambridge: Polity in association with Blackwell, 2002), 38–59.

7. Mala N. Htun, "Case Study: Latin America: Women, Political Parties and Electoral Systems in Latin America," in *Women in Parliament: Beyond Numbers*, rev. ed., eds. Julie Ballington and Azza Karam (Stockholm: International IDEA, 2006), 112–121.

8. Drude Dahlerup, "Increasing Women's Political Representation: New Trends in Gender Quotas," in *Women in Parliament: Beyond Numbers*, rev. ed., eds. Julie Ballington and Azza Karam (Stockholm: International IDEA, 2006), 141–153.

9. Shauna Shames, *3:1: Republican Women Are Outnumbered in Congress: Right the Ratio*, (Cambridge, MA: Political Parity and Hunt Alternatives, 2015), https://www.politicalparity.org/wp-content/uploads/2015/01/primary-hurdles -full-report.pdf.

10. Center for American Women and Politics (CAWP), "History of Women in the U.S. Congress." accessed July 13, 2016, http://www.cawp.rutgers.edu/history -women-us-congress; CAWP, "The Gender Gap: Voting Choices in Presidential Elections" (New Brunswick, NJ: Eagleton Institute of Politics, Rutgers University, 2017), http://www.cawp.rutgers.edu/sites/default/files/resources/ggpresvote.pdf.

11. See, for example, Karen Celis and Sarah Childs, *Gender, Conservatism and Political Representation* (Colchester, UK: ECPR Press, 2014), as well as individual contributions in the same edited volume.

12. Celis and Childs, *Gender, Conservatism and Political Representation*.

13. Ronald Inglehart and Pippa Norris, "The Developmental Theory of the Gender Gap: Women's and Men's Voting Behavior in Global Perspective," *International Political Science Review* 21, no. 4 (October 1, 2000): 441–463, accessed August 5, 2015, http://ips.sagepub.com/content/21/4/441.short?rss=1&ssource=mfc.

14. Celis and Childs, *Gender, Conservatism and Political Representation*.

15. CAWP, "Election 2014: Results for Women Candidates" (New Brunswick, NJ: National Information Bank on Women in Public Office, Eagleton Institute of Politics, Rutgers University, 2014), http://www.cawp.rutgers.edu/sites/default /files/resources/can2014results.pdf.

16. Jake Sherman and Anna Palmer, "GOP Poll of Women: Party 'in Past,'" Politico, August 29, 2014, accessed July 13, 2016, http://www.politico.com/story /2014/08/gop-poll-of-women-party-stuck-in-past-110398.

17. Republican National Committee (RNC), "Growth & Opportunity Project" (2013): 6, accessed July 10, 2016, http://goproject.gop.com/rnc_growth _opportunity_book_2013.pdf.

18. RNC, "Growth & Opportunity Project," 6.

19. RNC, "Growth & Opportunity Project," 19.

20. Abby Livingston, "House GOP's Effort to Elect More Women Gets Mixed Results," Roll Call, April 28, 2014, accessed July 13, 2016, http://www.rollcall .com/politics/house-gops-effort-to-elect-more-women-gets-mixed-results.

21. Shames, *3:1*, 25.

22. Shames, *3:1*, 4.

23. Shames, *3:1*, 4.

24. Unpublished data provided by Political Parity (Cambridge, MA: Hunt Alternatives, 2015).

25. EMILY's List, "Our History" (2016), accessed July 13, 2016, http://www .emilyslist.org/pages/entry/our-history.

26. Shames, *3:1*, 8.

27. Shames, *3:1*.

28. Shames, *3:1*, 8.

29. Shames, *3:1*, 8.

30. Shames, *3:1*, 8.

31. Shames, *3:1*, 8.

32. CAWP, "Summary of Women Candidates for Selected Offices" (New Brunswick, NJ: Eagleton Institute of Politics, Rutgers University, 2014), http:// www.cawp.rutgers.edu/sites/default/files/resources/can_histsum.pdf.

33. These committees include the Republican National Committee, Republican Governors Association, National Republican Senatorial Committee, National Republican Congressional Committee, Republican State Leadership Committee, and College Republican National Committee.

34. RNC Women, "Media Advisory: Republican Committees Launch 'Women on the Right UNITE' on Friday," GOP, June 26, 2013, accessed July 13, 2016, https://www.gop.com/media-advisory-republican-committees-launch-women -on-the-right-unite-on-friday.

35. Sharon Day, "Women on the Right Unite to Elect More Women," *BlogHer*, June 28, 2013, http://www.blogher.com/women-right-unite-elect-more-women.

36. Abby Livingston, "Republicans Circulate List of Top Female House Candidates," Roll Call, July 1, 2014, accessed July 13, 2016, http://www.rollcall.com /news/home/republicans-candidates-women-house-list-2014; Aaron Blake, "GOP Launches Programs to Recruit More Women," *Washington Post*, June 28, 2013, https:// www.washingtonpost.com/news/post-politics/wp/2013/06/28/gop-launches -programs-to-recruit-more-women.

37. Sharon Johnson, "13 Female House Challengers Carry the GOP Banner," Women's eNews, January 22, 2014, accessed July 13, 2016, http://womensenews .org/2014/01/13-female-house-challengers-carry-the-gop-banner.

38. Johnson, "13 Female House Challengers."

39. Barbara Palmer and Dennis Simon, *Breaking the Political Glass Ceiling: Women and Congressional Elections* (London: Routledge, 2008).

40. Shames, *3:1*.

41. Male party leader, unpublished data provided by Political Parity (Cambridge, MA: Hunt Alternatives, 2015).

42. Livingston, "House GOP's Effort."

43. Ali Weinberg, "Women Republicans Need to Downplay Compromise, GOPers Say," ABC News, January 21, 2015, accessed July 13, 2016, http:// abcnews.go.com/Politics/republicans-female-candidates-stop-compromise /story?id=28381518.

44. Unpublished data provided by Political Parity (Cambridge, MA: Hunt Alternatives, 2015).

45. Livingston, "House GOP's Effort."

46. Political Parity, "Get It Right with Margaret Hoover" (Cambridge, MA: Hunt Alternatives, 2015), accessed December 16, 2016, https://soundcloud.com /political-parity/get-it-right-primary-hurdles.

47. Personal communication.

48. personal communication.

49. Shames, 3:1, 32.

50. Jaime Fuller, "Monica Wehby Wins Republican Senate Primary in Oregon," *Washington Post*, May 21, 2014, https://www.washingtonpost.com/news /post-politics/wp/2014/05/21/monica-wehby-wins-republican-senate-primary-in -oregon; Mollie Reilly, "Monica Wehby Wins Primary in Oregon Senate Race," *Huffington Post*, May 20, 2014, http://www.huffingtonpost.com/2014/05/20 /monica-wehby-primary_n_5354366.html?; Philip Rucker, "Can Republicans Expand Their Reach in Blue States? Oregon Senate Race Provides a Test," *Washington Post*, June 1, 2014, https://www.washingtonpost.com/politics/can -republicans-expand-their-reach-in-blue-states-oregon-senate-race-provides-a -test/2014/06/01/c6d2d924-e791-11e3-8f90-73e071f3d637_story.html.

51. Elizabeth Titus, "Wehby Wins Oregon Senate Nod," Politico, May 21, 2014, accessed July 13, 2016, http://www.politico.com/story/2014/05/oregon -senate-primary-2014-wehby-106927.html.

52. Jason Pye, "NRSC Chair Says Nice Things about Big Government Republicans," United Liberty, June 3, 2013, accessed July 13, 2016, http://www .unitedliberty.org/articles/13887-nrsc-chair-says-nice-things-about-big-gov ernment-republicans; Alexandra Jaffe, "NRSC Requiring Candidates Get Mentors, Go through Campaign Boot Camp," The Hill, June 3, 2013, accessed July 13, 2016, http://thehill.com/blogs/ballot-box/senate-races/302989-nrsc -requiring-candidates-get-mentors-go-through-campaign-bootcamp-.

53. Personal communication.

54. Shames, 3:1.

55. Peter Roff, "Political Women," *U.S. News*, January 21, 2015, accessed July 13, 2016, http://www.usnews.com/opinion/blogs/peter-roff/2015/01/21/how-joni -ernst-and-nikki-haley-can-help-the-gop-maintain-its-majority?int=9e5708.

56. Shames, 3:1, 20.

57. Sam Levine, "Hayworth Falls Short," *Huffington Post*, November 5, 2014, http://www.huffingtonpost.com/2014/10/07/nan-hayworth-midterm-election -results_n_5948672.html.

58. Personal communication.

59. Nicole Puglise, "GOP Women's Recruitment Effort Adapts for 2016," Roll Call, July 12, 2016, accessed December 18, 2016, http://www.rollcall.com/news /home/gop-womens-recruitment-effort-adapts-2016.

60. Puglise, "GOP Women's Recruitment."

61. Simone Pathé, "Republican Gender Gap Could Grow in the House," Roll Call, December 6, 2016, accessed December 18, 2016, http://www.rollcall.com/news

/republican-gender-gaphouse?utm_name=newsletters&utm_source=weekendreads &utm_medium=email.

62. Elise Viebeck, "How These Powerful Women Learned to Love Fundraising," *Washington Post*, September 13, 2016, accessed December 18, 2016, https:// www.washingtonpost.com/news/powerpost/wp/2016/09/13/how-these-powerful -women-learned-to-love-fundraising.

63. Puglise, "GOP Women's Recruitment."

64. Rachael Combe, "Not with Her, but Not with Him: The Women of the *New* GOP," *Elle*, August 12, 2106, accessed December 18, 2016, http://www .elle.com/culture/career-politics/a37956/the-girls-are-all-right.

65. Jeremey W. Peters, "Emerging Republican Platform Goes Far to the Right," *New York Times*, July 12, 2016, accessed December 16, 2016, http://www.ny times.com/2016/07/13/us/politics/republican-convention-issues.html?_r=0; Jennifer Haberkorn, "Republicans Building Stronger Anti-Abortion Plank in Platform," Politico, November 7, 2016, accessed December 16, 2016, http:// www.politico.com/story/2016/07/republicans-abortion-platform-225391; Dan Balz, "Republican Platform Turns 2013 RNC Autopsy on Its Head," *Washington Post*, July 14, 2016, accessed December 16, 2016, https://www.washingtonpost.com /politics/republican-platform-turns-2013-rnc-autopsy-on-its-head/2016/07/14 /cae7cbc0-49cb-11e6-bdb9-701687974517_story.html.

66. Bill Gribbin, ed., "We Believe in America: 2012 Republican Platform," 2012 Republican National Convention, https://prod-static-ngop-pbl.s3.amazonaws. com/docs/2012GOPPlatform.pdf.

67. Bill Gribbin, ed., "Republican Platform 2016," 2016 Republican National Convention: 14, accessed December 16, 2016, https://www.gop.com/the-2016 -republican-party-platform.

68. Gribbin, "Republican Platform 2016."

69. Gribbin, "Republican Platform 2016," 35.

70. Gerhard Peters, "List of Opposition Responses to State of the Union Addresses," The American Presidency Project, eds. John T. Woolley and Gerhard Peters (Santa Barbara, CA: University of California, 1999–2017), accessed July 13, 2016, http://www.presidency.ucsb.edu/sou_response.php.

71. Christ Gentilviso, "Sarah Palin Endorses GOP Candidate with Controversial Planned Parenthood Past," *Huffington Post*, March 27, 2014, http://www .huffingtonpost.com/2014/03/27/sarah-palin-karen-handel_n_5042673.html.

72. Fritz Klug, "Terri Lynn Land Asks 'Really?' in 1st TV Ad about 'War on Women' Attack," MLive, April 22, 2014, accessed July 13, 2016, http://www.mlive .com/lansing-news/index.ssf/2014/04/terri_lynn_land_makes_fun_on_w.html.

73. Anna Palmer and John Bresnahan, "GOP Men Told How to Talk to Women," Politico, December 5, 2013, accessed July 13, 2016, http://www.politico. com/story/2013/12/gop-men-tutored-in-running-against-women-100701; Dahlia Lithwick, "How to Talk to Republican Congressmen: A Guide for Women," Slate, December 10, 2013, accessed July 13, 2016, http://www.slate.com/articles /double_x/doublex/2013/12/the_gop_is_teaching_candidates_how_to_talk _to_women_now_here_s_a_guide_for.html; Cheryl Chumley, "GOP Launches

Candidate Training: How to Talk to Women," *Washington Times*, December 5, 2013, accessed July 13, 2016, http://www.washingtontimes.com/news/2013/dec/5/gop-launches-candidate-training-how-talk-women.

74. Jackie Kucinich, "NRCC Urges Early Outreach to Women," *Washington Post*, August 18, 2014, https://www.washingtonpost.com/blogs/she-the-people/wp/2014/08/18/nrcc-urges-early-outreach-to-women.

75. *Washington Post*, "House GOP Candidates Reach Out to Women in Ads," filmed August 2018, YouTube video, 1:36, posted August 18, 2014, https://www.youtube.com/watch?v=GxNOg8QY72o.

76. Personal communication.

77. Rosalyn Cooperman and Melissa Deckman, "Republican Women Poised to Play a Key Role as Messengers in the 115th Congress," *Presidential Gender Watch Blog*, December 22, 2016, accessed December 22, 2016, http://presidentialgenderwatch.org/republican-women-poised-play-key-role-messengers-115th-congress/#more-12062.

78. *New York Times*, "Donald Trump Is Choosing His Cabinet: Here's the Latest List," December 15, 2016, accessed December 22, 2016, http://www.nytimes.com/interactive/2016/us/politics/donald-trump-administration.html.

79. Claire Zillman, "Hillary Clinton Had the Biggest Voter Gender Gap on Record," *Fortune*, November 9, 2016, accessed December 16, 2016, http://fortune.com/2016/11/09/hillary-clinton-election-gender-gap.

80. Republican Party of California, "California Republican Party Platform & Bylaws," accessed January 15, 2015, http://www.cagop.org/wp-content/uploads/2014/05/2012-2016-Platform.pdf; Utah GOP, "Utah Republican Party State Party Platform," March 20, 2015, accessed July 13, 2016, http://utah.gop/about/utah-republican-party-state-party-platform; Republican Party of Texas, "Report of Permanent Committee on Platform and Resolutions as Amended and Adopted by the 2014 State Convention of the Republican Party of Texas" (2014), http://www.texasgop.org/wp-content/uploads/2014/06/2014-Platform-Final.pdf.

81. Tennessee Republican Party, "Speaker Beth Harwell to Co-Chair Group Aimed at Recruiting More Women Candidates," May 23, 2013, accessed July 13, 2016, http://tngop.org/speaker-beth-harwell-to-co-chair-group-aimed-at-recruiting-more-women-candidates.

82. Kate Klunk, "RSLC's 'Right Women, Right Now' Announces 558 Candidates, Unveils '14 in '14 Races to Watch,'" August 16, 2014, accessed July 13, 2016, http://www.kateklunkforstaterep.com/rslcs-right-women-right-now-announces-558-candidates-unveils-14-in-14-races-to-watch.

83. Personal communication.

84. Personal communication.

85. Republican State Legislative Committee, "Right Women, Right Now," accessed December 22, 2016, http://rslc.gop/about_rslc/rwrn.

CHAPTER 2

Gendering Republican Party Culture

Catherine Wineinger

Women currently make up 19.4 percent of Congress, and the partisan divide is significant, with Democratic women holding 78 seats and Republican women holding only 26.[1] This gap is clear in the leadership realm as well, where Republican women hold only 5 committee chair positions (3 in the House and 2 in the Senate) and 2 conference leadership positions (Cathy McMorris Rodgers as House Republican conference chair and Mimi Walters as House Republican sophomore representative).[2] This is compared to 12 Democratic women ranking members and 7 Democratic Party leaders, including Nancy Pelosi as House minority leader. Recent scholarship on women's representation has sought to explain these partisan discrepancies, but few have turned specifically to an analysis of the impact of party culture.[3]

Contrary to the notion that the Republican and Democratic Parties are mirror images of one another, party culture literature suggests that the parties are two very different entities with different rules and dynamics.[4] Jo Freeman begins her analysis of party culture by turning to the *International Encyclopedia of the Social Sciences*, which defines political culture as

> the set of attitudes, beliefs and sentiments which give order and meaning to a political process and which provide the underlying assumptions and rules that govern behavior in the political system. It encompasses both the political ideals and the operating norms of a polity. Political culture is thus the manifestation in aggregate form of the psychological and subjective dimensions of politics. A political culture is the product of both the collective history of a political system and the life histories of the members of the system and thus it is rooted equally in public events and private experience.[5]

Freeman goes on to suggest that the political cultures of the Democratic and Republican Parties are not only different, but they affect how the two parties function in American politics. Both *attitudinal* and *structural* differences influence the way Democrats and Republicans gain power within their parties, reach out to potential voters, and interact with the broader political system.[6]

This chapter analyzes the evolution and gendered effects of Republican Party culture since the 1980s. Through a content analysis of congressional floor speeches and interviews with Republican Party leaders[7] and congresswomen,[8] I seek to unveil how GOP culture has changed over time, how it affects women's representation within the party, and how Republican women are navigating this culture. Findings suggest that certain aspects of Republican Party culture have gendered implications that can constrain both the electoral and institutional power of women in the party. Still, Republican congresswomen are working to pressure party leadership and represent women by strategically employing identity politics in a way that coincides with the structural and attitudinal norms of the party.

GENDERING REPUBLICAN PARTY CULTURE

As Rep. Virginia Foxx (R-NC) pointed out, "We've always had women. Did you know you know that the first five women elected to Congress were Republicans?"[9] Indeed, women have played a significant role in GOP politics throughout history, and examining the gendered implications of Republican Party culture can deepen our understanding of the current role of women in the party. Just as women are influenced by and must learn to navigate various institutional constraints in politics,[10] their influence and power is also affected by the cultural aspects of their parties. Here, I argue that Republican Party culture can account for many of the challenges that Republican women face as candidates and as lawmakers.

The election of Ronald Reagan in 1980 marked an era of cultural and ideological change for the GOP. Conservative activists were largely successful at capturing control of the Republican Party by appealing to the ideological philosophies of Republican politicians and voters, ultimately weeding out more liberal and moderate Republicans. As Matt Grossman and David A. Hopkins note, "the relationship between ideological identity and partisan affiliation strengthened further after Reagan's victory, to the point that claiming adherence to the conservative movement became a virtual requirement for national party officials to retain their credentials as Republicans in good standing."[11] I thus analyze how current Republican Party culture has evolved from Freeman's 1986 description. Examining party culture through a gender lens allows scholars to better understand not only how this culture affects the gender dynamics of a party, but also how women are working to navigate the institutional constraints of such a culture.

CONSISTENT CULTURAL CONSTRAINTS

An analysis of party culture literature and interviews with current members of Congress and party leaders suggests that several aspects of GOP culture have remained intact since the 1980s. The Republican Party, for example, remains an ideological party with a worldview rooted in broad philosophical principles rather than a coalition of group interests. An emphasis on family values, "masculine" policy issues, and individualism can result in electoral and institutional challenges for women in the party and can limit the way they represent women in the legislative arena. The party's top-down structure and leadership norms can also further constrain women as leaders within the party.

Ideology and Policy Priorities

While the Democratic Party is largely composed of a coalition of group activists, the Republican Party tends to "ignore group characteristics"[12] and reject identity politics.[13] Intraparty debates within the Democratic Party, then, often revolve around concrete policies and decisions about which groups to promote; debates within the Republican Party are frequently based on ideological homogeneity and whether policies and individuals are conservative enough.[14]

As George Nash notes,[15] the conservative ideology that unites the Republican Party is best described as what conservatives have called a "three-legged stool"—an ideology that unites the values of social conservatism, laissez-faire capitalism, and a strong national defense. While Hans Noel points out that this "modern conservative coalition" is not necessarily characteristic of all individual Republicans, it is still central to the culture of the party as a whole: "There are conservatives who accept only part of that package, but the package as a whole has a well-developed intellectual tradition and the Republican Party as a whole advances that package. The conservative ideology has become the core of the Republican Party."[16]

Certain aspects of social conservatism—an emphasis on "family values" and traditional gender roles, for example—are not only inherently gendered but can also create unique obstacles for Republican women in the public sphere. In a response to the feminist movement of the 1960s and 1970s, antifeminist women organized in opposition to what they perceived to be a threat to traditional gender roles and the nuclear family structure. Kira Sanbonmatsu notes that antifeminist activists worked to prevent the passage of the Equal Rights Amendment (ERA; see Glossary) and were part of a broader "pro-family" movement.[17] As Rebecca Klatch has argued, "the preservation of traditional gender roles is at the very core of the social conservative woman's activism."[18]

More recently, Melissa Deckman has argued "that the growing prominence of conservative women in American politics as leaders of the Tea Party and within the GOP suggests that many conservatives have actually softened their position on what constitutes 'appropriate' gender roles."[19] Indeed, as more women enter the workforce and become breadwinners,[20] Americans' views of the role of women as homemakers has also begun to shift.[21] Still, Republican Party elites and activists continue to be more likely than Democrats to value traditional gender roles.[22] This, I argue, can have an impact on the way Republican women are perceived both in the legislature and on the campaign trail.

When asked about the challenges she believes women face in the Republican Party, Rep. Marsha Blackburn (R-TN) mentioned the fact that some GOP men still do not value their female colleagues as equals: "I think it should be noted that some conservative men do not view women as full and equal partners in the workplace. And I know for some men that is never going to change. So, I don't look at it and say it is a stumbling block. I recognize it and I do my part to change their attitude every day by doing a very good job of what is put in front of me to do."[23]

While both Democratic and Republican women report having to work harder than their male colleagues to be taken seriously, the fact that Republican women must navigate an ideology that promotes "family values" and traditional gender roles can produce a unique obstacle within their own party. Rep. Kristi Noem (R-SD) spoke specifically about the challenges of building relationships in Congress not only as a woman, but as a mother:

> When I first got to D.C., I found it hard to build relationships because I had made the decision I wasn't going to go sit in bars at night. I had three young kids and a family and I *just didn't think it was a good perception for me to do that* [emphasis added]. So it got hard to build relationships with other members, and especially when the majority of the other members are men. . . . So it's more limiting for women. I think that maybe a group of guys can go out and go to a baseball game and maybe go out to a late dinner, but if I did

that with 15 other guys, people would look at that and say, "That's a little bit strange." I mean, I can do that but I always try to make sure that I'm not putting myself in a situation that just doesn't look good.[24]

Here, Noem is ultimately concerned about how she would be perceived if she went out after work with her male colleagues, especially with three young children at home. Again, while this can be a challenge for both Democratic and Republican women, the emphasis on moral traditionalism that is rooted in conservative ideology perhaps makes it a more prominent factor in the decisions of Republican women.

These socially conservative beliefs, aside from affecting how women are treated in Congress, have also presented electoral challenges for Republican women. Rep. Renee Ellmers (R-NC), who first won her election as a Tea Party–endorsed candidate in 2010, claims that women are disproportionately tasked with proving their credentials as both a serious public servant and a good mother:

> I think people are curious about, "Who is this person? Who is this woman who is a mom, who has a family back home, who wants to run and go to Washington every week? What does that say about that person?" So then automatically people start making assumptions about who you are, what your purpose is, what your agenda is. And, you know, they want to put you in a category or they want to label you as something. And none of it is accurate. And so we struggle with getting our message out. We struggle with telling the story of who we are, and why we care about what we are doing, and why we care about our constituents. I think it is a challenge, and I think it's more of a challenge for women than it is for men.[25]

As candidates, some Republican women struggle with the perception that they are careless mothers if they run for public office. One female Republican state party leader noted, "What frustrates me is that people say, 'She has kids. Can she manage this?' A lot often have kids at home and it doesn't cross their mind. This whole 'Can she manage being a wife, mother and an elected official?' We never care about men in that way."[26]

Indeed, a 2014 Public Opinion Strategies survey found that one-fourth of Republican voters rank "family values, someone who reflects good Christian values in office" as one of the most important qualities of a candidate running for office.[27] Moreover, Tiffany Barnes and Erin Cassese find that "other elites in the GOP—such as activists and donors—who act as 'policy demanders' and advocate for policy change, endorse traditional

beliefs about gender and women's roles."[28] Thus, when Republican mothers run for office, especially in conservative districts and primary elections,
they must learn to work within an ideology that often continues—perhaps
unintentionally—to limit women to the private sphere. While navigating
motherhood is undoubtedly challenging for candidates across the political spectrum,[29] it can be particularly tasking for Republican women, who
must often work within the confines of social conservatism.

The other two legs of conservative ideology—free market capitalism
and a strong national defense—have also posed specific challenges for
Republican women. The Republican and Democratic parties are viewed
by voters as "owning" different issues. Specifically, Republicans are seen
as more competent than Democrats on such issues as national security
and crime,[30] which are also issues primarily associated with masculine
traits.[31] An emphasis on fiscal conservatism, especially since the rise of
the Tea Party,[32] has also been a central tenet of Republican Party politics.
Nicholas Winter analyzes the intersection of gender stereotypes and party
images, arguing that the Republican Party is typically associated with
masculine traits, while the Democratic Party is associated with more feminine traits.[33] Again, this becomes particularly challenging for Republican
women, both legislatively and electorally, as they must work to credential
themselves as adequately conservative members of their party.

Rep. Kay Granger (R-TX) described her experience of working to make
sure she was not pigeonholed into only speaking about what scholars have
often deemed "women's issues" (see Glossary): abortion, health care, education, social welfare, and the like:

> When I first came to Congress, Newt [Gingrich] was the Speaker, and he
> really wanted more women in Congress. He wanted them to speak on bills.
> He wanted them to be in the chair. And his office would call and say, "We
> need you in the chair this week." But he called and he said, "Kay, we have
> a woman's issue coming up on the floor that we'd like you to address." And
> I said, "Oh, is it health care or education—which one is it?" And he said,
> "I knew you'd say that." So, I thought it was my job to say labor issues are
> ours; financial issues are ours. We're everywhere . . . and we should be in
> positions far greater than we are.[34]

This pressure to work primarily on women's issues has presented itself
as an obstacle for both Republican and Democratic women alike. Still,
the centrality of a cohesive conservative ideology in the Republican
Party makes it particularly important for Republican women, more than
Democratic women, to be able to credential themselves as competent on

"masculine" issues, as these issues are typically associated with Republican conservatism.

This is true not only in Congress but on the campaign trail as well. The fact that Republican women candidates are viewed by voters as more ideologically liberal than their Republican male counterparts[35] suggests that Republican women candidates must work harder to credential themselves as true conservative women. As Grossman and Hopkins note, "The Republican donor base is made up of ideological conservatives, whereas the Democratic donor base is a collection of policy issue activists, often motivated by social identity group concerns."[36] Even female Republican donors tend to value conservatism over gender.[37] The ideological homogeneity that is central to Republican Party culture inevitably impacts which campaigns are funded and, thus, who gets elected to public office.

Indeed, making it through Republican primary elections is perhaps one of the toughest challenges Republican women face in the political arena, largely due to difficulties in convincing a conservative base that they are, in fact, conservative enough.[38] An increase in conservative media outlets since the 1980s has also contributed to this problem. As Grossman and Hopkins note, distrust of the media establishment by conservatives dates back to the 1950s. It was not until the Reagan administration, however, that the Fairness Doctrine—"which required honest, equitable, and balanced programming" [39]—was eliminated, thus paving the way for an increase in successful conservative talk shows that have been able to mobilize a unified ideologically conservative voter base.

All of this has an impact not only on *whether* Republican women get elected but also *which kinds* of Republican women get elected. While Republican congresswomen have historically been more moderate than their Republican male counterparts, and while Republican women voters continue to be less ideologically extreme than Republican men,[40] analyses of recent Congresses suggest that Republican congresswomen are now ideologically indistinguishable from Republican congressmen.[41]

Individualism and a Rejection of Identity Politics

Throughout history, Republican Party elites have rewarded party loyalty over promotion of group interests. Gendered interests were no different in this regard. In 1937, Marion Martin was appointed the head of the RNC's Women's Division. In this capacity, Martin played a role in reining in the influence of various Republican women's clubs and promoting party discipline among them.[42] Moreover, Freeman points out that the National Federation of Republican Women, rather than being an influential platform for women's demands to the Republican Party, has instead worked to bring Republican Party messages to women.[43] And while feminists in the party did push for gender equality and party support for the ERA, Goldwater conservatives grew increasingly influential in the GOP throughout the 1960s and 1970s, eventually pushing feminists out of the party.[44]

By the 1980s, support for the ERA was no longer an aspect of the party platform, and, as historian Catherine Rymph points out, the GOP was promoting women who "displayed little gender consciousness at all but who instead championed their ability to succeed as individuals."[45] This gender blindness, or aversion to identity politics, remains a driving force in the Republican Party today.[46] Unlike the Democratic Party, which allows for the substantial influence of various group interests, the Republican Party's emphasis on individualism can make it difficult for women in the party to advocate for issues on behalf of and as women, even when they believe women bring a different and important perspective to policymaking. For example, when speaking about the lack of Republican women being elected, Catherine Brinkman, the former chair of the California Young Republicans, said, "There's not enough women, and there's definitely not enough—being a Republican, I don't want to say 'diversity' because it's not about that. . . . It's not about affirmative action. It's, can we have people who represent the counties, the cities, the parts of the country they're from? Can we do that ever? Or does it always have to be white guys?"[47]

Many Republican congresswomen, consistent with their party culture, actively reject the idea that there are specific "women's issues." Still, most of them believe that women can bring a unique perspective to the policymaking process. Rep. Ann Wagner (R-MO), when asked about the difference women make in Congress, said, "We bring a different perspective. I'm not a believer in women's issues. I think all issues are women's issues. We just may come at them from a different perspective and, from living our lives and the complexity of it all, we may have a different approach to so many different issues."[48] For many Republican women, there is a tension between valuing women as women and rejecting the premise of group identity politics.

This can be particularly challenging in the age of "war against women" rhetoric, which has been consistently used by the Democratic Party. The Republican Party, in an attempt to combat the image that they are antiwomen, has worked to put women at the forefront of party activity. Rep. Virginia Foxx told us, "The party wants to present an image that is accurate, which is that women are involved and that women are part of the process. Therefore, there are sometimes conscious efforts to say, 'Okay, we want people to know women are here.' We're not tokens, and I think that's important. We're not tokens, but people want to be sure that the outside world knows women are involved."[49] Unlike the Democratic Party, which actively promotes demographic groups, the Republican Party must find a delicate balance between rejecting group identity politics and promoting the voices of women.

Consistent with this culture of individualism, Rep. Martha Roby (R-AL) insisted that her gender was not a factor in her decision to run for office. She told us, "It never occurred to me when I decided to run for Congress that being a woman would make any difference. My dad told me I could be whatever I wanted to be, and I took him at his word. So, I often get asked about being a woman in Congress, but it wasn't a factor in my decision."[50] While this can indeed be an empowering perspective, it may also prevent Republican women from understanding and confronting the various gendered challenges of running a political campaign as a woman.[51] For example, a party culture that promotes individualism and rejects identity politics makes it difficult to address the structural obstacles that exist for women candidates.

When speaking about her experiences with candidate recruitment, one female state Republican leader highlighted the struggle many Republicans face in valuing women candidates while not overvaluing identity politics:

> I think it would benefit the party. I struggle with people trying to identify women for the sake of being women. Overall, we would benefit by having more women in office, especially in the legislature at the state and federal level, for the different perspective they bring. I think it is important, but it shouldn't be at the sake of everything else. If they're as qualified or more qualified, we should be promoting women.[52]

Similar sentiments were stressed by male federal Republican leaders as well, one of whom stated, "Again, I think to try to elect and recruit female candidates because they're female is a disservice to females. Having quality candidates is a priority."[53] Another claimed, "We have recruited female candidates, but not because they were female, because they were good candidates."[54] This explicit emphasis on quality over gender demonstrates the importance that members of the Republican Party place on individualism.

In reality, women candidates in both parties are just as qualified and, in fact, tend to be more qualified than their male counterparts.[55] The fact that Republican leaders feel the need to emphasize qualifications when discussing the recruitment of women candidates suggests that a desire to step away from a perception of identity politics remains central to Republican Party culture. This, in turn, can create structural limitations for Republican women, which can hinder their chances of winning elections compared to Democratic women.[56]

As candidates, many Republican women have also claimed to struggle with campaign fund-raising. One female federal Republican leader noted, "[Democrats] have more women running in general. I think it is because the Democratic Party has very strong women's organizations that support their women candidates from the outside. EMILY's List, NARAL, Planned Parenthood. All these organizations are dedicated to getting women elected, spend time and resources training women to be candidates, activists. They have amazing fund-raising ability."[57] While there are organizations—WISH List, Susan B. Anthony List, etc.—dedicated to electing Republican women, it is true that they are much less effective and have much less money than many prominent Democratic groups.[58] A reluctance to embrace the interests of specific demographic groups can make it more difficult for Republican women's groups to form and function effectively in support of women candidates. As Rosalyn Cooperman and Melody Crowder-Meyer find,[59] even donors who give to Republican women's groups value conservatism over demographics. It is important, therefore, not to discount the impact that Republican Party culture has on Republican women's descriptive political representation (see "Representation of Women," Glossary).

Top-Down Party Structure and Institutional Leadership

These attitudinal differences that distinguish Democrats from Republicans are related to the internal structures of the two parties.[60] While the Democratic Party is organized as a party that accepts policies and messaging from various demographic groups, the Republican Party's top-down structure is more hierarchical and leaves little room for influence from individual groups. In attempting to understand the advancement of women's interests and women's leadership within the party, it is important to take into consideration this aspect of Republican Party culture.

Freeman argues that "the different direction in the flow of power also creates different conceptions of legitimacy. In the Democratic Party legitimacy is determined by who you represent, and in the Republican Party by whom you know and who you are. . . . Legitimacy in the Republican Party is dependent on having a personal connection to the leadership."[61] This can be especially constraining for Republican congresswomen, given the current gender dynamics and the relatively small number of women in the party. Rep. Ileana Ros-Lehtinen (R-FL) reflected on her time in Congress:

> I got here 26 years ago, and it was a different environment. There weren't as many women and it was definitely a good ol' boys club. I think there is so much less of that, *but still, it's a boys club. There is no denying that* [emphasis added]. . . . I'm saddened that when I got here, I was the only Republican woman on the Foreign Affairs Committee and now, 26 years later, I'm still the only Republican woman on the Foreign Affairs Committee.[62]

While Ros-Lehtinen has clearly seen a change during her time in Congress, the fact that she still views the institution as a "good ol' boys club" suggests that women members may need to work harder than their male counterparts to break into existing legislative networks.[63] Indeed, while many men are able to build relationships with male party leaders in informal settings, women in Congress are often left out of these activities and rely more on the connections made in formal settings. For example, Rep. Virginia Foxx, who is the chair of the House Committee on Education and the Workforce and who was serving as House Republican Conference secretary at the time of our interview, told us, "I also happen to have a close relationship with the Speaker, a result of having served on his committee. So, you see, my relationship with him predates being in leadership because of the committee structure. I served on that committee from the time I got here and we got to be good friends from that."[64] Developed out of her formal committee position, this personal relationship with Speaker John Boehner has helped Foxx to become an active and influential woman in the party.

Still, as Freeman notes, there are consequences to having connections to the wrong people.[65] On September 25, 2015, Speaker Boehner announced that he would resign from the speakership. His term was wrought with battles with conservative Republicans who expected the Speaker to take hard-line positions on legislation. Some have suggested that these intraparty divisions played a significant role in Boehner's decision to resign. Shortly after his announcement, it was rumored that perhaps this may open the door to Republican women's leadership. Both Rep. Marsha Blackburn (R-TN) and Rep. Cathy McMorris Rodgers (R-WA) were expected to run either for Speaker or for majority leader. Ultimately, these women chose not to run. When asked about this decision, McMorris Rodgers cited her relationship with Speaker Boehner:

> At the end of several days of talking to the members, I concluded that at this time it was smarter and more effective for me to stay in my current position. *And part of it was for people to be able to see me separate from John Boehner* [emphasis added]. You know, he invited me on the leadership team, I've been on his leadership team, and although I'm very proud of the work that I have done and was excited about the vision and I'd put together a whole strategic plan for being majority leader, I found that I think people need to see me separate from John Boehner, at least my colleagues do for a while.[66]

McMorris Rodgers undoubtedly remains an influential actor in the Republican Party. Still, as someone who came to a leadership position through her formal, personal connection with John Boehner, McMorris Rodgers faced some consequences when the Speaker resigned. Her acknowledgment that it was necessary to separate herself from Boehner before running for majority leader highlights the challenges that a top-down party structure can present for all members of the Republican Party, but for women, in particular, as they find ways to navigate the male-dominated institution of Congress.

Another consequence of a top-down party structure, Freeman suggests, is that the leadership pool in the GOP is made up of people who can repackage the party's message to make it palatable to voters, rather than people who work to change the party message from the bottom-up.[67] This, paired with the party's individualistic culture, makes it more difficult for Republican women to use leadership roles to speak and act specifically on behalf of women. Indeed, McMorris Rodgers, who is the highest-ranking Republican woman in Congress, emphasizes that women are important in helping to make the Republican Party platform accessible to different kinds of voters. She says that "people are going to listen to what [women] have to say in a different way than perhaps they've heard from their male counterparts."[68] In other words, changing the *messenger*—not necessarily the message—is an important role for women in Republican leadership.

THE TEA PARTY EFFECT: A SHIFT IN CULTURAL NORMS?

In contrast to the more confrontational debates within the Democratic Party, Freeman notes that Republican Party politics is "closed, quiet, and consensual."[69] That is, the politics of the Republican Party, because it is rooted in a cohesive ideology with a top-down organizational structure, has made it easier to build consensus while being deferential to party leadership. Freeman further describes the importance of party loyalty in the GOP:

> The Republican Party sees itself as an organic whole whose parts are inter-dependent. Republican activists are expected to be good soldiers who respect leadership and whose only important political commitment is to the Republican Party. Since direction comes from the top, the manner by which one effects policy is by quietly building a consensus among key individuals, and then pleading one's case to the leadership as furthering the basic values of the party. Maneuvering is acceptable. Challenging is not.[70]

Yet while not completely gone, discipline and loyalty to party leadership seems to be eroding as one of the main tenets of Republican Party culture. This can be seen by the challenges faced by Speaker Boehner and, now, by Speaker Paul Ryan. Grossman and Hopkins point to the rise of the Tea Party in explaining why this shift may be occurring, arguing that "the Tea Party faction has encouraged a confrontational style of politics and moved the party even further to the right."[71] While more extreme in its positions, the Tea Party is still largely ideologically consistent with the Republican Party. What has changed is the more aggressive nature of the movement to push party leadership—both inside and outside of Congress—to the right.

It is important to pay attention to this possible shift in cultural norms, as it may work to further limit the voices of women in the party. Interviews with congresswomen show that Republican women, like Democratic women, place particular emphasis on building consensus both within their party and across the aisle. The small number of women in the GOP also makes it challenging for women as a group to be an effective con-frontational force within the party. Still, Republican women are finding ways to work as and on behalf of women by engaging in a specific form of identity politics that remains consistent with many of the main aspects of Republican Party culture. Understanding how women are working within the social and structural norms of their party can shine light on the role of women in the party and how they may be working to represent women in new and innovative ways.

NAVIGATING REPUBLICAN PARTY CULTURE: WOMEN'S REPRESENTATION

Recruiting Women and Running as Mothers

Due largely to the Republican Party's effort to stay away from group politics, GOP women often do not receive the structural support needed to be successful candidates. Still, many party leaders understand the importance of reaching out to women voters, if for nothing else than to combat the Democrats' "war against women" claim. Yet, while the party as a whole has created women's recruitment programs, it is Republican women who tend to lead them.

Ann Wagner (R-MO), for instance, talked about her role in the National Republican Congressional Committee's (NRCC) Project GROW, which was created to recruit Republican women candidates. As conference chair, Cathy McMorris Rodgers (R-WA) was also joined by seven other House Republican women to form the RISE Project, which was created to recruit new women candidates and support women incumbents in their reelection efforts. Elise Stefanik (R-NY) spoke about women's unique ability and determination to get more women involved in the Republican Party: "I think we understand the importance of reaching out to women voters very effectively and are trying to make sure that, frankly, all of Congress is focused on continuing to engage women in the process."[72] Republican women are working to recruit women and thus break down structural barriers, but they are doing so in a way that frames recruitment and mobilization as beneficial to the electoral goals of the party as a whole.

As previously discussed, the Republican Party's emphasis on conservative ideology and individualism can also limit the success of Republican women once on the campaign trail. As candidates, Republican women must work to degender themselves and also prove their conservative credentials and commitment to family values at the same time. Conservative women have taken different approaches to this, but one strategy involves emphasizing their identities as mothers. As Ronnee Schreiber points out in her analysis of conservative women activists, "Appeals to maternalism are often featured, with women claiming legitimacy as actors through their status as mothers, or by arguing that feminism devalues women's roles as primary caretakers."[73]

One example of a conservative Republican female candidate who chose to utilize her motherhood on the campaign trail is Rep. Mia Love (R-UT). A case study[74] of her campaign output reveals that Love made some reference to herself as mother, to her children, or to the fact that she is married in every section of her Web site. In one of her ads, titled "Give Back",[75] two of the words used to describe her were "mother" and "conservative." Consistent with previous analyses of Republican women's campaigns,[76] Love used her identity as a mother to advocate for conservative policy positions, including such "masculine" issues as the national debt. During her nomination speech at the Utah Republican Party Convention, for example, Love underscored the relationship between her experience as a mother and her conservative principles: "When I ponder the difficulties facing our nation, I don't just see dollar signs, debt, and deficits. I see my three children who will look at me and ask, 'How did we let this happen?' We cannot let this happen. We are Republican. . . . Conservative principles work. . . . I've applied the power of conservative principles as a mayor and as a mother."[77]

Indeed, Beail and Longworth point out that some conservative women candidates have framed themselves as "mama grizzlies" in an attempt "to reclaim issues traditionally thought of as 'masculine'—reducing the size of government, the economy, free markets, lower taxes—as areas where women were needed to protect the futures of their children."[78] Melissa Deckman, too, notes that both Tea Party and Republican women have engaged in motherhood rhetoric to frame traditionally masculine issues "as being pro-family."[79] Yet Ronnee Schreiber, in her analysis of 2010 congressional candidates, finds that Republican women—and, in particular, those endorsed by the Tea Party—were still less likely than Democratic women to invoke their motherhood status on the campaign trail.[80] Each of these findings highlights the complexities of navigating an ideology and party culture that emphasizes family values and also promotes traditionally masculine policy issues and a rejection of group identity politics.

Speaking as Women, Speaking on Behalf of Women

Once in office, Republican congresswomen have continued to find ways to represent women within the confines of their party culture. Again, the current political environment in which the Republican Party has been consistently deemed antiwomen by the left has led party leaders to promote some women as leaders and highlight them as spokespersons for the party.[81] Aside from this messaging tactic by Republican leaders, however, Republican women themselves are also finding ways to speak as and on behalf of women more broadly.

In my analysis of congressional floor speeches,[82] I find that Republican women are increasingly using their personal experiences of motherhood to express knowledge and authority across various policy areas that are not typically considered to be "women's issues." For example, Martha Roby (R-AL) spoke explicitly about her family life, stating, "I remind my constituents all the time that I'm Riley's wife and a mom to my two kids, Margaret and George. I'm putting gas in the car. I'm picking up carpool. I'm going to the grocery store."[83] She went on to say that these experiences as a mother and wife have allowed her to see the everyday negative impact that President Obama's energy policies have on the America people.

When speaking on immigration, Virginia Foxx noted, "As a mother and grandmother, I am moved by the plight of these young children. . . . Today, we can provide resources to secure the border and ensure that those who have already undertaken this journey can be speedily reunited with their families.[84] In support of Second Amendment rights, Vicki Hartzler (R-MO) reflected on her identity as a mother, stating, "The first person that taught me how to hunt and to carry a gun correctly was my grandmother. . . . This belief in the Second Amendment is critically important to South Dakotans, and I certainly appreciate the fact that I had the opportunity to enjoy it. Now I have the chance with my own kids and with my husband, Brian."[85] Speeches with these types of identity claims—speaking *as* women—have increasingly become a much larger proportion of Republican women's congressional floor speeches.

Republican women have also been challenging "war against women" rhetoric by attempting to reframe women's interests. In her interview, Kristi Noem (R-SD) stated, "Women are here and are actively participating in a lot of these big discussions when it comes to budgeting, to spending, to national defense. Every mom in the country, their number one priority is that their kids are safe. And that is central to the discussion that we need to have when it comes to national security and our military"[86] Marsha Blackburn (R-TN) shared a similar sentiment in one of her floor speeches, arguing that national security is a "women's issue" that is particularly important to mothers. She said, "Madam Speaker, when you talk about issues that are women's issues, right now national security is at the top of the heap. As we have talked about soccer moms and Walmart moms and all of these other iterations and descriptions during the years, right now we are looking at a category of security moms because the issue of security is what mothers are talking about."[87]

In the 1990s, motherhood claims made by Republican congresswomen were mainly used to discuss traditional "women's issues," such as family leave and education. In more recent Congresses, there is a shift in the motherhood narrative; these claims are used when discussing a wider variety of issues related to fiscal conservatism, limited government, and national security. Interestingly, this framework falls in line with a narrative that has been constructed mainly by Tea Party activists. As Melissa Deckman notes, "What has changed from previous eras of conservative activism in the twentieth century . . . is how Tea Party women activists frame their motherhood appeal. Rather than an overt, public focus on social issues, such as feminism, or religious issues, such as 'godless' communism, as being of utmost concern to American families, the Tea Party movement has made conservative economic policy a 'pro-family' cause— one to be championed by mothers."[88]

Deckman describes three main motherhood frames used by Tea Party women activists: (1) "kitchen table conservatives," (2) "generational theft," and (3) "limited government as family protection."[89] I find that the motherhood rhetoric used by conservative women in Congress does not diverge much from these three frames; on the contrary, it tends to map on quite well to the motherhood rhetoric used by Tea Party women activists.

The "kitchen table conservatives" frame is used by women to argue that mothers, who are often in charge of their family budgets, are best qualified to speak about the need for a balanced budget in Washington. Deckman turns to Jenny Beth Martin, a cofounder of the Tea Party Patriots, as an example of such rhetoric: "We are the ones, oftentimes, in the houses and families, who are balancing the checkbooks and buying the groceries. . . . When it comes to their own personal family checkbook, women are the ones who pay such close attention to it. And we are saying we want the government to do the same thing."[90] I find similar rhetoric used by Diane Black (R-TN) when, in a floor speech, she stated, "Long before I served on the Budget Committee, I got a crash course on budgeting 101 as a single mother."[91] In an interview, Kristi Noem (R-SD) emphasized, "A lot of the women that I know are juggling lots of different responsibilities. They are not just working jobs; they are caring for their parents, they are raising children, they are making their household budgetary decisions. . . . And that perspective needs to be at the table when we are talking about bills and legislation."[92]

"Generational theft," a term originally coined by Sarah Palin, is a second motherhood frame used by Tea Party women. As described by Deckman, this frame highlights the motivation that conservative mothers have "to save children from the large debt burden that they face."[93] We can see this frame carried out in Congress as well. For example, Marsha Blackburn (R-TN) argued during a debate, "Mr. Chairman, this is why it is important for us to have a budget that balances in 10 years. I have to tell you, as a mom and a grand mom, I look a lot at what is happening to our children and our grandchildren."[94]

Finally, Tea Party women tend to invoke motherhood as a way to highlight the conservative notion of "limited government as family protection." In this frame, as Deckman notes, Tea Party mothers discuss the detrimental effects they believe big government has had on their families.[95] This is also a narrative that is being used by Republican congresswomen, as is evident in speeches related to such government programs as the Affordable Care Act. Kristi Noem (R-SD), for example, argued,

"The 30-hour workweek instituted in Obamacare is limiting economic opportunity across the country. It is especially harmful for women when 63 percent of those who are most at risk are women. . . . If you want to talk about putting challenges in their way when they are trying to fulfill all the requirements of work, of paying their bills, of being with their children, of having successful family lives, this regulation is one of the worst."[96]

These specific rhetorical frames, born out of conservative activism but used in the legislative arena, are not only centered on the concerns and personal experiences of women; they also fit neatly into existing Republican Party culture. Engaging in this rhetoric works as a specific kind of identity politics—one that can be used to represent women, while promoting individualized experiences and emphasizing all aspects of conservative ideology. The clear influence of Tea Party rhetoric also suggests that Republican women in Congress—some of whom were endorsed by the Tea Party—may be engaging in other similar tactics. As the Tea Party actively challenges GOP leadership, how are congresswomen also seeking influence and representing women in the party, despite their small numbers?

Pressuring Leadership and Seeking Influence

In interviews conducted on behalf of the Center for American Women and Politics (CAWP) with women members of Congress, most of the Democratic women talked specifically about Nancy Pelosi and used her as an example of women's leadership and influence within the Democratic Party. Republican women, in contrast, cannot point to a woman who has ever held the highest-ranking position in Republican congressional politics. In the 114th Congress (2015–2016), formal leadership roles among women in the House extended to Cathy McMorris Rodgers as chair of the House Republican Conference, Lynn Jenkins as conference vice chair, Virginia Foxx as conference secretary, and a sole woman in committee leadership, Candice Miller as chair of the House Administration Committee. House Republican women may trail Democratic women in both numbers and leadership roles, but many of the Republican women we interviewed still say they that they have had an impact in Congress and in their conference.

One example of this is the creation of the Republican Women's Policy Committee (RWPC). In the 112th Congress (2011–2012), following the 2010 election, in which the Tea Party played a significant role, the 24 Republican women in the House of Representatives formed the RWPC. The committee is used to build coalitions among Republican women, to mentor newer women members, and to promote women's perspectives within their party. Renee Ellmers (R-NC), the chair of the RWPC in the 114th Congress, said, "We understand that there is power in numbers and that can we can empower each other and help promote each other, elevate each other, make each other aware of legislation that we are working on or, you know, just situations that are taking place where we can be a helpful voice and help promote each other."[97] Indeed, according to Diane Black (R-TN), the RWPC is doing what it was intended to do: promote the voices of Republican women in Congress. She says, "I think the accomplishment is the fact that we have raised the awareness that women being involved makes a better product. . . . I see a difference between when I came here five years ago and now, and my colleagues actually reaching out to us rather than us inserting ourselves. I have colleagues who actually reach out to me and say, what do you think about this?"[98]

Republican women have also used their leadership roles to empower women both within and outside of the institution. For example, Virginia Foxx, as secretary of the House Republican Conference and a member of the Rules Committee, uses her institutional power to promote the voices of women on the House floor. Cathy McMorris Rodgers (R-WA) said of Foxx, "[She], as the secretary of the conference, has really worked to get women involved in the debate. She's also on the Rules Committee so she's on the floor a lot, no matter what the legislation may be, and wants to have women engaged in the debate no matter what the issue." She went on to say that Renee Ellmers (R-NC) "will organize special orders on the House floor where we can go down and talk about a particular issue"[99] One special order set up by Ellmers and the RWPC focused on the issue of national security and its importance to American women.

Republican women may be lacking in numbers, but they are attempting to make up for it in organizational strength. They are building coalitions, making gendered claims on the floor, and pressuring leadership to listen to women's voices on all issues—not simply those typically deemed "women's issues." These strategies preserve conservative notions of gender roles, traditional family values, and fiscal conservatism while also promoting the lives and experiences of women. Whether this will successfully translate into women's substantive representation and increased women's leadership remains unclear.

Despite their use of Tea Party rhetoric, Republican congresswomen are not collectively engaging in a confrontational style of politics. They are still adhering to the cultural norm of "building consensus among key individuals, and then pleading [their] case to the leadership as furthering the basic values of the party."[100] While they are indeed voicing women's opinions, they are also working within the confines of traditional conservative issues and are taking the party's message to women, not simply women's message to the party. Finding ways to reach out to women voters and challenge "war against women" accusations while retaining the principles of Republican conservatism proved beneficial to the party as it attempted to regain control of the government. Since winning the presidency and a majority in both houses in the 2016 election, however, the GOP will likely be less focused on messaging strategies,[101] thus potentially limiting opportunities for women's representation within the party.

CONCLUSION

This chapter examines Republican Party culture through a gender lens. I have argued that unveiling the gendered implications of party culture is essential to fully understanding the role that women play in Republican Party politics. In analyzing how GOP culture has evolved since the 1980s, I find that several cultural aspects—a cohesive ideology, an emphasis on individualism, and a top-down party structure—have not only remained consistent over time but still present specific challenges and constraints for Republican women.

Yet, despite these cultural constraints and their small numbers, Republican women candidates and members of Congress are navigating their party culture to speak and act on behalf of women. Specifically, they are engaging in a type of identity politics that allows them to represent women while upholding the party's ideological principles and notions of individualism. We see this through their gendered campaign tactics, evolving floor speech rhetoric, and organizing strategies within the institution.

Not surprisingly, Rep. Ileana Ros-Lehtinen (R-FL) spoke optimistically of the role of women in the conference, saying, "We have a good working relationship with the GOP leadership, they take us seriously and they want us to have a very important role going forward."[102] However, the future of Republican congresswomen's influence in Republican congressional politics remains unclear after the 2016 election results. As the conservative wing of the GOP continues to confront leadership and move the party to the right,[103] and as the focus of the GOP moves away from messaging tactics and toward governing strategies,[104] women's representation may be placed on the backburner.

I call on scholars to continue to study the evolution and gendered implications of party culture. Understanding women's representation and the role that women play in the Republican Party means first and foremost understanding the political culture in which they must work. It is only then that we can paint a more accurate picture of the institutional challenges that women face as candidates and as lawmakers.

NOTES

1. Center for American Women and Politics (CAWP), "Women in the U.S. Congress 2017," http://www.cawp.rutgers.edu/women-us-congress-2017.

2. CAWP, "Women in Congress: Leadership Roles and Committee Chairs," http://www.cawp.rutgers.edu/women-congress-leadership-committees.

3. For an exception, see Jocelyn Jones Evans, *Women, Partisanship, and the Congress* (New York: Palgrave Macmillan, 2005).

4. Jo Freeman, "The Political Culture of the Democratic and Republican Parties," *Political Science Quarterly* 101, no. 3 (1986): 327–356; Jo Freeman, "Who You Know versus Who You Represent," in *The Women's Movements of the United States and Western Europe: Feminist Consciousness, Political Opportunity and Public Policy*, eds. Mary Katzenstein and Carol Mueller (Philadelphia: Temple University Press, 1987), 215–244; Matt Grossmann and David A. Hopkins, "Ideological Republicans and Group Interest Democrats: The Asymmetry of American Party Politics," *Perspectives on Politics* 13, no. 1 (2015): 119–139; Matt Grossman and David A. Hopkins, *Asymmetric Politics: Ideological Republicans and Group Interest Democrats* (New York: Oxford University Press, 2016).

5. Freeman, "The Political Culture," 327–328.

6. Freeman, "The Political Culture."

7. Interviews with state and federal party leaders were conducted in 2014 by Public Opinion Strategies, on behalf of Political Parity, a program of Swanee Hunt Alternatives. Ten interviews among party leaders were conducted. A *party leader* is identified as someone actively involved at senior leadership levels at national committees or in senior roles at the state level. Five interviews were conducted among party leaders at the national level and five interviews were conducted among party leaders at the state level. At the state level, the focus was on Indiana, Arizona, and Washington State as examples of states with more active local programs for women candidates. The interviews were conducted from March 25–April 21, 2014.

8. Interviews with women members in the 114th Congress (2015–2016) were conducted by the research team at the Center for American Women and Politics (CAWP) at Rutgers University. The CAWP Study of Women in the 114th Congress interviewed 83, or 77 percent, of all women serving in the 114th Congress. The response rate was 81 percent among women members of the U.S. House and 65 percent among women senators; 84 percent of Democrats and 59 percent of Republicans, including delegates, participated. Almost all of the interviews were conducted in person on Capitol Hill, although a few were conducted by phone to accommodate member schedules; the semistructured interviews ranged from 12 to 77 minutes in length, with the average interview lasting 29 minutes. The interviews took place between September 2015 and April 2017. All interviews

were on the record, although members could choose to go off the record at any point during the interview. Questions focused on representational goals, policy priorities and achievements, party polarization, and perceptions of gender and race dynamics within the 114th Congress. The study was made possible with funding from Political Parity, a program of Swanee Hunt Alternatives, Cambridge, Massachusetts.

9. Interview with Virginia Foxx, September 18, 2015.

10. Kelly Dittmar, *Navigating Gendered Terrain: Stereotypes and Strategy in Political Campaigns* (Philadelphia: Temple University Press, 2015); Jocelyn Jones Evans, *Women, Partisanship, and the Congress* (New York: Palgrave Macmillan, 2005); Mary Hawkesworth, "Congressional Enactments of Race–Gender: Toward a Theory of Raced–Gendered Institutions," *American Political Science Review* 97, no. 4 (2003): 529–550; Michele L. Swers, *The Difference Women Make: The Policy Impact of Women in Congress* (Chicago: University of Chicago Press, 2002); Michele L. Swers, *Women in the Club: Gender and Policy Making in the Senate* (Chicago: University of Chicago Press, 2013).

11. Grossman and Hopkins, "Ideological Republicans," 9.

12. Freeman, "The Political Culture," 336.

13. Grossman and Hopkins, "Ideological Republicans"; Grossman and Hopkins, *Asymmetric Politics*; Ronnee Schreiber, *Righting Feminism: Conservative Women and American Politics* (Oxford: Oxford University Press, 2012).

14. Grossman and Hopkins, "Ideological Republicans"; Grossman and Hopkins, *Asymmetric Politics*.

15. George H. Nash, *The Conservative Intellectual Movement in America since 1945* (Wilmington, DE: ISI Books, 2008).

16. Hans Noel, *Political Ideologies and Political Parties in America* (Cambridge: Cambridge University Press, 2014), 37.

17. Jo Freeman, "Feminism vs. Family Values: Women at the 1992 Democratic and Republican Conventions," *PS: Political Science and Politics* 26, no. 1 (1993): 21–27; Kira Sanbonmatsu, *Democrats, Republicans, and the Politics of Women's Place* (Ann Arbor: University of Michigan Press, 2004).

18. Rebecca E. Klatch, *Women of the New Right* (Philadelphia: Temple University Press, 1988), 10.

19. Melissa M. Deckman, *Tea Party Women: Mama Grizzlies, Grassroots Leaders, and the Changing Face of the American Right* (New York: New York University Press, 2016), 177.

20. Wendy Wang, Kim Parker, and Paul Taylor, "Breadwinner Moms," Pew Research Center, May 29, 2013, http://www.pewsocialtrends.org/2013/05/29/breadwinner-moms/.

21. Sanbonmatsu, *Democrats, Republicans*.

22. Tiffany D. Barnes and Erin C. Cassese, "American Party Women," *Political Research Quarterly* 70, no. 1 (2017): 127–141.

23. Interview with Marsha Blackburn, November 17, 2015.

24. Interview with Kristi Noem, November 17, 2015.

25. Interview with Renee Ellmers, December 2, 2015.

26. Shauna Shames, *3:1: Republican Women Are Outnumbered in Congress: Right the Ratio*, (Cambridge, MA: Political Parity and Hunt Alternatives, 2015), accessed June 2, 2017, https://www.politicalparity.org/wp-content/uploads/2015/01/primary-hurdles-full-report.pdf.

27. Shames, *3:1*, 36.

28. Barnes and Cassese, "American Party Women," 137.

29. Richard L. Fox, *Gender Dynamics in Congressional Elections* (Thousand Oaks, CA: Sage, 1997); Dittmar, *Navigating Gendered Terrain*.

30. John R. Petrocik, "Issue Ownership in Presidential Elections, with a 1980 Case Study," *American Journal of Political Science* 40, no. 3 (1996): 825–850; John R. Petrocik, William L. Benoit, and Glenn J. Hansen, "Issue Ownership and Presidential Campaigning, 1952–2000," *Political Science Quarterly* 118, no. 4 (2003): 599–626.

31. Leonie Huddy and Nayda Terkildsen, "Gender Stereotypes and the Perception of Male and Female Candidates," *American Journal of Political Science* 37, no. 1 (1993): 119–147.

32. Theda Skocpol and Vanessa Williamson, *The Tea Party and the Remaking of Republican Conservatism* (New York: Oxford University Press, 2016).

33. Nicholas J. G. Winter, "Masculine Republicans and Feminine Democrats: Gender and Americans' Explicit and Implicit Images of the Political Parties," *Political Behavior* 32 (2010): 587–618.

34. Interview with Kay Granger, January 7, 2016.

35. David C. King and Richard E. Matland, "Sex and the Grand Old Party: An Experimental Investigation of the Effect of Candidate Sex on Support for a Republican Candidate," *American Politics Research* 31, no. 6 (2003): 595–612.

36. Grossman and Hopkins, "Ideological Republicans," 115.

37. Danielle M. Thomsen and Michele L. Swers, "Which Women Can Run? Gender, Partisanship, and Candidate Donor Networks," *Political Research Quarterly* 70, no. 2 (2017): 449–463.

38. Kelly Dittmar, "Primary Problems: Women Candidates in U.S. House Primaries," Center for American Women and Politics, Rutgers University, October 3, 2013, http://www.cawp.rutgers.edu/sites/default/files/resources/primary-problems-10-1-13.pdf; Shames, *3:1*.

39. Grossman and Hopkins, "Ideological Republicans," 149.

40. Barnes and Cassese, "American Party Women."

41. Brian Frederick, "Gender and Roll Call Voting Behavior in Congress: A Cross-Chamber Analysis," *American Review of Politics* 34 (2016): 1–20; Danielle M. Thomsen, "Why So Few (Republican) Women? Explaining the Partisan Imbalance of Women in the U.S. Congress," *Legislative Studies Quarterly* 40, no. 2 (2015): 295–323.

42. Catherine E. Rymph, *Republican Women: Feminism and Conservatism from Suffrage through the Rise of the New Right* (Chapel Hill: University of North Carolina Press, 2006).

43. Freeman, "The Political Culture."

44. Rymph, *Republican Women*.

45. Rymph, *Republican Women*, 244.

46. Grossman and Hopkins, "Ideological Republicans"; Grossman and Hopkins, *Asymmetric Politics*.

47. Emily Crocket, "These Republican Women Say Their Party Abandoned Them Long Before Trump," *Vox*, November 8, 2016.

48. Interview with Ann Wagner, April 28, 2016.

49. Interview with Virginia Foxx.

50. Interview with Martha Roby, February 12, 2016.

51. Dittmar, *Navigating Gendered Terrain*.

52. Interview with female state Republican Party leader, March 25–April 21, 2014.

53. Interview with male federal Republican Party leader, March 25–April 21, 2014.

54. Interview with male federal Republican Party leader, March 25–April 21, 2014.

55. Kathryn Pearson and Eric McGhee, "What It Takes to Win: Questioning 'Gender Neutral' Outcomes in U.S. House Elections," *Politics & Gender* 9, no. 4 (2013): 439–462.

56. Pearson and McGhee, "What It Takes."

57. Interview with female federal Republican Party leader.

58. Rosalyn Cooperman and Melody Crowder-Meyer, "Can't Buy Them Love: How Party Culture among Donors Contributes to the Party Gap in Women's Representation," Paper presented at the annual meeting of the Midwest Political Science Association, 2015.

59. Cooperman and Crowder-Meyer, "Can't Buy Them Love."

60. Freeman, "The Political Culture"; Freeman, "Who You Know."

61. Freeman, "The Political Culture," 333–334.

62. Interview with Ileana Ros-Lehtinen, March 1, 2016.

63. Interview with Ileana Ros-Lehtinen, 336.

64. Interview with Virginia Foxx, September 18, 2015.

65. Freeman, "The Political Culture"; Freeman, "Who You Know."

66. Interview with Cathy McMorris Rodgers, December 4, 2015.

67. Freeman, "The Political Culture."

68. Interview with Cathy McMorris Rodgers.

69. Freeman, "The Political Culture"; Freeman, "Who You Know," 338.

70. Freeman, "Who You Know," 339.

71. Grossman and Hopkins, *Asymmetric Politics*, 104.

72. Interview with Elise Stefanik, October 20, 2015.

73. Schreiber, *Righting Feminism*, 17.

74. Author's note: I conducted an analysis of Love's 2014 campaign output, including content analyses of her social media feeds, Web site, online videos, and advertisements. This case study was used to determine the ways in which she navigated her gender and racial identities in the context of Republican Party culture.

75. Mia Love for United States Congress, *Love for Utah*, 2014, http://love4utah.com.

76. Linda Beail and Rhonda Kinney Longworth, *Framing Sarah Palin: Pit Bulls, Puritans, and Politics* (London: Routledge, 2013); Dittmar, *Navigating Gendered Terrain*; Deckman, *Tea Party Women*.

77. Mia Love for United States Congress, "Mia Love—UTGOP Convention Speech 2014," filmed April 2014, YouTube video, 6:52, posted April 27, 2014, https://www.youtube.com/watch?v=BTfkrELdOHA.

78. Beail and Longworth, *Framing Sarah Palin: Pit Bulls, Puritans, and Politics*, 144.

79. Deckman, *Tea Party Women*, 99.

80. Schreiber, "Mama Grizzlies Compete for Office," 549–563.

81. Deckman, *Tea Party Women*.

82. Author's note: I conducted an analysis of congressional floor speeches given by Republican women in the 103rd, 104th, 113th, and 114th Congresses to determine whether and how these speeches have changed over time. I specifically analyzed changes in the frequency and framing of gendered claims made on the House floor.

83. Rep. Roby, speaking on Affordable Energy, 113th Cong., 1st sess., *Congressional Record* 159, no. 92 (June 25, 2013): H4015.

84. Rep. Foxx, speaking on H.R. 5230, 113th Cong., 2nd sess., *Congressional Record* 160, no. 123 (August 1, 2014): H7208.

85. Rep. Hartzler, speaking on Second Amendment Rights, 113th Cong., 1st sess., *Congressional Record* 159, no. 58 (April 25, 2013): H2338.

86. Interview with Kristi Noem.

87. Rep. Blackburn, speaking on Imminent Threats to Our National Security, 114th Cong., 1st sess., *Congressional Record* 161, no. 109 (July 14, 2015): H5156.

88. Deckman, *Tea Party Women*, 117.

89. Deckman, *Tea Party Women*, 118–126.

90. Deckman, *Tea Party Women*, 118.

91. Rep. Black, speaking on H. Con. Res. 27, 114th Cong., 1st sess., *Congressional Record* 161, no. 50 (March 25, 2015): H1942.

92. Interview with Kristi Noem.

93. Deckman, *Tea Party Women*, 121.

94. Rep. Blackburn, speaking on H. Con. Res. 96, 113th Cong., 2nd sess., *Congressional Record* 160, no. 58 (April 9, 2014): H3076.

95. Deckman, *Tea Party Women*.

96. Rep. Noem, speaking on H.R. 2575, 113th Cong., 2nd sess., *Congressional Record* 160, no. 54 (April 3, 2014): H2871.

97. Interview with Renee Ellmers.

98. Interview with Diane Black, October 28, 2015.

99. Interview with Cathy McMorris Rodgers, December 4, 2015.

100. Freeman, "The Political Culture," 339.

101. Frances Lee, *Insecure Majorities: Congress and the Perpetual Campaign* (Chicago: University of Chicago Press, 2016).

102. Interview with Ileana Ros-Lehtinen.

103. Grossman and Hopkins, *Asymmetric Politics*.

104. Lee, *Insecure Majorities*.

CHAPTER 3

Women in the Tea Party and the GOP: A Natural Alliance?

Melissa Deckman

In 2008, millennial Keli Carendar was not happy with the direction of her country in the wake of the nation's recent fiscal meltdown that had been spurred by a housing bubble and driven many financial institutions to bankruptcy and many homeowners to foreclosure. A libertarian at heart, Carender was not only dismayed that the country appeared poised to elect Barack Obama, a Democrat, as the nation's next president, but she disagreed with the Targeted Asset Relief Program (TARP) that had been put into place by Republican president George W. Bush's administration earlier that year. TARP aimed to bring stability to the financial markets by bailing out the nation's largest financial institutions to stem their losses and offset what many economists believed would be the start of another Great Depression. These events prompted her to become involved in conservative political activism in her native city of Seattle:

> I personally saw what Candidate Obama was saying and thought he was a total radical and I couldn't understand why everyone thought he was a moderate. Not that I liked [John] McCain [the Republican nominee], but this guy [Obama] is totally far out in left field. What are you guys thinking? So, it spurred me to action and to do something.[1]

Shortly after Obama's inauguration, when Congress passed a major stimulus bill that increased government spending on infrastructure and established programs geared at helping homeowners avoid foreclosures on their mortgages, Carender held what she dubbed the "Porkulus Protest" in February 2009, as a protest against federal legislation that increased the national deficit. Many herald that protest as the nation's first Tea Party rally.[2] Carendar's role in spearheading the Porkulus Protest ultimately led her to become the national grassroots coordinator for Tea Party Patriots, one of the largest national Tea Party organizations founded as part of the larger Tea Party movement in America.

The Tea Party movement is not a politically monolithic entity; what binds its many grassroots and national organizations together is its advocacy for limited government that is rooted in a conservative interpretation of the Constitution. Reducing the federal debt, lowering taxes, and promoting American exceptionalism are key issues that dominate the movement.[3] The transformative nature of the election of America's first black president also spurred many Americans, particularly older people, to get involved in the Tea Party; indeed, studies find that "racial resentment" is an important predictor of which Americans are likely to support the movement.[4] In the age of Trump, concerns about immigration and national security also differentiate Tea Party supporters from other Americans, as they take a far more conservative view of such positions.

In many ways, the Tea Party invokes similar populist (see "Populism," Glossary) right-wing elements found in our nation's history, from anti–New Deal American groups opposed to FDR in the 1930s, to the anti-communist witch hunts led by Sen. Joseph McCarthy and the strongly conservative Cold War Republicans embodied by Barry Goldwater and Ronald Reagan.[5] However, one way that the Tea Party is unique compared to earlier conservative movements is the role that women are playing in it, a demographic not typically aligned with conservative causes. In earlier right-wing movements, such as the Christian Right, women often played important, but behind-the-scenes, roles.[6] By contrast, the Tea Party is distinct in that women have been just as likely—if not more so—to rise as leaders as men within the movement. Women, such as Jenny Beth Martin, lead national Tea Party organizations (Tea Party Patriots); many others have founded their own local Tea Party groups, and others still have developed new right-wing conservative social media groups geared specifically at women, such as Smart Girl Politics and As a Mom . . . a Sisterhood of Mommy Patriots.

Given that women have arrived as major movers and shakers within the Tea Party, why have we not seen a similar influx of conservative women rising as leaders and activists within the GOP? Why do many conservative women apparently find the Tea Party to be a better vehicle for their activism than the Republican Party? Are Tea Party women and Republican women fundamentally different in their beliefs and approaches to policy?

On the one hand, Tea Party women and Republican women share many commonalities in terms of their social backgrounds and attitudes about numerous social and economic issues. Tea Party women also realize that to enact their preferred policy changes, they need to work within the Republican Party in Congress and in state legislatures around the country. Indeed, many argue that the Tea Party has already made the GOP into a more conservative party on a variety of measures,[7] and my book *Tea Party Women* shows that some Tea Party women have been successful in influencing the messaging of the GOP, especially in its appeal to mothers in the electorate over economic concerns.[8]

On the other hand, the Tea Party has been a more welcoming space for many conservative women activists because strong differences remain between them and rank-and-file Republican women concerning their orientation to the federal government, more generally, and their skepticism of the Republican Party, more specifically—a skepticism that has long historical roots in earlier conservative populist movements in the United States. Unlike the GOP, which many Tea Party activists describe as too slow-moving and overly bureaucratic, the Tea Party is far more organizationally fluid, which allows these very conservative women to bypass such structures and form their own organizations. Additionally, Tea Party women have sometimes been rebuffed by local and state Republicans in their efforts to emerge as leaders themselves, describing the GOP as the consummate "old boys' network." Tea Party women, like their male counterparts, believe the Republican Party establishment is too willing to compromise on conservative principles, so, for many of these women, the Tea Party serves as an ideal outlet for their brand of very conservative activism.

Will the election of Donald Trump bring new opportunities for Tea Party women to shape the Republican Party? Possibly. As I demonstrate in this chapter, Trump's calls to deport illegal aliens, build a wall along the Mexican border, and limit immigration from Muslim countries are significantly more likely to find support among Tea Party women than Republican women nationally. While Trump's more populist economic views place him at odds with many members of his party, his nationalistic tendencies appeal to many Tea Party women. If Trump is successful in rebranding his party more in his image, as a populist champion bent on limiting free trade and promoting America first, this may potentially open the door for Tea Party women to find new ways to influence the Republican Party during his administration.

The Scope of Tea Party Women Nationally

In 2012 and 2013, I interviewed dozens of women active in the Tea Party about why they had become involved in the movement as well as several leaders of longer-standing conservative women's organizations to get a sense of their take on women's roles within the movement.[9] I also relied on participant observation at Tea Party events and textual analysis of Tea Party writings. To compare GOP women nationally with Tea Party women on a variety of public policy positions, I analyzed national survey data from the Public Religion Research Institute, a nonpartisan, nonprofit research institute.[10]

Despite the tremendous enthusiasm generated by the Tea Party among conservatives nationally, and the large level of media attention it generated, survey data shows that the movement never received the full support of most Americans. And, although women led many of the newly formed Tea Party organizations at the grassroots, state, and national levels, a gender gap emerged in the general public showing that men are significantly more likely than women to express support for the movement.[11] In other words, a breakdown of Tea Party members shows that about 60 percent are men, while about 40 percent are women.[12] Yet, among men and women who identify as part of the Tea Party, there are relatively few differences among them in terms of their attitudes on most public policies.[13] Simply put, the Tea Party attracts very conservative men and women to its causes.

Turning just to women, however, Figure 3.1 takes a look at American women's orientation toward the Tea Party over time, beginning in 2010 and through June 2016, based on data from the Public Religion Research

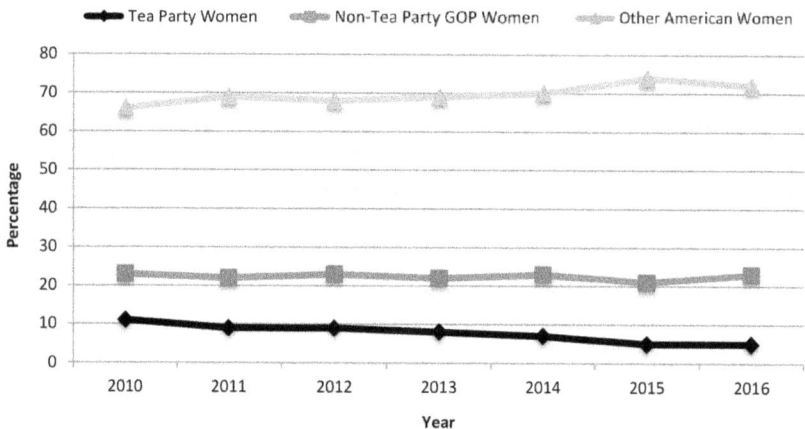

Figure 3.1 Percentage of Women Who Identify as Tea Party Members, Republicans Who Do Not Identify as Tea Party Members, and Other American Women, 2010–2016

Source: Data from Public Religion Research Institute (PRRI), 2010–2016.

Institute (PRRI), which has consistently asked Americans since 2010 whether they "consider themselves part of the Tea Party or not."[14] At the movement's highpoint of visibility in 2010, just 11 percent of American women claimed to be part of the Tea Party. By June 2016, however, that figure had dropped to 5 percent.

Instead, American women have been far more likely in each of these years to claim Republican Party identification while rejecting the Tea Party label (herewith known as Republican women). By 2016, for instance, 23 percent of American women identified as Republicans, but not as part of the Tea Party. Generally speaking, however, the percentage of Republican women has stayed consistent nationally, wavering between 21 percent and 23 percent since 2010.[15]

By and large, most American women are neither part of the Tea Party nor Republicans. This group of "other" American women has increased slightly over the same period; in 2010, for instance, 66 percent of American women identified as Democrats, independents, or with a third party. That percentage had increased to 74 percent by 2015, and then dropped slightly to 72 percent in 2016. The sheer fact that the majority of American women are not part of the Tea Party and do not identify as Republicans demonstrates the uphill work that both entities need to do to convince more American women to support their conservative brand of politics.

Tea Party Women: What Brought Them to the Movement?

In analyzing why the Tea Party appealed to many conservative women at its inception in 2009, most women activists I interviewed revealed that they were alarmed at the economic downturn of 2008 and the federal government's reaction to it. Nearly all the women I interviewed said they were motivated to become part of the Tea Party following the bailouts of Wall Street in late 2008 and the election of Barack Obama, who with a Democratically controlled Congress had enacted legislation that either grew the deficit, such as the American Recovery and Reinvestment Act of 2009 (the "Stimulus Bill"), or extended the size and scope of government, such as the Affordable Care Act, better known as Obamacare. In their minds, such government activism at the federal level represented a betrayal of the principles of the Founding Fathers, who they believe designed a federal government with far more limited powers in the Constitution. Many also believed that the Tea Party's message of lowering taxes, reducing government regulation, decreasing the federal budget deficit, and returning to a more limited scope of federal government was the formula for putting America back on a winning path.

Not surprisingly, given the importance that such issues played in motivating their involvement in the Tea Party, my analysis of PRRI data shows that Tea Party women hold conservative positions on a variety of economic issues (see Figure 3.2). However, Tea Party women look very similar to Republican women when it comes to these concerns—and notably quite different from other American women.[16] For instance, 64 percent of Tea Party women and 67 percent of Republican women say that lowering taxes is preferable to spending more government money on infrastructure and education when it comes to building the economy, according to the 2012 PRRI American Values Survey.[17] In the 2014 PRRI American Values Survey, slight majorities of both women disagree that the government should do more to reduce the gap between the rich and the poor, and both sets of women believe government policies for the poor are more likely to create a "culture of dependency where people are provided with too many handouts," as opposed to serving "as a critical safety net, which help people in hard times get back on their feet." Turning to more recent data, the 2015 PRRI American Values survey shows that both sets of women are reluctant to favor raising the minimum wage to $15 per hour. Both Tea

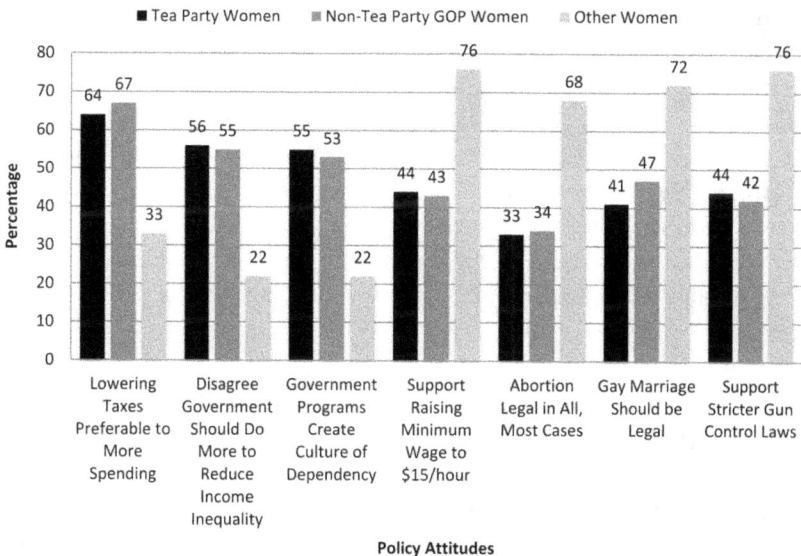

Figure 3.2   Similarities among Tea Party and Republican Women on Policy Attitudes

Source: Data from Public Religion Research Institute (PRRI), American Values Survey, 2012, 2014, 2015.

Party and Republican women are also united in their desire to not expand Obamacare or keep its current form (data not reported). On these economic measures, other American women hold far more liberal attitudes.

Similarly, on social issues that have long driven a wedge in American politics, Tea Party women and Republican women share similar opinions. Both sets of women are largely opposed to abortion rights, gay marriage, and gun control initiatives, again standing apart from other American women (see Figure 3.2). With respect to abortion and gay marriage, such predominately conservative views are not surprising, given that both sets of women are best described as theologically conservative. According to the 2015 PRRI American Values Survey, roughly half of both Tea Party women and Republican women who are not part of the movement describe themselves as born-again Christians. Both sets of women also attend church frequently, especially compared to other American women (data not reported).

Given such similarities between Republican women and Tea Party women, why did the latter group decide to become engaged in this larger political movement as opposed to situating their activism within the GOP? Part of the reason is connected to the hierarchical nature of the Republican Party. Many of the women I spoke with, such as Jenny Beth Martin of Tea Party Patriots, believe that the Tea Party gives women more opportunities to become leaders in conservative politics than the GOP:

> I would say more than anything, men and women and others who are active in the Tea Party, we don't have the same sort of bureaucracy that the Republican Party has. You don't have to cut through all of these different layers to become a leader in the Tea Party. We want as many leaders as we can possibly have. And we make it easy for people who have leadership goals to step up and become leaders.[18]

Social media has also presented these women with unprecedented networking opportunities and has allowed them to bypass more bureaucratic conservative organizations, particularly the Republican Party, to lead their own groups. In fact, many of the Tea Party women activists I spoke with fervently believe that the importance of social media to the Tea Party has especially allowed women to flourish as leaders on their own terms and in their own time. For instance, Lori Parker, the cofounder of As a Mom . . . A Sisterhood of Mommy Patriots—a social media organization devoted to raising political awareness among socially conservative women that was founded during the rise of the Tea Party—told me that the use of social media provided an outlet for conservative political activism that was simply unavailable to many busy mothers:

> Moms are so busy and their lives are so packed, to say let's meet Tuesdays at 7 o'clock doesn't work. Where, if we say, we have a meeting 24/7 going on online, pop in whenever you can, read the latest on the farm bill, it works. It conforms better to everyone's life because it is much easier to pop into your iPhone while you are waiting for junior to get done with piano lessons than it is to find a babysitter and show up to a meeting. We are social media. We wouldn't exist without social media, because that is how we completely run.[19]

Another cofounder of a statewide Tea Party organization in Maryland, who writes her own successful local blog, believes that social media is especially well suited to women's multitasking and communication skills in comparison to men, telling me that "women are willing to share details" about political organizing that are often neglected by men.[20] In the age of social media, busy conservative women have more options than working within their local or state party organizations, which can be more time-consuming and less flexible. Carrie Lukas, the managing director of the Independent Women's Forum, said that the huge influx of conservative women active in the Tea Party is linked to social media's ability to provide an alternative to traditional party activism:

> The main reason there has been a huge shift in political involvement and, in particular, women with children being more politically involved in the Tea Party, is that they can be. Most of our political dialogue now takes place on the Internet, through social media. So, if you are a stay-at-home mother of four or a working mom of four, you don't have time to go down to campaign headquarters, hand out leaflets and volunteer or do x, y, and z.[21]

The barriers to political entry with the Tea Party, as compared with the GOP, are far lower, which has allowed conservative women a new way to express their political views and become engaged in politics. And the reliance on social media as a major mechanism for political organization may also better suit women than men. As Lukas concluded, "Girlfriends are used to sharing with each other and tagging each other (on Facebook) . . . 'I thought this article was an interesting story that we should all pass around.' Women do this quite naturally, and I think men in general are more reticent to do stuff like that. And I think that that is the political basis for the organizational success of the Tea Party."[22]

Of course, many conservative women are not drawn to the Tea Party merely because it is more convenient than the traditional organizing work of political parties. Tea Party activists who are attempting to reshape the GOP into a more conservative party often complain about the tension between the "establishment" Republican Party and more conservative grassroots activists, or "authentic Republicans."[23] So several of the Tea Party women activists believed that the Tea Party offered a better avenue for women conservatives because of their unwillingness to compromise on their strong ideological principles.

At the same time, many of women activists I spoke with argue that the GOP has been particularly bad for women conservatives, and, thus, the Tea Party offers a far more welcoming environment. For example, Katrina Pierson, who cofounded the Garland Tea Party in Dallas, Texas, in 2009, told me,

> It used to be that men in the GOP or male leaders could take a woman's idea as their own—I have had this experience—but with social media women can be attributed, they can define their own brand, and define yourself and have your ideas heard. You don't have to go through the good old boys' club any longer and that has been huge for women.[24]

Pierson also cites the "lashing" that national women figures, such as Sarah Palin and Michele Bachmann, faced for "not agreeing with the party leadership" as more evidence that the Republican Party is not always welcoming of women to its leadership ranks. Pierson herself tried unsuccessfully to challenge Rep. Pete Sessions in the 2014 GOP congressional primary in her home district in Texas, only to face little support for her candidacy among party leaders. She told the *Dallas Daily News* that her campaign, which garnered about 30 percent of the vote, "exceeded expectations" and that her main goal was keeping the Republican establishment honest on conservative principles.[25]

Similar to Katrina Pierson, Jennifer Jacobs also faced hostility from "establishment" Republicans in her years of local political activism.[26] Jacobs started a county-based Tea Party organization in rural Maryland several weeks after the Tea Party phenomenon emerged in February 2009 when she realized that "no one else was doing it."[27] Jacobs, a small business owner and grandmother, did have prior political experience before founding her Tea Party group, having served for one term on her county's Republican Central Committee in the 1990s. However, she soon figured out, in her words, that "being a woman was a detriment" to party involvement. She told me, "The party tries to put you in a box, and if you think outside of the box or try and do things outside of the box, you are pun-ished." By contrast, she has found the Tea Party's warm welcome of men *and* women conservatives appealing: "It's all about the individual. This is what the Founders knew, it is what we women already know—our country is broken and it needs to be fixed."[28]

That Tea Party women are more conservative than Republican women and more skeptical about the GOP becomes clear in looking at other data comparing Tea Party and Republican women nationally. Figure 3.3 shows, for instance, that while both Tea Party women and Republican women are far more likely to consider themselves conservative compared to other American women, Tea Party women are more likely to do so than Republican women.[29] Moreover, they express far more skepticism about the Republican Party more generally than do rank-and-file Republican women: just 56 percent have a favorable view of the Republican Party, compared with 80 percent of Republican women.[30] Their attitudes about health care and the GOP's ability to improve Obamacare are also telling. Recall that angry Tea Party activists flooded town hall meetings the sum-mer of 2009 to protest Obamacare, enraged by the proposed legislation

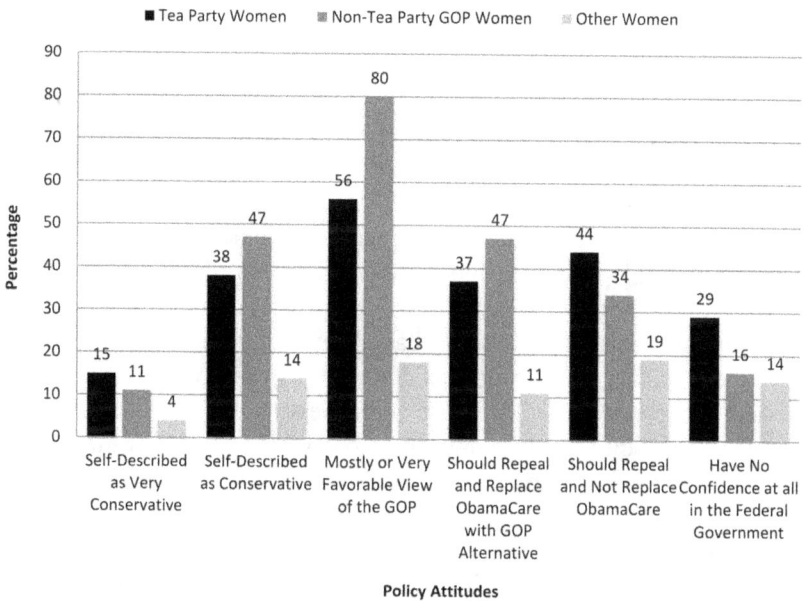

Figure 3.3 Differences among Tea Party and Republican Women: Ideology, the GOP, and Obamacare

Sources: PRRI/Brookings Immigration Survey, 2016; American ValuesSurvey, 2014.

that they decried as federal overreach. While Republican leaders also denounced the policy from the start, data from PRRI's 2014 American Values Survey shows that 47 percent of non–Tea Party Republican women felt that Obamacare should be repealed and "replaced with a Republican alternative," compared with just 37 percent of Tea Party women. Instead, 44 percent of Tea Party women expressed support for simply repealing the law and not replacing it.[31]

Not surprisingly, Tea Party women nationally hold far more negative views about the federal government more generally than other American women, and even Republicans. While Republicans have certainly always argued for limited government, especially compared to Democrats, who express more comfort in having the federal government play a larger role in Americans' lives, Tea Partiers generally hold more disdain toward Washington. Relatively few Americans expressed a great deal of confidence in the federal government according to the 2015 PRRI American Values Survey, but Tea Party women were nearly twice (29%) as likely as non–Tea Party Republican women (16%) to say "none at all" (see Figure 3.3).[32] Clearly, the data show that Tea Party women are more ideologically conservative and express greater skepticism about the federal government and the GOP than their Republican women counterparts.

TEA PARTY WOMEN IN THE AGE OF TRUMP

The surprising and unorthodox campaign of Donald Trump brought a new, divisive dimension to the Republican presidential campaign. Perhaps no other issue set Trump apart from his early rivals in the Republican Party presidential contest than immigration and national security. While many of Trump's Republican opponents in the nomination race similarly rejected comprehensive immigration reform supported by prominent Democrats and some Republican leaders in Congress that would have allowed undocumented immigrants a potential path to citizenship, none used such course, vitriolic language to express their opposition. Calling for America to build a wall along its border with Mexico, Trump said of our neighbors to the South, "When Mexico sends its people, they're not sending their best. . . . They're sending people that have lots of problems, and they're bringing those problems with us. They're bringing drugs. They're bringing crime. They're rapists. And some, I assume, are good people."[33] In December 2015, Trump was also heavily criticized by leaders in both parties when he called for a "total and complete shutdown of Muslims entering the United States until our country's representatives can figure out what is going on" a few days after two radicalized terrorists—an

American-born citizen of Pakistani descent and his Pakistani-born wife who was a permanent legal resident—opened fire and killed 14 people at a public health facility in San Bernardino, California.[34]

Concerns about immigration and national security highlight another area in which Tea Party women differ from Republican women more generally. As data from the 2016 PRRI/Brookings Institution Immigration Survey show, Tea Party women are more likely than their Republican women counterparts to find immigration to be a personally salient issue to them and to hold the most hard-line position on immigration. For instance, Tea Party women are nearly twice as likely as Republican women—44 percent to 24 percent, respectively—to "completely agree" that the United States should "make serious efforts to deport all illegal immigrants."[35] Tea Party women are significantly more likely to favor building a wall along the Mexican border as well, although differences between Tea Party women and their GOP women counterparts do not reach statistical significance when it comes to the temporary ban on Muslim immigrants (see Figure 3.4).

Tea Party women's opposition to immigrants is steeped in economic anxieties. Half of Tea Party women also believe that immigrants "mainly

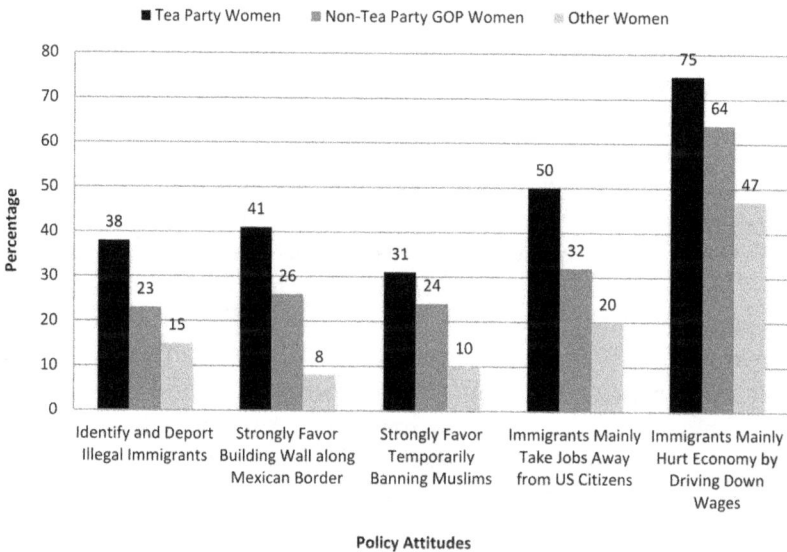

Figure 3.4 Differences among Tea Party and Non–Tea Party Republican Women on Immigration Policy Attitudes

Source: PRRI American Values Survey, 2015; PRRI Immigration Survey, 2016.

take jobs away from U.S. citizens," rather than mostly taking jobs that Americans do not want; they are significantly more likely to say so than Republican women.[36] Seventy-six percent of Tea Party women agree with the statement that immigrants "mainly hurt the economy by driving down wages," rather than helping the economy by providing low-cost labor; on all of these measures, other American women hold far less conservative views (see Figure 3.4).

That Tea Party women generally express the most conservative positions on immigration is not surprising given earlier work by political scientists Christopher Parker and Matt Barreto, who found that Tea Party identification is significantly related to anti-immigration attitudes.[37] Moreover, scholars Theda Skocpol and Vanessa Williamson found that many Tea Party activists express hostility toward immigrants because of the perception that such undocumented residents are a burden to public resources, such as public education and health care.[38] While the Democratic Party has championed comprehensive immigration reform in recent years, the Republican Party's reaction to such reform has been more divisive. In a nod to the growth of Latinos as part of the U.S. population, and in recognition that Latino voters overwhelmingly favor immigration reform, many Republican leaders have called for the GOP to champion such policies as a means to diversify and grow the party.[39] Yet, moves toward a more moderate immigration policy by the GOP, as this data reveal, are likely to be met with fierce resistance from very conservative activists at the grassroots level, including Tea Party women.

Combined, these last few statistics suggest that many Tea Party women were likely to embrace Donald Trump as their preferred nominee for president in 2016. In addition to his hard-line immigration stances, Trump routinely touted his appeal as a political outsider willing to challenge the Republican establishment. Indeed, his outsider status led several female leaders that are often linked with the Tea Party to endorse him, most notably Sarah Palin, arguably the first well-known Republican to back Trump in January 2016. In her endorsement speech, Palin hailed Trump as a political force that exposes the "complicity" of both sides of the political aisle in disenabling a "fundamental transformation of America." She argued that Trump has been able to "tear the veil off" the political system: "We need someone new, who has the power, and is in the position to bust up that establishment to make things great again."[40] Amy Kremer, a well-known Tea Party leader who for many years served as the executive director of Tea Party Express, a political action committee dedicated to electing Tea Party–style Republicans to various levels of political office, also endorsed Donald Trump and cofounded the Women for Trump PAC.[41]

Yet, when asked who their preferred nominee for president was in June 2016, shortly after the primary contests were over, the 2016 PRRI/ Brookings Institution Immigration Survey shows that just 28 percent of Tea Party women listed Trump as their preferred Republican nominee, compared with 34 percent of other Republican women. Instead, 50 percent of Tea Party women preferred U.S. senator Ted Cruz over Donald Trump; Cruz was the preferred nominee of just 35 percent of non–Tea Party Republican women (data not reported). In some ways, Ted Cruz is a natural selection for Tea Party activists. Although perhaps less extreme than Donald Trump in his language about immigration, Cruz has generally held very conservative views on the issue.[42]

The greater appeal of Cruz versus Trump among Tea Party women, however, was likely more linked to his religion. A devout Evangelical and social conservative, Cruz made religious liberty a cornerstone of his run for the presidency; the national data shows that Tea Party women, who are more theologically conservative than most American women, consider religious liberty a pressing political problem. Moreover, Cruz's efforts in 2013 to shut down the government over opposition to funding Obamacare, while enraging party leaders, endeared him to many Tea Party activists, who viewed his action as a principled stand against a policy they hated. In many ways, then, Ted Cruz can be viewed as just as "antiestablishment" as Donald Trump, though the two men differ in many policy arenas apart from immigration, especially concerning their views on the Constitution and on limited government (for instance, Trump said repeatedly during the campaign trail that he would not reduce entitlement spending on programs such as Medicare and Social Security, which does not align with most Tea Party groups)—issues that I found many Tea Party women view with primary importance.[43]

Many nationally known Tea Party figures, including Jenny Beth Martin, publicly rejected Donald Trump as the best candidate to uphold the values of the Tea Party movement. Speaking at the 2016 Conservative Political Action Conference before the primaries had finished, Martin said of Trump, "He loves himself more than our country. He loves himself more than the Constitution. . . . Donald Trump has no business thinking he is Tea Party."[44] Tea Party Patriot's political action committee instead endorsed Ted Cruz during the primaries, describing him as a man who "understands and loves our Constitution."[45]

Once the nomination campaign was done, though, most Tea Party women leaders quickly got in line to back Donald Trump, given that their views were in dire opposition to the policy stands of Hillary Clinton, the Democratic Party's nominee. Jenny Beth Martin's response to Trump's selection as her party's nominee sums up this pragmatic decision to back Trump for the White House: "Hillary Clinton stands opposed to everything the Tea Party stands for, on the policy, political and personal fronts. Donald Trump, on the other hand, has pledged to fight to uphold our core values. In making a choice between the two of them, there really is no choice at all—we choose Trump."[46] Notably, as exit polls demonstrate, despite many misgivings about Donald Trump, particularly in the wake of startling revelations about his behavior toward women, as embodied by the leaked *Access Hollywood* audiotape of an earlier interview in which he bragged about being able to sexually assault women, conservative women largely backed Trump at the polls.[47]

TEA PARTY WOMEN AND THE REPUBLICAN PARTY: SOME AREAS OF COMMON GROUND

As the Trump administration begins, can Tea Party women better shape the Republican Party? If past is prologue, I find that on areas of common ground with the Republican Party, Tea Party women have had some success in influencing the GOP. For instance, the past several election cycles have brought some very conservative women to prominence within the Republican Party, starting with the 2010 elections, in which a record number of Republican women ran for Congress and other races.[48] Indeed, many credit Sarah Palin, whose Sarah PAC endorses self-proclaimed "mama grizzlies" running for Congress and other offices, with inspiring more conservative women to run for office. While some Tea Party–backed women lost what pundits considered "winnable" general elections in several high-profile Senate races in 2010—Christine O'Donnell (Delaware) and Sharron Angle (Nevada) come to mind—other Republican women succeeded in getting elected to Congress, including nine women to the House and one woman to the Senate[49]—often with the encouragement and active campaigning of Tea Party activists.

Nikki Haley and Susana Martinez, both of whom also secured much Tea Party support as party outsiders in 2010, made history by becoming the first women of color to be elected as governors in South Carolina and New Mexico, respectively. In 2014, the Tea Party also helped usher in the election of several very conservative women at the federal level, including Iowa's first woman senator, Joni Ernst, and Mia Love (Utah), the first Republican African American woman elected to the House of Representatives. In that respect, conservative Republican women whose fortunes were helped by the Tea Party show that the GOP can be receptive to conservative women candidates.

Tea Party women's activism in helping elect more conservative women to Congress and into several governors' mansions is not the only way that the Tea Party has shaped the GOP into a more conservative party. Leading Republican women in Congress—whose presence sometimes predates the Tea Party—have used rhetoric to defend their policies as good for women and families, which Tea Party women first used successfully to galvanize their movement supporters. As political scientist Michele Swers argues in her work on women and Congress, the GOP often looks to its women members as surrogates to "reach out to women voters who tend to favor Republicans, such as white suburban married women, and to defend their party against Democratic accusations that Republican policies are harmful to women."[50]

In *Tea Party Women*, I identify several "motherhood frames" that many Tea Party women commonly use in their writing, speeches, or social media communications to explain why they have become politically active and to inspire other like-minded women to get involved with the Tea Party. While appealing to mothers to engage in politics is a time-honored tradition used by political activists on both the left and the right, what is new about Tea Party women's use of motherhood pleas is in its application to economic policy. I find that Tea Party women employ several motherhood frames to promote deficit and debt reduction. For example, Tea Party women often call on mothers to become engaged in politics as "kitchen table" conservatives—because moms have experience "balancing the budget" at home, those skills are needed to help balance the federal budget nationally. For example, Tami Nantz, the former editor in chief of Smart Girl Politics—a popular social media site geared at conservative women—believes that discussing the economic issues that confront families, such as grocery and utility costs, "is a huge way to reach women" to be supportive of the Tea Party cause.[51]

After the Tea Party's rise, many leading Republican women in Congress began employing similar household analogies in their defense of smaller federal budgets. At a press conference to announce the formation of the Women's Policy Committee in the House of Representative in May 2012, Rep. Diane Black of Tennessee touched on these themes: "As a wife, mother, and small business owner, I know firsthand about the importance of making a budget and living within one's means. This commonsense fiscal responsibility is sadly lost on the president and his party."[52] Several years later, Cathy McMorris Rogers, the chair of the House Republican Conference, defended the need to balance the federal budget in very personal terms as a mother. Speaking in March 2015, as House Republicans proposed a budget that would reduce federal spending, McMorris Rogers commented, "As a mom of three young kids, I know firsthand the challenge that comes with balancing the family budget. Women all across the country do the same thing—on average, they manage 84 percent of household income for their families—and they know better than anyone that a balanced budget leads to a better future."[53]

Another motherhood theme that Tea Party women often use to compel conservative women to become active in politics concerns the federal debt and the well-being of America's next generation, as described by Sarah Palin in her book *America by Heart*. She writes, "Moms can be counted on to fight for their children's future. And when politicians start handing our kids the bill for their cronyism and irresponsibility—when they engage in generational theft—moms rise up."[54] Tea Party women routinely insist that part of their motivation for getting involved in politics is to save children from the large debt burden that they face. Jenny Beth Martin, of Tea Party Patriots, agrees that motherhood is a powerful source of inspiration for their activism because parents are concerned with the fiscal health of the nation. She believes that many women are getting involved in the Tea Party because "they are looking at their children and thinking we have got to leave a country that is fiscally sound for their children; they deserve that. It is motherhood and it is looking at our children and making sure that we have or are leaving the right country for them."[55] This line of rhetoric concerning debt reduction and motherhood also appears to be influencing the argumentation of more "establishment" Republican women leaders. Rep. Cathy McMorris Rodgers described House Republican women on the conservative *RedState* blog—a Web site popular with Tea Party activists—as "mothers and grandmothers who want to eliminate the debt burden for the next generation" and as conservative reformers "committed to leaving America better for our children and grandchildren than it was for us."[56]

That the Republican Party relies on its women leaders—however small in numbers they are compared with the Democratic Party—to promote its "brand" or argue that their policies are better for American families is nothing new.[57] But the emphasis on motherhood appeals, for example, when calling for Congress to cut its spending and reduce the debt, takes a page out of the rhetorical playbook first used by Tea Party women. That such similar rhetoric on what is best for women and their families comes from both Tea Party women and an increasing number of elected Republican women officials should not be surprising, however, given how often these two groups of women have intermingled in recent years. For example, prominent Republican women are often featured speakers at events sponsored by Tea Party women's groups, such as the Smart Girl

Politics Summit, and GOP women are often profiled on the Web sites of conservative women's organizations, serving to inspire many right-wing women at the grass roots. The increasing use of gendered rhetoric by GOP women to promote conservative policy signifies that the Republican Party, pushed by the rise of women as conservative activists, is realizing that it needs a different message, and more diverse messengers, to better reach women voters across the country. In this respect, then, Tea Party women may have found a way to influence the Republican Party, despite the misgivings that some grassroots conservative women leaders have about the Republican Party more generally.

But can such influence on the Republican Party grow now that Donald Trump has entered the White House? The selection of former governor Nikki Haley as his ambassador to the United Nations shows that Trump is willing to promote some conservative women who secured earlier Tea Party backing into prominent spots within his administration. However, Trump trails recent presidents in the number of women he has selected to be part of his cabinet, and of the other three women he nominated—Elaine Chao at the Transportation Department, Linda McMahon at the Small Business Administration, and Betsy DeVos at the Education Department—none really have close ties to the Tea Party. Moreover, Trump's economic positions as a presidential candidate did not exactly subscribe to Tea Party principles. His unwillingness to reform Social Security and his promotion of far more government investment in the nation's infrastructure, indeed, seemed more likely to be drawn from the Democratic Party rather than the GOP platform. Moreover, his protectionist trade proposals also upset many free market organizations with close ties to the Tea Party.

However, if Trump changes the priorities of the GOP to place less emphasis on economic issues and instead to emphasize national security and immigration reform—issues that dominated his first few weeks as president as he signed a series of executive orders aimed at building a wall with the Mexican border, denying federal funding to "sanctuary cities,"[58] and stopping the immigration of refugees from Syria and immigrants from seven other predominately Muslim countries—then perhaps an opening for Tea Party women, who clearly hold more conservative positions on these matters than other Republican women nationally, to take a larger leadership role in the GOP may emerge.

While there are relatively few Republican women currently serving in either chamber in 2017, in the 115th Congress, (just 5 Republican women serving in the Senate and 22 Republican women serving in the House of Representatives), several now hold powerful committee chairs in the House, including Diane Black (Tennessee), chair of the Budget Committee, and Kay Granger (Texas), chair of the Defense Appropriations Subcommittee, which decides the spending priorities of the military.[59] Both Diane Black and Kay Granger quickly endorsed Trump's executive orders,[60] and Black has cosponsored legislation to withhold federal grants to sanctuary cities, noting in a press release that "Americans have compassion for our neighbors abroad but we know that our first responsibility is to protect our fellow citizens here at home. That is the core of President Trump's 'America First' agenda, and it is an agenda that families in my district are eager to see put to work."[61] Whether representatives such as Diane Black represent a vanguard of new conservative women to lead the GOP remains an open question, however.

CONCLUSION

Women who identify with the Tea Party are a small, diminishing minority in the United States. While close to 1 in 10 women claimed to be part of the movement in 2010, their numbers now rank at around 5 percent of the American public. By contrast, during this same period, the number of women who identified as Republicans—but who eschewed the Tea Party label—has stayed roughly consistent. Combined, however, both sets of women represent a relatively small slice of the population.

Although this chapter reveals some very real tension between Tea Party women activists and the Republican Party, mainly because Tea Party women have often felt that women have not always been welcome in the GOP's ranks or viewed the party as too willing to compromise with Democrats, this analysis shows that when it comes to most political issues, Tea Party women and Republican women who do not identify with the movement share far more in common in terms of their political views. Their similarities become especially striking considering that women who neither embrace the Tea Party nor the Republican Party look very differently in terms of their political attitudes. While tensions continue to simmer between the Tea Party and the Republican Party, it is important to remember that the Tea Party has in many ways turned the GOP into a more conservative party on numerous issues, particularly as they relate to economic policy. And, as this chapter briefly demonstrates, the Republican Party has embraced many of the same gendered arguments first used by Tea Party women to sell its model of smaller government to cast a wider appeal to women voters.

Ironically, though, the challenges that the right-wing Tea Party women I interviewed face in shaping the Republican Party are similar to those experienced by women representing the ideologically *moderate* flank of the party. As the Republican Party has become more conservative ideologically in the past few decades, work by political scientist Danielle Thomsen shows that GOP women state legislators, who have historically been more moderate than their male counterparts, have been reluctant to seek their party's nomination for Congress, given that primary voters are far more conservative than voters in the general election.[62] Experimental studies also show that Republican voters assume that their party's female candidates are less conservative than the male candidates,[63] which again may make it more difficult for women to be elected as Republicans. Coupled with the GOP's hesitancy to "do identity politics," or recruit and train women with the express goal of promoting more of them, it is little wonder that women who are elected to office are three times more likely to be Democrats than Republicans. The GOP's lackluster record in promoting women as candidates also spills over to its leadership ranks. In 2015, just 9 out of 50 state chairs of the Republican Party were women, which was a little less than half of the women represented as party chairs within the Democratic Party.[64]

These perceptions about Republican women, then, may have spillover effects for women in the Tea Party, despite their very conservative orientation: if Republican party leaders, most of whom are men, believe that women within the party are less conservative than men, Tea Party women may be hindered in their ability to wield influence within the GOP, making involvement in the Tea Party a more appealing alternative. Whether the election of Donald Trump, a populist president who is prioritizing national security and immigration as the leading issues of his administration, does more to advance the leadership opportunities of Tea Party women remains to be seen.

NOTES

1. Melissa Deckman, *Tea Party Women: Mama Grizzlies, Grassroots Activists, and the Changing Face of the American Right* (New York: NYU Press, 2016), 37.

2. Kate Zernike, *Boiling Mad: Inside Tea Party America* (New York: Times Books /Henry Holt and Co., 2010).

3. Deckman, *Tea Party Women.*

4. Christopher Parker and Matt A. Barreto, *Change They Can't Believe In: The Tea Party and Reactionary Politics in America* (Princeton, NJ: Princeton University Press, 2013).

5. Charles Postel, "The Tea Party in Historical Perspective," in *Steep: The Precipitous Rise of the Tea Party*, ed. Lawrence Rosenthal and Christine Trost (Berkeley: University of California Press, 2012), 25–56.

6. There are, of course, notable exceptions to this trend, especially the late Phyllis Schlafly, who gained national prominence as the architect behind the movement to ratify the Equal Rights Amendment in the 1970s. Schlafly maintained an active presence in conservative grassroots activism until her death in 2016.

7. Theda Skocpol and Vanessa Williamson, *The Tea Party and the Remaking of Republican Conservatism* (New York: Oxford University Press, 2012).

8. Deckman, *Tea Party Women*.

9. More detailed information about the interviews can be found in appendix A of my book *Tea Party Women*.

10. I draw most of my analysis from two surveys: the 2015 PRRI American Values Survey (N = 2695) and the 2016 PRRI/Brookings Institution Immigration Survey (N = 2607). In some cases, I present data featured in my book *Tea Party Women* (2016), which relies on a number of PRRI surveys conducted from 2012 through 2014, because similar questions were not featured in the two more recent PRRI surveys employed here. Where possible, I try to use the most recent data available.

11. Deckman, *Tea Party Women*.

12. Deckman, *Tea Party Women*.

13. Deckman, *Tea Party Women*.

14. Data for this question comes from the following surveys conducted by the Public Religion Research Institute (PRRI) in conjunction with the Brookings Institution: the 2010 American Values Survey; the 2011 American Values Survey; the 2012 American Values Survey; the 2013 Immigration Survey; the 2014 American Values Survey; the 2015 American Values Survey; and the 2016 Immigration Survey. For more information about how these surveys were conducted and to download the data, see PRRI's data vault: http://www.prri.org/data-vault.

15. Although the data are not reported here, it is important to recognize that while most Republican women nationally reject the Tea Party label, either a majority or plurality of women in the Tea Party still consider themselves Republican. For instance, in 2010, 59 percent of Tea Party women identified as Republicans; in 2016, it was 46 percent. The second most frequent party identification among Tea Party women was "independent." Relatively few American women who belong to the Tea Party identify as Democrats. See Deckman, *Tea Party Women*.

16. Notably, an analysis of gender differences within Tea Party members yields few statistically significant differences. In most of the policy attitudes examined in this chapter, I find that Tea Party women and Tea Party men are virtually indistinguishable. These findings echo my earlier analyses in *Tea Party Women*.

17. Deckman, *Tea Party Women*. These differences are not statistically significant according to a chi-square test conducted by the author.

18. Deckman, *Tea Party Women*, 38.

19. Deckman, *Tea Party Women*, 62.

20. Ellen Sullivan (pseudonym), author interview, Frederick, Maryland, February 4, 2013. In my book *Tea Party Women*, I use pseudonyms for most of the grassroots activists. For those activists leading national organizations or

those who have taken a higher profile, such as Katrina Pierson—who ran for Congress—I opted to use their real names.

21. Deckman, *Tea Party Women*, 69.

22. Deckman, *Tea Party Women*, 69.

23. Skocpol and Williamson, *The Tea Party and the Remaking of Republican Conservatism*.

24. Deckman, *Tea Party Women*, 46.

25. Pierson's high-profile involvement in the Tea Party led to her being hired as the national spokeswoman for the Donald Trump presidential campaign in early 2016.

26. I use a pseudonym here.

27. Jennifer Jacobs, author interview, Annapolis, Maryland, November 8, 2012.

28. Jennifer Jacobs, author interview.

29. Ideological differences between Tea Party women and Republican women are statistically significant according to a chi-square test at the $p < 0.10$ level ($p = 0.07$).

30. Differences regarding Tea Party women's and Republican women's views of the GOP and confidence in the federal government are also statistically significant, at the $p < 0.001$ and $p < 0.05$ levels, respectively, according to a chi-square test conducted by the author.

31. These differences are statistically significant at the $p < 0.01$ level according to a chi-square test.

32. These differences are statistically significant at the $p < 0.05$ level according to a chi-square test.

33. "Donald Trump's Presidential Announcement Speech," *Time*, accessed May 28, 2017, http://time.com/3923128/donald-trump-announcement.

34. Russell Berman, "Donald Trump's Call to Ban Muslim Immigrants," *The Atlantic*, December 7, 2015, accessed May 28, 2017, http://www.theatlantic.com/politics/archive/2015/12/donald-trumps-call-to-ban-muslim-immigrants/419298.

35. Differences between Tea Party and Republican women are statistically significant when it comes to views on deporting illegal immigrants ($p < 0.05$) according to a chi-square test.

36. These differences are statistically significant at the $p < 0.05$ level according to a chi-square test; however, differences between Tea Party and Republican women fail to reach statistical significance when it comes to their views on whether immigrants mainly hurt the economy by driving down wages ($p = 0.203$).

37. Christopher Parker and Matt A. Barreto, *Change They Can't Believe In: The Tea Party and Reactionary Politics in America* (Princeton, NJ: Princeton University Press, 2013).

38. Skocpol and Williamson, *The Tea Party and the Remaking of Republican Conservatism*.

39. Republican National Committee (RNC), "Growth & Opportunity Project," accessed July 10, 2016, http://goproject.gop.com/rnc_growth_opportunity_book_2013.pdf.

40. Kyle Blaine, "So, Uh, Here's the Full Text of Sarah Palin's Bizarre Trump Speech, BuzzFeed, January 19, 2016, accessed May 28, 2017, https://www.buzzfeed

.com/kyleblaine/so-uh-heres-the-full-text-of-sarah-palins-bizarre-trump
-spee?utm_term=.vuJ3LZZvD#.yyDVbxxmP.

41. Michelle Cottle, "Standing by Their Man," *The Atlantic*, June 13, 2016, accessed May 28, 2017, http://www.theatlantic.com/politics/archive/2016/06 /standing-by-their-man/486851.

42. For example, Ted Cruz openly criticized his fellow Republican U.S. sena- tors, such as John McCain and Marco Rubio, for helping shepherd a comprehen- sive immigration reform bill through the Senate in 2013 that would have allowed a path to citizenship for the roughly 11 million undocumented residents living in the United States. (The bill failed to pass the Republican-controlled House.) While Cruz initially did support increasing *legal* immigration for highly qualified workers in 2013, he always opposed "amnesty" for undocumented workers, as the bipartisan bill would have allowed if it had not failed in the House of Representa- tives. By the time that Cruz became a presidential candidate, however, his posi- tion on immigration turned more hard-line as he called for more border security and a temporary halt on all legal immigration.

43. Deckman, *Tea Party Women*.

44. Allegra Kirkland, "Tea Party Leader: Trump 'Has No Business Thinking' He's One of Us," Talking Points Memo, March 4, 2016, accessed May 28, 2017, http://talkingpointsmemo.com/livewire/jenny-beth-martin-slams-trump-cpac.

45. Jenny Beth Martin, "Tea Party Patriots Endorses Ted Cruz," *Washington Times*, February 1, 2016, http://www.washingtontimes.com/news/2016/feb/1/jenny -beth-martin-tea-party-patriots-endorses-ted-.

46. Alex Swoyer, "Tea Party Super Pac Endorses Donald Trump," *Breitbart News*, September 22, 2016, http://www.breitbart.com/2016-presidential-race/2016/09/22 /tea-party-super-pac-endorses-donald-trump/.

47. Michelle Cottle, "Why White Women Continue to Back Trump," *The Atlan- tic*, November 14, 2016, http://www.theatlantic.com/politics/archive/2016/11/white -women-support-gop/507617.

48. Beth Reingold and Jessica Harrold, "Women and the 2010 Midterm Elec- tions: A Mixed Bag," *Women's News and Narratives*, Spring 2011, http://www .womenscenter.emory.edu/aboutTheCenter/ourHistory/Online%20Magazine1 /SPRING11_Womens_News_and_Narratives/election_story.html.

49. Center for American Women in Politics (CAWP), "CAWP Elec- tion Watch," November 3, 2010, http://www.cawp.rutgers.edu/sites/default/files /resources/pressrelease_11-23-10.pdf.

50. Michele Swers, *Women in the Club: Gender and Policy Making in the Senate* (Chicago: University of Chicago Press, 2013), 245.

51. Deckman, *Tea Party Women*, 119. Nantz now served as a contributor to the conservative-leaning news Web site opportunitylives.com.

52. Diane Black, "Republicans Launch Women's Policy Committee in House: New Caucus Gives Voice to Key Group on Important Issues," May 22, 2015, https:// black.house.gov/press-release/republicans-launch-women's-policy-committee -house-new-caucus-gives-voice-key-group.

53. House Republicans, "Balancing Our Budget for American Families," March 17, 2015, https://www.gop.gov/balancing-our-budget-for-american-families.

54. Sarah Palin, *America by Heart: Reflections on Family, Faith, and the Flag* (New York: Harper, 2010), 130.

55. Deckman, *Tea Party Women,* 122.

56. Cathy McMorris Rodgers, "House Republican Women: Working for You," Red State, May 23, 2012, http://www.redstate.com/diary/congresswomancathy mcmorrisrodgers/2012/05/23/house-republican-women-working-for-you.

57. Swers, *Women in the Club.*

58. Sanctuary cities are cities that essentially refuse to cooperate with federal authorities to deport undocumented immigrants who live in them.

59. David Hawkings, "House Republican Women See a Boost in Authority," Roll Call, January 18, 2017, https://www.rollcall.com/news/hawkings/house -republican-women.

60. Alex Daugherty, "Texas Republicans Silent of Supportive of Trump's Immigration Order," *Charlotte Observer,* January 29, 2017, http://www.charlotteob server.com/news/politics-government/article129476954.html.

61. Diane Black, "Congressman Black Statement on President Trump's Immigration Orders," January 25, 2017, http://black.house.gov/media/press-releases /congressman-black-statement-president-trump-s-immigration-orders.

62. Danielle Thomsen, "Why So Few (Republican) Women? Explaining the Partisan Imbalance of Women in the U.S. Congress," *Legislative Studies Quarterly* 40, no. 2 (2015): 295–323.

63. David C. King and Richard E. Matland, "Sex and the Grand Old Party: An Experimental Investigation of the Effect of Candidate Sex on Support for a Republican Candidate," American Politics Research 31, no. 6 (2003): 595–612.

64. Data were calculated by the author from the RNC's Web site, which presents an interactive map with party leaders: https://www.gop.com/leaders/states. Women in 2015 make up 17 of the Democratic state party chairs. Data were calculated by the author from links found on the Democratic Party's Web site: http://asdc.democrats.org/state-parties.

CHAPTER 4

Republican Women, Then and Now: Ideological Changes in Congressional Candidates from 1980 to 2012

Danielle M. Thomsen

The underrepresentation of women in American politics has motivated more than three decades of political science research. At the national legislative level, the United States is ranked 104th worldwide, with women comprising only 19 percent of the House of Representatives.[1] The laggard status of women in American politics stands in stark contrast to levels of female representation cross-nationally (see "Women in Politics, Worldwide Rankings," in Glossary). The United States is well below the Nordic countries, where women hold approximately 40 percent of the national legislative seats, but the United States also trails behind much of the world. Just to reach the global average of 22.3 percent, all of the current female members would have to be retained, and an additional 18 women would need to be elected to congressional office. Most recently, it has taken five election cycles for the number of women in Congress to increase by such a margin.[2] And this is simply to achieve the global average; gender parity remains much further down the road.

Scholars have long sought to understand the extent to which the electoral environment hinders the advancement of women to congressional office. As a result, previous analyses of gender and electoral success have focused almost exclusively on differences between men and women. The main finding to emerge from this line of research was that "when women run, they win" at equal rates as their male counterparts.[3] Similarly situated women candidates attracted as many votes and raised as much money as their male counterparts, and the general conclusion was that "winning elections has nothing to do with candidate sex."[4] Based on these general indicators, gender scholarship in the 1990s suggested that the electoral environment was largely *gender neutral*. Most of the earliest studies concerned general election outcomes, but those on primary victory rates also analyzed differences between men and women.[5]

Less attention, however, has been devoted to variation across women candidates and shifts in the makeup of women candidates over time. It is of course clear that the women elected to congressional office have changed dramatically in recent years. The female legislators in Congress are first and foremost partisans who in large part resemble their male counterparts. Over the last three decades, the ideological gulf between Democratic and Republican women has increased with nearly each election cycle, and the distance between female members now exceeds that between men.[6] But previous studies of officeholders include only those who won both the primary and general elections, and there are no empirical analyses of the ideological makeup of the full pool of male and female congressional candidates over time. Understanding which women run for office has direct consequences for policy outcomes, and particularly for debates around women's issues (see Glossary). While women's issues have historically been associated with feminist values, conservative women in office are instead likely to pursue policies that are linked with traditional family values.[7]

This chapter draws on a new dataset of U.S. House candidates to examine ideological changes in male and female candidates from 1980 to 2012. The main takeaway is that male and female primary and general election candidates, winners and losers alike, have become more polarized over time. The percentage of ideologically moderate women candidates has declined dramatically in both parties in recent years. In addition, a much smaller number of Republican women are running as incumbents, which contributes to the growing partisan disparity among women in Congress (see Figures I.1 and I.2 in the Introduction). The findings extend our understanding of ideology and gender in the current context, and they have important implications for the types of policies that women in the contemporary Congress are likely to pursue. The chapter concludes by discussing how these changes in the types of women who run for office matter for the substantive representation of women in American politics.

GENDER, IDEOLOGY, AND CANDIDATE EMERGENCE

The lack of available data has long hindered the study of candidate ideology. Poole and Rosenthal constructed DW-NOMINATE scores to trace historical changes in the ideology of members of Congress, but there were no measures that placed all congressional candidates, both winners and losers, on a common ideological scale.[8] Ansolabehere, Snyder, and Stewart developed the first comprehensive solution to this problem by comparing the policy positions of candidates running in races where the two candidates had a voting record, and they supplemented these data with responses to Project Vote Smart's National Political Awareness Test (NPAT).[9] Others have done snapshot analyses of candidate ideology that are similar to the NPAT, and more recently, Burden conducted the Candidate Ideology Survey (CIS), which asked candidates running in 2000 to place themselves on a left-right ideological scale.[10] But none of these data allowed for a comparison of the ideology of winners as well as losers across multiple election cycles.

Gender scholars have thus overwhelmingly examined changes in male and female candidates with respect to incumbents.[11] Rogowski and Langella trace changes in the ideology of incumbent and nonincumbent congressional candidates from 1980 to 2012, but their focus is on primary rules, and they do not explore gender differences.[12] Our specific interest here is how ideological patterns of candidate emergence vary across male and female Republicans and Democrats as well as over time. It is possible that candidate entry differs by gender and party in light of previous research showing that men and women are perceived in stereotypically gendered ways.[13] For example, Koch demonstrates that women candidates are not only seen as more liberal than their male counterparts, but they are also perceived to be more liberal than they actually are.[14] In addition, King and Matland find that GOP voters are less likely to vote for a hypothetical female Republican candidate than a hypothetical male candidate but Democrats and Independents are more likely to do so.[15] Patterns of candidate emergence may be different for Republican women than for Republican men and Democratic women if they expect to incur an additional penalty in the primary and receive an additional benefit in the general election.

Yet, it is also possible that gender differences in candidate emergence have varied over time and that they have diminished in the current partisan era. In a recent experimental study of gender stereotypes, Brooks finds that female candidates are no longer assumed to be more liberal than male candidates.[16] Hayes and Lawless additionally demonstrate that media coverage and voter evaluations today primarily stem from partisanship and ideology, not the sex of the candidate.[17] And in one of the most comprehensive studies of gender and voting behavior, Dolan shows that vote choice is shaped by partisanship and incumbency rather than candidate sex.[18] Any gender differences that used to be apparent may have diminished over time as the two parties drifted further apart ideologically. Due to previous data limitations, we know very little descriptively about how the ideological makeup of female and male candidates has evolved in recent decades.

DATASET OF MALE AND FEMALE CONGRESSIONAL CANDIDATES

The analyses are based on primary and general election candidates for the U.S. House of Representatives from 1980 to 2012. Election results were obtained from the Federal Election Commission (FEC) and the *America Votes* series.[19] There are 24,228 primary candidates and 13,547 general election candidates (Republicans and Democrats) in this dataset. I merged these data with the Database on Ideology, Money in Politics, and Elections (DIME).[20] The DIME dataset includes the ideology and gender of those who ran for congressional office from 1980 to 2012. Bonica uses campaign finance records from state and federal elections to estimate the ideology of a wide range of political actors.[21] Existing ideological measures, such as DW-NOMINATE scores, only allow for an analysis of incumbent members of Congress; one advantage of using Bonica's estimates here is that we can analyze congressional candidates who won as well as those who lost.

There are 17,681 primary candidates and 12,518 general election candidates who appear in both the *America Votes* series or FEC election returns data and the DIME dataset. These figures are lower than the total number of candidates who were on the primary and general election ballots in these years because not all congressional candidates are in the DIME dataset. Of the full sample of those who appeared on the ballot, 73 percent of the primary candidates and 92 percent of the general election candidates have Bonica ideology scores.[22] Of the primary candidates, 8,818 are Democrats and 8,863 are Republicans; of the general election candidates, 6,463 are Democrats and 6,055 are Republicans.

Candidate gender was obtained from the Bonica dataset and through additional online and newspaper searches.[23] The gender breakdown of primary candidates is virtually the same as that in Lawless and Pearson, which provides further validation.[24] A total of 3,041 and 1,745 women ran in congressional primaries and general elections, respectively, and women comprised 12.6 percent of all primary candidates and 12.9 percent of all general election candidates. This figure is higher than the average of 8 percent reported by Lawless and Pearson due to the difference in time periods under consideration.[25] Of the full sample of primary and general election female candidates, 2,383 and 1,636 have Bonica ideology scores (78% and 94%, respectively). Because the main concern is ideological changes in male and female candidates over time, this chapter examines only those with available ideology scores.

Table 4.1 shows the number of male and female candidates by election year and party. The number of candidates varies across cycles, with a low of 850 primary candidates in 1990 and 651 general election candidates in 1980 and a high of 1,399 primary candidates in 2010 and 809 general election candidates in 1996. On average, there are 1,040 primary candidates and 736 general election candidates per cycle.[26]

We can see that the differences between Republican and Democratic women are especially striking. Throughout the 1980s, women were equally distributed between the parties, and in 1984, Republican women candidates even outnumbered Democratic women. In 1990, the trajectory of Republican and Democratic women began to split. The "Year of the Woman" elections in 1992 led to the first significant jump in women candidates in both parties, but what is perhaps more notable is that the number of women in the Democratic pool has increased steadily since then. Women comprised 16 percent of Democratic primary candidates in 1992, 21 percent in 2002, and 27 percent in 2012. Similarly, women were 16 percent of Democratic general election candidates in 1992, 21 percent in 2002, and 28 percent in 2012. The proportion of female candidates in the GOP has instead stagnated during this time. Women made up 10 percent of the Republican primary pool in 1992, 11 percent in 2002, and 12 percent in 2012. They constituted 9 percent of Republican general election candidates in 1992, 12 percent in 2002, and 11 percent in 2012. Thus, although women have increased their ranks in both the Republican and Democratic pools since the 1980s, Democratic women have been more successful than their Republican counterparts.

Victory rates do not differ as markedly between Republican and Democratic women. Of these female Democratic general election candidates, 50 percent won in 1992, 51 percent won in 2002, and 53 percent won in 2012 (33, 37, and 58 women, respectively). Of the female Republican general election candidates, 36 percent won in 1992, 51 percent won in 2002, and 47 percent won in 2012 (12, 21, and 20 women, respectively). However, these dramatic differences in the number of Republican and Democratic women candidates have important implications for the widening of the partisan gap among women in Congress.[27] There is now a record high of 62 Democratic women in the U.S. House, and women comprise one-third of the Democratic caucus. The percentage of women

Table 4.1 Number of Male and Female Primary and General Election Candidates by Party and Cycle

Primary Candidates

	1980	1982	1984	1986	1988	1990	1992	1994	1996	1998	2000	2002	2004	2006	2008	2010	2012
Female Republicans	27	31	44	37	33	25	69	72	67	54	49	53	64	53	52	102	81
Female Democrats	28	35	37	40	43	52	108	90	113	89	89	99	106	126	134	121	160
Male Republicans	406	427	366	372	362	375	602	548	558	434	440	434	428	392	448	772	586
Male Democrats	455	520	452	454	454	398	561	448	472	351	361	365	353	432	433	404	434
Total	916	1,013	899	903	892	850	1,340	1,158	1,210	928	939	951	951	1,003	1,067	1,399	1,261

General Election Candidates

	1980	1982	1984	1986	1988	1990	1992	1994	1996	1998	2000	2002	2004	2006	2008	2010	2012
Female Republicans	21	22	34	30	25	22	33	37	40	39	37	41	47	35	35	45	43
Female Democrats	19	27	29	24	31	37	66	67	74	66	72	72	82	90	95	89	110
Male Republicans	289	311	304	302	299	299	350	364	364	311	333	311	315	296	312	364	345
Male Democrats	322	364	365	363	358	332	344	310	331	275	290	276	281	305	316	304	276
Total	651	724	732	719	713	690	793	778	809	691	732	700	725	726	758	802	774

Source: Data compiled by the author from the America Votes series, the Federal Election Commission, and the DIME dataset (Scammon, Richard M., Alice V. McGillivray, and Rhodes Cook. *America Votes 19–27: A Handbook of Contemporary American Election Statistics.* Washington, DC: CQ Press, 1990–2006; Federal Election Commission Election Data, "Election Results for the U.S. House of Representatives." Washington, DC, 2008–2012. https://transition.fec.gov/pubrec/electionresults.shtml; Bonica, Adam. "Mapping the Ideological Marketplace," *American Journal of Political Science* 58, no. 2 [2014]: 367–387). These figures include candidates who appear in both the America Votes series or FEC election results dataset and the DIME dataset.

in the Democratic Party is six times larger than it was just 25 years ago. By contrast, the percentage of women in the Republican Party has hovered between 6 percent and 10 percent since the mid-1980s, and women currently make up 9 percent of the GOP delegation (22 of 247 members).

We can also examine differences in incumbency status for Republican and Democratic women over time. Of the full sample of Democratic primary candidates, 3,714 are incumbent members of Congress and 5,104 are nonincumbents. Of the full sample of Republican primary candidates, 3,077 are incumbent members of Congress and 5,786 are nonincumbents. Table 4.2 shows the number of incumbent and nonincumbent female candidates by election cycle and party. There are 2,383 women in the sample of primary candidates (913 Republicans and 1,470 Democrats) and 1,636 women in the sample of general election candidates (586 Republicans and 1,050 Democrats). Of the female Republican primary candidates, 230 are incumbents and 683 are nonincumbents; of the general election candidates, 226 are incumbents and 360 are nonincumbents. Of the female Democratic primary candidates, 483 are incumbents and 987 are nonincumbents; of the general election candidates, 474 are incumbents and 576 are nonincumbents.

We again see the same partisan trends in Table 4.2. Similar numbers of incumbent and nonincumbent Republican and Democratic women ran in the 1980s, but these figures began to diverge in the 1990s. Since the 2000s, the number of Democratic women candidates often doubles that of Republican women. The partisan disparity among incumbents is especially noteworthy because these individuals are the most likely to be elected to congressional office. Among Democratic general election candidates, women comprised 5 percent of Democratic incumbents in 1982, 8 percent in 1992, 19 percent in 2002, and 27 percent in 2012. By contrast, among Republican general election candidates, women made up 5 percent of Republican incumbents in 1982, 7 percent in 1992, 9 percent in 2002, and 10 percent in 2012. The plateau in the number of Republican women running as incumbents has important effects for aggregate trends in women's representation.

In sum, although both Republican and Democratic women have increased their ranks in both parties, Democratic women dramatically outnumber Republican women in the candidate pool. These data provided a general overview of changes in the number of female incumbent and nonincumbent candidates over time and by party. Yet, what they do not reveal are the dramatic changes in the ideology of the Republican and Democratic women candidates who ran for Congress between 1980 and 2012. In fact, the Republican women who were incumbents in the 1980s

Table 4.2 Number of Female Incumbents and Nonincumbents by Party

								Primary Candidates									
	1980	1982	1984	1986	1988	1990	1992	1994	1996	1998	2000	2002	2004	2006	2008	2010	2012
Republican Nonincumbents	22	23	34	27	22	17	60	62	53	38	34	36	44	31	35	87	58
Republican Incumbents	5	8	10	10	11	8	9	10	14	16	15	17	20	22	17	15	23
Democratic Nonincumbents	18	25	24	30	31	37	90	57	86	56	53	60	70	83	85	67	115
Democratic Incumbents	10	10	13	10	12	15	18	33	27	33	36	39	36	43	49	54	45
Total	55	66	81	77	76	77	177	162	180	143	138	152	170	179	186	223	241

								General Election Candidates									
	1980	1982	1984	1986	1988	1990	1992	1994	1996	1998	2000	2002	2004	2006	2008	2010	2012
Republican Nonincumbents	17	14	24	20	14	14	24	28	26	23	22	24	27	13	18	30	22
Republican Incumbents	4	8	10	10	11	8	9	9	14	16	15	17	20	22	17	15	21
Democratic Nonincumbents	9	17	17	14	19	22	49	34	48	34	36	35	46	49	46	36	65
Democratic Incumbents	10	10	12	10	12	15	17	33	26	32	36	37	36	41	49	53	45
Total	40	49	63	54	56	59	99	104	114	105	109	113	129	125	130	134	153

Source: Data compiled by the author from the America Votes series, the Federal Election Commission, and the DIME dataset (Scammon, Richard M., Alice V. McGillivray, and Rhodes Cook. *America Votes 19–27: A Handbook of Contemporary American Election Statistics*. Washington, DC: CQ Press, 1990–2006; Federal Election Commission Election Data, "Election Results for the U.S. House of Representatives." Washington, DC, 2008–2012. https://transition.fec.gov/pubrec/electionresults.shtml; Bonica, Adam. "Mapping the Ideological Marketplace," *American Journal of Political Science* 58, no. 2 [2014]: 367–387). These figures include candidates who appear in both the America Votes series or FEC election results dataset and the DIME dataset.

and 1990s are completely different from those who were incumbents in the 2000s, whereas many of the Democratic women who were incumbents in the 1990s remained in office through the 2000s. In the next section, we look specifically at ideological shifts across male and female candidates during this period.

DESCRIPTIVE TRENDS IN CANDIDATE IDEOLOGY

Figure 4.1 shows the average ideology of male and female primary and general election candidates from 1980 to 2012.[28] The Bonica ideology scores range from approximately −1.5 to 1.5, with higher values indicating more conservative positions. The trends are similar across primary and general election candidates. Republican women candidates were to the left of their male counterparts in the 1990s ($p < 0.01$), but this pattern was not evident in the 1980s. This is somewhat surprising given that the Republican women who held office in the 1980s were more liberal than the Republican men.[29] GOP female primary candidates had an average ideology score of 0.79 and 0.76 in the 1980s and 1990s, respectively, compared to 0.81 and 0.84 for Republican men. Gender differences again disappeared by the mid-2000s. Since then, women running in the primary or general election have been as conservative as their male counterparts. The average ideology score of female and male Republican primary candidates in the 2000s was identical, at 1.00 and 1.00, respectively. Patterns among general election candidates are similar, with Republican women having an average ideology score of 0.80, 0.77, and 0.93 in the 1980s, 1990s, and 2000s, respectively. The average score of male Republican general election candidates was 0.80 in the 1980s, 0.84 in the 1990s, and 0.94 in the 2000s.

On the Democratic side, women candidates in both primary and general elections have remained to the left of their male copartisans throughout this period, and the disparity is significant in every election ($p < 0.01$). Female Democratic primary candidates had an average score of −0.84 in the 1980s and −0.87 in the 1990s, respectively, compared to −0.51 and −0.59 for Democratic men. The gap has been similar in recent elections as well, with female and male Democratic primary candidates having an average score of −1.10 and −0.88, respectively, in the 2000s. Trends do not differ markedly for general election candidates. The average ideology score for Democratic women was −0.79 in the 1980s, −0.93 in the 1990s, and −1.11 in the 2000s, and the average score for Democratic men was −0.55 in the 1980s, −0.63 in the 1990s, and −0.86 in the 2000s.

What is clear from Figure 4.1 is that Republican and Democratic candidates, men and women alike, are moving away from the ideological

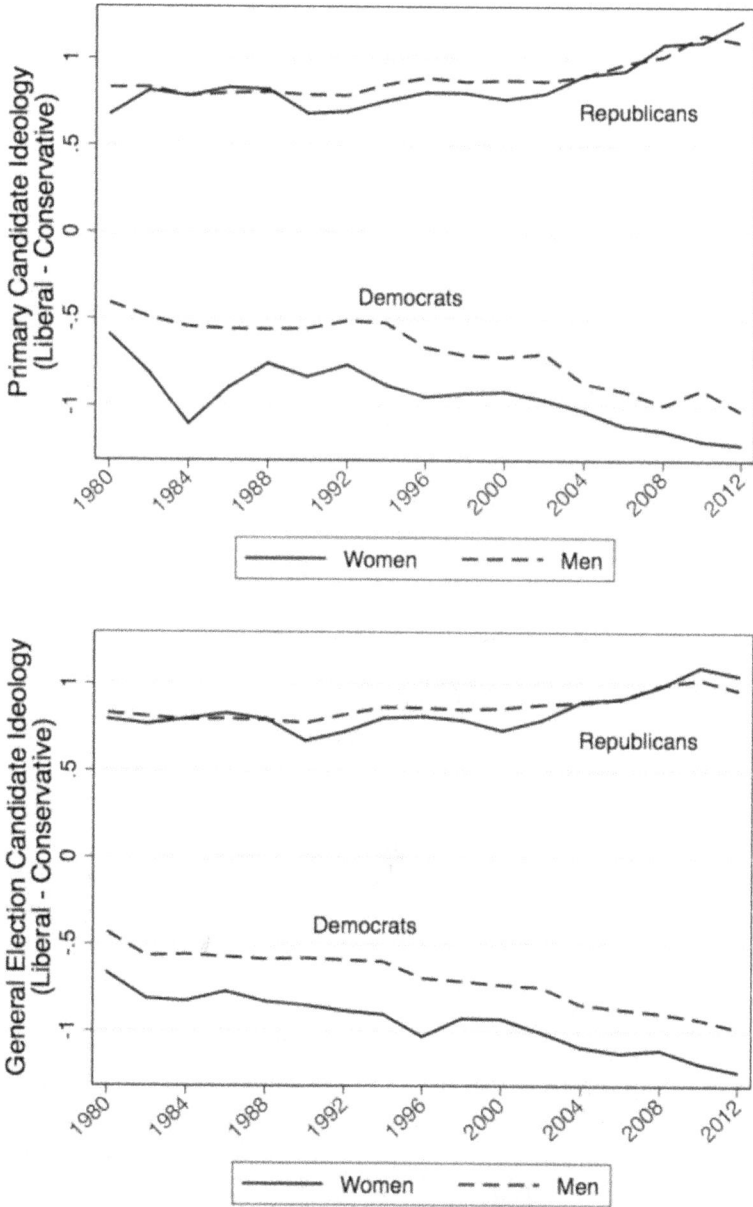

Figure 4.1 Ideology of Primary and General Election U.S. House Candidates, 1980–2012

Source: Data compiled by the author from the America Votes series, the Federal Election Commission, and the DIME dataset (Scammon, Richard M., Alice V. McGillivray, and Rhodes Cook. *America Votes 19–27: A Handbook of Contemporary American Election Statistics.* Washington, DC: CQ Press, 1990–2006; Federal Election Commission Election Data, "Election Results for the U.S. House of Representatives." Washington, DC, 2008–2012. https://transition.fec.gov/pubrec/electionresults.shtml; Bonica, Adam. "Mapping the Ideological Marketplace," *American Journal of Political Science* 58, no. 2 [2014]: 367–387). These figures include candidates who appear in both the America Votes series or FEC election results dataset and the DIME dataset.

center. This trend emerges among all primary candidates as well as those who advance to the general election. Indeed, if we look within groups, the changes over time are more dramatic than the gender disparity at any specific point in time. Female Republican primary candidates had an average ideology score of 0.68 in both 1980 and 1990, but this figure increased to 0.77 in 2000 and 1.10 in 2010. Similarly, the average score of male Republican primary candidates was 0.83 in 1980 and 0.79 in 1990, versus 0.88 in 2000 and 1.14 in 2010. These patterns are mirrored on the Democratic side. The average ideology score of Democratic women was –0.59 in 1980, –0.83 in 1990, –0.92 in 2000, and –1.20 in 2010. Democratic men also became more liberal, with scores of –0.41 in 1980, –0.56 in 1990, –0.72 in 2000, and –0.91 in 2010. In short, male and female candidates in both parties have become increasingly polarized over the last 30 years.

We can also examine how the number of ideologically moderate women candidates has declined during this time. Figure 4.2 shows the total number of women candidates who resemble former moderate Republican Connie Morella (MD) and former moderate Democrat Blanche Lincoln (AR) and the number of women who resemble current conservative Republican Marsha Blackburn (TN) and current Democratic minority leader Nancy Pelosi (CA).[30] The data are presented by decade.

We can again see that Democratic women candidates greatly outnumber Republican women, especially in the 1990s and 2000s. But in both parties, it is also clear that the number of Connie Morellas and Blanche Lincolns has not kept pace with the number of Marsha Blackburns and Nancy Pelosis. The decline in moderates is even more apparent when we examine these figures as proportions rather than raw numbers. Women who are at least as liberal as Morella made up 10 percent of female Republican primary candidates in the 1980s (18 of 172), 14 percent in the 1990s (40 of 287), and 6 percent in the 2000s (27 of 454). Women who are at least as conservative as Lincoln constituted 20 percent of female Democratic candidates in the 1980s (37 of 183), 15 percent in the 1990s (69 of 452), and 8 percent in the 2000s (64 of 835). The numbers have only continued to decline. In 2010, those resembling Morella made up a meager 4 percent of female GOP primary candidates (4 of 102), and those resembling Lincoln made up 7 percent of female Democrats (8 of 121).

By comparison, the number of Blackburns and Pelosis has soared in recent years. Women who are at least as conservative as Blackburn comprised 20 percent of the GOP pool of women in the 1980s (34 of 172), 25 percent in the 1990s (71 of 287), and 38 percent in the 2000s (171 of 454). On the Democratic side, women who are at least as liberal as Pelosi made up 22 percent of the GOP pool of women in the 1980s (40 of 183),

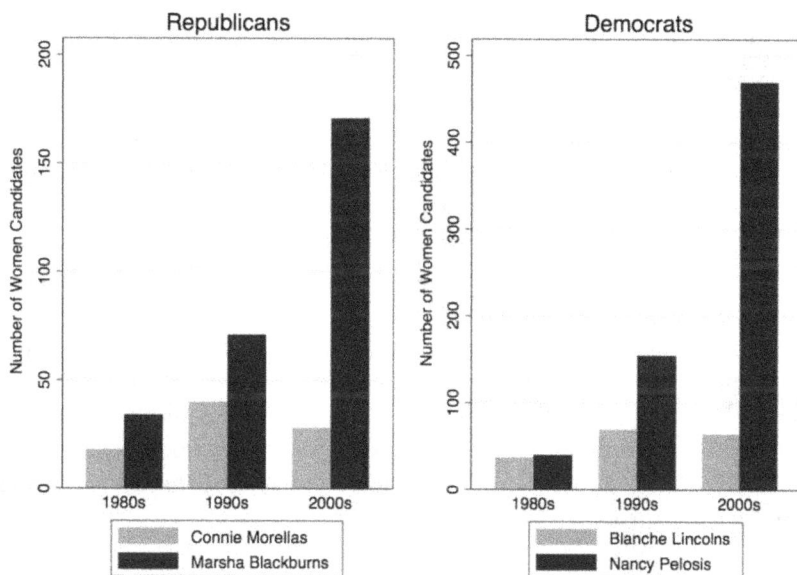

Figure 4.2 Number of Moderate and Ideological Women Candidates, by Party and Decade

Source: Data compiled by the author from the America Votes series, the Federal Election Commission, and the DIME dataset (Scammon, Richard M., Alice V. McGillivray, and Rhodes Cook. *America Votes 19–27: A Handbook of Contemporary American Election Statistics.* Washington, DC: CQ Press, 1990–2006; Federal Election Commission Election Data, "Election Results for the U.S. House of Representatives." Washington, DC, 2008–2012. https://transition.fec.gov/pubrec/electionresults.shtml; Bonica, Adam. "Mapping the Ideological Marketplace," *American Journal of Political Science* 58, no. 2 [2014]: 367–387). These figures include candidates who appear in both the America Votes series or FEC election results dataset and the DIME dataset.

34 percent in the 1990s (155 of 452), and 56 percent in the 2000s (470 of 835). In 2010, women resembling Blackburn and Pelosi made up 50 and 58 percent of Republican and Democratic women candidates, respectively (51 of 102; 70 of 121).

As discussed above, the decline in moderates among incumbents is especially important because these women are the most likely to be elected to office. Among female Republican primary candidates, women like Morella constituted 20 percent of GOP women incumbents in the 1980s (9 of 44) and 14 percent in the 1990s (8 of 57), but this figure declined dramatically to a mere 3 percent in the 2000s (4 of 129). Among female Democratic primary candidates, women like Lincoln made up 29 percent of women incumbents in the 1980s (16 of 55), 14 percent in the 1990s (18 of 126), and 3 percent in the 2000s (10 of 302).

The significant retention of Democratic women has resulted in a huge increase in the number of liberal Democratic women running as incumbents. Democratic women at least as liberal as Nancy Pelosi made up 13 percent of female Democratic incumbents in the 1980s (7 of 55), compared to 41 percent of female Democratic incumbents in the 2000s (123 of 302). By comparison, many of the conservative Republican women candidates who ran during this period did not have the perks of incumbency. In fact, of the female Republican incumbents who ran in the 1980s, not a single one resembled Blackburn (0 of 44), and even in the 2000s, only 13 percent of female Republican incumbents were at least as conservative as Blackburn (17 of 129). In short, there are very few moderate incumbents running in either party, and a growing number of liberal Democratic women are doing so, which further contributes to the disparity between Republican and Democratic women in Congress.

DISCUSSION AND CONCLUSION

This chapter draws on a new dataset of U.S. House candidates from 1980 to 2012 to examine partisan and gendered patterns of candidate emergence over time. The clear pattern is that the percentage of ideologically moderate men and women has diminished dramatically over the last 30 years. The women who run for Congress in the contemporary partisan era are more polarized than they were 30 years ago, and they are even more polarized than their male counterparts. These dramatic shifts in the ideological makeup of women candidates play a key role in determining which women are ultimately elected to office. Many more conservative and liberal women enter congressional office today due to different patterns of selection into congressional contests. On the Republican side, the Martha Robys (AL) and Marsha Blackburns of today have replaced the Connie Morellas and Nancy Johnsons (CT) of yesterday. And among Democrats, the Blanche Lincolns and Beverly Byrons (MD) have been replaced by women who instead resemble Nancy Pelosi and Debbie Wasserman Schultz (FL).

Ideology plays an increasingly prominent role in contemporary patterns of women's representation. Understanding the linkages between ideology and gender is crucial for considering various remedies to the continued dearth of women in office as well as the content of policy outcomes. Reproductive health care offers a particularly stark example of how the policy preferences of Republican and Democratic women in office have changed over time. During her tenure in office, Republican Senator Olympia Snowe (ME) had a consistently pro-choice record and had long supported the federal funding of family planning programs. At an awards ceremony in 2014, Cecile Richards, the president of Planned Parenthood, called Snowe one of the "bravest and fiercest defenders of women in American history."[31] By comparison, virtually all of the Republican women in office today are pro-life, and Blackburn has been at the forefront of recent Republican efforts to defund Planned Parenthood.[32] Blackburn has a 100 percent lifetime rating from the National Right to Life Committee and a 0 percent rating from Planned Parenthood and NARAL.[33] Similarly, former Democratic Representative Beverly Byron (MD) was pro-life, and she often broke with her party on reproductive issues when she was in office.[34] By comparison, Nancy Pelosi is a strong supporter of abortion rights, and in virtually all of the Congresses in which she has served, Pelosi has received a 100 percent rating from Planned Parenthood and NARAL and a 0 percent rating from the National Right to Life Committee.[35]

Changes in the distribution of female candidates have also had important implications for the ability of Democratic and Republican women to climb the career ladder. The comparatively low turnover of Democratic women is one reason that the number of Democratic women has continued to grow steadily over the last three decades. Unlike their female counterparts in the GOP, the carryover of Democratic women has enabled them to rise to increasingly powerful positions. Nancy Pelosi reached new heights as the former Speaker of the House and current minority leader. And when the Democrats held the majority in the 110th and 111th Congresses (2007–2011), there were 4 and 3 House committees, respectively, that were chaired by women. However, in the 114th Republican-controlled Congress (2015–2016), only 1 of the 21 committee chair positions is held by a woman. Candice Miller (R-MI) heads the lower-tier House Administration Committee, but even her initial appointment in 2012 came days after the first 19 positions had all been doled out to men.[36] Having a greater number of women not only in elected office but also in positions of influence is important for the substantive representation (see "Representation of Women," Glossary) of women as well.

More generally, scholars are increasingly suggesting that there are crucial differences across women that must be taken into account. As Elder claims, "The more important measure of women's power is arguably their representation within their respective party delegations."[37] Republican women in Congress have policy priorities and concerns that differ from both Democratic women and Republican men, but they lack the numerical strength to influence their party's policy direction.[38] There is reason to be concerned about the laggard status of Republican women, particularly in light of the advancements made by women in the Democratic Party. The dearth of Republican women candidates seriously constrains the influence that women can have in Congress, and the decline in moderate candidates in both parties opens a new chapter in women's representation in the contemporary partisan era. Ideology has become a central part of American politics, and we can gain a better grasp of gender politics as well as party politics by examining how these forces interact and intersect to shape women's representation in the 21st century.

NOTES

1. Inter-Parliamentary Union (IPU), "Women in National Parliaments," 2017, http://www.ipu.org/wmn-e/classif.htm.

2. Center for American Women and Politics (CAWP), "Women in the U.S. Congress Fact Sheet," 2015, http://www.cawp.rutgers.edu/women-us-congress-2015.

3. Barbara C Burrell, *A Woman's Place Is in the House: Campaigning for Congress in the Feminist Era* (Ann Arbor: University of Michigan Press, 1994); Robert Darcy, Susan Welch, and Janet Clark, *Women, Elections, and Representation* (Lincoln: University of Nebraska Press, 1994); Richard A. Seltzer, Jody Newman, and Melissa Voorhees Leighton, *Sex as a Political Variable: Women as Candidates and Voters in U.S. Elections* (Boulder, CO: Lynne Rienner, 1997).

4. Seltzer, Newman, and Leighton, *Sex as a Political Variable*, 79.

5. Burrell, *A Woman's Place Is in the House*; Ronald Keith Gaddie and Charles S. Bullock III, *Elections to Open Seats in the U.S. House: Where the Action Is* (Lanham, MD: Rowman & Littlefield, 2000); David King and Richard Matland, "Sex and the Grand Old Party: An Experimental Investigation of the Effect of Candidate Sex on Support for a Republican Candidate," *American Politics Research* 31, no. 6 (2003): 595–612; Jennifer L. Lawless and Kathryn Pearson, "The Primary Reason for Women's Underrepresentation? Reevaluating the Conventional Wisdom," *Journal of Politics* 70, no. 1 (2008): 67–82; Barbara Palmer and Dennis Simon, *Women & Congressional Elections: A Century of Change* (Boulder, CO: Lynne Rienner, 2012).

6. Brian Frederick, "Are Female House Members Still More Liberal in a Polarized Era? The Conditional Nature of the Relationship between Descriptive and Substantive Representation," *Congress & the Presidency* 36, no. 2 (2009): 181–202.

7. Tracy L. Osborn, *How Women Represent Women: Political Parties, Representation, and Gender in the State Legislatures* (New York: Oxford University Press, 2012); Michele L. Swers, "Representing Women's Interests in a Polarized Congress," in *Women and Elective Office: Past, Present, and Future*, eds. Sue Thomas and Clyde Wilcox (New York: Oxford University Press, 2014), 162–180.

8. Keith T. Poole and Howard Rosenthal, *Ideology and Congress* (New Brunswick, NJ: Transaction Publishers, 2007).

9. Stephen Ansolabehere, James M. Snyder Jr., and Charles Stewart III, "Candidate Positioning in U.S. House Elections," *American Journal of Political Science* 45, no. 1 (2001): 136–159.

10. Morris P. Fiorina, *Representatives, Roll Calls, and Constituencies* (Lexington, MA: Lexington Books, 1974); Robert S. Erikson and Gerald C. Wright Jr., "Voters, Candidates, and Issues in Congressional Elections," in *Congress Reconsidered*, 3rd ed., eds. Lawrence C. Dodd and Bruce I. Oppenheimer (Washington, DC: Congressional Quarterly Press, 1985), 91–116; Barry Burden, "Candidate Positioning in U.S. Congressional Elections," *British Journal of Political Science* 34, no. 1 (2004): 211–227.

11. Frederick, "Are Female House Members."

12. Jon C. Rogowski and Stephanie Langella, "Primary Systems and Candidate Ideology: Evidence from Federal and State Legislative Elections," *American Politics Research* 43, no. 5 (2014): 846–871.

13. Deborah Alexander and Kristi Andersen, "Gender as a Factor in the Attribution of Leadership Traits," *Political Research Quarterly* 46, no. 3 (1993): 527–545; Leonie Huddy and Nayda Terkildsen, "Gender Stereotypes and the Perception of Male and Female Candidates," *American Journal of Political Science* 37, no. 1 (1993): 119–147; Monika McDermott, "Race and Gender Cues in Low Information Elections," *Political Research Quarterly* 51, no. 4 (1998): 895–918; King and Matland, "Sex and the Grand Old Party."

14. Jeffrey Koch, "Do Citizens Apply Gender Stereotypes to Infer Candidates' Ideological Orientations?" *American Journal of Political Science* 62, no. 2 (2000): 414–429; Jeffrey Koch, "Gender Stereotypes and Citizens' Impressions of House Candidates' Ideological Orientations," *American Journal of Political Science* 46, no. 2 (2002): 453–462; see also McDermott, "Race and Gender Cues."

15. King and Matland, "Sex and the Grand Old Party."

16. Deborah Jordan Brooks, *He Runs, She Runs: Why Gender Stereotypes Do Not Harm Women Candidates* (Princeton, NJ: Princeton University Press, 2013).

17. Danny Hayes and Jennifer L. Lawless, "A Non-Gendered Lens? Media, Voters, and Female Candidates in Contemporary Congressional Elections," *Perspectives on Politics* 13, no. 1 (2015): 95–118.

18. Kathleen A. Dolan, *Voting for Women: How the Public Evaluates Women Candidates*, (Boulder, CO: Westview Press, 2004).

19. Richard M. Scammon, Alice V. McGillivray, and Rhodes Cook, *America Votes 19–27: A Handbook of Contemporary American Election Statistics* (Washington, DC: CQ Press, 1990–2006).

20. Adam Bonica, "Mapping the Ideological Marketplace," *American Journal of Political Science* 58, no. 2 (2014): 367–387.

21. See Bonica, "Mapping the Ideological Marketplace," for a full description of the data and validation.

22. The DIME dataset includes candidates who filed with the Federal Election Commission. Candidates who do not exceed the $5,000 threshold of campaign

fund-raising are not required to file. Those who are excluded are thus more likely to be long-shot candidates, but it is not clear that they are more likely to be extremists. Even so, these excluded candidates constituted only 8 percent of primary winners and 0.04 percent of general election winners, so they are highly unlikely to have an influence on policy outcomes or levels of women's representation. Furthermore, the DIME dataset provides the best publicly available measures of the ideological positions of congressional winners and losers over time.

23. Candidate sex was unable to be identified in 13 cases (0.01 percent of the sample). These individuals are excluded from the analysis.

24. Lawless and Pearson, "The Primary Reason for Women's Underrepresentation."

25. Lawless and Pearson, "The Primary Reason for Women's Underrepresentation."

26. Again, these figures include only those with Bonica ideology scores.

27. Danielle M. Thomsen, "Why So Few (Republican) Women? Explaining the Partisan Imbalance of Women in the U.S. Congress," *Legislative Studies Quarterly* 40, no. 2 (2015): 295–323.

28. These averages include races in which candidates do and do not face opposition.

29. Susan Welch, "Are Women More Liberal Than Men in the U.S. Congress?" *Legislative Studies Quarterly* 10, no. 1 (1985): 125–134; see also Frederick, "Are Female House Members."

30. This figure does not include all female Republican and Democratic candidates, as 60 percent of Republican women candidates were between Morella and Blackburn and 43 percent of Democratic women candidates were between Lincoln and Pelosi. However, the general purpose is to compare the decline of the moderates of yesteryear and the rise in the conservatives and liberals of today.

31. Matt Goodman, "At Planned Parenthood Luncheon, Former GOP Senator Says Partisanship Damages Women's Healthcare," *Dallas/Fort Worth Healthcare Daily*, April 8, 2014, accessed June 9, 2016, http://healthcare.dmagazine.com/2014/04/08/at-planned-parenthood-luncheon-former-gop-senator-says-partisanship-damages-womens-healthcare.

32. Cortney O'Brien, "'Disturbed' by Planned Parenthood Video, House GOP Launch Investigation," *Townhall*, July 15, 2015, http://townhall.com/tipsheet/cortneyobrien/2015/07/15/house-gop-disturbed-by-planned-parenthood-video-launch-investigation-n2025903. Accessed 9 June 2016.

33. Project Vote Smart, "Candidate Ratings and Endorsements," accessed June 9, 2016, https://votesmart.org/candidate/evaluations/25186/marsha-blackburn#.WS2Wz45ffm8.

34. Office of History and Preservation, Office of the Clerk, U.S. House of Representatives, *Women in Congress, 1917–2006*, 108th Congress, 1st sess., 2007, H. Doc. 108-223 (Washington, DC: GPO, 2006), 583–585, https://www.gpo.gov/fdsys/pkg/GPO-CDOC-108hdoc223/content-detail.html.

35. Project Vote Smart, "Candidate Ratings and Endorsements," accessed June 9, 2016, https://votesmart.org/candidate/evaluations/26732/nancy-pelosi# .WS2acI5ffm8.

36. Jake Sherman, "Candice Miller to Lead House Panel," *Politico*, November 30, 2012, accessed June 9, 2016, http://www.politico.com/story/2012/11 /with-candice-miller-appointment-woman-will-lead-house-committee-after -all-084460.

37. Laurel Elder, "Whither Republican Women: The Growing Partisan Gap among Women in Congress," *The Forum* 6, no. 1 (2008): Article 13.

38. Burrell, *A Woman's Place Is in the House*; Michele L. Swers and Carin Larson, "Women in Congress: Do They Act as Advocates for Women's Issues?," in *Women and Elective Office: Past, Present, and Future*, eds. Sue Thomas and Clyde Wilson (New York: Oxford University Press, 2005), 110–128.

PART 2

Elections and Candidates

Competitive, free, and fair elections are so fundamental to our modern vision of democracy that we regularly use their presence or absence to determine whether a country can be called democratic.[1] Different democracies, however, structure their elections quite differently, and the United States has several unique quirks in its electoral setup that make our elections unusual, especially party primaries and political action committees (PACs). This section examines the impact of these and other factors on the electoral fortunes of Republican female candidates.

In chapter 5, Shauna L. Shames focuses on party primaries, finding multiple reasons why congressional primaries particularly disadvantage Republican women as compared to women in the Democratic Party. In chapter 6, Rosalyn Cooperman and Melody Crowder-Meyer also find that Republican women face more challenges, particularly in raising money through PACs (independent groups not run by, but typically aligned with, parties; see Glossary). In particular, the absence of a powerful women's PAC, such as EMILY's List (which raises money for pro-choice Democratic female candidates), is a real detriment for women on the Republican side of the aisle. Finally, in chapter 7, Kelly Dittmar examines the 2016 electoral results in-depth, focusing on how Republican women fared.

NOTE

1. Freedom House, "Methodology," accessed June 1, 2017, https://freedomhouse.org/report/freedom-world-2016/methodology; Center for Systemic Peace, "The Polity Project," accessed June 1, 2017, http://www.systemicpeace.org/polityproject.html.

CHAPTER 5

Higher Hurdles for Republican Women: Ideology, Inattention, and Infrastructure

Shauna L. Shames

In the 114th Congress of the United States, looking only at the women, Democrats outnumber Republicans by about three to one. This is a rather astonishing ratio, and it raises a major question: why aren't there more Republican women elected to national office in this country? This odd split certainly has not always been the case. Up until about the early-1990s, elected women were pretty evenly split across the two major parties. If we look at a chart showing the divergence, we can see that the real movement away from an equal split started in the early 1990s and that it further increased fairly recently. Figure I.1 in the Introduction shows the number of women in their respective party's caucuses in the U.S. House of Representatives over time. The gray and black bars are about even until the "Year of the Woman" elections in 1992 (see Glossary), when the Democratic women suddenly shoot ahead.

Looking at these numbers as percentages, women reached about 10 percent of the Republican Party by the early 2000s and then stayed there instead of increasing further (even losing some seats lately), while women in the Democratic Party in the House reached 20 percent in the early 2000s and then shot up past 30 percent after the 2012 elections. The largest recent period of divergence was after 2008, as the Tea Party took root in the Republican Party and began systematically challenging moderate Republicans, particularly through primary battles. The Democrats, in that same period, redoubled their efforts to recruit and promote women as candidates. The result is a startling picture of difference for women across parties.

So, what is going on? In multiple ways, it turns out, Republican women are at a distinct disadvantage. In electoral races, the hurdles appear to be higher for women running as Republican Party candidates. This chapter harnesses findings from multiple studies to explain and illustrate this story of "higher hurdles." These findings are drawn from original research conducted by Political Parity, a program of Swanee Hunt Alternatives, a private foundation based in Cambridge, Massachusetts, between 2012 and 2014, when I was the research fellow there. In 2012, we at Political Parity assembled a team of researchers to study the barriers facing Republican female candidates, in particular.[1] We divided the research question into several subquestions, focusing on key aspects of the problem, with some researchers looking quantitatively into campaign fund-raising, others looking more qualitatively at the actions of party leaders and recruiters, and yet others conducting case study analysis on successful and unsuccessful Republican female candidates.[2] I am grateful to Swanee Hunt Alternatives for granting permission to use the original data as well as the narrative framing in writing this chapter.

AREN'T WOMEN WOMEN? WHY SHOULD PARTY MATTER?

For decades, advocates for gender equality in politics have decried the relative lack of women elected to positions of power in the U.S. government. We like to think of ourselves as a leader among countries, but in truth, the United States now ranks 101st in the world (just ahead of Kyrgyzstan and Madagascar and behind nearly every other postindustrial democracy) in terms of the number of elected women in its national parliament, according to the Inter-Parliamentary Union (IPU; see Glossary, "Women in Politics, Worldwide Rankings.") This is largely because most other comparable countries have seen fit to introduce gender quotas in some way into their candidacy, party, or government structures to be sure that women are included, and the United States (for the most part) has not.[3] The one exception is that both parties in the United States do have internal party quotas for representation at national conventions, where half of all delegates in both parties must, by party rules, be women. So, it is a lie to say that we have no quotas or that we in this country are simply against quotas; both parties have quotas that they use internally. But there are no quotas in terms of elected officials or candidates.

The reasons that other countries have introduced party-based candidate quotas or reserved-seat quotas for women in legislative bodies are varied. In some countries, the rationale has been the historical exclusion of women; in others, there are continuing barriers to their ascension because men have filled the available seats and then pass those seats along to other men. Additionally, as women and politics research has made clear, the inclusion of women as political candidates and officeholders has positive implications both for policy outcomes and for the political interest and activity of the female half of the population (see "Representation of Women," in Glossary). In India, where women's participation in politics is mandated by constitutional amendment, the rationale behind the quota movement was simple: "Democracy without women is not democracy," the women proposing the amendments successfully argued. The resulting quotas mean, among other things, that one-third of officials on village panchayat (councils) must be women. This has made an enormous difference; councils that are at least one-third women, a major research study found, are far more likely to ensure that the village gets public goods, such as clean drinking water.[4]

If true democracy requires the involvement of women as well as men, does it also require Republican as well as Democratic women? Well, if women in the general population are not solely concentrated in the Democratic Party, the answer is yes. Our republican system of democracy is based on the idea of representation; our elected officials are supposed to represent our interests and preferences and fight it out with other elected officials representing other interests. The near total exclusion of women's perspectives and interests that existed in many countries (including ours) for a very long time makes for a highly unrepresentative democracy. Now that we have begun to increase the number of women in elective office, we should be concerned that they are being disproportionately drawn from one party rather than both, especially given the general population party breakdown (discussed below). If about a third of women are Democrats, another third Republicans, and a third in the middle, that Democratic third is by far the most represented. Even still, women are underrepresented compared to men—or, as I believe we should say, men are overrepresented in Congress compared with their proportion in the overall population. (Men are 49% of the U.S. population but about 80% of Congress.)

THE PRIMARY ITSELF AS THE PRIMARY PROBLEM

Why do Democratic women so vastly outnumber Republican women in Congress? A brief exploration of the numbers describing where women run and win over time—in what party and at what level—gives us some useful context for better understanding the question. What the numbers show is that not only do Democratic women run more than Republican women, but they also win more. For example, based on data collection from FEC filings performed by Political Parity in 2015, in the 2014 midterm elections, 249 women filed as primary candidates for House seats: 154 Democrats (62% of women filers) and 95 Republicans (38%). Of these, 159 became general election nominees, with an even greater partisan split (69% of the women winning nomination were Democrats). Then, of all female general election candidates, 84 were elected to the House. Of these, 62 (74% of overall winners) were Democrats and just 22 (or 26%) were Republicans. Overall, then, Republican women started out as over a third of candidates but ended as only about a quarter of winners.

Further, beyond being more likely to run in the first place, Democratic women are far more likely to win their primaries than Republican women. Look for example at the 2014 Senate races; female candidates of both parties ran in near equal numbers in the 2014 Senate primary: 15 Democrats and 16 Republicans. Of the total 31 female candidates for Senate in 2014, about half (48%) won their party's nomination. But female Democratic Senate candidates outperformed GOP women in the primary and were twice as likely to become their party's nominee; 66 percent of Democratic women won their primaries, compared with 31 percent of Republican women. Interestingly, Republican women then went on to do better in the general elections than their Democratic female counterparts; for them, the highest hurdle was the primary.

Figure I.2 in the Introduction shows the number of women in both parties who have filed to run for the U.S. House and the number who have been nominated by their party for the general election. Looking across time, we can see that Democratic women run more often than female Republicans. The year 2010 is something of an interesting exception, as the number of Republican women filing jumped because of a bunch of new Tea Party women running, but the number of Republican women filing fell off in the next electoral cycle and continued to drop in 2014. Democratic women are also more likely than Republican women, over time, to win their primary races. Based on the last two election cycles, they are also more likely, once nominated, to win the general election. The party gap, however, is starkest during the primary.

The lack of primary victories for female Republican candidates may be caused in part by, and is certainly exacerbated by, their relative lack of incumbency status. Incumbency for all types of candidates is usually the major determinant of winning. Incumbents generally win reelection at a rate of 90 percent or more. For GOP women, however, the lack of incumbency status becomes a vicious cycle. With few female Republican incumbents, most Republican female candidates are running as either challengers or open-seat candidates, and there are a decreasing number of open seats available over time. This leaves Republican women concentrated in the "challenger" category, which is the group least likely to win. Add to this the fact that existing officeholders (mostly long-serving men) are very likely to win reelection, and it means that Republican women face high hurdles indeed.

Beyond incumbency, however, three other areas of "higher hurdles" help explain the small number of Republican women who win primaries, especially when comparing them with both their Republican male and their Democratic female counterparts: ideology, inattention, and infrastructure. This chapter explores each category of barriers in turn.

HIGHER HURDLE 1: IDEOLOGY

With the Republican Party ideology moving to the political right, the bulk of those in the party (especially women) who are more moderate are left out of their own party and are thus considered ineligible (or less "electable") as candidates in a primary-centric system. Writing about this trend in 2005, Christie Todd Whitman, the former governor of New Jersey and the EPA administrator under George W. Bush, wrote, "The GOP cannot afford to eliminate its most popular potential candidates from contention because they don't pass the favorite litmus test of the far right."[5] As a whole, however, the party has not taken her advice.

With the rise of the Tea Party since 2008, moderate candidates are less and less likely to be chosen as their party's nominees for congressional seats. One telling symbol of this trend is threats by the Tea Party to "primary" (used as a verb rather than a noun) more moderate officeholders, meaning they challenge sitting Republican incumbents by running a very conservative challenger against them in their own party's primary. This threat, even when not carried out, can serve to move candidates as a whole further to the right, as incumbents might shift policy positions in a more conservative direction to avoid being "primaried." Indeed, in chapter 4, Danielle M. Thomsen documents the change in ideological scores for candidates in both parties; as she shows, the parties are diverging ideologically, with the Republican Party candidates becoming increasingly right wing in issue positions. This trend has the potential to create difficulties for Republican women in at least two ways.

First, a strong rightward shift could lessen the number of women calling themselves Republicans. With most women in the party not espousing far-right positions on most issues, and more than a third of women in the general population calling themselves Independents rather than

Percentage

0% 10% 20% 30% 40% 50% 60% 70% 80% 90% 100%

All Elected Female Senators

All Elected Congresswomen

Female General Election Winners for House Seats

Female Primary Winners for House Seats

Female Primary Candidates for House Seats

Women in General Population

☐ Percent Democratic   ■ Percent Independent   ■ Percent Republican

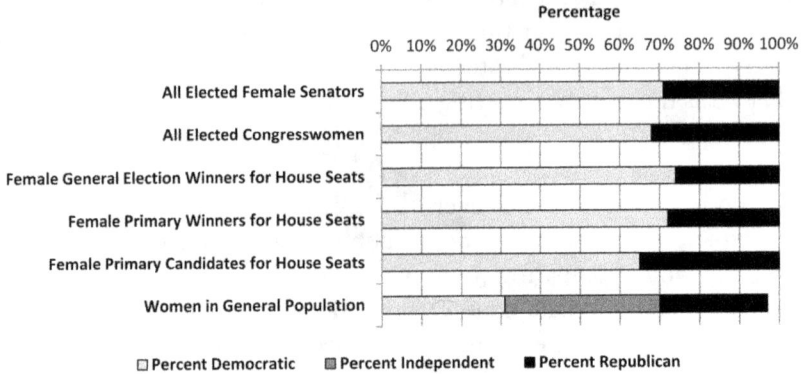

Figure 5.1   Party Identification across Levels, 2012

Sources: Data from Political Parity Program, "Primary Hurdles for Republican Women" (Cambridge, MA: Swanee Hunt Alternatives, 2015), accessed January 3, 2017; the Center for American Women and Politics (CAWP), "2012 Elections," CAWP public data, available at http://www.cawp.rutgers.edu/facts/elections/past_candidates#e2012, accessed September 29, 2017; and the Pew Research Center's 2012 Values Survey, available at http://www.people-press.org/values/, accessed September 29, 2017.

Note: Total in "Women in General Population" does not add to 100% due to inclusion of other parties.

Republicans or Democrats (see Figure 5.1), the pool of women who could be candidates is small (see chapter 4 for more on this idea).

But also, for those women who do run, we know from the previous literature that women are often perceived to be more moderate politicians than men, even if they are not.[6] This was not true of the female Republican candidates studied over time in the research; they were just as conservative as their male counterparts. Comparing women to men within party, the big difference was not on the Republican side, but on the Democratic side, where women continue to be somewhat more liberal than men. But the quantitative data analyses also suggested that the more conservative candidate usually wins the Republican primary. With a shift toward the far right among the Republican electorate, particularly primary voters, GOP women may have to struggle to overcome the gendered stereotype that they are more moderate, even when it is untrue.

Beyond the recent shift in party ideology, however, there is a more fundamental reason why Republican women have a more difficult time of it. Politics in most democracies has historically, until fairly recently, excluded women's formal participation (although of course women have always acted behind the scenes and sometimes broken in to take center stage). Still, in this country at least, until the 1970s, most of the women who held office got there through "the widow's route" (taking the seat of a husband, brother, or father who was killed or incapacitated). Those who are more conservative politically also hold more conservative gender roles, and some still see politics as being a more appropriate space for men than for women. The number of people who believe this, or are willing to admit to believing this, has dwindled in the past few decades, but it is not completely zero, even now.

In an original poll commissioned for this project, conducted by Nicole McCleskey, Republican voters were asked one question: "Do you prefer a male or female candidate if all other qualifications appear equal?" Subsequent questions asked the same thing for what the respondents thought their spouse, and then their friends, would want in terms of a candidate's gender. Not surprisingly, most people (over 70%) said that the hypothetical candidate's gender made no difference to them—but about 25 percent thought it did matter. Some of these, about one-fifth, preferred a female candidate, but the large majority preferred a man. Moreover, these people mostly thought their spouse and friends would agree, with nearly 20 percent thinking their spouse (and over 20% thinking their friends) would want a male rather than a female candidate. Sex bias, in other words, is not as popular as it once was, but it is not exactly gone either. Democratic voters, however, either do not have or will not admit to having anywhere near these levels of outright gender preference. Of course, they still may harbor bias and just not want to tell pollsters about it, but it seems likely, given the data that we have, that outright sex bias is more of a problem for Republican than Democratic women.

HIGHER HURDLE 2: INATTENTION

Deeply related to ideology are a set of practical considerations that we termed "inattention." By this, we meant a lack of focus on the recruitment, support, and development of female candidates. Here, the party's internal culture, as discussed in chapters 2 and 11, is relevant. By orientation, the Democratic Party embraces the ideal of diversity and believes that identity and diversity issues (particularly around race, gender, and sexual orientation) are important; the Republican Party opposes group-based thinking, preferring instead to think of people as individuals rather than group members. Such a difference puts Republican women seeking party support for candidacy at a disadvantage, as there is little party support for women as a group.

Relatedly, as Rosalyn Cooperman and Melody Crowder-Meyer show in chapter 6, there is far less PAC support for the mere election of women on the Republican side of the aisle. As they note, the group-based feminist perspective that particularly motivates donors to contribute to EMILY's List simply does not exist in PACs on the Republican side. And the GOP itself (at the state and national levels) is simply far less interested in promoting women as candidates for the sake of increasing women's representation, although they will often engage in the "identity politics" game by making sure women legislators are often the public face of the party "women's issues" (see Glossary). While some recent efforts have sprung up to train and support women, they are meager and half-hearted compared to the rather robust set of groups and initiatives existing in the Democratic Party.

In studying inattention, the qualitative research, particularly one-on-one interviews with both national and state party leaders (names are withheld for confidentiality), yielded fruitful data. One female Republican state party leader, for instance, suggested in an interview performed by Political Parity in 2015 that women's initial reluctance about running for office often leaves space for men to jump in first. "Guys instinctively say yes," she explained. "It takes more energy to recruit a woman candidate than a male candidate. Women think more globally about how hard it will be on their family, their work. They think that through more deeply on the front end than most male candidates."

Our interviews with elected Republican women and party leaders suggest that the GOP struggles to recruit, coach, and retain women. There's no significant structure to shepherd female candidates through a primary election. And with little candidate development at the local level or explicit party engagement in primaries, Republicans are not establishing a pipeline of future federal officeholders. In another interview for Political Parity in 2015, a female Republican national party leader explained, "We haven't spent time developing a farm team. The Democrats have done a better job of encouraging women to run for municipal and state office, and it puts them in a position to run in congressional seats."

Women are also harder to recruit than male candidates. They are not asked to run as often, are less likely to be asked multiple times, and are more likely to need intense recruitment. Party leaders surmise that fewer Republican women run for Congress because there are not many at the state or local levels willing and able to move up the ranks. One Republican congresswoman explained to Political Parity researchers in 2015, "I think there are more Democratic women who are active in the party and become local officeholders and move through the ranks. We don't have enough of a bench."

Many others also stated that candidate development needs to be a focus. The Lugar Training Series and broader "Excellence in Public Service Series" (which includes programs in multiple states) provide women candidates with the skills and tools to manage a primary campaign. These programs are expanding, but are not yet national in scope. Yet, it was clear that party leaders at the national level are aware of the difficulties Republican women are having at the primary stage and the adverse effects this can have for the party as a whole. One such party leader told Political Parity in a 2015 interview, "I think there is a difference between what a primary voter is looking for and what a general election voter is looking for. Primary voters tend to be male, white. There are more married women. The general electorate is more diverse and includes more single women. It may be harder for some people to get through the primary, but they might be more successful and a stronger general election candidate."

HIGHER HURDLE 3: INFRASTRUCTURE

Running for office is no small feat. Every candidate, even an incumbent, works hard to win elections. The costs involved—financial as well as time and effort—are staggering and grow with each passing cycle.[7] This hurdle only becomes harder to scale as the costs of running a political campaign rise (currently about $1.5 million for a House seat and $10.4 million for the Senate[8]), and women have less access to big money.[9]

For various reasons, however, the costs are higher for women than for men. Our research found that although all women encounter obstacles, Republican women tend to face higher hurdles, particularly in primary elections. In particular, it appears that female Republican candidates have greater difficulty raising money than their Democratic counterparts, mainly because of fragmented sources of support (see chapter 6).

As illustrated in Figure 5.2, which examines financial data from the 2014 congressional (House) races, female Democratic candidates had demonstrably more success fund-raising than their female Republican counterparts.

Looked at as percentages of each type of candidate, to control for the fact that more women ran as Democrats, we can see that the Democratic women were about twice as likely as Republican women to have raised money from their party. Other categories of fund-raising success tell a similar story. Democratic women were far more likely than Republican women to have raised at least $10,000 from PACs and to have raised at least $80,000 by the end of the second quarter of 2014. Democratic women

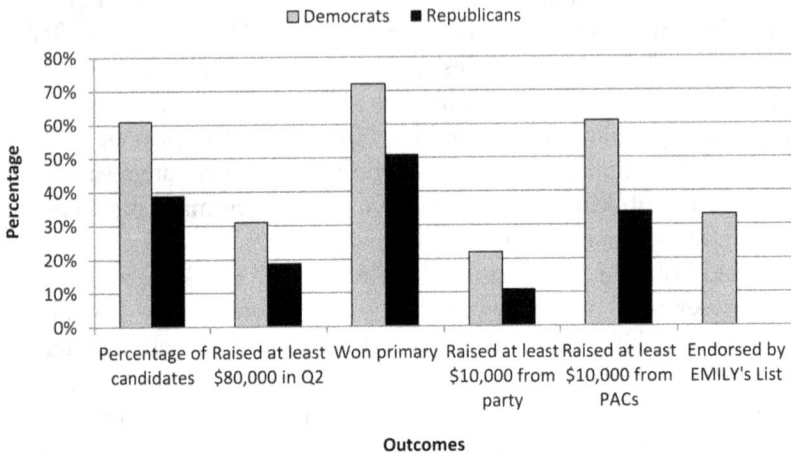

Figure 5.2   Female House Candidate Outcomes: Electoral and Financial (2014 Averages)

Source: Based on original FEC and other data collected by Political Parity; Political Parity Program, "Primary Hurdles for Republican Women" (Cambridge, MA: Swanee Hunt Alternatives, 2015), accessed January 3, 2017.

were also significantly more likely than Republican women to have won their primaries—which is not exactly surprising, given the financial data.

Because political parties are hesitant to get involved in primary elections, a significant percentage of campaign funds come from PACs. In 2014, super PACs reported total receipts of nearly $700 million and total independent expenditures of nearly $350 million.[10] As Cooperman and Crowder-Meyer also point out in chapter 6, the role of EMILY's List is critical here. EMILY's List provides direct support for pro-choice female Democratic candidates and serves as a strong "stamp of approval" that helps endorsed candidates leverage other funding. Our analysis of Republican women's fund-raising groups suggests that the presence of EMILY's List—and the absence of a comparable entity on the GOP side—is a serious structural deficit for female Republican candidates; the lack of a comparable strong, centralized PAC for Republican women specifically is a large reason for the Democratic women's relative level of success. While there are several PACs that raise money for Republican women, such as Maggie's List and VIEW PAC, none has the size or stature to serve this same function for female GOP candidates.

Our analysis of data from the Federal Election Commission and the Center for Responsive Politics does not show major differences in receipts of party money by women versus men within parties. By the end of Q2 filings for 2014, candidates in general had received little direct party money. Nonparty money, however, is not readily available for Republican women; in many cases, they do not receive PAC money until they become the party nominee. This presents a paradox: without money, female GOP candidates struggle to win their primaries, but they generally do not receive much party money until they do. This catch-22 led one Republican congresswoman to observe, in a 2015 interview with Political Parity, "When we have a quality leader running, there needs to be a commitment to get her through the primary. We've always adopted a hands-off approach to primaries. That changed in 2014. . . . There's a growing recognition that we can't sit out primaries."

CONCLUSION

Improving our political system requires greater female representation on both sides of the aisle as well as legislative bodies that reflect the true diversity of our country. Somewhat more women continue to identify as Democrats than Republicans in the general population. But these differences in party identification are nowhere near the extreme disparity in female elected officials in high-level offices. More women also identify as Independent than as Republican, suggesting opportunity for the GOP to pick up new voters and seats.

In her political memoir, former governor Whitman lamented her party's lack of support from those who are not white or male:

> I have talked about the problem the Republican Party has in attracting the votes of African American and other minority voters. Our actions have not always been true to our legacy as the party of Lincoln. I believe, however, that moderates can chart a new course for the party in appealing to and attracting minority voters to our ranks—and that will benefit not just the party but the country as well.[11]

The same could and should be said about gender. Involving women more strategically and systematically as candidates, particularly by helping them through the primary process, would make for not just a stronger party but a more representative democracy overall.

NOTES

1. See Political Parity Program, "Primary Hurdles for Republican Women" (Cambridge, MA: Swanee Hunt Alternatives, 2015), accessed January 3, 2017, http://www.politicalparity.org/research/primary-hurdles.

2. More detailed information on the methodology of each research team and subproject is available in the report issued by Swanee Hunt Alternatives in 2015, cited above. Also, several of the researchers involved in the original research project, including Rosalyn Cooperman, Melody Crowder-Meyer, Kelly Dittmar, Kira Sanbonmatsu, and Danielle Thomsen, are included as authors in this volume. Special thanks go to Nicole McCleskey and Bob Carpenter, political consultants and researchers, who, respectively, conducted the interviews and collected the 2014 campaign financial data.

3. See the Quota Project (a project of International IDEA, the Inter-Parliamentary Union, and Stockholm University) at http://www.quotaproject .org for excellent research and analysis on this point as well as lists of countries with and without quotas.

4. Raghabendra Chattopadhyay and Esther Duflo, "Women as Policy Makers: Evidence from a Randomized Policy Experiment in India," *Econometrica* 72, no. 5 (2004): 1409–1443.

5. Christine Todd Whitman, *It's My Party Too: The Battle for the Heart of the GOP and the Future of America* (New York: Penguin Press, 2005), 9

6. Leonie Huddy and Teresa Capelos, "Gender Stereotyping and Candidate Evaluation: Good News and Bad News for Women Politicians," in *The Social Psychology of Politics*, ed. Victor C. Ottati et al. (New York: Kluwer Academic Press, 2002), 29–53; Leonie Huddy and Nayda Terkildsen, "Gender Stereotypes and the Perception of Male and Female Candidates," *American Journal of Political Science* 37 (1993): 119–147; Kira Sanbonmatsu and Kathleen Dolan, "Do Gender Stereotypes Transcend Party?," *Political Research Quarterly* 62, no. 3 (2008): 485–494.

7. See also Shauna L. Shames, "The Costs of Running," in *Out of the Running: Why Millennials Reject Political Careers and Why It Matters* (New York: NYU Press, 2017), 35–69.

8. Campaign Finance Institute, "Vital Statistics," accessed August 26, 2015, www.cfinst.org/pdf/vital/VitalStats_t1.pdf.

9. Sarah Bryner and Doug Weber, "Sex, Money, and Politics," Center for Responsive Politics, September 26, 2013, accessed May 30, 2017, https://www .opensecrets.org/news/reports/gender.php; see also National Council for Research on Women, CAWP, and Center for Responsive Politics, "Money in Politics with a Gender Lens," accessed May 30, 2017, https://www.icrw.org/publications /money-in-politics-with-a-gender-lens.

10. Open Secrets, "2014 Financial Activity for Super PACs," Center for Responsive Politics, accessed May 30, 2017, https://www.opensecrets.org/outside spending/summ.php?cycle=2014&disp=O&type=S&chrt=V.

11. Whitman, *It's My Party, Too*, 232.

CHAPTER 6

A Run for Their Money: Republican Women's Hard Road to Campaign Funding

Rosalyn Cooperman and Melody Crowder-Meyer

[Bernie Sanders] thinks that they should stop with identity politics—
the Democratic Party. Whoa. He can call, we'll tell him how to do
that and win.

—Kellyanne Conway[1]

Although women comprise nearly half of Republican identifiers in the
American public, Republicans in elected office are disproportionately
male. Women hold fewer than 10 percent of the Republican seats in
Congress and are poorly represented at other levels of office as well.[2] Furthermore, the gender disparity among officeholders is much larger in the
Republican Party than the Democratic Party.[3] Democratic women's representation is over three times higher than Republican women's representation in the 115th Congress, with women holding about 33 percent of
Democratic seats in Congress.

For decades, women's political action committees (PACs; see Glossary)
have worked to increase women's political representation (see "Representation of Women," Glossary) by explicitly engaging in identity politics, that is, drawing attention to candidates' status as women running
for elected office. These PACs have raised millions of dollars on behalf
of women candidates, and yet their influence within the Republican and
Democratic Parties remains understudied. In this chapter, we fill this gap
by outlining the activities and funding capacities of women's PACs and
highlighting significant differences between liberal and conservative

PACs. In doing so, we offer an explanation for women's greater representation among Democratic than Republican elected officials.

We argue that donor support of Republican and Democratic women is
a key—and understudied—factor limiting the representation of Republican women. While scholars have shown that party differences in the pool
of candidates, candidate ambition, elite recruitment activities, electoral
context, and legislative professionalism all suppress Republican women's
candidacies,[4] very little work has considered the role that donors play in
this equation.[5] While money does not guarantee a victory on Election
Day, most agree that financial support plays a significant part in a candidate's electoral success.[6] Research also suggests that women considering a
candidacy may be particularly concerned about the fund-raising requirements of seeking elected office, making the presence of adequate funding
especially important for female candidate emergence and women's representation in office.[7] Consequently, in this chapter, we examine the funding infrastructure available to female Republican candidates and compare
it to the funding sources available to women seeking office as Democrats
to demonstrate why Democratic women have been more successful at
seeking and attaining office than Republican women.

We draw on our collection of PAC finance data to examine the electoral activity of eight women's PACs in 2012 and 2014.[8] While each PAC
has a stated goal of electing more women to federal office, these PACs
undertake different strategies in pursuit of that goal, with consequences
for women's representation. We reveal that liberal women's PACs are
more effective at promoting women's representation in the Democratic
Party than conservative women's PACs are in the Republican Party. Liberal women's PACs embrace the identity politics of progressive women
running for elected office. Liberal women's PACs have closer ties to those
in their associated party, raise more funds, and spend more money to support female candidates than their conservative women's PAC counterparts. In contrast, conservative women's PACs are less comfortable with
overt displays of identity politics. They instead typically emphasize how
Republican women candidates embody fiscal and social conservatism and
just happen to also be women. These differences lay the foundation for
Republican women's underrepresentation in political office.

We identify three main challenges that complicate Republican women's
bids for Congress relative to Democratic women. First, the development
of women's PACs over the last several decades has resulted in stronger
ties between liberal women's PACs and the Democratic Party than those
between the Republican Party and conservative women's PACs. While all
women's PACs share a foundational frustration with both parties' limited

recruitment and support of women candidates, liberal women's PACs represent a key Democratic Party constituency—progressive women—that gives these groups clout within the party not enjoyed by conservative women within the Republican Party. The differing political cultures of the Democratic and Republican parties also made it easier for liberal women's PACs to develop a closer relationship with the Democratic Party than conservative women's PACs have with the Republican Party. As the Democratic Party is more receptive to group-based claims and progressive gender roles, the policy demands of that key constituency are more likely to be heard.[9]

Second, we demonstrate that even in a favorable electoral context, conservative women's PACs cannot effectively compete against liberal women's PACs, specifically EMILY's List, in the resources they provide to endorsed candidates. Overall, conservative women's PACs raise and distribute significantly less money compared to liberal women's PACs. Additionally, they allocate their funds in ways that are less beneficial to Republican women candidates, particularly as Republican women are more likely than Democratic women to run in congressional districts as challengers against incumbents. Conservative women's PACs do not always endorse Republican women in contested primary elections, when fund-raising is vital; do not increase their giving power by bundling contributions from individual members to endorsed candidates; and do not help build their preferred party with direct contributions to state and federal party organizations—all practices in which the largest liberal women's PAC, EMILY's List, regularly engages. Liberal women's PACs provide resources to endorsed Democratic women candidates to grow their campaigns at critical junctures and demonstrate the depth of their commitment to demanding greater representation for progressive women. In contrast, conservative women's PACs provide more modest and supplemental, but not essential, resources to endorsed Republican women candidates. Theirs is more of a suggestion, not a demand, to the Republican Party for more women's representation.

Finally, by analyzing the flows of independent expenditures of the largest liberal and conservative women's PACs, EMILY's List and Susan B. Anthony List, respectively, we reveal that monies allocated by the conservative women's PAC are spent in a way that does not bolster, and may even hinder, women's representation. Specifically, Susan B. Anthony List spends far less money than EMILY's List on supporting women candidates. Susan B. Anthony List is more likely than EMILY's List to spend money opposing women candidates who do not share its policy goals; they deliberately fund Republican men candidates to defeat and therefore *decrease* the number of Democratic women officeholders. EMILY's List, on the other hand, spends the majority of its funds supporting women candidates or opposing men running against women candidates. These differing strategies, which are notably consistent with the party loyalty versus group interest cultures some have attributed to the Republican and Democratic Parties, mean that while Democratic women candidates have organizations they can turn to for funding due to both their gender *and* party identities, Republican women candidates must compete for funding against a much broader group of candidates, even when appealing to conservative "women's PACs."

Our examination of the funding infrastructure of women's PACs makes clear that Republican women are disadvantaged when compared to their Democratic counterparts in obtaining funding for their campaigns overall, and early funding specifically. The lack of early funds for Republican women candidates is a barrier to conservative women's PACs effectively demanding greater representation for women. All these differences lay a foundation for the party gap in women's candidacy as well as the representation gap between Democratic and Republican women in Congress.

WOMEN'S REPRESENTATION POLICY DEMANDERS AND POLITICAL PARTY CULTURE

There are two theories that inform our expectations regarding the relationship between women's PACs, women candidates, and the Democratic and Republican Parties. The first is the group-centered theory of political parties that states that the parties are made up of groups motivated by intense policy demands coupled with a desire for their preferred parties to win elections. Cohen et al. define policy demander groups as characterized "by their demands, not their social or demographic characteristics."[10] By this standard, a women's group is not a group composed of women, but a group demanding women's inclusion in the decision-making and political processes. In this theory of parties, policy demander groups cannot blindly champion their demands to the exclusion of others, but they must instead balance their demands within the framework of their preferred political party to win elections. Thus, once a policy demander group is integrated into the broader party apparatus and believes it can pursue its policy goals through the party, the groups should strongly support the party's candidates and help them win elections to achieve the groups' policy goals.[11] We argue that women's PACs are present as policy demanders in both parties. However, the sets of other policy demanders within each party, and the cultures shaping party elites' behavior, enhance the influence and power of liberal women's PACs while restricting the activities of conservative women's PACs.[12]

The political culture theory of political parties posits that the cultures of the Democratic and Republican Parties are very distinct. Freeman characterizes the Democratic Party as more decentralized, with power flowing upward among constituencies that compete for attention and resources from the party. In contrast, the Republican Party is more hierarchical, with power flowing downward to groups who will prioritize party loyalty over its group-specific claims.[13] The Democratic Party is essentially organized to hear and respond to group-based demands. Not so for the Republican Party. According to Freeman, Republicans would view these same group demands as "disloyal and unnecessary" because the group is prioritizing its own interests over those of the Party.[14] Thus, groups making policy demands will have an easier time pressing their claims in the Democratic Party than in the Republican Party.

In 2014, we conducted a survey of donors—the National Supporter Survey (NSS)—which offers some support for the persistence of these party cultures among both party and women's PAC donors.[15] Specifically, we find that Democratic donors are less likely than Republican donors to prioritize party loyalty when asked to compare party and group interests. In the NSS, we asked donors how much they agreed or disagreed with this statement: "It is best to minimize disagreement among individuals and groups within the party for the sake of party loyalty." Even when we include donors to women's PACs in our calculations, a party difference is clear: over half of Republican donors (53.5%) compared to only 40 percent of Democratic donors agree or strongly agree with this statement (a difference statistically significant in a chi-squared test at $p = 0.000$). If we focus only on the donors in our sample who donated to party campaign committees (rather than women's PACs), the distinction is even larger. Among Republican donors, over 59 percent agreed or strongly agreed that party loyalty should be promoted over individual and group disagreements, while only 41 percent of donors to the Democratic campaign committees expressed this same preference ($p = 0.026$).

Examining the motivations for political activity among donors also reveals differences between Democrats and Republicans in their orientations toward issues and group demands. In the NSS, we asked, "In 2011–2012, how much of your overall political activity was motivated by whether 'I wanted to work for an issue or for some particular group.'" Even among those donors selected for our sample, *because* they had donated to a women's PAC, Republicans were less likely to express they had acted due to this motivation. Specifically, 57 percent of Republicans compared to 64 percent of Democrats indicated that "a lot" of their activity was motivated by working for an issue or particular group ($p = 0.067$). The distinction is even broader among our sample of party donors—those who donated to one of the party congressional campaign committees. Among these donors, Republican donors (48.7%) were 10 percentage points less likely than Democratic donors (58.7%) to indicate that "a lot" of their activity was motivated by an issue or group interest ($p = 0.088$).

These results from our survey of campaign donors suggest further evidence of disparate party cultures.[16] We propose that these cultures lead to very different levels of fund-raising success and candidate support activities by one type of intense policy demander—women's PACs—within each political party. Women's PACs in both parties seek to increase the number of women running for and holding office. However, our collection of data from the 2012 and 2014 election cycles reveals that both the strategies used by liberal and conservative women's PACs and their success in supporting women candidates vary. Therefore, Republican and Democratic women candidates face substantially different fund-raising landscapes, which likely have consequences for both their decisions to seek office and their success in achieving elected office.

DATA

To evaluate the fund-raising capacities and strategies of liberal and conservative women's PACs, we gathered data identifying the fund-raising activities of women's PACs during the 2012 and 2014 election cycles. We referenced publicly available PAC campaign finance reports through the Federal Election Commission Web site and also summary PAC campaign finance totals from the Center for Responsive Politics. By examining these two cycles, we capture the activities of women's PACs in electoral contexts that were favorable and less favorable for each party's candidates. Specifically, the 2012 election cycle was a presidential election year that resulted in the reelection of Democratic incumbent Barack Obama and Democratic seat gains in both the U.S. Senate, where Democrats retained a majority, and the U.S. House, where Republicans maintained a majority. The 2014 election cycle was a midterm election year that resulted in the Republican Party regaining majority party status in the Senate and strengthening its majority in the House. Drawing on data from both election cycles enables us to identify clear patterns in the fund-raising amounts and allocation decisions made by liberal and conservative women's PACs and confirms that these patterns are not just due to the strength of a particular party's candidates in a specific election cycle.

THE DIVERGING DEVELOPMENT OF LIBERAL AND CONSERVATIVE WOMEN'S PACS

The evolution of women's PACs and the strategies they employ did not develop independent of politics and parties, but in response to them. Tracing the history of women's PACs is therefore important in identifying when women's PACs split to independently pursue the election of Democratic and Republican women candidates. Doing so also sheds light on why liberal women's PACs, EMILY's List in particular, developed a closer relationship, if not alliance, with the Democratic Party, while conservative women's PACs developed under the radar of the Republican Party and its donors.

Women's PACs were formed by women out of a frustration with *both* the Democratic and Republican Parties, who largely ignored women candidates, denied women candidates party funds, or placed them in hopeless races as challengers against popular incumbents.[17] The first group of women's PACs, which included NOW, focused on supporting pro-choice and pro-ERA candidates, regardless of party affiliation or whether a woman candidate's race was competitive. But their support was clearly focused on boosting the candidacies of progressive women; anti-ERA or pro-life women candidates would be neither endorsed nor funded. They also sought allies from sympathetic men. NOW and its contemporaries funded, and continue to fund, select friendly male candidates.[18] This original group of women's PACs was established before the parties took up opposing sides on the ERA and women's reproductive rights, more broadly. In addition to funding Democratic women candidates, NOW funded pro-choice, pro-ERA Republican women candidates because they were present in the Republican Party at that time. Women's PACs initially existed during a time when demanding women's representation was not considered an overtly partisan act.

Yet, as the parties polarized (see "Party Polarization," Glossary) on social issues, by the 1980s, women's PACs had become more closely identified with the Democratic Party than Republican Party.[19] This occurred most notably through the development of EMILY's List, which refined the demand for women's representation generally to a focus on supporting competitive, Democratic, pro-choice women. A few years after EMILY's List's founding, a women's PAC focused on supporting Republican women—Republicans for Choice—also emerged. However, EMILY's List's strategy remained distinct in several ways: it developed practices that ensured its support of female candidates would be more likely to accomplish its goal of electing more progressive women into office.

First, EMILY's List was selective in which women candidates it promoted. To gain an EMILY's List endorsement, Democratic women candidates had to demonstrate they were competitive and had the ability to independently raise funds. This requirement assured both EMILY's List and the Democratic Party that they were putting resources behind candidates who could effectively run their own campaigns and who had a good chance of electoral success. This vote of confidence signaled to other donors and campaign supporters that the candidate was worthy of their investment. Additionally, to boost women's candidacies, EMILY's List often endorsed women early in their election cycle to maximize the opportunity to raise funds from its members in both their primary and general elections. The decision by EMILY's List to get involved early in a woman candidate's election cycle is strategically sound; women candidates are significantly more likely than their male counterparts to face a contested primary.[20]

Second, EMILY's List worked to develop a relationship with the Democratic Party to ensure that the competitive, progressive women EMILY's List was supporting would also receive specialized attention, resources, and financial support from the broader party. As abortion became an issue on which the parties clearly diverged, EMILY's List reinforced that divergence by refusing to fund pro-choice Republican women candidates or Democratic women candidates who were not sufficiently pro-choice. It chose a party and used that affiliation to build party support for its chosen candidates. EMILY's List further established itself as a powerful donor group by strategically addressing federal campaign finance laws (which limit direct PAC contributions to $5,000 per candidate per election), leveraging the power of its highly motivated, progressive female membership base and introducing the concept of bundling smaller funds from members to endorsed candidates.[21] EMILY's List also directed funds to the national party's congressional committees, DCCC and DSCC, as well as state parties with particularly competitive congressional contests. While EMILY's List is at odds, on occasion, with the Democratic Party—funding pro-choice Democratic women candidates in contested primaries even as the party remains neutral—it nonetheless offers a fund-raising division of labor to the Democratic Party that we will show is unmatched by any other women's PAC.

The funds EMILY's List raises and distributes are tremendously valuable, as they allow supported candidates to expand their campaign donor bases beyond what they have established on their own, often during the early stages of their campaigns. These monies also enable the Democratic Party to direct their funds to other key contests to which they might not otherwise be able to contribute.[22] And, finally, direct contributions by EMILY's List to the Democratic Party's congressional committees and state party outlets also allow the party to marshal its funds to boost turn-out in competitive states and contests. Over time, these contributions to the Democratic Party reaffirmed EMILY's List status as an ally and promi-nent policy demander in the Democratic coalition, even as it pressed the party with demands for women's greater representation.

It is important to note that liberal women's PACs did not merely fade into the background as EMILY's List increased its standing within the Democratic Party. For example, NOW continues to endorse and fund pro-gressive women candidates. However, as we will show in Table 6.1, NOW does not raise funds on behalf of or bundle member contributions to endorsed candidates, nor does it contribute directly to the national Dem-ocratic Party or its party affiliates in the states. Instead, its fund-raising activity is generally limited to contributing directly to endorsed candi-dates, the majority of whom are Democratic women incumbents running for reelection.[23] Thus, while other liberal women's PACs join EMILY's List as policy demanders in the Democratic Party coalition, they do not consistently engage in all of the funding strategies used by EMILY's List.

In light of the success of EMILY's List, subsequent women's PACs have attempted to replicate elements of the EMILY's List playbook to demand women's representation for their own preferred subgroups and within the Republican Party. These PACs, however, formed independent of efforts by the Republican Party to recruit women candidates and have little for-mal relationship with the party. As such, conservative women's PACs are essentially invisible to the Republican Party, even as they work to promote the party's women candidates.[24] Republicans for Choice formed shortly after EMILY's List in 1989, and a few years later, WISH List formed after the 1992 "Year of the Woman" election (see Glossary) that ushered in 25 new Democratic women (out of 28 new women total).[25] Both PACs aimed to increase representation of pro-choice Republican women. By 2010, however, most pro-choice Republican women incumbents retired or were defeated, and the typical Republican woman candidate and office-holder were significantly more conservative.[26] Consequently, WISH List disbanded and merged with Republicans for Choice.

The remaining conservative women's PACs emphasized different issues they valued while demanding women's representation. Susan B. Anthony List formed in 1993 to elect pro-life women, but they have also funded pro-life men candidates. The Value in Electing Women (VIEW) PAC formed in 1997 to elect women who ran under the Republican Party label. Interestingly, the two most recent conservative women's PACs, Maggie's

List and ShePAC, formed in 2010 and 2012, respectively, identify economic conservatism as the most important issue in determining which women candidates to endorse, and they do not ask preferred candidates their positions on social issues. ShePAC's status as a conservative women's PAC was short-lived; it disbanded after the 2014 elections.[27]

None of these conservative women's PACs provide the same level of support to endorsed Republican women candidates as liberal women's PACs, particularly EMILY's List, provide to Democratic women candidates. Table 6.1 demonstrates this disparity by outlining the endorsement criteria and campaign finance activity of the eight existing women's PACs, which express the goal of increasing women's representation and raised sufficient funds to be required to file FEC reports in 2012 and 2014. EMILY's List raises funds for endorsed candidates, bundles funds from member contributions to their campaigns, raises independent expenditures in unlimited quantities to support or oppose candidates, and gives money to the national Democratic Party and its state affiliates for voter outreach and mobilization. In contrast, starting with the least active conservative women's PAC, Republicans for Choice supports Republican pro-choice candidates but does not engage in any of the remaining specified campaign finance activities. The other four conservative women's PACs occasionally endorse Republican women candidates in contested primaries, but they initially did not fund Republican women in their primaries even when the primary was uncontested. VIEW PAC provides no assistance to endorsed Republican women candidates beyond hard money contributions that max out at $5,000 per election. ShePAC adds some funds for independent expenditures in its activities, but the amounts spent in such expenditures are very modest. Maggie's List and Susan B. Anthony List are the most active conservative women's PACs, endorsing Republican women candidates in primaries, bundling funds from members, and raising funds for independent expenditures. However, none of the conservative women's PACs make direct contributions to the Republican Party, its congressional committees, or state parties.

In all, despite the work of conservative women's PACs to promote Republican women candidates, they have not been able to develop the close relationship with the Republican Party that EMILY's List has developed with the Democratic Party over its history.[28] This disparity likely has several causes. In the remainder of this chapter, we outline the gap in resources commanded by EMILY's List and other liberal women's PACs versus those marshalled by conservative women's PACs. We propose that this gap, when combined with the distinctions in PAC activities outlined here, make EMILY's List a more powerful player in the Democratic Party

Table 6.1 Women's PAC Endorsement Criteria and Campaign Funding Activities in 2012 and 2014

Women's PAC	Endorsement Criteria	Endorse Candidates in Primary Elections	Make Direct Contributions to Political Parties	Bundle Member Funds to Endorsed Candidates	Raise and Spend Independent Expenditures
EMILY's List	Democratic, pro-choice woman candidate in a competitive race	Yes	Yes	Yes	Yes
NOW	Federal feminist candidate endorsed by state NOW chapter	Yes	No	No	No
Planned Parenthood	Pro-choice, pro-family planning candidates for federal office	Yes	Yes	No	Yes
Maggie's List	Fiscally conservative Republican women federal candidates	Yes	No	Yes	Yes
Republicans for Choice	Pro-choice Republican candidates	No	No	No	No
ShePAC	Conservative women congressional candidates	Yes	No	No	Yes
Susan B. Anthony List	Pro-life women or pro-life men candidates who oppose pro-abortion women candidates	Yes	No	Yes	Yes
VIEW PAC	Republican women candidates to Congress	Yes	No	No	No

Source: Information compiled by authors.

coalition than any women's PACs in the Republican coalition. Additionally, this disparity is consistent with the party cultures theories we previously outlined. Because the Democratic Party culture is more supportive of group interests and progressive gender roles than the Republican Party culture, EMILY's List has access to a donor base supportive of women's representation as a goal and to other policy demanders within the party open to the influence of women's PACs.[29] Unless conservative women's PACs can make themselves as essential to the Republican Party as EMILY's List has become to the Democratic Party—likely requiring changes in the Republican Party culture and the funding available to Republican women's PACs from Republican donors—we expect the historical pattern of women's PAC integration in the two parties to continue. We find little reason to expect conservative women's PACs will gain power in the near future.

HOW MUCH MONEY DO WOMEN'S PACS SPEND?

The historical development of women's PACs in each party and distinctions in party culture among Republican and Democratic donors appear to have produced a clear distinction in the funding capacities of liberal and conservative women's PACs. Conservative women's PACs raise significantly less money than liberal women's PACs. This disparity means conservative women's PACs either endorse fewer candidates or direct smaller sums to the candidates they support. Consequently, Republican women candidates have less access to funds based on their status as women than do Democratic women candidates. This interparty funding disparity serves as an additional barrier for Republican women considering a run for office.

Table 6.2 lists the receipts, direct candidate contributions, and disbursements for each of the eight women's PACs included in the National Supporter Survey. Simply looking at the raw totals of funds raised and disbursed, it is clear that EMILY's List and Planned Parenthood PACs have a fund-raising advantage unmatched by any of the conservative women's PACs. EMILY's List distributed more than $2 million in funds to endorsed candidates in 2012 and distributed more than $1.6 million in funds in 2014. During that same period, Planned Parenthood PAC distributed about a million dollars each cycle. NOW's fund-raising totals are significantly less than what the other two liberal women's PACs raise, but together the amounts raised by liberal women's PACs far exceed total receipts raised by conservative women's PACs. Republicans for Choice raised slightly more than a quarter of a million dollars in both 2012 and

Table 6.2 Women's PAC Campaign Finance Receipts and Expenditures in 2012 and 2014

Women's PAC	2012 Receipts	2012 Direct Candidate Contributions	2012 Disbursements	2014 Receipts	2014 Direct Candidate Contributions	2014 Disbursements
EMILY's List	$36,677,350	$2,046,384	$33,973,836	$44,206,357	$1,650,622	$44,878,361
NOW	$137,438	$62,803	$141,023	$140,070	$27,671	$101,999
Planned Parenthood	$1,157,202	$943,398	$1,029,871	$1,130,327	$906,541	$727,247
Maggie's List	$173,647	$73,905	$170,156	$188,915	$35,859	$205,395
Republicans for Choice	$261,326	$0	$268,048	$253,212	$0	$249,815
ShePAC	$163,972	$6,000	$116,493	$64,586	$3,500	$112,065
Susan B. Anthony List	$462,167	$422,991	$446,991	$335,067	$241,862	$329,216
VIEW PAC	$346,263	$170,713	$325,657	$474,600	$270,500	$462,836

Source: Federal Election Commission.

2014, but they did not directly fund a single Republican pro-choice candidate. Maggie's List and ShePAC formed in 2010 and 2012, respectively, and raised funds as new PACs on the political scene. By that standard, Maggie's List was significantly more successful than ShePAC and distributed over $100,000 in funds to endorsed Republican women candidates. Facing little success, ShePAC disbanded after the 2014 election cycle.

VIEW PAC and Susan B. Anthony List were the most successful of the conservative women's PACs during this period. Over the 2012 and 2014 election cycles, VIEW PAC distributed nearly $500,000 to endorsed Republican women candidates. VIEW PAC does not fund Republican men; its contributions went solely to Republican women candidates. During that same time, Susan B. Anthony List distributed nearly $700,000 in funds to endorsed pro-life candidates.

As Table 6.1 demonstrates, liberal women's PACs can also offer more money to each individual candidate they support than conservative women's PACs because of their broader methods of supporting candidates. The largest liberal women's PAC, EMILY's List, maximizes contributions to endorsed candidates by distributing both direct *and* bundled contributions to Democratic women candidates. If EMILY's List endorses a candidate in her primary, the PAC will make a hard money contribution of up to $5,000 in the primary election, and often in the general election as well if the candidate wins her primary. Plus, by providing bundled funds from individual contributors to candidates, EMILY's list is able to ensure supported candidates receive significantly more than the $5,000 EMILY's List is restricted to contribute as a PAC.

Additionally, EMILY's List uses its status within the Democratic Party and friendly funding circles to further assist endorsed women candidates. EMILY's List has built a formidable reputation within its party and donor base of supporting high-quality candidates. Consequently, an EMILY's List endorsement carries more weight than an endorsement by other groups among donors—most (61%) of whom indicate that affecting the outcome of an election is a very important reason they contribute.[30] In fact, as we note in other work, our National Supporter Survey demonstrates that EMILY's List is very well-known among Democratic donors.[31] Virtually all (93%) of Democratic donors who completed our survey reported that they had at least heard of NOW and EMILY's List.

In contrast, we find that a supermajority of Republican donors have "never heard of" most of the conservative women's PACs. Specifically, we reveal in other work that between 68 percent and 92 percent of Republican donors report they have *never heard of* Maggie's List, ShePAC, or VIEW PAC. Even the better-known conservative women's PACs are still unknown to many Republican donors. Among donors to the Republican congressional campaign committees in our survey, about half reported they had never heard of Susan B. Anthony List (45%) or Republicans for Choice (50%). Further, among Republican donors to conservative women's PACs, between 20 percent and 28 percent reported they had never heard of those two groups.[32]

These distinctions in familiarity help to explain why an endorsement from a liberal women's PAC such as EMILY's List carries so much more weight than an endorsement from a conservative women's PAC and results in more significant gains in other fund-raising. Specifically, research shows that during primary election campaigns, Democratic women candidates endorsed by EMILY's List raise significantly more money than nonendorsed women candidates.[33] In contrast, Republican women have a harder time than Republican men raising money in primaries, regardless of whether they have been endorsed (or not) by a women's PAC.[34] Since conservative women's PACs raise less money, often do not augment direct PAC contributions with bundled funds from members, and are less well-known to their party's donors, Republican women candidates do not receive the same fund-raising boost as Democratic women from a women's PAC endorsement.

In sum, by examining the funds raised and disbursed by women's PACs, and the benefits that come with an endorsement by one of these groups, we see that Democratic and Republican women candidates receive very different benefits from women's PAC support. More funds are available to Democratic than Republican women due to the far greater amounts of money raised by liberal than conservative women's PACs and to the different strategies these groups use when disbursing funds (e.g., through bundling or not). Additionally, because of the reputation of liberal women's groups among Democratic donors, an endorsement from a liberal women's PAC can bring with it further contributions from other donors. On the other hand, conservative women's PACs are largely unknown to other donors in their party, making their support less beneficial to candidates they endorse. This finding alone would strongly suggest that female Republican candidates are disadvantaged relative to female Democratic candidates when it comes to fund-raising—at least in terms of raising money due to their identity as women. Examining precisely how funds are spent by conservative and liberal women's PACs further clarifies this disparity and highlights that Democratic women have access to funds intended primarily for female candidates while Republican women are competing with male candidates even for funds from supposedly "women's PACs."

WHERE DOES THE MONEY GO?

While each of the groups discussed in this chapter can be categorized as "women's PACs" based on their published endorsement criteria and statements regarding their support for female candidates, a closer examination of the candidates each group supports demonstrates that—consistent with the party cultures theories we have outlined—liberal women's PACs are more focused on promoting women's representation with their resources than conservative women's PACs. We draw this conclusion based on an investigation of the use of independent expenditures by liberal and conservative women's PACs. Independent expenditures are an important gauge of a PAC's priorities, as PACs have the opportunity to direct unlimited funds to the candidates and contests they most value. Independent expenditures are typically spent on campaign advertising directed at voters to give them a reason to turn out to vote or stay home on Election Day. We find that the largest liberal women's PAC, EMILY's List, focuses more of its resources on supporting women candidates than the largest conservative women's PAC, Susan B. Anthony List. In fact, Susan B. Anthony List allocates more money in support of preferred male candidates or against female candidates in the opposing party than toward female Republican candidates. Instead of forcefully supporting women candidates, with its allocation of independent expenditures, the largest conservative women's PAC actually works to depress women's representation by focusing funds on opposing Democratic women candidates.

Figure 6.1 identifies the funds raised in 2012 and 2014 for the two women's PACs with the largest amounts of independent expenditures, EMILY's List and Susan B. Anthony List.[35] In 1995, EMILY's List created a separate entity, WomenVote!, to mobilize women voters and raise independent expenditures.[36] In 2012, Susan B. Anthony List created Women Speak Out to mobilize pro-life voters and raise independent expenditures.[37] These Super PACs are the main entities through which each organization collects and distributes independent expenditures. For EMILY's List and Susan B. Anthony List, we group these funds into three categories: those used to support female candidates in the PAC's preferred party, those spent opposing women in the PAC's opposing party, and those spent to assist or oppose male candidates.

Figure 6.1 demonstrates that EMILY's List significantly outraises Susan B. Anthony List in independent expenditures and reserves more of its funds to support women candidates in its preferred party. In 2012 and 2014, EMILY's List raised more than twice the amount of money (about $8 million) Susan B. Anthony List raised (about $3 million) for independent

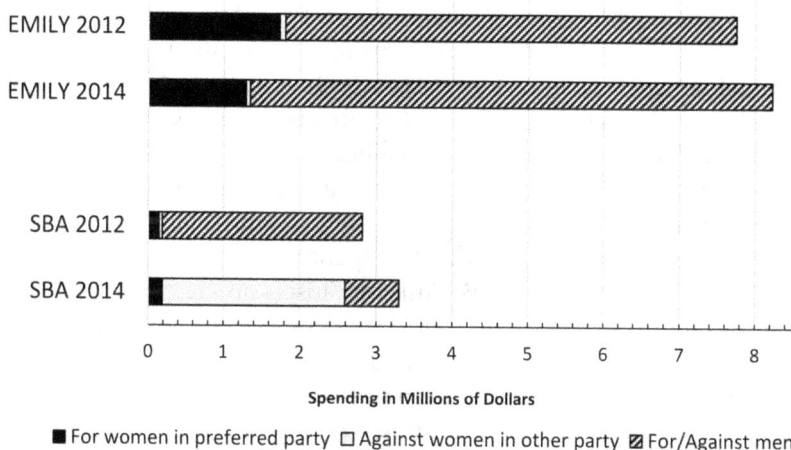

Figure 6.1 Independent Expenditures Distributed by EMILY's List and Susan B. Anthony List in 2012 and 2014

Source: Federal Election Commission.

expenditures. Both PACs raised more money during the midterm election cycle than the presidential election cycle. Each group also allocated its funds differently, depending on the election cycle. In 2012, only 5 percent of Susan B. Anthony List's independent expenditures, less than $150,000, were reserved to support Republican women candidates. During that same time, EMILY's List allocated 22 percent of its independent expenditures, roughly $1.7 million dollars, in support of Democratic women candidates. In 2014, Republican women candidates fared slightly better, as Susan B. Anthony List reserved 6 percent of its independent expenditures, nearly $190,000, for their campaigns. EMILY's List spent significantly more money in support of Democratic women candidates, nearly $1.3 million, constituting 16 percent of the total independent expenditures funds they raised.

Both PACs direct a majority of their independent expenditures to contests featuring men candidates, but the reasons they do so differ in ways that have significant consequences for women candidates. In 2012, Susan B. Anthony List raised nearly $3 million in independent expenditures, with over 90 percent of that sum allocated to contests with male candidates. Specifically, Susan B. Anthony List spent nearly $1.5 million against the Democratic incumbent, President Barack Obama, and over $500,000 earlier in the election cycle in support of its preferred

Republican presidential nominee, Rick Santorum. In 2014, Susan B. Anthony List reserved a much smaller percentage of its funds, 21 percent, for contests with male candidates, focusing most of its spending instead on opposing female Democratic candidates. In both election cycles, then, the majority of Susan B. Anthony List independent expenditure funding was allocated either to help Republican men or oppose Democratic women. Assisting Republican women was a minor portion of their independent expenditures.

In both election cycles, EMILY's List spent three-fourths of its funds—and more money than Susan B. Anthony List—on elections with male candidates. But there are important differences in *why* these groups direct money to favor or oppose male candidates. When EMILY's List spends money on male candidates, it does so to support female Democratic candidates. In *all* of the election contests where EMILY's List spent money on male candidates, it did so to oppose a male candidate running against an EMILY's List–endorsed Democratic female candidate.[38] The same cannot be said for how Susan B. Anthony List allocates its funds; it consistently prioritized spending money on pro-life candidates in competitive races, the majority of whom are Republican men, not women.

Additionally, Susan B. Anthony List dedicated many of its independent expenditure funds to *oppose* Democratic women candidates. EMILY's List does allocate independent expenditures to oppose Republican women candidates, but it does so in quantities that add up to less than 1 percent of total funds raised, and spends against Republican women only in contests with an EMILY's List–endorsed woman Democratic candidate. In contrast, in 2014, Susan B. Anthony List spent nearly three-quarters of its independent expenditures (more than $2.4 million) to oppose Democratic women candidates. Susan B. Anthony List spent more than a million dollars targeting one race, the North Carolina U.S. Senate race featuring Democratic incumbent Kay Hagan against Republican challenger Thom Tillis. Tillis defeated Hagan in the 2014 general election. In this example, Susan B. Anthony List worked to intentionally decrease (Democratic) women's representation in Congress. In other words, the historical split in women's PACs, through which they became clearly aligned with one or the other party, has resulted in some women's PACs using funds to assist their party even if that means opposing women's representation in the other party.

EMILY's List and Susan B. Anthony List raise millions of dollars in independent expenditures to provide further financial support to their most preferred candidates or in competitive electoral contests. And these electoral contests are not randomly selected. In their allocation of independent expenditures, EMILY's List and Susan B. Anthony List engage in a candidate proxy war with one another. In congressional elections, Susan B. Anthony List directs a majority of its funds to support candidates, mostly Republican men, who run against EMILY's List–endorsed pro-choice women Democrats. In contrast, EMILY's List directs a majority of its funds to support pro-choice women Democrats who have been targeted by Susan B. Anthony List. In billing itself as the "anti-EMILY's List",[39] Susan B. Anthony List's executive director aptly captured the organization's actions. In opposing EMILY's List, Susan B. Anthony List often opposes Democratic women's representation, and even supports men candidates to do so. In pursuing this strategy, Susan B. Anthony List is acting consistently with the party cultures theories proposing that the Republican Party culture values party loyalty over group claims. Susan B. Anthony List is also acting consistently with the demands of other policy demanders within the Republican Party that shape that party's culture. Social conservatives are an important constituency within the Republican Party, and advancing a pro-life agenda is an important part of their identification as Republicans.[40] As such, demanding greater representation for pro-life candidates is an issue-based claim that is faithful to a strongly pro-life Republican Party platform. Endorsing pro-life *women* candidates is a secondary bonus.

CONCLUSION

When it comes to money—specifically money aimed at increasing women's representation—Republican women are significantly disadvantaged when compared to their Democratic women counterparts. Women's PACs are not created equal; the liberal PACs that support Democratic women candidates are more generous and more strategically helpful than the conservative PACs that support Republican women candidates. These differences are entrenched and will not be solved by simply advising conservative women's PACs to raise more money as long as the Republican Party—its operatives and donors—believes that intentionally supporting women candidates is negatively equated with identity politics. Thus, these findings have important implications for Republican women considering a bid for elected office at all levels of government.

Several factors contribute to Democratic women's advantage in funding over Republican women. Liberal women's PACs are deeply embedded in the Democratic Party because of a culture that is receptive to group-based interests, progressive gender roles, and a demand for greater representation of women as candidates. They have ample funds and donor support that enables them to raise more money and distribute funds to grow Democratic women's campaigns early on in an election cycle, when funding is crucial. In comparison, conservative women's PACs remain reluctant to endorse Republican women in contested primaries, raise substantially less money overall, and are largely unknown within the Republican Party. Perhaps donors who contribute funds to conservative women's PACs, due to party culture, are less motivated to increase the number of Republican women candidates and officeholders. Consequently, Republican women candidates do not enjoy this same breadth of resources, as they lack major sources of funding based on their identity as women. This is particularly evident in the case of Susan B. Anthony List, a PAC that self-identifies as a pro-life women's PAC, which allocates more of its independent expenditures to support pro-life Republican men than women candidates. Stated plainly, Republican women have to compete with Republican men to get funding from the largest conservative women's PAC.

It is likely that the different orientations of liberal and conservative women's PACs and donors to the two parties toward supporting candidates due to their *gender* as well as their policy positions negatively affects prospective Republican women who are already significantly underrepresented as officeholders. Republican women must establish their social and fiscal conservative credentials, but they cannot draw attention to the obvious fact that they are women running under their party's label. Democratic women are not similarly burdened and have more dedicated resources to help with the heavy lifting of fund-raising than Republican women candidates.

Healthy democracies need capable and dedicated citizens from all backgrounds to participate in politics. Women are not monolithic in their preferences, and it is hard to press a claim of playing identity politics for women when they comprise a majority of the voting population. Women benefit when other women who share their identity run for office.[41] The hard road to Republican women's campaign finance may have the effect of especially discouraging qualified, competent Republican women from throwing their hats in the ring.

NOTES

1. Tom McCarthy, "Conway: New Trump Appointments 'Could Come This Week.'" *The Guardian*, November 21, 2016, https://www.theguardian.com/us-news/live/2016/nov/21/donald-trump-mike-pence-appointments-cabinet-candidates.

2. Center for American Women and Politics (CAWP), "Women in the U.S. Congress 2016," 2016, http://www.cawp.rutgers.edu/women-us-congress-2016; CAWP, "Women Mayors in U.S. Cities 2016," 2016, http://www.cawp.rutgers

.edu/levels_of_office/women-mayors-us-cities-2016; Kira Sanbonmatsu, *Where Women Run: Gender and Party in the American States* (Ann Arbor: University of Michigan Press, 2006).

3. Laurel Elder, "The Partisan Gap among Women State Legislators," *Journal of Women, Politics, & Policy* 33, no. 1 (2012): 65–85; Laurel Elder, "Whither Republican Women: The Growing Partisan Gap among Women in Congress," *The Forum* 6, no. 1 (2008), https://doi.org/10.2202/1540-8884.1204.

4. Melody Crowder-Meyer and Benjamin E. Lauderdale, "A Partisan Gap in the Supply of Female Potential Candidates in the United States," *Research & Politics* 1, no. 1 (2014): 1–7; Melody Crowder-Meyer, "Gendered Recruitment without Trying: How Local Party Recruiters Affect Women's Representation," *Politics & Gender* 9, no. 4 (2013): 390–413; Jennifer Lawless and Richard L. Fox, *It Still Takes a Candidate: Why Women Don't Run for Office* (New York: Cambridge University Press, 2010); Sanbonmatsu, *Where Women Run.*

5. Though see Sarah Bryner and Doug Weber, "Sex, Money, and Politics," Center for Responsive Politics, September 26, 2013, https://www.opensecrets.org/news/reports/gender.php; Karin E. Kitchens and Michele L. Swers, "Why Aren't There More Republican Women in Congress? Gender, Partisanship, and Fundraising Support in the 2010 and 2012 Elections," *Politics & Gender* 12, no. 4 (2016): 1–29.

6. Kelly Dittmar, Navigating Gendered Terrain: Stereotypes and Strategy in Political Campaigns (Philadelphia: Temple University Press, 2015); Henry A. Kim and Brad L. Leveck, "Money, Reputation, and Incumbency in U.S. House Elections, or Why Marginals Have Become More Expensive," *American Political Science Review* 107, no. 3 (2013): 492–504; Robert Biersack and Paul S. Herrnson, "Political Parties and the Year of the Woman," in *The Year of the Woman: Myths and Realities*, eds. Elizabeth Adell Cook, Sue Thomas, and Clyde Wilcox (Boulder, CO: Westview Press, 1994), 161–180.

7. Susan J Carroll and Kira Sanbonmatsu, *More Women Can Run: Gender and Pathways to the State Legislatures* (Oxford: Oxford University Press, 2013); Lawless and Fox, *It Still Takes a Candidate*; Shannon Jenkins, "A Woman's Work Is Never Done? Fund-Raising Perception and Effort among Female State Legislative Candidates," *Political Research Quarterly* 60, no. 2 (2007): 230–239; Georgia Duerst-Lahti, "The Bottleneck: Women Becoming Candidates," in *Women and Elective Office: Past, Present, and Future*, eds. Sue Thomas and Clyde Wilcox (New York: Oxford University Press, 1998), 15–25.

8. EMILY's List, Maggie's List, NOW, Planned Parenthood, Republicans for Choice, ShePAC, Susan B. Anthony List, and VIEW PAC—we selected these PACs based on two criteria: they explicitly mention the group goal of increasing women's representation in Congress by endorsing and funding women candidates, and they raised sufficient funds to require the filing of campaign finance reports with the Federal Election Commission at routine intervals during the aforementioned election years.

9. Jo Freeman, "The Political Culture of the Democratic and Republican Parties," *Political Science Quarterly* 101, no. 3 (1986): 327–356; Matt Grossmann and David A. Hopkins, "Ideological Republicans and Group Interest Democrats:

The Asymmetry of American Party Politics," *Perspectives on Politics* 13, no. 1 (2015): 119–139; Melody Crowder-Meyer and Rosalyn Cooperman, "Can't Buy Them Love: How Party Culture among Donors Contributes to the Party Gap in Women's Representation," *Journal of Politics*, forthcoming.

10. Marty Cohen, David Karol, Hans Noel, and John Zaller, *The Party Decides: Presidential Nominations before and after Reform* (Chicago: University of Chicago Press, 2008), 31.

11. Kathleen Bawn, Martin Cohen, David Karol, Seth Masket, Hans Noel, and John Zaller, "A Theory of Political Parties: Groups, Policy Demands, and Nominations in American Politics," *Perspectives on Politics* 10, no. 3 (2012): 571–597.

12. Crowder-Meyer and Cooperman, "Can't Buy Them Love."

13. Freeman, "The Political Culture of the Democratic and Republican Parties," 345; Grossmann and Hopkins, "Ideological Republicans and Group Interest Democrats."

14. Freeman, "The Political Culture of the Democratic and Republican Parties," 332.

15. The NSS is a national survey of individuals who contributed money to one of the Democratic or Republican Party congressional campaign committees (NRCC, NRSC, DCCC, DSCC) or a women's PAC around the 2012 U.S. federal election cycle. Due to the widely varying numbers of supporters for each organization, our sample differed by organization. For groups with the fewest donors (VIEW PAC, NOW), we sent surveys to all donors in their FEC reports from the 2010 and 2012 election cycles as well as 2013. For groups with somewhat more donors (ShePAC, Maggie's List, Republicans for Choice, and Planned Parenthood), we sent surveys to all donors in the 2012 election cycle and 2013 FEC reports. Finally, for groups with the largest donor base (EMILY's List, Susan B Anthony List, and the NRCC, NRSC, DCCC, and DSCC), we surveyed a sample of donors from the 2012 postprimaries election cycle. We surveyed donors to both liberal women's PACs (EMILY's List, NOW, Planned Parenthood) and conservative women's PACs (Maggie's List, Republicans for Choice, ShePAC, Susan B. Anthony List, VIEW PAC). Federal campaign finance regulations require that PACs routinely file reports to disclose fund-raising sources and beneficiaries, which are made publicly available on the Federal Election Commission's (FEC) Web site. From these reports, we contacted over 3,700 donors via postal mail to complete an online survey or its paper equivalent.

Our National Supporter Survey had a response rate of 21 percent and is, to our knowledge, the most comprehensive survey of donors to women's PACs conducted to date. By comparing information about those in our survey sample to other data we gathered from FEC filings, we find little evidence of nonresponse bias that would affect our findings. Those from whom we received completed surveys are a close, if not perfect, representation of campaign committee and women's PAC donors. More details on our sample, response rates, and nonresponse bias calculations are available from the authors and in Crowder-Meyer and Cooperman, "Can't Buy Them Love."

16. See also Crowder-Meyer and Cooperman, "Can't Buy Them Love."

17. Barbara Burrell, "Political Parties and Women's Organizations: Bringing Women into the Electoral Arena," in *Gender & Elections: Shaping the Future of American Politics*, 3rd ed., eds. Susan J. Carroll and Richard L. Fox (Cambridge: Cambridge University Press, 2014), 211–240.

18. Like NOW, Planned Parenthood PAC has always funded men candidates, and as its first priority is to fund pro-choice candidates, it is not as strictly a women's representation policy demander as groups such as EMILY's List. Planned Parenthood PAC does, however, primarily fund Democratic women candidates and exhibits other electoral strategies similar to a key women's representation policy demander, EMILY's List, which is why it is included in this analysis.

19. Christina Wolbrecht, *The Politics of Women's Rights: Parties, Positions, and Change* (Princeton, NJ: Princeton University Press, 2000); Kira Sanbonmatsu, *Democrats/Republicans and the Politics of Women's Place* (Ann Arbor: University of Michigan Press, 2002).

20. Jennifer Lawless and Kathryn Pearson, "The Primary Reason for Women's Underrepresentation? Reevaluating the Conventional Wisdom," *The Journal of Politics* 70, no. 1 (2008): 67–82.

21. Jamie Pimlott, *Women and the Democratic Party: The Evolution of EMILY's List* (New York: Cambria Press, 2010).

22. Rosalyn Cooperman, "Emily's Friends: The Emerging Relationship between Emily's List, Organized Labor, and Women Candidates in U.S. House Elections, 2002–2008" (paper presented at the Annual Meeting of the American Political Science Association, Washington D.C., September 2010).

23. Additionally, other liberal women's organizations such as EMERGE America have formed to support Democratic women seeking office. However, they do not engage in any of the fund-raising activities embraced by EMILY's List. Instead, they seek to encourage women's candidacies by offering candidate training to interested women.

24. Crowder-Meyer and Cooperman, "Can't Buy Them Love."

25. CAWP, "Women Candidates for Congress 1974–2014," 2014, http://cawp .rutgers.edu/sites/default/files/resources/canwincong_histsum.pdf.

26. Danielle Thomsen, "Why So Few (Republican) Women? Explaining the Partisan Imbalance of Women in the U.S. Congress," *Legislative Studies Quarterly* 40, no. 2 (2015): 295–323.

27. Founding dates for all the specified women's PACs were identified from the PAC's Web sites or from statement of organization paperwork that is on file with, and publicly available from, the Federal Election Commission.

28. One additional measure of closeness outside the scope of this project is that EMILY's List and the Democratic Party will hire one another's staff in subsequent elections. Since the 1990s, several senior staff members from EMILY's List have worked for the Democratic National Committee or its congressional campaign committees. The same is not true for conservative women's PACs and the Republican Party. See Cooperman, "Emily's Friends."

29. See Freeman, "The Political Culture of the Democratic and Republican Parties"; Grossmann and Hopkins, "Ideological Republicans and Group Interest

Democrats"; Wolbrecht, *The Politics of Women's Rights: Parties, Positions, and Change*; Crowder-Meyer and Cooperman, "Can't Buy Them Love."

30. Peter Francia, John Green, Paul Herrnson, Lynda Powell, and Clyde Wilcox, *The Financiers of Congressional Elections: Investors, Ideologues, and Intimates* (New York: Columbia University Press, 2003).

31. Crowder-Meyer and Cooperman, "Can't Buy Them Love."

32. Crowder-Meyer and Cooperman, "Can't Buy Them Love."

33. Peter Francia, "Early Fundraising by Nonincumbent Female Congressional Candidates: The Importance of Women's PACs," *Women & Politics* 23, no. 1 (2002): 7–20.

34. Kitchens and Swers, "Why Aren't There More Republican Women in Congress?"

35. Save for Planned Parenthood, the remaining women's PACs do not have a significant independent expenditure presence. Planned Parenthood does raise and distribute independent expenditures in support of pro-choice candidates; indeed, in 2012, a significant portion of these funds were spent in support of President Obama's reelection efforts. NOW does not raise funds for independent expenditures. There is no conservative women's PAC that comes remotely close to SBA List's independent expenditure totals. Maggie's List and ShePAC, the other two conservative women's PACs that raise independent expenditures, distributed less than $5,000 combined in 2012 and 2014.

36. EMILY's List, "WomenVote!," 2016, https://www.emilyslist.org/pages/entry /women-vote.

37. Susan B. Anthony List, "Women Speak Out Super PAC Launches," 2012, https://www.sba-list.org/newsroom/press-releases/women-speak-out-super -pac-launches.

38. In most cases, the men candidates EMILY's List opposed were Republicans, though in 2012 and 2014, EMILY's List spent less than 1 percent of independent expenditure funds ($315,154 total) against six Democratic men candidates who were running against Democratic women. Figures were compiled by the authors from EMILY's List's campaign finance reports filed with the Federal Election Commission.

39. Author interview with then Susan B. Anthony List executive director Jennifer Bingham, August 6, 2003.

40. Kimberly Conger, Rosalyn Cooperman, Gregory Shufeldt, Geoffrey L. Layman, John C. Green, Richard Herrera, and Kerem Ozan Kalkan, "Group Commitment among Republican Factions: A Perspective from National Convention Delegates," 2016; see also Wolbrecht, *The Politics of Women's Rights: Parties, Positions, and Change*; Crowder-Meyer and Cooperman, "Can't Buy Them Love."

41. Susan Carroll, *The Impact of Women in Public Office* (Bloomington: Indiana University Press, 2001); Michele Swers, *Women in the Club: Gender and Policy Making in the Senate* (Chicago: University of Chicago Press, 2013).

CHAPTER 7

Republican Women in the 2016 Election: Progress or Same Old Patterns?

Kelly Dittmar

In 2016, Republicans' electoral success was widespread. Donald Trump won a highly contested race for the presidency; Republicans maintained the majority in the U.S. House and Senate; the number of Republican governors rose to a level only matched 94 years prior; and Democrats made few inroads against the Republican dominance of state legislatures nationwide. But, as in previous years of Republican gains, Republican women remained on the sidelines of this success story. The number of Republican women dropped in the U.S. House and Senate, in state legislatures, and in statewide elected executive posts from 2016 to 2017. At the presidential level, just one woman, Carly Fiorina, competed among the 17 candidates in the Republican Party primary, and she dropped out of the race by February 2016, after just two states' nomination contests. In all, the Republican Party did little to close the partisan gender gap in candidacy or representation in election 2016.

Perhaps this is unsurprising. As the contributors to this volume have made clear, there are multiple challenges facing women in the Republican Party, and there appeared to be little concerted effort to address them in election 2016. Efforts to combat women's underrepresentation require that it be recognized, defined, and problematized. In 2014, House Republican women launched Project GROW to "empower, engage and encourage female candidates and women voters."[1] In discussing the impetus for their effort, Rep. Ann Wagner told CNN that the GOP needed to do a better job messaging to women, "both to motivate women in the electorate, but also to motivate women to run for public office."[2] In Project GROW's first cycle, Republicans saw a net gain of two women in the House and two new Republican women won U.S. Senate seats.[3] But even before these modest successes, the Republican National Committee chairman, Reince Priebus, denied that his party even had a women's representation problem. In October 2014, he told a crowd at George Washington University that the Republican Party had done "a very good job" of electing women to Congress at a time when just 23 Republican women served, representing 4.3 percent of all members and 8.2 percent of all Republicans in the 113th Congress. He went on to say, "We've got [women] leaders all over the country. . . . I think sometimes we do a really bad job bragging about it."[4] At that time, Republican women were 11.6 percent of all statewide elected executive officials and 8.7 percent of state legislators nationwide.

A similar type of amplification may explain the results of an October 2016 survey by the Public Religion Research Institute (PRRI), which found that only 37 percent of Republicans agree that the country would be better off with more women holding public office.[5] This statistic might be better explained, however, by party members' disavowal of "identity politics." That ideological aversion starts at the top. House Speaker Paul Ryan (R-WI) has repeatedly characterized identity politics as a threat to democracy, telling a national audience in July 2016,

> I would argue that the left basically perfected identity politics. It's very effective, but it's very divisive, and we on the right should not come anywhere close to it. I believe in inclusive, aspirational politics that speaks to our common humanity, that speaks to the principles that unify us, and that to me is the kind of leadership that people in this country are begging for that we are endeavoring to try and offer. I believe we need to be inclusive and aspirational. That means talk to virtues within people, prey not on darker emotions, but prey on what unites us. That means reject identity politics in every way, shape or form.[6]

While his opposition to identity politics focuses on voter targeting, his rejection of identity politics "in every way, shape or form" explains the reluctance of party leadership at the national and state levels to conduct targeted recruitment or provide directed support of women candidates. That ideological approach seemed to dominate national recruitment efforts in the 2016 election, when Project GROW was absorbed back into the National Republican Campaign Committee's (NRCC) Young Guns program to recruit emerging Republican leaders—male and female. In July 2015, NRCC recruitment chair Richard Hudson (R-NC) told *Roll Call*, "The goal now is not to just go find female candidates and throw money at them, but to bring female candidates into the Young Guns program, so that we're helping them to develop as candidates so they can be more successful."[7]

At the state level, there was at least greater recognition of the gender-specific challenges confronting women candidates in 2016. The Republican State Leadership Committee (RSLC) continued its Right Women, Right Now (RWRN) program, launched in 2012, to recruit and support women candidates for state-level offices. RWRN had limited success in 2012 and 2014, but it sought to recruit 500 new women candidates for state-level office and to see at least 150 of them serving in 2017.[8] While they may have met those goals, the numbers of women in state-level offices did not rise between 2016 and 2017.

In addition to an ideological resistance to and limited expanse of identity-based efforts, the 2016 presidential election also encouraged strategic caution when it came to Republican messaging and behavior on women's representation. In a year when a Democratic woman came so close to making presidential history, Republican claims against identity politics served to discredit Hillary Clinton's candidacy, and advocacy for greater gender parity in officeholding could be misconstrued as support for the woman seeking to break the highest, hardest glass ceiling in American politics.

The gendered context of the presidential election presented another challenge to Republican candidates, especially women. In nominating Donald Trump, a man with a documented history of making sexist remarks and a campaign strategy that embraced hypermasculinity, Republicans upheld an electoral environment in which power was defined in masculine terms and allocated along gender lines. Female candidates, particularly those running for federal office, were confronted with questions about balancing their party allegiance with their principles of gender equality and respect for women.

In this context, Republican women's electoral gains at individual and state levels were overshadowed and underemphasized by their persistent (and even growing) deficit in representation nationwide. For Republican women in 2016, the dominant narrative was more of the same, even in a political context where the emerging reality seemed anything but.

U.S. HOUSE

Without a concerted effort to recruit women candidates in 2016, the number of Republican women filing to run for the U.S. House fell short of the record high that filed in 2010. According to the Center for American Women and Politics (CAWP), 95 Republican women filed to run for the House in 2016, 1 more than filed in 2014, but 33 short of the 128 women who filed for U.S. House races in 2010.[9] Forty-six Republican women were nominees for House seats in 2016, down from the record high of 50 in 2014. Of those nominees, 21 women won their races, 3 short of the previous high of 24 Republican women House winners.

Republican women continued to represent the minority of women candidates running and winning House seats in election 2016. As Table 7.1 shows, they were 35 percent of the women who filed as major party candidates for House races, 28 percent of women nominees, and just one-quarter of the women who won in November 2016. Despite Democratic women's majority representation among women, they represented

Table 7.1   2016 Women Candidates by Party and Status, Various Levels

		Percent of Women Candidates Who Are Democrats	Percent of Women Candidates Who Are Republicans	Percent of Democratic Candidates Who Are Women	Percent of Republican Candidates Who Are Women
House	Filed	65.07%	34.93%	24.55%	11.22%
	Nominees	72.29%	27.71%	28.10%	10.57%
	Winners	74.70%	25.30%	31.96%	8.71%
Senate	Filed	67.50%	32.50%	27.27%	11.11%
	Nominees	73.33%	26.67%	31.43%	12.12%
	Winners	83.33%	16.67%	41.67%	4.55%
State Legislature	Nominees	65.19%	33.98%	36.70%	19.24%
	Winners	59.99%	39.16%	36.15%	17.96%
Statewide Executive	Filed	61.90%	38.10%	28.26%	18.32%
	Nominees	65.00%	35.00%	36.11%	18.42%
	Winners	52.63%	47.37%	33.33%	19.15%

Source: Center for American Women and Politics (CAWP), Rutgers University.

Note: House and Senate counts include only major party candidates. State legislative counts also include incumbent candidates of any party and nonpartisan candidates from the state of Nebraska. Statewide executive counts include only major party and nonpartisan candidates.

just one-quarter of all Democrats who filed for House contests in 2016, though they were 32 percent of all Democratic winners. Republican women fared worse within their party; they were 11 percent of Republicans who filed for House seats and just 9 percent of all Republican House winners in 2016.

Republican women were slightly less successful than their male counterparts in making it through their primary races; 48 percent of Republican women, compared to 52 percent of Republican men, were successful (see Table 7.2). In contrast, 68 percent of Democratic women candidates won their primary races to become House nominees, compared to 56 percent of Democratic men. Just one female Republican incumbent, Renee Ellmers (NC-2), was defeated in her primary; however, her defeat may be symbolic. Ellmers was the lead advocate for Republican women's work to elect

Table 7.2 2016 Win Rates for Candidates, Various Levels

		Democrats		Republicans	
		Women	Men	Women	Men
House	Primary	67.8%	56.43%	48.42%	51.73%
	Incumbent	98.18%	99.14%	95.00%	99.00%
	Non-incumbent	54.10%	44.86%	36.00%	34.48%
	General	51.67%	43.00%	45.65%	56.56%
	Incumbent	100.00%	98.26%	100.00%	96.98%
	Nonincumbent	12.12%	9.90%	7.41%	14.21%
Senate	Primary	40.74%	33.33%	30.77%	27.88%
	Incumbent	100.00%	100.00%	100.00%	100.00%
	Nonincumbent	38.46%	27.27%	18.18%	10.71%
	General	45.45%	29.17%	25.00%	72.41%
	Incumbent	100.00%	100.00%	50.00%	95.00%
	Nonincumbent	40.00%	5.56%	0.00%	22.22%
State Legislature	General	53.21%	54.48%	66.67%	72.54%
	Incumbent	94.57%	93.93%	94.50%	96.89%
	Nonincumbent	23.79%	13.60%	35.83%	29.52%
Statewide Executive	Primary	66.67%	46.46%	58.33%	57.94%
	Incumbent	88.89%	100.00%	100.00%	100.00%
	Nonincumbent	60.00%	40.45%	41.18%	51.09%
	General	38.46%	43.48%	64.29%	61.29%
	Incumbent	62.50%	90.00%	85.71%	93.33%
	Nonincumbent	27.78%	30.56%	42.86%	42.17%

Source: Center for American Women and Politics (CAWP), Rutgers University.

more women to the House in 2014, and she spoke out publicly about the importance of women's voices in legislative debates within the Republican caucus. In January 2015, for example, she stood up to male caucus leaders against their plans to bring a 20-week abortion ban with no exception for rape or incest to the House floor (see chapter 10). Ellmers's resistance ended up contributing to her demise, as her primary opponent characterized it as a betrayal to her party and to true conservative ideology. Susan B. Anthony List, a political action committee (PAC) that had endorsed and funded Ellmers in each of her congressional campaigns, responded by shifting their support to her primary opponent, George Holding, who defeated her in the Republican primary by 30 percentage points.

Ellmers's loss contributed to the slight gender disparity in primary win rates between Republican men and women candidates, as Republican women nonincumbents actually won at a rate just slightly higher than men; 36 percent of Republican women and 35 percent of Republican men competing in House primaries were successful in 2016 (see Table 7.2). That rate would have been higher if Christine Jones had not been defeated by just 27 votes in the primary race for Arizona's safely Republican 5th congressional district seat. Jones, a former executive at GoDaddy and 2014 gubernatorial candidate, ran against the party establishment and in line with presidential candidate Trump. Her opponent, Andy Biggs, was endorsed by the retiring incumbent, Matt Salmon, and was the early favorite in the race. However, Jones spent just over $2 million of her own money to put up a fight against Biggs, resulting in the razor thin, and court-decided, outcome in the primary election. Interestingly, some of the only outside support that Jones received was from Values in Electing Women (VIEW) PAC, an organization committed to electing qualified Republican women to federal office, who gave their maximum donation of $10,000 to her primary campaign.

Liz Cheney, one of only two nonincumbent Republican women elected to Congress in 2016, had little trouble earning her party's nomination or maintaining Republican control of Wyoming's at-large congressional seat. She won her primary by 18 points and the general election by 32 points, nearly doubling the votes of her Democratic opponent.

No other nonincumbents fared so easily. Just 7.4 percent of Republican women nonincumbent nominees won on Election Day, compared to 14.2 percent of Republican men, 12.1 percent of Democratic women, and 9.9 percent of Democratic men running for open seats or as challengers in general election House races. Even those newcomer women deemed as most competitive by organizations such as VIEW PAC and the NRCC faced uphill battles to electoral success. VIEW PAC provided their maximum level of support to three nonincumbent Republican women candidates other than Jones: Denise Gitsham (Calif.-52), Amie Hoeber (Md.-6), and Tonia Khouri (Ill.-11). Each of these women were identified as "Young Guns" by the NRCC, but they also confronted unlikely odds for success as challengers to incumbents.

Like Jones, Hoeber's ability to self-fund boosted her chances in the primary. She defeated six male opponents and ultimately contributed just under $1 million to her campaign. Sparking controversy, she also benefited from spending by Maryland USA, a Super PAC to which her husband had donated nearly $4 million in the 2016 cycle. In addition to emphasizing her national security expertise as a former deputy undersecretary of the army under President Reagan, Hoeber also presented herself as a women's advocate, touting her leadership in the National Women's Political Caucus and efforts to advance women in national security. That work, which encompassed a vaguely centrist position on abortion, distinguished Hoeber from her Republican opponents, but it appeared to do little to help her in her general election race against Democratic incumbent John Delaney. He defeated her by 16 points on Election Day.

Hoeber's standing as a women's advocate was also put into question when she was pushed to respond to the release of the *Access Hollywood* tape in which Republican presidential nominee Donald Trump admitted to sexually assaulting women. Hoeber, like many Republicans, disavowed Trump's behavior without rejecting his candidacy: "Having spent much of my professional life in a male-dominated world, I am . . . no stranger to being subjected to the attitude he expressed. The proper response is a rejection of the sexist, abusive attitude. It is not, in my view, appropriate to respond by subjecting our great country to the damage it would suffer under a Hillary Clinton presidency."[10]

Tonia Khouri, the Republican nominee challenging incumbent Bill Foster in Illinois's 11th congressional district, took a similar approach. Khouri maintained that she would vote for Trump, but she was "personally offended" by the comments made by him. "Locker room banter is something I, and many other hardworking women, have been subjected to throughout our lives," she said. "It is unacceptable and demeaning to those of us who have worked tirelessly to better our families, our community and the businesses we lead."[11] Khouri emphasized her role as a wife, mother, and business owner throughout her campaign, noting that each of these roles would provide her with unique perspectives on issues ranging from national security to economic policy. After winning the Republican primary by less than 400 votes, Khouri was defeated by Foster in the general election by 20 points.

The gap was only slightly smaller in Denise Gitsham's challenge to incumbent Scott Peters in California's 52nd congressional district. Gitsham, a daughter of immigrants from China and Canada, focused on foreign policy issues in much her campaign. She took moderate positions on various issues, including immigration, and strenuously avoided making any comments about her support (or not) of nominee Trump. Gitsham did "reject Donald Trump's degrading and objectifying statements about women," calling his words "an embarrassment to our party" and "utterly antithetical to my faith and values."[12] However, when asked to denounce Trump's candidacy outright, Gitsham repeated that she wanted to focus on her campaign.

While these women candidates were 3 among just 22 House candidates who received direct contributions from the NRCC in 2016, receiving $5,000 each, the party committee spent no money on their behalf through independent expenditures. The only nonincumbent Republican woman to receive significant NRCC support in 2016 was Claudia Tenney (N.Y.-22), who received a small direct contribution and over $2 million in combined outside spending for her campaign and against her opponent, Kim Myers. Tenney also received support from RightNOW Women PAC, VIEW PAC, and Susan B. Anthony List.

Tenney and Myers were competing for a congressional seat vacated by GOP incumbent Richard Hanna. In the primary, Tenney was outspent by organizations that she associated with the "establishment," but she built upon the far right and Tea Party support that earned her New York Assembly seat in 2010. She praised her coalition of antiestablishment voters for helping her to defeat the Republican primary candidate endorsed by Hanna, explaining that they "know that the cabal between the establishment in both parties is destroying this country and . . . need someone who's going to be strong and stand up for them."[13] As a single mother of a marine and a small business owner, Tenney could also relate with the "regular people" of her district. In that way, she aligned herself with the populism and antielitism espoused by Trump's presidential campaign and presented herself as an "independent, conservative" leader.

While her campaign seemed to distance itself from Trump in the final weeks before Election Day, Tenney never pulled back her own support of the GOP nominee. After the release of the *Access Hollywood* tape, Tenney responded, "Donald Trump's comments towards women are offensive and crude. Unfortunately, we have a choice between someone whose words are disgusting, and someone whose actions make her completely unfit for office in Hillary Clinton." She warned that Hillary Clinton would "jeopardize national security, undermine the rule of law and taint the presidency with scandal and corruption," and that her tax, regulatory, and trade politics would "further devastate upstate New York's economy."[14] Tenney's success may have come in part due to her loyalty to the top of the ticket, but likely even more because of the strength of their shared antiestablishment message. With the help of significant Republican Party support in the general election, Tenney defeated Myers by eight points on Election Day and prevented Democrats from taking this Republican seat in 2016.

Tenney is one of the 21 Republican women who were sworn in to the House of Representatives on January 3, 2017. This was one fewer Republican woman representative than served at the end of the 114th Congress.[15] Notably, Republican women represented a higher proportion of all Republican House members a decade ago, revealing the static trend in Republican women's House representation. Moreover, just three of the 21 Republican women serving in the 115th Congress are women of color, representing 9 percent of all women of color in the U.S. House. While no new Republican women of color were elected in 2016, 6 of 8 female Democratic newcomers to the House were women of color.

Lastly, there was a slight boost in Republican women's positional power in the 115th Congress, despite the drop in numbers. After Candice Miller, the only woman to serve as a committee chair in the 114th Congress, retired, Rep. Virginia Foxx (NC-5) was selected to chair the House Education and Workforce Committee in 2017, and Rep. Diane Black (Tenn.-6) became the first woman chair of the House Budget Committee.

U.S. SENATE

There was a loss of one Republican woman in the U.S. Senate from the 114th to the 115th Congress. The proportion of women in the Senate Republican caucus is just under 10 percent in 2017, down from 11 percent in the 114th Congress. Democratic women, in contrast, are 35 percent of their party's senators, a 3 percentage point increase from the previous Congress. As with the House data, the trend for Democratic women's growth within the party has been positive, while Republican women senators' representation within their party has remained flat for more than a decade. While four Democratic women of color serve in the 115th Congress, no Republican woman of color has ever served in the U.S. Senate. Republican women also saw no gains in positional power in 2017. No Republican women senators serve among the six designated leadership positions in the majority, and just one standing Senate committee and one special committee are chaired by a Republican woman.

The dearth of progress for Republican women in the Senate can be explained, in part, by their scarcity among candidates and nominees. Thirteen Republican women filed as candidates in 11 U.S. Senate contests in 2016. In the same year, when 34 Senate races were held, 27 Democratic women and 104 Republican men filed as candidates for Congress' upper chamber. While the number of Democratic women filing for Senate races in 2016 was nearly double the number that filed in 2014, the number of Republican women filing for Senate contests dropped by 3 from 2014 to 2016. Republican women candidates for the Senate fell short of the record high of 17 filed candidates set in 2010.

Just four Republican women were nominees for Senate seats in 2016, including two incumbents (Senators Kelly Ayotte (N.H.) and Lisa Murkowski (Alaska)); one challenger (Wendy Long (N.Y.)); and one candidate running for an open, albeit Democratic-leaning, seat (Kathy Szeliga (Md.)). Just one of those four nominees, incumbent Sen. Lisa Murkowski (R-AK), won on Election Day, unlike in 2014, when three of five Republican women nominees were successful.[16] Democratic governor Maggie Hassan edged out incumbent Republican senator Kelly Ayotte by under 1,000 votes in New Hampshire in one of the most hotly contested Senate races of 2016.

As Table 7.1 also shows, Republican women were one-third of women who filed as major party candidates for Senate seats, 27 percent of female nominees, and 17 percent of women who won Senate seats in 2016. They were 11 percent of Republicans who filed, 12 percent of Republican nominees, and just 5 percent of Republican winners in 2016 Senate elections. Democratic women, on the other hand, were 42 percent of all Democratic Senate winners in a year when Democratic success was limited. Democratic women nominees competed in some of the most competitive Senate races of 2016, and five nonincumbents won.

Republican women were slightly more likely than their male counterparts to make it through their Senate primaries, though the difference in win rates is small (see Table 7.2). In the general election, however, only one-quarter of Republican women were successful compared to nearly three-quarters of male Republican Senate nominees. While 40 percent of Democratic nonincumbent women and 22 percent of Republican nonincumbent men won on Election Day, no nonincumbent Republican women won Senate seats in 2016. Democratic women, unlike their Republican peers, outpaced the success of their male counterparts at every phase and in each type of Senate contest.

Wendy Long (N.Y.) and Kathy Szeliga (Md.) were the only nonincumbent Republican women to become Senate nominees in 2016. Long, who had no previous political experience aside from her 2012 loss to incumbent senator Kirsten Gillibrand (D-NY), received no significant support from the party or from voters. She consistently polled over 40 points behind incumbent Chuck Schumer, who bested her by 43 points and nearly 3 million votes on Election Day.

Unlike Long, Kathy Szeliga did win the support of Republican women's PACs, including RightNOW Women and VIEW PAC, in her bid for Maryland's open senate seat. Szeliga, a Maryland state legislator and businesswoman, included among her arguments for voter support a reminder that Maryland could emerge from election 2016 without any women in its congressional delegation were she not successful. This was a message used by Democratic primary candidate Donna Edwards, who emphasized the importance of keeping a woman in Barbara Mikulski's long-held seat. At a candidate forum, Szeliga joked, "When Barbara Mikulski was retiring, I thought, let's put a taller, younger Polish girl from Baltimore in the U.S. Senate."[17] She also criticized Democrat Chris Van Hollen for "mansplaining" to voters about "what women want and need," seeking to rebut assumptions that Democratic policies are inherently better for women.[18] Unlike House winner Claudia Tenney, Szeliga emphasized her willingness to work across party lines despite her conservative record. Like Tenney, though, she sought to present herself as "regular mom," albeit one that rides a motorcycle, providing an important contrast to career politicians.

Szeliga was unable to overcome the two-to-one deficit for Republicans among Maryland's registered voters and was defeated by Van Hollen by 24 points. She was given no financial support from the National Republican Senatorial Committee (NRSC), making the hill she needed to climb that much steeper. Finally, Hillary Clinton defeated Donald Trump by 26 points in Maryland, demonstrating the challenges of any GOP candidate running statewide. Szeliga spent little time aligning herself with Trump, but she never rejected his candidacy. In response to the *Access Hollywood* video, she issued a statement calling on Trump to "sincerely apologize to all women immediately," and she called both Trump and Clinton "seriously flawed" candidates.[19] Still, Szeliga pledged to vote for Trump, allowing her Democratic opponent to use Trump's unpopularity in the state against her.

The Republican woman candidate who appeared most hurt by Trump, however, was incumbent senator Kelly Ayotte (N.H.). Ayotte faced off against Gov. Maggie Hassan in one of the most competitive Senate races of 2016. Over $120 million was spent in the race that resulted in a difference of less than 1,000 votes. Both Hassan and Ayotte were among the top beneficiaries of spending by their party committees, and the

Republican PAC Granite State Solutions spent close to $25 million on the New Hampshire Senate race.[20] Hassan outmatched Ayotte in spending by women's organizations. EMILY's List's independent expenditure Women Vote! spent $3.2 million against Ayotte, in addition to the $1.5 million spent on Hassan's behalf by Planned Parenthood and NARAL combined.[21] While Ayotte received $10,000 of direct contributions from both RightNOW Women PAC and VIEW PAC, they came nowhere near matching the targeted support provided to Hassan by a stronger women-focused infrastructure for Democrats. Antigun groups, including Michael Bloomberg's Independence USA PAC, also contributed millions of dollars to defeat Ayotte, so that, by Election Day, she faced a larger financial deficit with her Democratic opponent than Republicans in any other targeted Senate race of the 2016 cycle.[22]

Hassan benefited significantly from her close ties to the Clinton campaign and its funders. In contrast, Ayotte struggled throughout the Senate campaign to position herself clearly in relation to her party's presidential nominee. The New York Times described Ayotte's "delicate dance" around Trump's candidacy as generating negative attention and much fodder for attacks by Hassan, who repeatedly called on Ayotte to denounce Donald Trump.[23] For most of the cycle, Ayotte said that she would support her party's nominee, but she never endorsed Donald Trump. She did not campaign with him but was also reluctant to reject him. In a debate in early October 2016, she said when asked that Trump was "absolutely" a role model, only to walk back the comment after receiving significant backlash. It was not until the Access Hollywood video was released that Ayotte officially renounced Trump's candidacy and told voters that she would be writing in Mike Pence on her presidential ballot.

While Ayotte tried to characterize her decision as evidence of her independence, a value especially important to New Hampshire voters, Hassan and other critics used it as evidence of political opportunism. Ayotte tried to make clear why this was her breaking point, telling reporters, "He's talking about assault of women, and I thought about years from now when my daughter, Kate, is old enough to know what is in those tapes and understand what he is talking about, I want her to know where I stood. I want my daughter to know that that is more important to me than winning any election."[24] In the end, however, it is unclear whether it was Ayotte's break from Trump or the fact that it took her so long that was most damaging to her campaign.

Importantly, the Trump challenge was not the only one that Ayotte faced, nor the only hurdle en route to her reelection. She sought to tout her bipartisanship with New Hampshire's important independent voters, but she was criticized for partisan loyalty evident in her Senate voting record. Relatedly, Ayotte needed to maintain her party base by maintaining conservative positions on abortion and guns, both of which contributed to targeted outside spending against her. The distinct political culture of New Hampshire cannot be denied as a significant factor in Ayotte's struggle, but some of the challenges she faced were also tied to the distinctly different environments faced by Republican and Democratic women candidates in 2016.

STATE LEGISLATURE

As Elder notes in chapter 8, the distinct political contexts within states have also influenced geographic patterns in Republican women's state legislative representation. Consistent with her findings, Republican women make up the largest proportion of their party's state legislators in Hawaii and Alaska in 2017.[25] They fare worst in Alabama, representing just 5 percent of Republican legislators in the state. Women are 10 percent or less of Republican state legislators in other southern states, including Mississippi, Virginia, and South Carolina, as well as Utah and Wyoming. Women are one-fifth or less of all Republican legislators in 29 states. Of the states with Republican control of both chambers, Alaska (40%), Arizona (33%), Minnesota (25%), and Kansas (24%) have the highest proportion of women members in the GOP majority.

Nationwide, the number of Republican women in state legislative office dropped by a net of 4 from the end of 2016 to the start of 2017; there was a net loss of 12 Republican women in state Houses and a net gain of 8 Republican women in state Senates between 2016 and 2017. The proportion of women among all Republican state legislators dropped slightly from 2016 to 2017, from 17.2 percent to 16.8 percent, and the proportion of Republicans among women state legislators dropped from 39.1 percent to 38.4 percent. The proportion of women among Democratic state legislators increased slightly between 2016 and 2017, and Democratic women saw a net gain of 27 state legislative seats after the 2016 election.[26]

Less than 1 percent of Republican state legislators are women of color. Just 28 of the 433 women state legislators of color at the start of 2017 were Republicans; 19 served in state Houses and just 8 held state Senate seats. There were 30 Republican women state legislators of color in 2016. Two Republican women are Speakers of state Houses in 2017, the same number who led lower chambers in 2016. In state Senates, the number of Republican women in the top leadership positions dropped from 9 to 7 after the 2016 elections.

When evaluated individually, there were 17 states that saw a net gain and 17 states that saw a net loss in Republican women legislators between 2016 and 2017. Another 15 states saw no change in the representation of Republican women in their legislatures, including the states that did not hold state legislative elections in 2016. Overall, the gains and losses among Republican women state legislators were modest overall and within individual states. Moreover, both gains and losses were evident in states across regions, showing no clear pattern of advancement or regression by geographic location.

Consistent with federal patterns, the dearth of Republican women candidates is the key contributor to these stagnant trends. Despite efforts from such organizations as the RSLC to recruit more women candidates for state legislative offices in 2016, the 900 Republican women nominees for state legislatures was 14 less than the record high 24 years prior, in an election year where the same number of state legislative chambers held elections. Republicans were 34 percent of all women nominees for state legislative offices, while they were 56 percent of men on state legislative ballots in 2016.[27] Both Democratic and Republican women were underrepresented as a proportion of their party's nominees, but Republican women fared significantly worse. Women were 37 percent of Democratic nominees for state legislative contests in 2016, while women were 19 percent of Republican nominees (see Table 7.1).

Democratic women were also a larger proportion of their party's winners in 2016; 36 percent of Democratic winners and 18 percent of Republican winners for state legislative seats were women. But, in a year where Republicans fared better than Democrats in state legislative contests nationwide, Republican women nominees still won their races at a higher rate than their Democratic counterparts. Of the 900 Republican women nominees for state legislative offices in 2016, 600—or two-thirds—won their races. In contrast, 53 percent of Democratic women nominees were successful (see Table 7.2). Republican women fared especially better than Democratic women in races for open state legislative seats; nearly two-thirds of Republican women nominees won open seat contests, while 44 percent of Democratic women nominees were elected.

Among all Republican nominees, men outperformed their female counterparts; nearly three-quarters of all male nominees for state legislative seats in 2016 won on Election Day. However, Republican women fared *better* than Republican men as nonincumbent candidates; 35.8 percent of nonincumbent GOP women and 30 percent of nonincumbent GOP men won state legislative seats. The win rates among Democratic men and women were nearly equal in 2016 state legislative elections, though

Democratic nonincumbent women fared better than Democratic nonincumbent men (see Table 7.2).

These data, while limited in their capacity to control for district competitiveness and contextual factors, reveal the dearth of Republican women among state legislative nominees as more significant to expanding their representation in state legislatures nationwide than disparities in their rates of success.

STATEWIDE ELECTED EXECUTIVE

Over the past two decades, the smallest partisan gaps in women's representation have been at the statewide elected executive level. Moreover, it is only at this level of office that Republican women have surpassed Democratic women in seats held. In 2017, Republican women are 55.4 percent of women in statewide elected executive offices. They hold 41—or 13.1 percent—of 312 statewide elected executive offices nationwide, the same number that served in 2016.[28] In 2016, two new Republican women won positions as state superintendents of public instruction in Indiana (Jennifer McCormick) and Montana (Elsie Arntzen), and incumbent state auditor Suzanne Crouch (R-IN) won her race to become Indiana's lieutenant governor. Incumbent comptroller Leslie Munger (R-IL) lost her bid for reelection against another woman, Democrat Susanna Mendoza. Mendoza was one of five new Democratic women to win statewide elected executive office in 2016.

Mendoza was also the only new woman of color to be elected to statewide executive office in 2016. In 2017, just seven women of color serve in statewide elected executive offices, down from nine in 2016. Three women of color are Republicans, including incumbent governor Susana Martinez (New Mexico), and incumbent lieutenant governors Jenean Hampton (Kentucky) and Evelyn Sanguinetti (Illinois).

Despite making up a larger proportion of women in statewide elected executive office, Republicans were a smaller proportion of women who filed, won primary contests, and won general election races for statewide executive office in 2016. The success of incumbent Republican women, as well as the dominance of Republicans among female holdovers, ensured that Republican women maintained their representational advantage over Democratic women after election 2016. As Table 7.1 shows, Republican women were 38 percent of women who filed as major party or nonpartisan candidates for statewide executive contests, 35 percent of female nominees, and 47 percent of women who won statewide executive office in 2016.

They were 18 percent of Republicans who filed, 18 percent of Republican nominees, and just 19 percent of Republican winners in statewide executive contests. Though Democratic women were better represented among their party's candidates, they had the lowest general election win rates among all statewide executive candidates in 2016. In contrast, nearly two-thirds of Republican women nominees won their races for statewide elected executive office, more than their Democratic or male counterparts (see Table 7.1).

Still, the only possibility for gains by Republican women at the statewide elected executive level came from four open-seat nominees and three general election challengers. Political newcomer Deborah Bucknam lost the general election race to become attorney general of Vermont by 37 points. Nora Espinoza, who was unopposed in her primary, drew upon 10 years of experience in the state legislature in her bid to become New Mexico's secretary of state. She was defeated by 13 points by Maggie Toulouse Oliver, who retook an office that had been held by Democrats from 1931 to 2010. Elsie Arntzen, on the other hand, became the first Republican in nearly 30 years to become Montana's superintendent of public instruction, defeating Melissa Romano by 3 percentage points, or 16,000 votes. Arntzen's success came in the face of heavy spending by the state's teacher's union, but she likely benefited from high Republican support in Montana's 2016 elections. Trump won Montana by 20 points, almost doubling the lead that Romney had over Obama in 2012. But Arntzen's campaign made very little, if any, mention of Trump, and it benefited significantly from her own name recognition and the statewide support that she had gained over 12 years in the state legislature.

Trump's success may have been more influential to statewide races in Indiana, where Jennifer McCormick defeated Democratic incumbent superintendent of public instruction Glenda Ritz. Ritz bested McCormick in both campaign finances and name recognition statewide, but her advantage was fragile in the face of strong Republican headwinds. Ritz entered the 2016 race as the only sitting Democrat among Indiana's statewide elected executive officials, and her campaign felt the side effects of a Republican presidential campaign that targeted the state. Trump won Indiana by 19 points, almost double Romney's lead in 2012. That margin benefited the Republican gubernatorial ticket as well, ensuring that Suzanne Crouch, the sitting state auditor, would continue her service as the state's lieutenant governor.

Unlike in the congressional contests, these Republican women candidates faced few questions about their allegiance to or alignment with Donald Trump. Instead, their successes and defeats were more directly related to the political context and cultures statewide as well as the down-ballot effects of turnout at the top of the ticket.

PRESIDENCY

Republican women's underrepresentation persisted at the presidential level in the 2016 election. Carly Fiorina was the sole woman among 17 Republican contenders for the presidential nomination. Only 1 woman competed against 5 men for the Democratic nomination in 2016, but Hillary Clinton entered the race as the strong favorite to be the party's nominee. Fiorina, on the other hand, announced her candidacy in early May of 2015, with very low name recognition and little previous political experience.

In fact, Fiorina was the first female major party candidate for president with no experience in elected or appointed office. The Republican women who sought the presidency before her include U.S. Senator Margaret Chase Smith, two-time presidential cabinet appointee Elizabeth Dole, and U.S. Representative Michele Bachmann. Fiorina's candidacy was the longest of any Republican woman's to date, but not the most successful. Over nine months, Fiorina's polling average in the Republican primary never topped 12 percent, and she dropped out of the race after finishing in seventh place in the first two primary contests in Iowa and New Hampshire. While Margaret Chase Smith also fared poorly in New Hampshire's 1964 primary and lost every other primary contest in which she competed that year, she did earn 25 percent of the vote in Illinois, allowing her to become the first and only Republican woman to have her name placed in nomination for president after a six-month campaign. Elizabeth Dole dropped out of the 2000 race before competing in any primary contests, and Michele Bachmann ended her bid for the presidential nomination after coming in sixth place in the Iowa caucuses, the first nomination contest of the 2012 campaign.

Though she had never held elected or appointed office, Fiorina was not a complete newcomer to the political scene. In 2010, she ran for the U.S. Senate in California, but she was defeated by Democratic incumbent senator Barbara Boxer by 12 points. In 2008 and 2012, she served as an adviser to Republican presidential nominees' campaigns, and in 2014, she launched her own political action committee to support Republican candidates in the midterm elections by targeting independent women voters.[29] Unlocking Potential PAC spent more than $1.5 million in the 2014 cycle, targeting key Senate races, such as those in Iowa, New Hampshire, and North Carolina.[30]

Fiorina's gender focus continued in her 2016 campaign. Even before she formally launched her campaign, Fiorina positioned herself as the best candidate to contrast likely Democratic nominee Hillary Clinton. She explained in April 2015, "I think that if Hillary Clinton were to face a female nominee, there are a whole set of things that she won't be able to talk about. She won't be able to talk about being the first woman president. She won't be able to talk about a war on women without being challenged. She won't be able to play the gender card."[31] In arguing that having two women candidates would somehow neutralize gender as a factor in the 2016 election, Fiorina overlooked the reality that gender has long shaped presidential politics in the United States for men and women candidates alike; presidential candidates have been playing the gender card for over a century, most commonly in the ways they have performed and affirmed their masculinity. An all-female race would not avoid the deeply rooted gender norms of the American presidency, nor would it prevent candidates from addressing gendered realities that both candidates and voters face. In arguing that she was distinctly positioned to combat Clinton *because* of her gender, Fiorina proved this point and contradicted her own claims of a gender-free campaign environment.

But Fiorina's complicated approach to gender in 2016 was reflective of the Republican Party's rejection of "identity politics." In the same April 2015 remarks where she touted her gender as an electoral asset, Fiorina said that her ability to nullify the role of gender in the campaign would ensure an election based on substance, adding, "I think that's what elections should be run on—not identity politics, not what you look like, but who you are, and what you believe, and what you've done, and what you will do."[32] Less than three weeks later, she launched her candidacy with a Web video that opened with her watching Clinton's announcement video and pivoted to Fiorina asking voters to join her if they believed "that it's time to declare the end of identity politics."[33]

That video also called on citizens to "stand up to the political class," a recurrent theme throughout Fiorina's campaign, where she sought to use her outsider status as a positive contrast to her Republican and Democratic opponents instead of a potential weakness of her candidacy. On the campaign trail, she repeatedly vowed to "take our country back" from "professional politicians" and emphasized her experience with executive decision making in the private sector. Fiorina touted her path "from secretary to CEO," noting that she became the first woman to lead a Fortune 20 company, Hewlett-Packard (HP), in 1999 and oversaw a major merger with Compaq during her six-year tenure there.[34] As Fiorina learned in her Senate campaign, there was risk in touting her business experience.

HP suffered significant job and profit losses during her tenure, and the company sent jobs overseas under her watch. Her controversial tenure at HP did become fodder for campaign coverage and attacks in 2016, but it was the relative inattention to her candidacy in comparison to her many opponents that was likely most damaging to her campaign.

Interestingly, and contrary to her derision of playing the gender card, Fiorina garnered the greatest attention when her gender was made salient by her or her opponents. One month after launching her campaign, Fiorina began "a conversation on the state of women in America," arguing "we still can make our country a better place by fully tapping the potential of every woman."[35] In a conference call with reporters, she noted, "I do think that I'm in a unique position to have this conversation because of the experiences that I've had in my life."[36] Those experiences informed claims she made in a *Medium* post in June 2015. Feminism in America, she argued, must be redefined to celebrate women's independence and empowerment instead of being "used as a political weapon to win elections."[37] Fiorina's feminist focus was evident in July 2015 when she participated in a much-circulated *Buzzfeed* video about sexism in the workplace. In the video, titled "If Men Were Treated Like Women in the Office with Carly Fiorina," Fiorina comedically reenacts scenarios of sexism she had experienced in her professional life, ultimately using her experience *as a woman* as a site for empathy with women voters.[38]

That empathy earned Fiorina both attention and praise again in a September 2015 GOP debate when she was asked about Donald Trump's comments to *Rolling Stone* about her attractiveness.[39] Asked for a response to his critique, Fiorina simply stated, "I think women all over this country heard very clearly what Mr. Trump said."[40] That line, as well as her strong performance in that debate, gave Fiorina the largest boost in support that she saw throughout her presidential campaign. When her appearance was attacked again by the cohosts of *The View* in October 2015, she told them to "man up" and appeared on their show to confront them directly, again earning her a boost in media attention that focused on the double standard that she argued conservative women face.[41]

Fiorina's candidacy did not only earn attention due to her gender. Pundits credited her success in an August 2015 undercard debate for boosting poll numbers and ensuring that she made the main stage in September's GOP primary debate, where she made news with her effective rebuttal to Trump. Fifty-two percent of viewers said that she won the September debate, and she jumped up to second place in the CNN/ORC poll taken the following week.[42] In both debates, Fiorina emphasized her executive experience, her contrast to the professional political class, and

the importance of military and foreign policy strength. Proving her stereotypically masculine credentials, she sternly stated in the September
debate, "We need the strongest military on the face of the planet, and
everyone has to know it." During the same debate, Fiorina also made one
of her most impassioned pleas on the issue of abortion. She dared Hillary Clinton and Barack Obama to watch tapes released by the antiabortion Center for Medical Progress that implied that Planned Parenthood
was engaged in tissue harvesting of live fetuses. The video she referenced
mashed audio from conversations with Planned Parenthood employees
with graphic video footage taken from elsewhere, a fact revealed after the
debate.[43] Thus, even in her most substantively successful moments of the
2016 campaign, Fiorina's messages were never devoid of gender dynamics.

Fiorina participated in three more main stage debates, but she failed
to garner as much praise or even opportunity to put forth her message or
agenda. She did not qualify for the final prime-time debates ahead of contests in Iowa or New Hampshire, despite claims by her campaign that her
exclusion was unfair. Those claims were not bolstered by any significant
efforts by women's organizations, contrary to the petition launched by the
conservative women's organization Smart Girl Politics to urge Fox News
to include Fiorina in the first prime-time GOP debate in August 2015.[44]
The absence of any distinct advocacy of Fiorina's candidacy by women
or women's organizations is consistent with both the Republican Party's
aversion to identity-based politics and the dearth of a significant gender-
focused support infrastructure for Republican women candidates.

In an interview with CNN on the eve of the New Hampshire primary,
Fiorina made a final pitch for primary votes that illuminated the awkward
ways in which she sought to disparage identity politics while emphasizing
the importance of her own gender identity throughout her campaign:

> Hillary Clinton wants to talk about the historic nature of her candidacy,
> she wants to talk about being first woman president and there are peo-
> ple out there—lots of people, men and women—who think it's time for a
> woman president. My message to them will be, "Look, how about an hon-
> est woman, a competent woman? How about a qualified woman?" But I'm
> never going to ask for people's support because I'm a woman. I'm going to
> ask for their support because I'm the most qualified candidate to beat Hill-
> ary Clinton and to do the job.[45]

In the end, Republican voters did not view Fiorina as the most qualified
candidate to defeat Clinton. It would be unfair to blame Fiorina's gender for her defeat, as there were multiple factors that created significant

hurdles to her campaign's success. But it would also be inaccurate to claim that gender played no role in Fiorina's campaign. Fiorina emphasized her gender as an electoral advantage and sought to use her own gendered experiences to gain empathy from women voters and as evidence of resilience in the face of obstacles to leadership. She benefited from others' attention to her gender throughout the campaign, even when negative, and focused some of her strongest substantive messages on issues with high levels of gender saliency. Of course, all of this occurred while Fiorina sought to align with Republican ideological norms that reject gender as a relevant factor in candidate credentials or as a legitimate motivation for candidate support. Like many Republican women candidates for office, navigating this conflict between gender reality and the party's approach to gender proved challenging for Fiorina and shed light on the distinct hurdles that Republican women face across levels of political office.

CONCLUSION

While the political context, especially at the federal level, was far from ordinary in 2016, the challenges to and outcomes for Republican women candidates across levels of office confirmed many of the findings revealed in this volume. Party leaders doubled down on their philosophical aversion to identity politics, deterring any targeted efforts to recruit, support, and elect women. The feeble infrastructure built to increase Republican women's representation, whether via recruitment or financial support, was further weakened and could do little to influence the dynamics or outcomes of the 2016 cycle. Most significantly, it appeared to have little effect on the numbers of Republican women running and winning elected office in state and federal races. Instead, the gender disparity among Republican candidates, nominees, and elected officials remained the same, and the partisan gap in women's candidacy and representation continued across levels and types of offices.

When Donald Trump took office in 2017, he maintained the masculine dominance that characterized his campaign. From his own rhetoric to the overrepresentation of men in his cabinet selections, Trump has sent a message from the de facto head of the Republican Party that gender parity in power is not a priority. That message matters in creating the conditions for women's advancement within the Republican Party. It also affects the likelihood for women's representational gains across party lines and, ultimately, whether prevailing patterns preventing gender parity in American government will be disrupted.

NOTES

1. NRCC, "NRCC Announces New Women's Initiative," June 28, 2013, https://
www.nrcc.org/2013/06/28/nrcc-announces-new-womens-initiative-project-grow.

2. Laurie Ure and Dana Bash, "GOP Attacks Its Female Deficit in Congress," CNN,
July 31, 2013, http://www.cnn.com/2013/07/30/politics/women-congress-gop.

3. Valerie Dowling, "GOP Celebrates Republican Women Milestones,"
GOP.com, January 7, 2015, https://www.gop.com/gop-celebrates-republican-women
-milestones.

4. Eddie Scarry, "RNC Chair Priebus: 'We Do a Really Bad Job Bragging' about
Women in GOP," *Mediaite*, October 2, 2014, http://www.mediaite.com/online
/rnc-chair-priebus-we-do-a-really-bad-job-bragging-about-women-in-gop.

5. Betsy Cooper, Daniel Cox, Rachel Lienesch, and Robert P. Jones, "The
Divide over America's Future: 1950 or 2050?" *Public Religion Research Institute*,
October 25, 2016, http://www.prri.org/research/poll-1950s-2050-divided-nations
-direction-post-election.

6. CNN, "CNN Town Hall with House Speaker Paul Ryan," July 12, 2016.

7. Nicole Puglise, "GOP Women's Recruitment Effort Adapts for 2016," Roll
Call, July 6, 2015, accessed May 30, 2017, http://www.rollcall.com/news/home
/gop-womens-recruitment-effort-adapts-2016.

8. RSLC, "RSLC's Right Women, Right Now Launches State-Level Political Education Series," August 11, 2015, http://rslc.gop/blog/2015/08/11/rslcs
-right-women-right-now-launches-state-level-political-education-series.

9. All 2016 candidate, nominee, and success data reported in this chapter
comes from the Center for American Women and Politics (CAWP) at Rutgers
University.

10. Amie for Congress, Facebook post, October 8, 2016, https://www.facebook
.com/plugins/post.php?href=https%3A%2F%2Fwww.facebook.com%2Famieforc
ongress%2Fposts%2F543874065806679&width=500.

11. Tonia Khour, "Tonia Khouri Statement on Donald Trump Recording,"
October 8, 2016, http://toniakhouri.com/tonia-khouri-statement-donald-trump
-recording.

12. Denise for Congress, Facebook post, October 7, 2016, https://www.face
book.com/deniseforcongress/posts/1811064365808252.

13. Patrick Howley, "Underdog Conservative Claudia Tenney Beats Establishment in New York Primary," Breitbart, June 28, 2016, http://www.breitbart
.com/2016-presidential-race/2016/06/28/underdog-conservative-claudia
-tenney-beats-establishment-new-york-primary.

14. Time Warner Cable News, "22nd Congressional District Candidates React
to Trump Video," October 9, 2016, http://www.twcnews.com/nc/north-carolina
/top-stories/2016/10/9/22nd-congressional-district-candidates-react-to-trump
-video.html.

15. In addition to the loss of incumbent Renee Ellmers in a contested primary,
incumbents Cynthia Lummis (Wyo.; at-large congressional district) and Candice
Miller (Mich.; 10th congressional district) retired.

16. CAWP, "Women Candidates 2014," http://cawp.rutgers.edu/sites/default /files/resources/cansum14.pdf.

17. Josh Hicks, "Facing Long Odds in Senate Bid, Kathy Szeliga—as Usual—Rolls Up Her Sleeves," *Washington Post*, October 31, 2016, https://www .washingtonpost.com/local/md-politics/facing-long-odds-in-senate-bid-kathy -szeliga--as-usual--rolls-up-her-sleeves/2016/10/30/492cfd5a-8fc9-11e6-9c85 -ac42097b8cc0_story.html?utm_term=.6a18e760cbd2.

18. John Fritze, "Kathy Szeliga, Chris Van Hollen Clash in Only Televised Senate Debate," *Baltimore Sun*, October 26, 2016, http://www.baltimoresun. com/news/maryland/politics/2016-senate-race/bs-md-senate-debate-sun-wjz -20161026-story.html.

19. Josh Hicks, "Szeliga, GOP Senate Candidate, Condemns Trump Remarks but Will Vote for Him," *Washington Post*, October 8, 2016, https://www.washing tonpost.com/local/md-politics/szeliga-md-senate-candidate-says-shes-appalled-by -trump-remarks/2016/10/08/15fe5f96-8d62-11e6-875e-2c1bfe943b66_story.html.

20. Center for Responsive Politics, "New Hampshire Senate Race," https:// www.opensecrets.org/races/indexp.php?cycle=2016&id=NHS1&spec=N.

21. Center for Responsive Politics, "New Hampshire Senate Race."

22. Center for Responsive Politics, "New Hampshire Senate Race."

23. Katharine Q. Seelye, "Maggie Hassan Unseats Kelly Ayotte in New Hampshire Senate Race," *New York Times*, November 9, 2016, https://www.nytimes .com/2016/11/09/us/politics/new-hampshire-senate-hassan-ayotte.html.

24. John DiStaso, "Ayotte Cites Daughter in Explaining Why She Withdrew Support for Trump," WMUR, October 9, 2016, http://www.wmur.com/article /updated-ayotte-cites-daughter-in-explaining-why-she-withdrew-support-for -trump/5235605.

25. All state legislative data reported in this chapter is as of January 13, 2017, from the CAWP at Rutgers University.

26. Thirty-eight more Democratic women served in state Houses at the start of 2017 than in 2016, though 11 fewer Democratic women served in state Senates postelection.

27. Candidate counts exclude third-party nonincumbent candidates, but they include nonpartisan candidates from Nebraska.

28. South Carolina governor Nikki Haley, first elected in 2010, served for three weeks in January 2017, until being confirmed as President Trump's U.S. ambassador to the United Nations.

29. Jackie Kucinich, "Fiorina to Head New PAC Aimed at Recruiting More Women to the GOP," *Washington Post*, June 30, 2014, https://www.washington post.com/blogs/she-the-people/wp/2014/06/30/fiorina-to-head-new-pac-aimed -at-recruiting-more-women-to-the-gop/?utm_term=.0db4761d1272.

30. Center for Responsive Politics, "Unlocking Potential PAC," https://www .opensecrets.org/pacs/lookup2.php?strID=C00564534&cycle=2014.

31. Alexandra Jaffe, "Carly Fiorina: Clinton Can't Play 'Gender Card' against Female Opponent," CNN, April 16, 2015, http://www.cnn.com/2015/04/16 /politics/carly-fiorina-hillary-clinton-gender-card.

32. Jaffe, "Carly Fiorina."

33. Carly Fiorina, "I'm Running for President," YouTube video, 1:04, posted May 4, 2015, https://www.youtube.com/watch?v=JjT6zQaJ6Uc.

34. CarlyFiorina.com, "Meet Carly," https://carlyfiorina.com/meet-carly.

35. Competitive Enterprise Institute, "Excerpts from Carly Fiorina's Address at CEI's Annual Dinner," June 18, 2015, https://cei.org/blog/excerpts-carly-fiorinas-address-ceis-annual-dinner.

36. Tessa Berenson, "Here's How Carly Fiorina Wants to Redefine Feminism," TIME, June 11, 2015, http://time.com/3918014/carly-fiorina-feminism.

37. Carly Fiorina, "Redefining Feminism: The State of Women in America," Medium, June 24, 2015, https://medium.com/@CarlyFiorina/redefining-feminism-19d25d8d8dfc#.1m1w4xkp1.

38. "If Men Were Treated Like Women in the Office with Carly Fiorina," BuzzFeed, July 16, 2015, https://www.youtube.com/watch?v=Tq5OQafDVxc.

39. Paul Solotaroff, "Trump Seriously: On the Trail with the GOP's Tough Guy," Rolling Stone, September 9, 2015, http://www.rollingstone.com/politics/news/trump-seriously-20150909.

40. Andrew Rafferty, "Fiorina: Women 'Heard Very Clearly' What Trump Said," NBC News, September 17, 2015, http://www.nbcnews.com/politics/2016-election/fiorina-women-heard-very-clearly-what-trump-said-n428786.

41. Fox News, "Fiorina Talks CNBC Debate, Clinton, Attack from 'The View,'" November 1, 2015, http://video.foxnews.com/v/4590410953001/?#sp=show-clips.

42. Eric Bradner, "Poll: Fiorina Rockets to No. 2 behind Trump in GOP Field," CNN, September 21, 2015, http://www.cnn.com/2015/09/20/politics/carly-fiorina-donald-trump-republican-2016-poll.

43. Lauren Carroll, "At CNN Debate, Carly Fiorina Urges Others to Watch Planned Parenthood Videos," Politifact, September 17, 2015, http://www.politifact.com/truth-o-meter/statements/2015/sep/17/carly-fiorina/cnn-debate-carly-fiorina-urges-others-watch-planne.

44. Teri Christoph, "Tell Fox News: Let Carly Debate!" Smart Girl Politics, May 29, 2015, http://www.smartgirlpolitics.com/tell-fox-news-let-carly-debate.

45. Tom LoBianco, "Carly Fiorina: Clinton Calls Everyone Sexist," CNN, December 28, 2015, http://www.cnn.com/2015/12/28/politics/carly-fiorina-hillary-clinton-sexism.

PART 3

State Legislators

In the U.S. federalist political system, state governments are important governing bodies in their own right, and they also serve as stepping stones to national office for ambitious politicians. This section examines the state legislatures with an eye to the representation and advancement of Republican women. As both chapters in this section note, this is a story of stagnation and underrepresentation. Why is this the case?

Chapter 8, by Laurel Elder, examines both the causes and consequences of the disproportionately low number of Republican women in state legislatures. She begins by pointing out the surprising nature of this lack of elected women in the GOP at the state level; as she notes, despite an electoral and political environment highly favorable to Republicans, a growing pool of qualified women candidates, and a growing number of politically active conservative women and conservative women's organizations, the representation of women within the Republican Party has remained at a standstill for two decades. Yet, as her quantitative analyses show, it appears that the conservative ideology of the Republican Party itself is the largest barrier to women's representation within the party. She also finds that Republican women are less likely to be in professionalized legislatures. The consequences of having so few Republican women in state legislatures, she writes, are negative for the image, viability, and functioning of the party as well as for full representation of women as a whole.

In Chapter 9, H. Abbie Erler investigates the (lack of) advancement of Republican women from local to state to national office. Erler is particularly concerned with state legislative "pipelines" to Congress. As she notes, political pipelines can become either clogged or leaky, both of which damage women's ability to move up to reach offices at higher levels. Erler finds that Republican and Democratic women in local and state offices are equally ambitious for higher level offices, but that Republican women are more likely to live (and serve in lower office) in states that lack functioning pipelines.

CHAPTER 8

Why So Few Republican Women in State Legislatures? The Causes and Consequences

Laurel Elder

State legislatures are well-established pipelines for higher-level office as well as crucial arenas of policy making. In recent years, states have been policy innovators on minimum wage, health care, and criminal justice reform, as well as being on the forefront in restricting reproductive rights. Over the past couple of decades, however, the number of women in state legislatures has stagnated, leaving women as a minority voice in debating and shaping these policies, many of which have a disproportionate impact on women. As this edited volume underscores, and prior research documents,[1] the chronic underrepresentation of women in state legislatures is a particular problem among Republicans.

This chapter explores three issues related to the underrepresentation of Republican women in state legislatures. First, it documents trends in state legislative office holding among Republican women over the past three decades and provides answers to the following questions: When did Republican women make their greatest gains in state legislatures, and when did their momentum begin to stall and even reverse? In which states and regions of the country have Republican women made the greatest gains, and in which parts of the country have they faced the toughest barriers? Second, the chapter draws on multivariate analysis to explore the factors that help and hinder the representation of Republican women. Finally, the chapter explores the consequences of having so few Republican women in state legislatures. Republican women hold diverse views, but in the aggregate they hold perspectives, positions, and priorities that are distinct from both Democratic women and Republican men. Thus, their sustained and dramatic underrepresentation holds serious consequences, not only for the image and functioning of the Republican Party, but for substantive representation.

TRENDS IN THE REPRESENTATION OF REPUBLICAN WOMEN STATE LEGISLATORS

To understand trends in state legislative office holding among Republican women, it is useful to begin by considering trends in women's representation in state legislatures as a whole. Although some decades have yielded greater gains than others, women have made important inroads into state legislatures. According to the Center for American Women and Politics (CAWP), from 1985 through summer 2016, the time frame for this study, women increased their representation in state legislatures from 16 percent to 24 percent, showing slow but steady progress.

Figure 8.1 breaks down these trends by party. In other words, it shows women as a percent of Democratic versus Republican state legislators

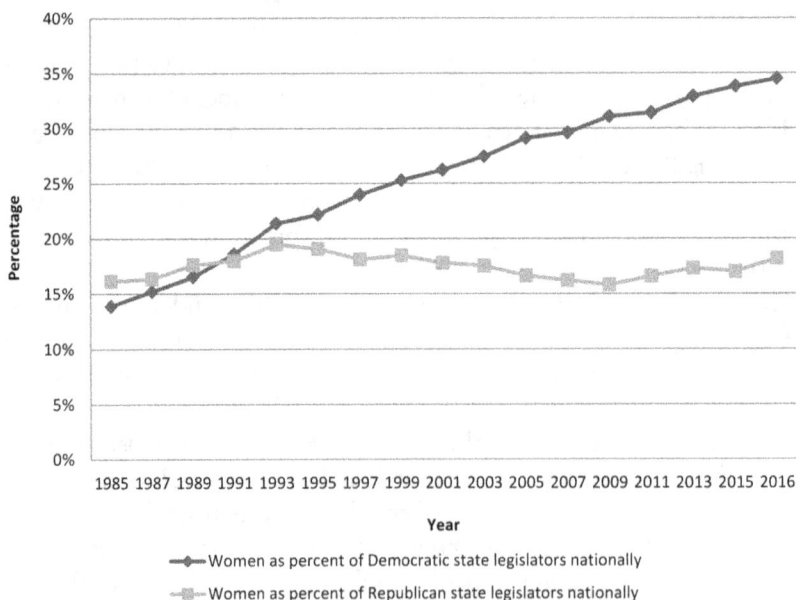

Figure 8.1 Women as a Percent of Republican and Democratic State Legislators, 1985–2016

Source: Calculated by author using data from Center for American Women and Politics, *Book of the States,* and National Conference of State Legislators.

over the past three decades and reveals that trends in women's representation vary dramatically by party.[2] The 1980s were characterized by steady growth and rough parity for Republican and Democratic women legislators. Starting in the 1990s and accelerating in the 21st century, however, the dynamics of representation for Republican and Democratic women diverged. The trend line for Democratic women has been consistently positive. Year after year, Democratic women have increased their numbers and, as of summer 2016, women are slightly more than one-third of Democratic state legislators nationally. In contrast, the representation of Republican women legislators hit its high point in 1993 and has gone down slightly since then. In other words, as of 2016, women represent only 18 percent of Republican legislators, a smaller share than they did two decades ago. Figure 8.1 underscores the extent to which research seeking to understand trends in women's representation in state legislatures as a whole misses an important reality: that their stalled progress is driven solely by dynamics within the Republican Party.[3]

The lack of progress for Republican women is surprising for several reasons. First, women have made significant progress in terms of educational and professional attainment across the past several decades. Women now graduate from college at higher rates than men, and women are attending law school and entering careers that are common launching pads for political careers at similar or higher rates than men.[4] In other words, women are better represented in what scholars have labeled the eligibility pool of candidates than ever before.[5] It is surprising that the broadening pool of women candidates has not turned into increasing representation for Republican women legislators.

Second, the lack of progress for Republican women as legislators is surprising because it has occurred across a time period when the Republican Party has flourished at the state level. According to statistics from the National Council of State Legislatures, Republicans have gained close to 1,000 state legislative seats over the past three decades, and today Republicans hold the largest number of state legislative seats at any time since 1920. Yet, as Republicans seized openings and turned state legislatures from blue to red, women in the party were not able to use these strategic opportunities to increase their presence among Republican legislators. For example, a large portion of Republican gains came as a result of the 2010 and 2014 state legislative elections, but these two elections had no meaningful effect on women's level of representation within the Republican Party (see Figure 8.1). Women came away from these Republican tidal-wave elections just as marginalized among Republican state legislators as they had been previously.

Finally, the dwindling numbers of Republican women in state legislatures is surprising given the robust, policy-oriented, grassroots activism
and leadership among conservative women. While women have been
active within the Republican Party and conservative causes across the
20th century, Ronnee Schreiber documents how conservative women's
organizations became particularly active in the 1980s, advocating for a
range of policies that they view as helping women and families.[6] And with
the emergence and prominence of the Tea Party movement in the 21st
century, conservative women have become what scholar Melissa Deckman refers to as a "visible force with which to be reckoned."[7] Yet, surprisingly, this grassroots activism by traditionally conservative as well as Tea
Party women has not resulted in significant inroads into state-level elective office by Republican women.

To summarize, Figure 8.1 reveals that despite an electoral and political
environment highly favorable to Republicans, a growing pool of qualified
women candidates, and a growing number of politically active conservative women and conservative women's organizations, the representation
of women within the Republican Party has remained at a standstill for
two decades. Figure 8.1 also reveals that women's inroads among Republican legislators stalled at the same time the Republican Party shifted to
the right in terms of its overall ideology as well as on issues specifically
related to the appropriate role and place of women. Indeed, it appears
that the rightward movement of the Republican Party and its current
conservative culture has undermined its ability to produce, recruit, and
support women state legislators.[8] As Susan Carroll and Kira Sanbonmatsu
aptly summarize, "Because Republican women legislators have been much
more likely to hail from the moderate wing of the Republican Party, the
increasing difficulty that moderates face in reaching office has disproportionately affected women."[9] Danielle Thomsen shows that the same phenomenon is occurring at the congressional level (see chapter 6).[10] Thus,
either because Republican women are less likely to view themselves as a
good fit for their party or because increasingly conservative Republican
leaders are reluctant to recruit women, starting in the 1990s and continuing through the present, the growing pool of qualified Republican women
are not pursuing legislative careers.

THE GEOGRAPHY OF REPUBLICAN WOMEN'S REPRESENTATION

Table 8.1 shows the percent of women among Republican as well as
Democratic state legislators for each state, organized by geographic

Table 8.1   Women as a Percent of Democrats versus Republicans in State Legislatures in 2016 and Change over Time

Region/State	Percent of Democrats who are women in 2016	Percent change in Democrats who are women, 1986–2016	Percent of Republicans who are women in 2016	Percent change in Republicans who are women, 1986–2016
The Northeast	**33**	**+15**	**26**	**+5**
Connecticut	31	+12	25	−2
Maine	38	+17	21	−6
Massachusetts	26	+11	23	+2
New Hampshire	43	+2	19	−11
New Jersey	34	+26	23	+11
New York	33	+16	14	+10
Pennsylvania	18	+14	19	+13
Rhode Island	28	+16	25	−2
Vermont	48	+18	27	+5
The South	**29**	**+21**	**13**	**+3**
Alabama	37	+30	5	−1
Arkansas	19	+12	20	+12
Delaware	32	+14	12	−5
Florida	36	+19	20	−6
Georgia	47	+38	13	+2
Kentucky	19	+12	14	+8
Louisiana	20	+16	12	+12
Maryland	38	+19	20	+3
Mississippi	21	+19	9	+9
North Carolina	34	+23	17	+3
Oklahoma	21	+13	12	+1
South Carolina	20	+13	10	+7
Tennessee	29	+23	13	0
Texas	30	+22	15	+5
Virginia	40	+26	7	+7
West Virginia	12	−6	17	+1
The Midwest	**40**	**+25**	**17**	**+4**
Illinois	40	+28	21	−2
Indiana	38	+22	14	+4
Iowa	39	+23	9	−4
Kansas	64	+44	20	+3
Michigan	32	+19	14	+6

(Continued)

Table 8.1 *(Continued)*

Region/State	Percent of Democrats who are women in 2016	Percent change in Democrats who are women, 1986–2016	Percent of Republicans who are women in 2016	Percent change in Republicans who are women, 1986–2016
Minnesota	41	+25	26	+13
Missouri	45	+31	18	+6
North Dakota	32	+18	12	+2
Ohio	39	+28	19	+12
South Dakota	25	+12	20	+5
Wisconsin	42	+24	16	−4
The West	**38**	**+19**	**22**	**+4**
Alaska	18	+1	38	+17
Arizona	44	+30	28	+6
California	24	+12	29	+16
Colorado	55	+27	29	+6
Hawaii	26	+13	50	+10
Idaho	52	+23	21	+5
Montana	53	+31	16	+9
Nevada	41	+28	25	+7
New Mexico	30	+28	24	−1
Oregon	42	+19	16	0
Utah	59	+49	7	+1
Washington	39	+14	29	+7
Wyoming	31	−14	10	−7

Note: Statistics combine data on lower and upper chambers and are calculated by author using data from the Center for American Women and Politics, *The Book of the States,* and the National Conference of State Legislatures.

region, as well as the total percentage point change in women's representation within each party over the past three decades. This 30-year time frame was chosen because it allows for a comparison of a time period when Republican and Democratic women were at rough parity with one another in terms of representation, with a time period where the dynamics of representation across party clearly differ. This table allows us to explore which states and regions of the country appear more or less hospitable to gains by Republican women.

As of summer 2016, women represent a dramatically smaller share of Republican legislators than Democratic legislators in all regions of the country: the Northeast, the South, the Midwest, and the West. One stunning theme in Table 8.1 is that in close to 30 percent of states, 14 total, the representation of women among Republican state legislators is the same or lower than it was three decades ago.

Barbara Norrander and Clyde Wilcox's research shows that the Northeast was the early leader in terms of women's representation in state legislatures,[11] and indeed Table 8.1 shows that the Northeast remains the region of the country most welcoming to Republican women legislators. Women represent 26 percent of Republican legislators in the Northeast as compared to 22 percent in the West, 17 percent in the Midwest, and just 13 percent in the South. Republican women have also made their biggest inroads into state legislatures in the Northeast over the past three decades, although the rate of progress is underwhelming across the board. Women's representation among Republican legislators in the Northeast increased by 5 percentage points, as compared to 4 percentage points in the West and Midwest and 3 percentage points in the South.

While Republican women have achieved relative success in the Northeast, the Northeast is also the region where Republicans exert the least influence as a party. The majority of state legislatures in the Northeast are controlled by the Democratic Party.[12] Thus, Republican women have their strongest voice in the region where their party holds the least power and has the least opportunity to shape the agenda or policy outcomes. Additionally, even in a number of states in the Northeast, the representation of Republican women has decreased rather than increased over the past three decades. The decline of Republican women in much of New England, in particular, is consistent with the theory discussed previously that the growing conservatism of the party has made legislative office particularly unwelcoming to moderate Republican women.[13]

Even though Republican women face challenges in all regions, they clearly face their biggest roadblocks in the South. It is striking that two decades into the 21st century, there remain three states in the South where women form less than 10 percent of Republicans: Alabama, Mississippi, and Virginia. These three Southern states join two others, Utah and Iowa, where women also form less than 10 percent of Republican legislators. Historically the conservative culture of the South has posed a challenge for women seeking office across the board; however, Table 8.1 shows that Democratic women have in fact posted impressive gains in this region. As a result, there is now a stunning gap between the representation of Republican and Democratic women legislators in a number of Southern states. In Alabama, for example, women form 37 percent of Democratic legislators but only 5 percent of Republican legislators; in Virginia, the comparison is 40 to 7; and in Georgia, women compose an impressive 47 percent of Democratic legislators compared to just 13 percent of Republican legislators. Thus, whatever is holding women back in the South is operating exclusively on the Republican side of the aisle.

Samantha Bradshaw and Rosalyn Cooperman sought to understand the dearth of Republican women in one particular Southern state legislature, Virginia.[14] Their study concludes that the Republican Party of Virginia makes no effort to explicitly recruit women candidates, but rather encourages interested self-starter candidates to find the party. Other studies reach similar conclusions that the Republican Party overall and Republican men in particular exhibit "low levels of commitment to remedying existing gender inequalities" and see no need to make explicit efforts to recruit women.[15] Such a system disadvantages women because women are more reliant on encouragement from others, especially party leaders, to consider running.[16] In other words, it appears that across the nation, and in Virginia in particular, the large number of well-educated, well-qualified Republican women are simply not being asked or encouraged to run for office.

There are two states where women form more than 30 percent of Republican legislators, Alaska and Hawaii, and thus represent comparative bright spots, as well as potential case studies, for how Republican women can succeed. At 50 percent, women form their highest share of Republican legislators in Hawaii. However, this success must be qualified by the reality that Hawaii is an overwhelmingly Democratic state. According to the National Council of State Legislators, as of 2016, only 8 of the 76 state legislative seats in Hawaii are held by Republicans, and of these 8 seats, 4 are held by women. Thus, the absolute number of Republican women in Hawaii is quite small, and the influence of Republicans in shaping policy in Hawaii is minimal. In fact, the case of Hawaii seems consistent with research suggesting that Republican women have the best opportunities to gain power in states where political positions are seen as less valuable.[17]

The other state where Republican women do well is Alaska, where women form 38 percent of Republican legislators. Women's sizable presence among Republican legislators in Alaska is a more meaningful accomplishment because Republicans control both houses of the legislature. Moreover, a woman, Rep. Charisse Millett, is the House majority leader. Thus, Republican women are in a strong position to shape legislative priorities and outcomes in Alaska. It is interesting to consider that Alaska has also had a Republican woman governor, Sarah Palin, and currently has a Republican woman as one of its two U.S. senators. Why Republican women have done particularly well in Alaska and the impact they are having on shaping policy outcomes are topics worthy of future investigation.

WHY SO FEW REPUBLICAN WOMEN?

This chapter next explores more systematically the factors that help or hinder the representation of Republican women in state legislatures and seeks to answer the following questions: Are Republican women well represented within states controlled by their party, or does conservative state culture act as a barrier to their representation? Do more women in the candidate pool, as traditionally defined, lead to greater numbers of Republican women legislators? Finally, do strong parties, term limits, and the professionalism of the legislature create opportunities or close doors for Republican women?

Table 8.2 presents the results of OLS multivariate regression analysis predicting the percent of women among Republican legislators, combining both lower and upper houses, across the states in 2016. The representation of women within the Republican Party is modeled as a function of

Table 8.2   Predictors of Percent Women among Republicans in State Legislatures, 2016

	Percent of Women among Republican Legislators
Partisanship of State Electorate (Republicanism)	−0.439**
	(0.108)
South	−0.060*
	(0.029)
Percent of Women in the Workforce	−0.003
	(0.003)
Full-time/Professional Legislature	−0.052*
	(0.025)
Term Limits	0.034
	(0.022)
Party Organization Strength	−0.009
	(0.006)
Constant	0.641**
	(0.197)
Observations	49
R-squared	0.461

Note: Cell entries are unstandardized coefficients.

Standard errors in parentheses.

$*p < 0.05$; $**p < 0.01$ two-tailed tests.

factors that previous research leads us to expect will help or hinder women's success in state legislatures, including the state's ideology/partisanship, as measured by the state's vote for Republican presidential candidate Mitt Romney in 2012[18]; whether the state is in the South or not; women's presence in the candidate pool, as measured by 2009 U.S. Census figures for the percent of women in the workforce; whether a state has term limits in effect and whether a state has a full-time/professional legislature, both based on 2016 information from the National Conference of State Legislatures; and a measure of party strength developed by David Mayhew and used in previous studies on women's representation in state legislatures.[19]

Studies consistently find that the ideology and partisanship of a state's electorate is associated with the representation of women. States with more Republican and more conservative voters have fewer women in their legislatures.[20] More recent studies find that the dampening effect of a conservative and Republican electorate constrains opportunities for office holding only among Republican women and has no impact on the fate of Democratic women, which makes sense given the polarization of the parties and the increased concentration of conservatism in the Republican Party.[21]

Table 8.2 shows that, as of 2016, the Republicanism of a state's electorate remains a strong, significant predictor of fewer women among Republican legislators. This finding is stunning, as it suggests that *the Republican Party itself* and the increasingly conservative ideology it has come to embrace is the biggest barrier to women's representation within the party. Whether it is that Republican women in very conservative states do not feel they are the right fit for their party or that the perceived value of seats in highly Republican states works against women candidates, the reality is that Republican Party strengths work against the representation of Republican women. This has serious implications for substantive representation, as discussed in the final section of this chapter.

In addition to the Republicanism of the electorate predicting fewer women, being a legislature in the South also predicts fewer women, a finding consistent with the results in Table 8.1. Even after state ideology/partisanship is controlled, Republican women are having a particularly hard time breaking into Southern legislatures. This result supports prior studies showing that the regional realignment of the parties has contributed to the stalled progress of Republican women elected officials.[22] Over the last several decades, the regional base of the Republican Party at the state level has undergone a dramatic shift toward the South. In 1985, Republicans held only 454 seats in Southern legislatures,[23] less than in any other region of the country. Since then, Republicans have made massive gains in the South, increasing their numbers to 1,345. In other words, three decades ago, Republicans held only 20.5 percent of state legislative seats in Southern states, and today they hold a stunning 87 percent. The party has made its biggest gains in the region of the country least hospitable to Republican women's candidacies. The pronounced underrepresentation of Republican women in Southern states is particularly concerning because the South has become the power center of the Republican Party and represents one of the leading areas of opportunity for higher office and leadership.

Another well-established factor influencing the representation of women in state legislatures is the number of women in the eligibility pool for state legislative office—the jobs that have traditionally led to political careers. In comparison to several decades ago, most women are now in the workforce full-time, which provides them with the resources, networks, and experiences that are typically prerequisites of political careers. Kira Sanbonmatsu's analysis of pooled data from the lower house of state legislatures from 1971 to 1999 found that women's labor force participation helped boost the representation of Democratic women legislators but not Republican legislators,[24] a finding confirmed by more recent studies.[25]

Table 8.2 reveals a similar result, in that the number of women in the workforce is not a significant predictor of women's representation among Republican legislators. In other words, the pipeline and social networking effects of being in the workforce are not operating in a positive way for women within the Republican Party. There are a couple explanations for this lack of effect. The first may be rooted in the realignment the parties have undergone in terms of their platforms and public rhetoric concerning the appropriate role of women and their response to the women's movement.[26] While the Republican Party does not vilify working women and women's involvement in public office, it also, not so subtly, emphasizes the desirability of more traditional roles for women.[27] As a result, Republican women who work, especially mothers who work, may feel less encouraged to run for office within their party. The research of Melody Crowder-Meyer and Benjamin Lauderdale reveals a second related factor.[28] In the aggregate, Republican and Democratic women are making different choices concerning education, career, and lifestyle, and as a result, there are dramatically fewer Republican women, compared to their Democratic counterparts, who have the backgrounds typical of those seeking state legislative office, an imbalance that is on track to continue growing bigger. While there are still millions of conservative women who could in theory run for state legislative office, the sizable partisan gap in the pipeline most likely contributes to the underrepresentation of Republican women in state legislatures.

Previous research has also found that professionalized legislatures have fewer women. Barbara Norrander and Clyde Wilcox speculate that this is because "full time legislatures attract a stronger pool of male competitors who make electoral victory more difficult."[29] Research disaggregating women's representation by party, however, shows that the exclusionary effects of highly paid, professional legislatures only inhibit the representation of Republican women and that Democratic women have made significant inroads into full-time and part-time legislatures alike.[30] The results in Table 8.2 show, consistent with this prior research, that as of 2016 full-time, well-paid legislatures predict fewer Republican women. One reason that Republican women may do comparatively poorer in highly professional legislatures is because full-time legislative work is less consistent with the Republican Party's more conservative position on the appropriate role of women. Alternatively, it may be that Republican women are less likely to be recruited or encouraged for these highly desirable seats. In either case, the poorer performance of Republican women in professional legislatures magnifies the problem of their underrepresentation by reducing their voice in the most powerful legislatures.

Also included is a measure of party organization strength, as previous analyses have found strong party organization to negatively impact the representation of women among legislative candidates and elected officials.[31] While party strength does have a negative coefficient in Table 8.2, consistent with previous research, it is not statistically significant. Finally, the model includes a measure of whether the state has term limits. Since incumbency is one of the biggest barriers to entering political office for all previously excluded groups, the implementation of term limits may offer more opportunities for women to break into state legislatures. The term limit variable, however, is not significant in Table 8.2. This is not that unexpected as previous explorations of this issue have produced mixed results.[32] This lack of result underscores an important point: without a sustained and concerted efforts to encourage more women to run, open seats create opportunities but do not automatically result in greater numbers of women in legislatures.

CONSEQUENCES OF SO FEW REPUBLICAN WOMEN

Finally, this chapter explores the consequences of having so few Republican women in state legislatures for the image, viability, and functioning of the party. First, the small, and in many states dwindling, number of

Republican women legislators limits the pool of Republican women well positioned to mount successful campaigns for higher-level office. As of summer 2016, there are six women governors, three Republican and three Democrat, and the majority in both parties served in their state's legislature before becoming governor.[33] Moreover, while fewer Republican women state legislators may be choosing to run for Congress than their counterparts, state legislative office remains the most common pipeline to congressional office, especially for Republican women.[34] According to data from the Center for American Women and Politics (CAWP), four of the six Republican women serving in the 114th U.S. Senate and a majority (13 of 22) of the Republican women in the U.S. House served in state legislatures. Thus, the paucity of Republican women state legislators is not only a major factor behind the small number of Republican women in Congress and statewide office, but it suggests that the representation of Republican women in high-level offices is unlikely to increase meaningfully in the coming years. Similarly, given the trends shown in this chapter, it is not at all surprising there was only one woman, Carly Fiorina, among the 17 candidates for the Republican presidential nomination, and that this one woman did not have prior elective experience.

The small number of Republican women legislators also has consequences for the image and functioning of the party. As the second decade of the 21st century comes to a close, many question whether a party that remains overwhelmingly male, with over 80 percent of its state legislators as men, can effectively speak to and about women's issues and, in turn, remain viable. This concern resonates within the party as well. A number of Republican Party elites describe recruiting and electing more women as, quite simply, a matter of party survival.[35] Indeed, many of the high-profile women the Republican Party has been turning to in order to counter accusations that the party is antiwoman or to showcase its diversity—such as Sen. Joni Ernst, Gov. Nikki Haley, Gov. Mary Fallin, and U.S. Rep. Cathy McMorris Rodgers—have taken on their current positions only after serving in their state legislatures, and, once again, there are not many women following in their footsteps.

Beyond the viability and image of the party, there are serious policy consequences of having so few Republican women legislators. According to the National Conference of State Legislatures, as of 2016, Republicans controlled 30 state legislatures, compared to just 11 for Democrats. Given the polarized functioning of legislative bodies, this means that Republicans alone are setting agendas and shaping policy in a majority of U.S. states. And, as this chapter has emphasized, there are few Republican women involved in this process. As Table 8.2 reveals, Republican women's representation is inversely related to their party's strength in a state. In other words, Republican women have their lowest levels of representation in states where the Republican Party exerts its greater power over agenda setting and legislating. This means that as Republican-controlled legislatures push for a range of policies, including policies disproportionately or differentially impacting women, women have a small seat at the table. While the views of Republican women are not monolithic, in the aggregate, their priorities, policy views, and approaches to issues are distinct from Republican men,[36] and these distinctive viewpoints are significantly underrepresented. Looking at recent state legislative policy making on two issues, reproductive rights and health care, illustrates this point.

State legislators have introduced, debated, and passed a large amount of pro-life/anti-choice legislation in recent years. It will come as no surprise that states passing the most restrictive abortion laws have been states controlled by the Republican Party. What is sometimes overlooked, though, is that there are very few women among the Republicans introducing, debating, and voting on these policies. Women form only 15 percent of Republican legislators, lower than their already low national average, in states that, according to the National Association for the Repeal of Abortion Laws (NARAL) Report Cards on Women's Reproductive Rights, have passed the most anti-choice legislation in 2015 and 2016. In fact, in regression analysis, not shown here, women's representation among Republican lawmakers is a strong, *inverse* predictor of more restrictive abortion policy. In other words, the fewer women there are among the Republican legislators, the more anti-choice legislation the state has passed recently, a relationship that remains substantively strong and highly significant even when party control of the legislature is included in the model.

The most obvious implication of this is that policies having to do with the regulation of women's bodies, and choices are being introduced, debated and passed with very few women's voices having input. This is particularly problematic as there is evidence that Republican women have different views and approaches to this issue than their men colleagues. Even as Republican women legislators have become more conservative over the past two decades, they remain significantly less conservative on the issue of abortion than their male counterparts.[37] Moreover, there is evidence that even among the growing number of pro-life Republican women legislators, they approach, frame, and craft pro-life policy in significantly different ways than their male colleagues.[38]

A couple recent examples illustrate this finding. In spring of 2016, several pro-life, Republican women lawmakers in Indiana spoke out strongly against restrictive abortion legislation passed by their male colleagues and signed into law by Republican governor Mike Pence, arguing it was too punitive toward women.[39] Another example can be seen in Oklahoma, where in spring 2016, the highly pro-life Republican governor, Mary Fallin, vetoed a law passed by her state's heavily Republican and heavily male legislature (see Table 8.1) that would essentially ban abortions, as she did not feel it was a sensible approach to the issue. Once again, these Republican women are in fact pro-life, but their approach to the issue is meaningfully different than their male colleagues. And, on the flip side of the issue, it is interesting to note that Alaska, a state with a Republican-controlled legislature and the highest portion of women among those Republicans, is rated by NARAL as having passed meaningful pro-choice legislation across its 2015–2016 term.

One additional issue that highlights the substantive implications of so few Republican women can be seen in health care. One of the major provisions of the Affordable Care Act, or Obamacare, was the expansion of Medicaid eligibility to low-income adults. While this provision was intended to apply nationally, the Supreme Court ruling in 2012 made it optional for states. As a result, according to the Kaiser Family Foundation, as of summer 2016, 31 states have adopted the Medicaid expansion and 19 states have chosen not to do so. The decision about whether to expand Medicaid under Obamacare has been a highly politicized one, with states controlled by Democrats more likely to expand Medicaid than Republican states.

The decision is also a gendered one, in that it has disproportionate impact on women. Women not only have different and often more serious health needs, but they are overrepresented among the group of low-income individuals who get covered in states that expand Medicaid, and, conversely, they are disproportionately among those without coverage in states than do not.[40] A comparison of means tests shows that women represent only 14 percent of Republican legislators in the states that have decided not to expand Medicaid. This is not to say that the outcome would be different if more Republican women were in these state legislatures, but rather that this decision, which disproportionately and differentially affects women, is being made without many Republican women offering their distinctive perspective.

LOOKING AHEAD: WHITHER REPUBLICAN WOMEN IN STATE LEGISLATURES?

Looking to the future, prospects are not promising for the representation of Republican women in state legislatures. The reasons why there are so few Republican women legislators are not due to the political climate, lack of opportunities, or some other factor outside of the control of the Republican Party. Rather, it is the Republican Party itself that appears to be constraining opportunities for Republican women. As the party moved to the right ideologically and developed its power base in the South, progress for Republican women legislators stalled. Today, Republican women have their lowest levels of representation in Southern states and in states where the Republican Party is the strongest.

Carroll and Sanbonmatsu demonstrate that women's decision to run for office cannot be understood by the traditional ambition model, but rather a relationally embedded candidacy model, which means women need to be asked and encouraged to run by others. While elements of the Republican Party leadership have identified the recruitment of more women candidates as a strategically important goal for the party, commitment to this goal is not part of the culture of the party, nor universally endorsed by party elites and voters. This is a particular problem for the Republican Party, given that they cannot rely, as the Democratic Party can, on a well-established network of independent organizations dedicated to recruiting and supporting women candidates.[41] As a result, the marginalized status of women within the Republican Party seems likely to persist, and with that the distinctive voices and perspectives of Republican women will continue to be marginalized. The limited number of Republican women legislators constrains opportunities for women at higher levels of elective office and also the ability of the party to counter the image, hardened as a result of the 2016 presidential election, that the party is antiwoman.

NOTES

1. Susan J. Carroll and Kira Sanbonmatsu, *More Women Can Run: Gender and Pathways to the State Legislatures* (New York: Oxford University Press, 2013); Laurel Elder, "Contrasting Party Dynamics: A Three Decade Analysis of the Representation of Democratic versus Republican Women State Legislators," *Social Science Journal* 51, no. 3 (2014): 377–385; Laurel Elder. "Whither Republican Women in New England?," *New England Journal of Political Science* 7, no. 2 (2014b): 161–193; Laurel Elder, "The Partisan Gap among Women State Legislators," *Women, Politics & Policy* 33, no. 1 (2012): 65–85; Laurel Elder, "Whither Republican Women: The Growing Partisan Gap among Women in Congress," *The Forum* 6, no. 1 (2008). doi: 10.2202/1540-8884.1204

2. Data on the number of Republicans and Democrats in state legislatures were drawn from *The Book of the States*, produced by the Council of State Governments, for 1986, and from the National Conference of State Legislatures for 2016. Data on the number of Republican and Democratic women in state legislatures were gathered from the Center for American Women and Politics (CAWP) fact sheets.

3. Caroline Heldman and Lisa Wade, "Sexualizing Sarah Palin: The Social and Political Context of the Sexual Objectification of Female Candidates," *Sex Roles* 65, no. 3 (2011): 156–164; Barbara Norrander and Clyde Wilcox, "Change and Continuity in the Geography of Women State Legislators," in *Women and Elective Office: Past, Present and Future*, 2nd ed., eds. Sue Thomas and Clyde Wilcox (Oxford UK: Oxford University Press, 2005), 176–196; Pamela Paxton, Matthew A. Painter II, and Melanie M. Hughes, "Year of the Woman, Decade of the Man: Trajectories of Growth in Women's State Legislative Representation," *Social Science Research* 38, no.1 (2009): 86–102; Wilma Rule, "Why Are More Women State Legislators?," in *Women in Politics: Outsiders or Insiders?*, ed. Lois Duke Whitaker (Upper Saddle River, NJ: Prentice Hall, 1999), 190–202.

4. Council of Economic Advisors, "Women's Participation in Education and the Workforce," Executive Office of the President of the United States (2014), https://obamawhitehouse.archives.gov/sites/default/files/docs/womens_slides_final.pdf.

5. R. Darcy, Susan Welch, and Janet Clark, *Women, Elections and Representation* (Lincoln: University of Nebraska Press, 1994).

6. Ronnee Schreiber, *Righting Feminism: Conservative Women and American Politics* (New York: Oxford University Press, 2012).

7. Melissa Deckman, *Tea Party Women: Mama Grizzlies, Grassroots Leaders, and the Changing Face of the American Right* (New York: New York University Press, 2016), 2–3.

8. Elder, "Contrasting Party Dynamics"; Elder, "The Partisan Gap."

9. Carroll and Sanbonmatsu, *More Women Can Run*, 92.

10. Danielle M. Thomsen, "Why So Few (Republican) Women? Explaining the Partisan Imbalance of Women in the U.S. Congress," *Legislative Studies Quarterly* 40, no.2 (2015): 295–323; Danielle M. Thomsen, "Ideological Moderates Won't Run: How Party Fit Matters for Partisan Polarization in Congress," *Journal of Politics* 76, no. 3 (2014): 1–12.

11. Barbara Norrander and Clyde Wilcox. "The Geography of Power: Women in State Legislatures," in *Women and Elective Office: Past, Present, and Future*, eds. Sue Thomas and Clyde Wilcox (Oxford, UK: Oxford University Press, 1998), 103–117.

12. As of summer 2016, Democrats control six of the nine Northeastern state legislatures. The two Northeastern state legislatures that have Republican majorities, New Hampshire and Pennsylvania, have Democratic governors, thereby diminishing the power of Republicans in those states.

13. Elder, "Whither Republican Women in New England?"

14. Samantha Bradshaw and Rosalyn Cooperman, "Where Are the Women? Women as Candidates in the Republican Party of Virginia," *Virginia Social Science Journal* 46 (2011): 19–38.

15. Carroll and Sanbonmatsu, *More Women Can Run*, 92; Kira Sanbonmatsu, *Where Women Run: Gender & Party Politics in the American States* (Ann Arbor: University of Michigan Press, 2006).

16. Carroll and Sanbonmatsu, *More Women Can Run*, 69.

17. Elder, "Contrasting Party Dynamics"; Stephen J. Stambough and Valerie R. O'Regan, "Republican Lambs and the Democratic Pipeline: Partisan Differences

in the Nomination of Female Gubernatorial Candidates," *Politics & Gender* 3, no. 3 (2007): 349–368.

18. This variable, the percent of vote for Mitt Romney in the 2012 election, is highly correlated with several other variables that would be theoretically interesting to include in the model but cannot be due to issues of multicollinearity, including Republican control of the legislature in 2016 (correlation is 0.77); the proportion of state legislative seats held by Republicans in the prior term (correlation is 0.841) and the conservatism of a state as measured by William Berry, Evan Ringquist, Richard Fording, and Russell Hanson, "Measuring Citizen and Government Ideology in the States," *American Journal of Political Science* 42, no. 1 (1998): 327–348 (correlation is 0.78).

19. Elder, "The Partisan Gap"; Sanbonmatsu, *Where Women Run*.

20. Darcy, Welch, and Clark, *Women, Elections and Representation*; Norrander and Wilcox, "Change and Continuity" and "Geography of Power."

21. Elder, "The Partisan Gap"; Elder, "Contrasting Party Dynamics."

22. Carroll and Sanbonmatsu, *More Women Can Run*, 92; Elder, "Whither Republican Women."

23. Data on the number of Republicans in southern state legislatures is based on *The Book of the States* for 1985 and the National Conference of State Legislatures for 2016 as well as calculations by the author.

24. Kira Sanbonmatsu, "Political Parties and the Recruitment of Women to the State Legislatures." *Journal of Politics*. 64, no. 3 (2002): 791–809.

25. Elder, "Contrasting Party Dynamics"; Elder, "The Partisan Gap."

26. Carroll and Sanbonmatsu, *More Women Can Run*, 83–91; Laurel Elder and Steven Green, *The Politics of Parenthood: Causes and Consequences of the Politicization and Polarization of the American Family* (Albany, NY: SUNY Press, 2012), 23–48; Christina Wolbrecht, *The Politics of Women's Rights: Parties, Positions, and Change* (Princeton, NJ: Princeton University Press, 2000).

27. Starting in 1980, the Republican Party dropped its support for the Equal Rights Amendment and in its place began championing the vital role of homemakers. The 1992 Republican platform accuses Democrats of "forcing millions of women into the workplace" and declares that "the well-being of children is best accomplished in the environment of the home," not in child care centers. The party has also opposed policies, including the Family and Medical Leave Act (FMLA) and publicly funded child care, aimed to support working mothers.

28. Melody Crowder-Meyer and Benjamin E. Lauderdale, "A Partisan Gap in the Supply of Female Potential Candidates in the United States," *Research and Politics* 1, no. 1 (2014): 1–7.

29. Norrander and Wilcox, "Change and Continuity," 187.

30. Elder, "The Partisan Gap."

31. Elder, "The Partisan Gap"; Sanbonmatsu, *Where Women Run*; Sanbonmatsu, "Political Parties and the Recruitment of Women."

32. Susan J. Carroll, "The Impact of Term Limits on Women," *Spectrum: The Journal of State Government* (Fall 2001): 19–21; Susan J. Carroll and Krista

Jenkins, "Unrealized Opportunity? Term Limits and the Representation of Women in State Legislatures," *Women & Politics* 23, no. 4 (2001): 1–30; Susan Carroll and Krista Jenkins, "Increasing Diversity or More of the Same? Term Limits and the Representation of Women, Minorities, and Minority Women in State Legislatures," *National Political Science Review* 10, no. (2005): 71–84; Elder, "The Partisan Gap."

33. Women governors who have state legislative experience include Oregon governor Kate Brown, a Democrat; Oklahoma governor Mary Fallin, a Republican; South Carolina governor Nikki Haley, a Republican; and New Hampshire governor Maggie Hassan, a Democrat. Susana Martinez (R-NM) and Gina Ralmondo (D-RI) both have previous elective office experience, as a county district attorney and state treasurer, respectively, but they did not serve in their state legislatures.

34. Elder, "Whither Republican Women."

35. Laurel Elder, "Women and the Parties: An Analysis of Republican and Democratic Strategies for Recruiting Women Candidates" (paper presented at the American Political Science Association Conference, Washington D.C., August 28–31, 2014); Republican National Committee (RNC), "Growth & Opportunity Project" (2013), http://www.documentcloud.org/documents/624293-republican-national-committees-growth-and.html.

36. Carroll and Sanbonmatsu, *More Women Can Run*, 81; Tracey Osborn, *How Women Represent Women: Political Parties, Gender, and Representation in the State Legislatures* (New York: Oxford University Press, 2012).

37. Carroll and Sanbonmatsu, *More Women Can Run*, 79–81

38. Beth Reingold, Rebecca Kreitzer, Tracy Osborn, and Michele L. Swers, "Antifeminism and Women's Representation in the States" (paper presented at the American Political Science Association, San Francisco, CA, September 3–5, 2015).

39. Dominique Mosbergen, "Female Republican Lawmakers Slam Indiana Abortion Bill as 'Overreaching'; House Approved It Anyway," *Huffington Post*, March 11, 2016, http://www.huffingtonpost.com/entry/indiana-abortion-bill_us_56e28901e4b0b25c918184d9; Chelsea Schneider and Tony Cook, "Pence Signs New Abortion Restrictions into Law with a Prayer," *Indy Star*, March 25, 2016, http://www.indystar.com/story/news/politics/2016/03/24/pence-signs-new-abortion-restrictions-into-law-prayer/82225890.

40. The American College of Obstetricians and Gynecologists, Committee on Health Care for Underserved Women, "Benefits to Women of Medicaid Expansion through the Affordable Care Act," Number 552, January 2013, http://www.acog.org/Resources-And-Publications/Committee-Opinions/Committee-on-Health-Care-for-Underserved-Women/Benefits-to-Women-of-Medicaid-Expansion-Affordable-Care-Act; Usha Ranji, Yali Bair, and Alina Salganicoff, "Medicaid and Family Planning: Background and Implications of the ACA," Kaiser Family Foundation, February 3, 2016, http://kff.org/report-section/medicaid-and-family-planning-the-aca-medicaid-expansion-and-family-planning.

41. Bradshaw and Cooperman, "Where Are the Women?"; Elder, "The Partisan Gap."

CHAPTER 9

Moving Up or Getting Out: The Career Patterns of Republican Women State Legislators

H. Abbie Erler

The 2016 election helped solidify the Republican Party's dominance over every level of government. Republicans can boast of unified party control at the federal level and in 25 states; they hold the presidency and governorships in 33 states. Republicans have picked up 11 Senate seats and 66 House seats since the last time the Democratic Party controlled both houses of Congress (2009–2011). Similarly, at the state level, Republicans control 69 out of 99 legislative chambers. However, one group within the Republican Party that has not benefited from this electoral supremacy is Republican women. Republican women have made few gains in Congress. They comprise 11.5 percent of Republican seats in the Senate and only 8.8 percent of the Republican Party's delegation in the House. Of the 4 new female senators elected in 2016, none were Republicans, and only 2 of the 8 newly elected female House members were Republicans. At the state level, where Republican lawmakers have made significant gains, the number of seats held by Republican women has only increased by 33 since 2011. Women make up 17.1 percent of all Republican state legislators, and Republican women comprise only 39 percent of all women state legislators.

Why are there so few Republican women in elective office when the Republican Party is electorally so strong? While several explanations have been proposed for why Republican women suffer greater underrepresentation than Democratic women, this chapter explores the role that political ambition plays. I argue that Republican women have a harder time reaching the halls of Congress because they are more likely to hold elective office in states that lack political pipelines to more prestigious positions. While Republican women may be just as ambitious for higher office as Democratic women, the states where they hold office offer few possibilities for political advancement.

Many studies of women and politics have focused on the eligibility pool as an important part of the puzzle in explaining the underrepresentation of women in political office.[1] The eligibility pool refers to individuals who are in the types of professions that typically lead to careers in politics, such as business, law, and political activism. They are people who have credentials, resumes, and experiences that would make them credible candidates for political office. As Darcy, Welch, and Clark state, "The gender composition of the eligible pool of candidates will eventually determine the gender composition of elected bodies."[2] State legislators are especially promising candidates for higher office. Women can leverage valuable resources that they gain as state legislators, such as policy expertise, campaign experience, and political connections, to launch successful runs for Congress or other statewide offices.[3] Service in the state legislature may "serve as a spring board into higher office"[4] in that they provide women with the credentials and skills they need to make a credible run for higher office.[5]

It is useful to think of the structure of political offices within a state as a pipeline. Women often enter the pipeline at a low level, such as city council member or state representative, and then move up the pipeline to higher and higher levels of office. If the pipeline functions effectively, women flow to these higher offices at a steady stream while more women enter the bottom of the pipeline to replace those who have moved further along in the pipes. As women increased their numbers in state legislatures in the early 1990s, some predicted that these gains would reverberate to higher levels of office, as these lower offices would create a pipeline, funneling women into higher office. As Stambough and O'Regan explain, "Success breeds success. In politics, success at one level often breeds success at the next levels."[6] If the political pipeline functions smoothly, it can help funnel women through the hierarchy of available offices. A well-developed pipeline can pave the way for successful female candidates by building networks among women across different levels of office and convincing party leaders and voters that women can run and win these offices. However, there is much that can go wrong with this political plumbing. Clogs can develop, leaving women stuck in the pipeline at low levels of office. Leaks might emerge, with women leaving the pipeline before reaching higher levels of office. Further, a state may have a political pipeline for some groups of women, such as Democratic women, but not others.

While the existence of state political pipelines is important for increasing women's representation (see "Representation of Women," Glossary), we know little about what facilitates the development of such pipelines. Many studies on the development of a political pipeline focus on candidate emergence and the factors that increase the likelihood that women will initially enter the electoral fray.[7] While these studies have produced valuable insights into the nature of women's political ambition, they have neglected to examine the actual workings of the pipeline. For example, we know little about the career patterns of women once they gain seats in the state legislature, including, importantly, whether they rise up the pipeline to higher levels of office. While getting more women into the pipeline is important, if the pipeline is clogged or has sprung a leak, few women will advance. Left unanswered in the literature are central questions such as: What state-level factors facilitate the development of functioning political pipelines in the U.S. states? Are these factors the same for Republican women and Democratic women? Do Republican women seek higher office and win higher office at the same rates as Democratic women?

This chapter begins to answer these questions by exploring whether political pipelines exist in the states for both Republican and Democratic women. It does so by examining the career moves of women legislators in the lower houses of 41 state legislatures from 2002 to 2008. I find that there are partisan disparities in the existence of political pipelines for women lawmakers. Few states have political pipelines that serve incumbent women of both political parties. Instead, incumbent Republican women are less likely to run for higher state legislative office than their Democratic counterparts, less likely to win their reelections bids and contests for higher office, and more likely to retire from legislative service. This chapter explores the factors that account for why Republican women lawmakers exhibit less progressive ambition than Democratic women and what institutional and demographic factors facilitate the pipelines for higher office for Republican and Democratic women.

AMBITION, POLITICAL PARTIES, AND WOMEN'S REPRESENTATION

What determines the existence of a political pipeline? Ambition is one necessary ingredient for the establishment of a political pipeline. For service in lower state offices to act as a springboard for higher political offices, those in these lower offices must have, at a minimum, a desire for a more prestigious position. In his early study of political careers, Schlesinger identifies three categories of political ambition: discreet, static, and progressive.[8] Legislators with discreet ambition have little desire to make a career out of politics. They typically serve in the state legislature for one or two terms before stepping down to return to private life. In contrast, legislators with static ambition are content to serve in their current office indefinitely. They run for, and frequently win, reelection again and again, but never attempt to move up the career ladder to higher office. Finally, legislators with progressive ambition ascend the hierarchy of offices within their states, running for offices that are more prestigious than the ones they currently hold. A functioning political pipeline depends on the presence of state lower house members with progressive ambition, willing to risk losing their seat in the state assembly to run for a seat in the state senate or beyond.

Yet, political ambition, and consequently a legislator's career path, is determined by more than just a personal desire for higher office. While political ambition depends on psychological factors, it is also shaped by institutional context. Studies of state legislatures find that they tend to be dominated by individuals who display similar types of political ambition. Legislative institutions attract individuals who hold a specific type of political ambition, and, in turn, these individuals choose legislative institutions that help facilitate that type of ambition.[9] In this way, legislative institutions and political ambition reinforce each other. For example, a legislature dominated by members with static ambition will structure legislative institutions in a way that promotes and rewards that ambition, such as a rigid seniority system and strong committee chairs. As a result, certain types of legislatures will be more attractive to some individuals than others based on the type of ambition that person holds.

There is a positive feedback mechanism at work. For example, seats in a professionalized legislature, with their heavy time demands and increased responsibilities, are likely to be seen as desirable only to individuals who are interested in running for higher office. The resources and skills that legislators acquire in these types of legislatures make them formidable candidates for higher office. In contrast, individuals with discreet ambition are more likely to run in states with legislatures where the demands on a legislator's time and energy are minimal.

The relationship between political ambition and legislative structure has important implications for women's representation and the development of a political pipeline for higher office. Despite the many studies of ambition and politics, little is known about whether there are gender or partisan differences in the manifestation of political ambition. Previous research has produced mixed results on whether women legislators are more ambitious for higher office than their male peers. Early studies found that women state legislators were just as ambitious for higher office as men, reporting similar levels of political ambition.[10] But more recent studies have challenged this conclusion, finding that women state legislators are less likely to run for Congress and are less likely to find holding higher office desirable.[11] Fewer studies have examined party differences in women's political ambition. We currently do not know whether Republican women have similar levels of progressive ambition as Democratic women, nor whether Republican female state legislators are as likely to run for higher office as Democratic female state legislators. However, despite this lack of empirical evidence, there are several theoretical reasons for why Republican women would pursue different career trajectories than Democratic women. I expect the factors that facilitate the development of progressive ambition in state legislators impact Republican and Democratic women differently. Chief among these factors are legislative professionalization, party organization strength, and term limits.

Legislative Professionalization

State legislators in highly professionalized legislatures are more likely to display progressive ambition than those who serve in less professionalized legislatures and are more likely to be recruited by party leaders to run for Congressional seats.[12] In part, this disparity is due to the fact that service in a highly professionalized legislature prepares members for runs for higher office. Elections for seats in a highly professionalized legislature approach the competitiveness of those for a seat in the House of Representatives. Members of professionalized legislatures already have experience raising early money, cultivating fund-raising contacts, soliciting contributions, and assembling professional campaign staffs. These are all skills that are transferrable to a run for higher office.[13]

In addition, members of professionalized legislatures have more time and resources available for performing constituency service and are more likely to have multiple district offices then members of less professionalized legislatures.[14] They also have greater connections with interest groups because they have more influence over policy than members of citizen-legislatures.[15] Because of these prior investments in campaign resources and constituency service, these members can quickly enter a campaign for higher office, if an opportunity arises, and be formidable candidates. As a result, individuals who are interested in making a career out of politics and moving up the political ladder to higher office are more often found in highly professionalized legislatures.

The increased competitiveness for seats in highly professionalized legislatures and the all-encompassing nature of the legislative work within them may discourage Republican women, more so than Democratic women, from serving in these types of legislatures. Republican women are more likely to have traditional views of their role in the family and as caregivers from their children.[16] As such, they may find service in a high-paced, demanding job that requires them to be away from their families for long stretches of time incompatible with their role as mothers. Dodson argues that the time demands of professionalized legislatures makes them less compatible with primary caregiving responsibilities than citizen legislatures. While she finds that in every type of legislature there is a substantial gap between the percentage of men legislators and women legislators with children under 18, this gap is largest for professionalized legislatures; 27 percent of the male members had minor children compared to just 8 percent of the female members.[17]

Republican women are also less likely than Democratic women to have the education, occupational, and other socioeconomic characteristics found in newly elected members to Congress.[18] Because of the demands of family and child-rearing, Republican women are less likely than Democratic women to be found in feeder professions for professionalized state legislatures, such as law. The only profession where Republican women are more prevalent than Democratic women is business. Yet, being a business owner is more compatible with service in a less professionalized legislature because the time demands of legislative service are much less than they are for more professionalized legislatures. Members of citizen legislatures can retain their private-sector jobs, whereas those in professionalized legislatures must choose between being a legislator and running a business.[19]

If Republican women are less likely to serve in professionalized legislatures, this has consequences for their advancement to higher levels of political office. As discussed above, service in less professionalized legislatures rarely prepares members for making the jump to higher office. Republican women may be serving in state legislatures where the opportunity for political advancement is limited.

Party Organization

The strength of state party organizations should also affect the prevalence of a political pipeline for Republican and Democratic women. Recruitment by party leaders is crucial for encouraging women to initially enter politics as well as for encouraging current female legislators to run for higher office.[20] Studies of candidate recruitment have found that men are more likely than women to be contacted by party leaders about running for office. Despite their success in winning office, party leaders often do not consider women candidates as electorally viable as men. This gender bias in recruitment is particularly evident in the Republican Party.[21] In addition, the Republican Party has become less hospitable to women's candidacies.[22] As the Republican Party has become increasingly conservative, Republican women have found themselves more and more out of step with the ideology of their party, as they tend to be more moderate.[23]

In addition, Republican women candidates have a difficult time overcoming the gender stereotypes held by Republican voters. Republican partisans are more likely to judge Republican woman harshly, seeing them as less conservative and less competent than a male candidate.[24] Both of these factors harm their prospects for advancing to higher office, especially statewide and congressional seats. Given this, I expect that states with strong party organizations should be less likely to have a pipeline for higher office for Republican women.

Term Limits

Term limits for state legislators alter the calculus of running for higher office and, as a result, facilitate progressive ambition. Since 1990, 15 states have imposed legislative term limits on their members. Term limits decrease the costs of running for higher office by eliminating the opportunity costs associated with the possibility of retaining one's former seat.[25] Previous research has found that term limits have encouraged progressive ambition among state legislators, as evidenced by the increase in the number of house members running for higher office after being termed out of their current office.[26] Term limits, however, place a strain on the available supply of potential candidates for office. Term limits require political parties to recruit potential candidates more frequently to run for the open seats that become available as incumbents are termed out of office. This may place Republican women at a disadvantage compared to Democratic women because the Democratic Party is more enthusiastic about facilitating women's candidacies.[27]

In addition, state house members hoping to run for an open state senate seat may face the possibility of running against a fellow state house member in the primary, as multiple state house districts are often nestled in a single state senate district. In these situations, where multiple incumbents run from the same party, Republican women candidates may be more likely to be discouraged from running by party leaders.[28] While states with term limits should be more likely to have a political pipeline for both Democratic and Republican women, I expect the impact of term limits to be greater on the progressive ambition of Democratic women.

CAREER PATHS OF REPUBLICAN WOMEN

The career trajectories of Republican and Democratic women state house members follow different paths. In the period examined here, there were more Democratic women serving in state legislatures than Republican women. Of the women legislators in the sample, 62.3 percent were Democrat, and only 37.7 percent were Republican. Republican women were more likely than Democratic women to retire from office. Over the four election cycles examined, 44.5 percent of Republican women who left office did so due to retirement, compared to 38.9 percent of Democratic women. Democratic women, on the other hand, were more likely to be forced out of office by term limits. Of the women legislators examined in this study who were forced out of office by term limits, 25.2 percent were Republicans, and 33.2 percent were Democrats.

Female state legislators are generally successful in their bids for reelection, but female Democratic state house members have slightly higher reelection rates than Republican women. In total, 95.3 percent of Democratic women and 90 percent of Republican women won their reelection bids. Party differences are also apparent in runs for higher office. Democratic women were more likely to attempt the move from the lower house to the state senate, comprising 58.7 percent of all female lower house members who ran for state senate. However, Republican women lower house members were slightly more likely to run for other higher offices, making up 52 percent of female house members who ran for statewide office or Congress. Republican women had slightly lower win rates for state senate than Democratic women. While 73.2 percent of Democratic female house members won their races for the state senate, only 68.4 percent of Republican women were successful at moving to higher offices. Women state house members had much lower win rates for other higher offices. Only 23.4 percent won their bids for statewide office or Congress. Democrats fared better, with 29 percent of Democratic women winning their races compared with 18 percent of Republican women. However, Democrats and Republicans termed out of office were equally likely to run for higher office. Of those women facing term limits, 32.3 percent of Democratic women and 32.9 percent of Republican women ran for higher office.

VARIATION IN THE DEVELOPMENT OF STATE POLITICAL PIPELINES

To determine whether a pipeline for higher office exists within a state, I develop political pipeline measures for both Republican and Democratic female lower house members in each state. A state's pipeline measure conveys two pieces of information: first, whether Republican (Democratic) women in the lower house ran for higher offices and, second, the extent or magnitude of progressive ambition exhibited by Republican (Democratic) women. These two components measure flow and volume, respectively. For a state to have a functioning pipeline for higher office, women in the lower house must consistently run for higher offices; women must steadily flow up the pipeline each election year and in sufficient volume, or numbers, to be meaningful. This study develops separate pipeline measures for runs for state senate and runs for all other higher offices, such as statewide elective office and Congress. In total, four pipeline measures are calculated for each state: Republican (Democratic) women running for the state senate and Republican (Democratic) women running for other higher offices.

Political pipeline measures are not equivalent to measures of the amount of ambition legislators possess, such as those found in survey research. However, they do capture the extent to which legislators manifest their ambition. It may be the case that some legislators are highly ambitious, but they choose not to act on that ambition for some reason. Because of this, the pipeline measures developed here may underestimate the amount of ambition that legislators possess. If we find lower pipeline measures for Republican (Democratic) women, this may indicate lower levels of progressive ambition, or it may indicate that these women are not as able to act on their ambition as Democratic (Republican) women.

This study develops a multivariate model to predict which factors are more likely to promote a political pipeline for Republican and Democratic women. As discussed above, I expect term limits, legislative professionalization, and party organization strength to have the biggest impact on whether a state has a pipeline for higher office for Republican and Democratic women. Information on the data used to construct this study's pipeline measures as well as the specifics on the model estimated can be found in this chapter's Appendix.

Examining scores on the state pipeline measures reveal that most states do not have functioning pipelines for either Republican or Democratic women. For Republican women, 67 percent of the pipeline measures for state senate are 0, indicating that no Republican state house member ran for state senate during that election in the state. For runs for statewide and congressional offices, 84.2 percent of the pipeline measures are 0 for Republican women. Democratic women fare only slightly better. For the pipeline measures for state senate, 58.5 percent are 0, and for the pipeline measures for statewide and congressional offices, 85.4 percent are 0. No state has a pipeline for state senate for Republican women for every election year in the sample. Only four states have pipelines every election for Democratic women running for the state senate (California, Missouri, Montana, and Oregon). Of the states in the analysis, nine do not have a pipeline for Republican women, and six lack a pipeline for Democratic women in any election from 2002 to 2008. New Mexico and South Carolina do not have a pipeline for either Democratic or Republican women; for the four elections examined here, no woman lower house member ran for state senate in these states. Less than half of the states have political pipelines for the state senate in two elections or more. For Republican women, 41 percent of states have a pipeline for two or more elections, while 46 percent of states have a pipeline for two or more elections for Democratic women.

As Table 9.1 shows, the factors that influence the development of a political pipeline for higher office differ for Republican and Democratic women. As discussed above, states are more likely to have a political pipeline for state senate for Democratic women than Republican women.

The likelihood that a pipeline for state senate exists in a state is 37.7 percent for Democratic women, but only 19.1 percent for Republican women. The chances of having a pipeline for higher statewide or congressional offices is even smaller. For Democratic women, the likelihood that a pipeline for statewide or congressional offices will exist in the state is only 13.2 percent; for Republican women, this likelihood is 11.2 percent. It is interesting to note that the difference in the likelihood that a state will have a pipeline for Republican women compared to Democratic women is smaller in the model for higher office runs than it was when looking at the state senate pipelines. This indicates that there are fewer partisan differences between women in runs for these types of offices; women of both parties are equally unlikely to run for these higher offices.

States with term limits are more likely to have a pipeline for the state senate, although the magnitude of this effect is greater for Democratic women. States with term limits have a 68.2 percent likelihood of having a pipeline for Democratic women, but only a 35.7 percent likelihood of having a similar pipeline for Republican women. The chances of having a pipeline increase by 15.6 percentage for Republican women and 30.5 percentage points for Democratic women moving from a state without term

Table 9.1   Republican and Democratic Pipelines for Office for Women
Lower House Members, 2002–2008

	Rep. Pipeline (State Senate)	Rep. Pipeline (Other Offices)	Dem. Pipeline (State Senate)	Dem. Pipeline (Other Offices)
Republican	0.02	0.01	−0.04	−0.06
Pres. Vote	(0.02)	(0.02)	(0.03)*	(0.03)**
Party Strength	0.14	−1.78	−0.22	−1.3
	(0.47)	(0.74)***	(0.58)	(0.68)**
Term Limits	0.81	0.99	1.3	1.2
	(0.30)***	(0.61)*	(0.44)***	(0.41)***
Two-Year	1.3	−0.066	−0.36	−1.7
Senate Term	(0.40)***	(0.62)	(0.47)	(0.74)**
Part-Time	−0.82	0.39	0.47	0.80
Legislature	(0.45)*	(0.53)	(0.50)	(0.58)
State Senate	0.03	−0.05	0.07	0.03
Turnover	(0.02)*	(0.03)*	(0.02)***	(0.03)
Seat Ratio	−0.70	−0.41	0.72	0.25
	(0.61)	(0.80)	(0.78)	(0.50)
Redistricting	1.2	0.98	0.16	−0.87
	(0.37)***	(0.58)*	(0.43)	(0.55)
Adjusted R-Squared	0.15	0.11	0.18	0.17

***$p < .01$; **$p < .05$; *$p < .1$

limits to a state with term limits.[29] Term limits also increase the likelihood that a state will have a pipeline for higher statewide and congressional offices for both Republican and Democratic women. However, term limits have less of an impact on runs for statewide and congressional offices than they do for the state senate. States with term limits have a 33.5 percent likelihood of having a pipeline for higher offices for Democratic women and a 25.2 percent likelihood of having a similar pipeline for Republican women. The chances of having a pipeline increase by 14 percentage points for Republican women and 20.3 percentage points for Democratic women moving from a state without term limits to a state with term limits.[30]

A state's level of professionalization negatively impacts the development of a pipeline for state senate for Republican women, but it has no effect on the pipeline for Democratic women. Legislative professionalization does not impact the pipeline for higher levels of offices for Republican or Democratic women. States with a part-time legislature have only a 9.4 percent chance of having a state senate pipeline for Republican women. This is almost 10 percentage points less than state with a full-time legislature (19.1%).[31]

The strength of a state's party organization also impacts the pipeline for higher office, but it only affects the pipeline for statewide and congressional office. This makes sense, as states with strong party organizations are defined as those that use a statewide nominating convention to choose candidates for these offices. States with strong party organizations are much less likely to have a pipeline for higher office than states with weak party organizations. This effect is more pronounced for Republican women than Democratic women. In states with strong party organizations, the likelihood of having a pipeline for statewide offices for Democratic women is 4 percent. For Republican women, the chances of having a pipeline for these higher offices in states with strong party organizations drops to 2 percent. For women in both parties, this is 9.2 percentage points lower than states with weak party organizations.[32] Term limits mitigates this effect somewhat for Democratic women, but not for Republican women. In states with term limits and a strong party organization, the chances that a Democratic pipeline will exist are 12.8 percent. The chances that a Republican pipeline will exist given these characteristics is only 5.2 percent.

In addition, several of the control variables included in the models impact the likelihood that a state will have a pipeline for women. The level of turnover in the state senate positively affects whether a state will have a pipeline for Republican and Democratic women. States where senate turnover is one standard deviation above the mean increase their likelihood of having a pipeline for Democratic women by 20 percentage points (37.7% compared to 57%). This effect is slightly less for states with term limits. In term-limited states, increasing the turnover in the state senate by one standard deviation above the mean increases the chance of having a pipeline for Democratic women by 14.6 percentage points.[33] State senate turnover also has an impact on the likelihood that a state will have a political pipeline for its Republican women. A one standard deviation increase in state senate turnover increases the chances that a Republican pipeline will exist from 19.1 percent to 25.2 percent, a 6.1 percentage point increase.[34] In the models for the pipeline for statewide and congressional offices, state senate turnover only impacts the pipeline for Republican women. There is no relationship between state senate turnover and the pipeline measure for Democratic women. State senate turnover decreases the pipeline measure for Republican women, indicating that state senate offices may be more appealing to Republican women than higher statewide offices. Increasing state senate turnover by one standard deviation above the mean decreases the pipeline for statewide and congressional offices for Republican women by 4.7 percentage points (11.2% to 6.5%).[35]

Likewise, redistricting has an effect on the development of a pipeline for Republican women, but not Democratic women. States are more likely to have pipelines for state senate and for statewide and congressional offices for Republican women in elections following redistricting. The magnitude of this effect is especially pronounced for the state senate. In elections following redistricting, the likelihood that a state will have a pipeline for Republican women increases by 23.9 percentage points (19.1% to 43%). The chances of having a Republican pipeline for statewide and congressional offices also increases in elections following redistricting, jumping from 11.2 percent to 25.1 percent.[36]

There is no relationship between the percentage of the vote for the Republican presidential candidate and the likelihood that a state has a pipeline for Republican women. The coefficients on these variables fail to reach conventional levels of statistical significance. However, a pipeline for Democratic women is less likely to develop in states with strong support for the Republican presidential candidate. States where the Republican presidential vote is one standard deviation above the mean have only a 29.4 percent likelihood that a pipeline for state senate will exist. A similar effect is found for the pipeline for higher levels of office. In states where support for the Republican presidential candidate is one standard deviation above the mean, the chance of a pipeline for higher office drops to 8.2 percent.[37]

CONCLUSION

This study finds that Republican women and Democratic women lower house members have substantially different career paths, even after taking into account institutional and state-level factors. Overall, few states have political pipelines for either Republican or Democratic female legislators, but more states have functioning pipelines for Democratic women than Republican women. This means that Democratic women lawmakers are more likely to run, and win, higher levels of office than Republican women. In addition, the factors that facilitate the development of a pipeline for higher office differ for Republican and Democratic women. Both Republican and Democratic women legislators run for state senate and higher statewide offices in states with term limits, but term limits encourage progressive ambition more so in Democratic women than Republican women. This is likely due to the Democratic Party's greater focus on recruiting women for higher office. In addition, higher state senate turnover encourages both more Republican and Democratic women in the lower house to run for state senate, although turnover levels have a smaller influence on runs for statewide and congressional offices. The strength of a state's party organization depresses women's progressive ambition for statewide elective office for both parties. However, legislative professionalization negatively impacts Republican women but not Democratic women, while elections following redistricting and states with two-year senate terms see more Republican women run for higher office but not Democratic women.

While past research on women's representation has argued that the key to increasing the number of women in higher office rests on increasing women's presence in lower-tiered offices, the findings here call this claim into question, at least for Republican women. States where Republican women are more likely to hold office are also those states where women are less likely to run for higher office. There is a gap between the supply of strong Republican women candidates and a pipeline for moving them to higher office. In the sample of states examined here, Republican women averaged more than 45 percent of the entire female membership in 15 states. However, those states that have the highest percentages of Republican women also have low pipeline measures for Republican women. In 5 of these states, there is no pipeline for Republican women in any of the elections in the sample, and 6 states have a pipeline for Republican women in only one of the four elections. States with large contingents of Republican women also tend to have less professionalized legislatures. Of those states with the highest percentage of Republican women, only three have highly professionalized state legislatures (Florida, Pennsylvania, and Wisconsin).

If Republican women are going to increase their numbers in statewide and congressional offices, they need to increase their presence in those legislatures that act as springboards for higher office. While Republican women have had success winning state legislative seats in such places as Idaho, South Dakota, and Delaware, service in these state legislatures rarely acts as a stepping-stone to more prestigious offices. In part, the reason for this is that the opportunity structure in these states is highly constricted. Delaware and South Dakota only have one congressional district, while Idaho has two. The options for higher offices to run for are limited for women who serve in these state legislatures, regardless of their party affiliation. In contrast, a large state such as California has 53 congressional districts that lower house members can run for. However, on average, only 22.2 percent of its women members are Republicans. Republican women will never break the glass ceiling if they continue serving in state legislatures that are essentially dead-end jobs.

APPENDIX

Data and Sources

Information on state legislative career patterns was obtained from membership rosters published annually by the Council of State Governments. From these rosters, I identified those members who were successfully reelected to office and those who left their current office at the end of the legislative session. For each legislator who left office, the reason for their exit was coded: defeated in the primary or general election, ran for higher office, ran for lower office, retired, term-limited, or died in office. Information on a member's reason for leaving office was obtained from state election results and local newspapers. In total, 16,936 career moves for legislators in 41 states from 2002 to 2008 were coded. States with four-year terms for their state house members were excluded because there are fewer opportunities to observe the career decisions of members in these bodies. New Hampshire and Vermont were excluded from this study due to the difficulty of determining why legislators in these states left office. Nebraska is excluded because of its unicameral legislature.

Estimation of Pipeline Measures

A state's pipeline measure for Republican (Democratic) women in the lower house is found by dividing the number of Republican (Democratic) women who ran for higher office that election year by the total number of Republican (Democratic) women in the lower house. Using the number of Republican (Democratic) women in the lower house as the denominator for this measure allows us to gauge how ambitious Republican (Democratic) women are as a group within that state. Measuring ambition in this way most closely resembles the idea of a pipeline.

Model Specification

To account for the presence of legislative term limits, a variable is coded 1 for states that have term limits and 0 for those that do not. Currently, 15 states have imposed legislative term limits on members of the house and state senate. To control for legislative professionalization, a variable is coded 1 if a state has a part-time legislature and 0 otherwise. States are classified as having a part-time legislature if the time that legislators spend doing legislative work—including time in session, committee work, and constituency service—is approximately half (or less) of a full-time job. Of the states examined here, 11 have part-time legislatures. The strength of a state's party organization is measured by whether political parties use a state convention to nominate candidates for statewide offices. In states with nominating conventions, the parties have a greater opportunity to play a gatekeeping function, screening potential candidates for office. Eleven states in the sample utilize state nominating conventions for statewide offices.

In addition, this model controls for several other variables that are expected to impact a legislator's career path, although I do not expect them to have differential effects for Republican and Democratic women. The type of ambition that a legislator displays is shaped by her state's opportunity structure. A state's opportunity structure refers to the number of available offices a legislator can run for or "the proliferation of outlets for political ambition."[38] States with many seats in their state senate and congressional delegation afford members a greater chance of winning higher office than states with fewer seats and more competition for these seats. A state's seat ratio measures the extent of its opportunity structure. This is found by dividing the number of seats in the state lower house by the number of state senate and congressional seats in each state. To minimize the large differences that exist across states on this measure, I use the nature log of this variable in the model (Powell 2000).[39] States with larger seat ratios have pipelines that narrow more rapidly than states with lower seat ratios.

Another variable that captures the opportunities for advancement up the political pipeline is the level of turnover in the state senate. States with high levels of turnover in their state senate have more open seat races and greater opportunities for women to advance up the political pipeline. Levels of state senate turnover were obtained from the *Book of the States*. To account for the political character of each state, the percentage of the Republican vote won in the state by the previous presidential candidate is included. Finally, a variable is included that indicates whether the state has a two-year term for members of the state senate and whether the election followed a redistricting year. Separate models are estimated for Republican and Democratic women and for state senate runs and all other higher office runs. Models are estimated using logistical regression with clustered standard errors.

NOTES

1. Susan J. Carroll and Kira Sanbonmatsu, *More Women Can Run: Gender and Pathways to the State Legislature* (New York: Oxford, 2013); R. Darcy, Susan Welch, and Janet Clark, *Women, Elections, and Representation* (Lincoln: Nebraska

University Press, 1994); Jeanne J. Kirkpatrick, *Political Women* (New York: Basic Books, 1974); Jennifer L. Lawless and Richard L. Fox, *It Still Takes a Candidate: Why Women Don't Run for Office* (New York: Cambridge University Press, 2010).

2. Darcy, Welch, and Clark, *Women Elections and Representation*, 119.

3. Linda L. Fowler and Robert McClure, *Political Ambition* (New Haven: Yale University Press, 1989); Cherie D. Maestas, Sarah Fulton, Sandy Maisel, and Walter J. Stone, "When to Risk It? Institutions, Ambitions, and the Decision to Run for the U.S. House," *American Political Science Review* 100, no 2 (2006) 195–208.

4. Barbara Palmer and Dennis Simon, "Political Ambition and Women in the U.S. House of Representatives, 1916–2000," *Political Research Quarterly* 56, no. 2 (2003): 127–138.

5. Georgia Duerst-Lahti, "The Bottleneck: Women as Candidates," in *Women and Elective Office*, eds. Sue Thomas and Calvin Wilcox (New York: Oxford University Press, 1998), 15–25; Susan J. Carroll, *Women as Candidates in American Politics*, 2nd ed. (Bloomington: Indiana University Press, 1994).

6. Stephen J. Stambough and Valerie R. O'Regan, "Republican Lambs and the Democratic Pipeline: Partisan Differences in the Nomination of Female Gubernatorial Candidates," *Politics & Gender* 3, no. 3 (2007): 349–368.

7. Richard L. Fox and Jennifer L. Lawless, "Gendered Perceptions and Political Candidacies: A Central Barrier to Women's Equality in Electoral Politics," *American Journal of Political Science* 55, no.1 (2011): 59–73; Lawless and Fox, *It Still Takes a Candidate*; Palmer and Simon, "Political Ambition and Women in the U.S. House"; Barbara Palmer and Dennis Simon, *Breaking the Political Glass Ceiling: Women and Congressional Elections* (New York: Routledge, 2006); Kira Sanbonmatsu, "Do Parties Know That 'Women Win'? Party Leader Beliefs about Women's Electoral Chances," *Politics & Gender* 2, no. 4 (2006): 431–450.

8. Joseph A. Schlesinger, *Ambition and Politics: Political Careers in the United States* (Chicago: Rand Nally, 1966).

9. Hibbing, *Congressional Careers*; Schlesinger, *Ambition and Politics*; Peverill Squire, "Career Opportunities and Membership Stability in Legislatures," *Legislative Studies Quarterly* 17, no.1 (1988): 211–227; Squire, "Legislative Professionalization and Membership Diversity."

10. Susan J. Carroll, "Political Elites and Sex Differences in Political Ambition: A Reconsideration," *Journal of Politics* 47, no.4 (1985): 123–143.

11. Fox and Lawless, "It Still Takes a Candidate"; Fulton et al., "Sense of a Woman"; Maestas et al., "When to Risk It?"; Mariani, "A Gendered Pipeline?"; Palmer and Simon, "Political Ambition and Women in the U.S. House of Representatives"; Palmer and Simon, *Breaking the Political Glass Ceiling*.

12. Michael Berkman, "Former State Legislators in the U.S. House of Representatives: Institutional and Policy Master," *Legislative Studies Quarterly* 18, no.1 (1993): 77–104; Michael Berkman and James Eisensetin, "State Legislators

as Congressional Candidates: The Effects of Prior Experience on Legislative Recruitment and Fundraising," *Political Research Quarterly* 52, no.3 (1999): 481–498; Maestas et al, "When to Risk It?"

13. Paul Herrnson, "Campaign Professionalism and Fund-Raising in Congressional Election," *Journal of Politics* 54, no.3 (1992): 859–870; Robert E. Hogan, "Campaign War Chests and Challenger Emergence in State Legislative Elections," *Political Research Quarterly* 54, no.4 (2001): 815–830; Cherie D. Maestas and Cynthia Rugeley, "Assessing the 'Experience Bonus' through Examining Strategic Entry, Candidate Quality, and Campaign Receipts in U.S. House Elections," *American Journal of Political Science* 52, no. 3 (2008): 520–535; Peverill Squire and John R. Wright, "Fundraising by Nonincumbent Candidates for the U.S. House of Representatives," *Legislative Studies Quarterly* 15, no. 1 (1990): 89–98.

14. Gary W. Cox and Scott Morgenstern, "The Increasing Advantage of Incumbency in the U.S. States, "*Legislative Studies Quarterly* 18, no. 4 (1993): 494–514; John M. Carey, Richard G. Niemi, and Lynda W. Powell, "Incumbency and the Probability of Reelection in State Legislative Elections," *Journal of Politics* 62, no. 3 (2000): 671–700; Robert E. Hogan, "Challenger Emergence, Incumbent Success, and Electoral Accountability in State Legislative Elections," *Journal of Politics* 66, no. 4 (2004): 1283–1303.

15. O. G. Abbe and Paul Hernnson, "Campaign Professionalism in State Legislative Elections," *State Politics & Policy Quarterly* 3, no. 3 (2003): 223–245.

16. Carroll and Sanbonmatsu, *More Women Can Run.*

17. Debra L. Dodson, "Change and Continuity in the Relationship between Private Responsibilities and Public Officeholding: The More Things Change, the More They Stay the Same," *Policy Studies Journal* 25, no. 4 (1997): 569–584.

18. Melody Crowder-Meyer and Benjamin E. Lauderdale, "A Partisan Gap in the Supply of Female Potential Candidates in the United States," *Research & Politics* 1, no. 1 (2014): 1–7.

19. Carey, Niemi, and Powell, "The Effects of Term Limits"; H. W. Jerome Maddox, "Opportunity Costs and Outside Careers in U.S. State Legislatures," *Legislative Studies Quarterly* 29, no. 4 (2004): 517–544.

20. Fox and Lawless, *It Still Takes a Candidate*; Kira Sanbonmatsu, "Gender Stereotypes and Vote Choice," *American Journal of Political Science* 46, no. 1 (2002): 20–34; Sanbonmatsu "Do Parties Know"; Maestas et al. "When to Risk It?"

21. Melody Crowder-Meyer, "Gendered Recruitment without Trying: How Local Party Recruiters Affect Women's Representation," *Politics & Gender* 9, no. 4 (2013): 390–413.

22. Danielle M. Thomsen, "Ideological Moderates Won't Run: How Party Fit Matters for Partisan Polarization in Congress," *Journal of Politics* 76, no. 3 (2014): 786–797; Carroll and Sanbonmatsu, *More Women Can Run*; Kathryn Pearson and Eric McGhee, "What It Takes to Win: Questioning 'Gender Neutral' Outcomes in U.S. House Elections," *Politics & Gender* 9, no. 4 (2013): 439–462.

23. Brian Frederick, "Gender and Patterns of Roll Call Voting in the U.S. Senate," *Congress & the Presidency* 37, no. 2 (2010): 103–124; Sarah Poggione, "Exploring Gender Differences in State Legislators' Policy Preferences," *Political Research Quarterly* 57, no. 2 (2004): 305–314.

24. David C. King and Richard E. Matland, "Sex and the Grand Old Party: An Experimental Investigation of the Effect of Candidate Sex on Support for a Republican Candidate," *American Politics Research* 31, no. 6 (2003): 595–612; Kira Sanbonmatsu and Kathleen Dolan, "Do Gender Stereotypes Transcend Party?," *Political Research Quarterly* 62, no. 3 (2009): 485–494.

25. Jeffrey Lazarus, "Term Limits' Multiple Effects on State Legislators' Career Decisions," *State Politics & Policy Quarterly* 6, no. 4 (2006): 357–383; Richard J. Powell, "The Impact of Term Limits on the Candidacy Decisions of State Legislators in U.S. House Elections," *Legislative Studies Quarterly* 25, no. 4 (2000): 645–661; Jennifer A. Steen, "The Impact of State Legislative Term Limits on the Supply of Congressional Candidates," *State Politics & Policy Quarterly* 6, no. 4 (2006): 430–447.

26. John M. Carey, Richard G. Niemi, Lynda W. Powell, and Gary Moncrief, "The Effects of Term Limits on State Legislatures: A New Survey of the 50 States," *Legislative Studies Quarterly* 31, no. 1 (2006): 105–134; Rebekah Herrick and Sue Thomas, "Do Term Limits Make a Difference? Ambition and Motivations among U.S. State Legislators," *American Politics Research* 33, no. 5 (2005): 726–747.

27. Sanbonmatsu, "Do Parties Know."

28. David Niven, "Party Elites and Women Candidates: The Shape of Bias," *Women and Politics* 16, no. 2 (1998): 97–107; Marjorie Sarbaugh-Thompson, Lyke Thompson, Charles D. Elder, John Strate, and Richard C. Elling, *Political and Institutional Effects of Term Limits* (New York: Palgrave Macmillan, 2004).

29. The coefficients on this variable are significant at the 99 percent level in both models.

30. The coefficients on this variable are significant at the 90 percent level in the model for Republican women and the 99 percent level in the model for Democratic women.

31. The coefficient on this variable is significant at the 90 percent level.

32. The coefficient on this variable is significant at the 95 percent level in the model for Democratic women and the 99 percent level in the model for Republican women.

33. The coefficient on this variable is significant at the 99 percent level.

34. The coefficient on this variable is significant at the 90 percent level.

35. The coefficient on this variable is significant at the 90 percent level.

36. The coefficient on this variable is significant at the 99 percent level and 90 percent level, respectively.

37. The coefficients on this variable are statistically significant at the 90 percent and the 95 percent level, respectively.

38. Alan Rosenthal, "State Legislative Reform: Determinants and Policy Consequences," *American Politics Quarterly* 7, no. 1 (1974): 51–70; Squire, "Career Opportunities."

39. Richard J. Powell, "The Impact of Term Limits on the Candidacy Decisions of State Legislators in U.S. House Elections," *Legislative Studies Quarterly* 25, no. 4 (2000): 645–661.

PART 4

Congresswomen

How do elected women discuss and legislate on women's issues? Much existing literature looks at this question by comparing women to men, tacitly assuming (or empirically testing) that women as a group will behave in a certain way. The chapters in this section assume instead that Republican women face different pressures than Democratic women in regard to speech and action on policy issues relating to women, gender, feminism, and reproduction.

In chapter 10, Michele L. Swers looks at the changing gender composition of Congress since the 1990s, analyzing the specific role of Republican women in debates over major policy issues, including family and medical leave, welfare reform, equal pay, violence against women, and abortion. The positions they take on these issues, she writes, are impacted by a series of key factors, including party polarization, ideology, constituent pressure, the expressed position and agenda of the president, and whether Republicans have control of the chamber under study. Increasingly, she finds, the GOP has called upon its female congress members and senators to rebut charges that the party is "antiwomen," and a growing conservative contingent of Republican women are ready and willing to serve such a partisan role, particularly on abortion.

Similarly, in chapter 11, Christina Xydias wonders whether Republican women in the U.S. House stick to their party's "script" or diverge from it in speaking out on issues of women's rights and interests. Xydias takes a different methodological approach, focusing deeply on the words of GOP female members' speeches in the 113th Congress (2013–2014) and using an innovative quantitative research design to determine what the party script was for that term and how closely Republican women followed it. Overall, she finds, the party ideology dominated; women elected to the House as Republicans in that term did not diverge from their party's positions on women's issues.

CHAPTER 10

From the Republican Revolution to the Tea Party Wave: Republican Women and the Politics of Women's Issues

Michele L. Swers

From the moment it was signed into law, Republicans have made repealing and replacing the Affordable Care Act (Obamacare), President Obama's expansive health insurance reform, a top policy goal. They rode this promise to a historic takeover of the congressional majority in 2010 and continued to rail against the law in the 2012, 2014, and 2016 elections. President Trump strongly denounced the law throughout his campaign and made repeal and replace his first domestic policy priority when he came to office. With Democrats unified in their support of the law, Republicans would have to rely entirely on their own ranks to pass a bill. Moving from campaign promise to policy became exceptionally difficult as policy disagreements emerged among different factions of the party and constituents who gained insurance from the program mobilized to protect their benefits.[1] Raucous town halls in which angry constituents accused representatives of taking away their health care and jeopardizing their lives made for viral videos, raising the stakes of the debate.[2]

After the House finally passed a bill, Senate Republicans immediately rejected it in favor of starting from scratch and crafting their own bill. Senate majority leader Mitch McConnell (R-KY) appointed a 13-member working group that would bring together hard-line conservatives, such as 2016 presidential candidate Ted Cruz (R-TX), with more moderate Republicans, such as Rob Portman (R-OH), whose state had expanded

Medicaid and was concerned about protecting the health benefits of these constituents.[3] One group that was conspicuously absent from the appointed panel was Republican women. Immediately, the media questioned why no women were included in a working group that would decide the contours of insurance regulations regarding maternity care and other women's health issues. Democratic senators piled on. California Democrat Kamala Harris tweeted, "The GOP is crafting policy on an issue that directly impacts women without including a single woman in the process. It's wrong."[4]

Throughout the development of the Affordable Care Act, Democratic women had played a pivotal role as advocates for women's health needs. Democratic women made sure that women could not be charged more than men, and pregnancy, contraception, and maternity care were included among the essential health benefits that insurance plans must cover.[5] As of this writing, Republicans are committed to dismantling Obamacare and creating a new system. Will gender-based considerations impact how Republican women approach reform? Will Republican women focus on how proposals impact various groups of women? Will they try to protect provisions of Obamacare that benefit women or seek to maintain coverage for vulnerable populations, such as low-income children or people with preexisting conditions? Alternatively, will Republican women prioritize conservative principles and seek to lower costs of insurance and reduce the federal government's role in guaranteeing health care coverage?

In this chapter, I examine how Republican women have approached legislation dealing with women's issues since the early 1990s and trace the advancement of Republican women into Congress. Over the past 25 years, as more women are elected to Congress, the number of Republican women has lagged behind the representation of women in the Democratic Party. Additionally, the ideological makeup of Republican women has changed as moderate Republican women hailing from the Northeast and Midwest were increasingly replaced by more conservative women from the South and West. Given these electoral dynamics, I analyze the role of Republican women in long-standing debates over women's issues, including family and medical leave, welfare reform, equal pay, violence against women, and the most frequently debated women's issue in Congress, abortion.

My analysis shows that the positions Republican women have taken on women's issues are influenced by many factors, including their own ideology, constituent interests, whether the women are serving in the majority or minority party, and the partisanship and agenda of the president. The decision to engage women's issues is also impacted by increasing partisan polarization and the emergence of women's issues as a central focus of party conflict. As a result, Republican women are increasingly called on to defend their party against Democratic accusations that the Republican Party is harmful to women and their families.

I find that, over time, moderate Republican women have advocated for women's rights and the advancement of policies protecting women, children, and families. However, these moderate Republican women are careful to balance their policy views against the imperative to protect their party. Thus, they try to avoid alienating fellow party members who oppose their stances on women's issues and refrain from making statements that could bolster Democratic arguments that the Republican Party does not support women's rights. Meanwhile, conservative women vary in their approach to women's issues. Some conservative women ignore these issues, preferring to focus on policies more central to the Republican Party, such as reducing regulations or cutting taxes. Since the Tea Party wave of 2010, more conservative women are entering Congress and looking to champion socially conservative positions on women's issues, particularly abortion. These women both embrace the call to serve as defenders of the party against Democratic attacks and seek leadership roles in drafting and implementing policies to restrict abortion.

WHY SO FEW REPUBLICAN WOMEN IN CONGRESS?

A significant obstacle to Republican women's institutional power is their small numbers in Congress. When majority leader Mitch McConnell (R-KY) was putting together the working group on health care reform, there were only five Republican women serving in the Senate. To date, women remain dramatically underrepresented in Congress, constituting only 19 percent of the members in the House of Representatives and 21 percent of the Senate.[6] However, there is a dramatic partisan gap in women's representation. In the current 115th Congress (2017–2018), Democratic women make up one-third of their party caucuses in the House and Senate. Democratic women have leveraged their numbers and seniority to earn leadership positions within the party and the committee system, most notably the election of Nancy Pelosi (D-CA) as Speaker of the House (2007–2010) and current minority leader. By contrast, just under 10 percent of Republican members in the House and Senate are women.[7] Most of the Republican women serving in Congress were elected after 2010, limiting their influence in an institution where seniority strongly influences advancement to positions of power on committees.

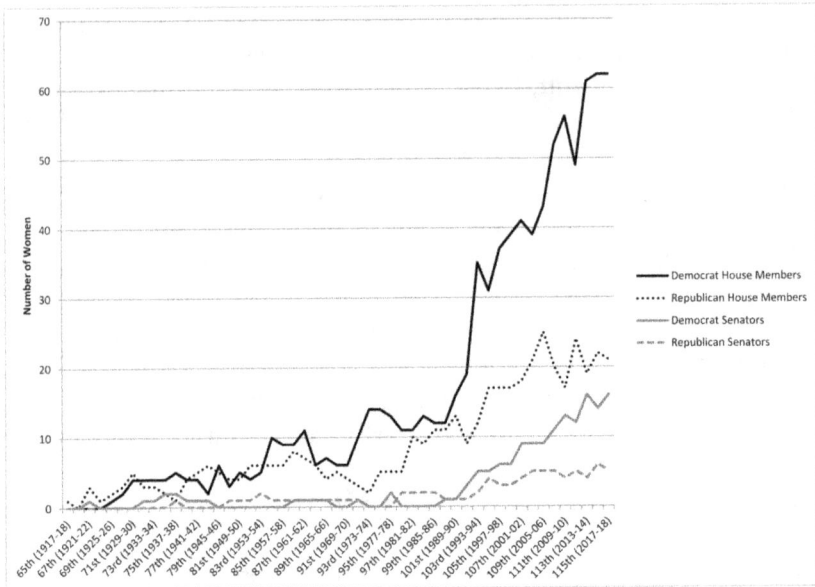

Figure 10.1   Women in the House and Senate by Party, 1917–2018

Source: Center for American Women and Politics (CAWP). "History of Women in the U.S. Congress." http://www.cawp.rutgers.edu/history-women-us-congress.

The partisan gap in women's representation emerged in the early 1990s and continues to grow. Figure 10.1 tracks the number of women in Congress over time. Prior to the 1970s, only a handful of women had served in Congress. Many of these women were widows of members that had been urged to run to keep the seat in party control until party leaders could coalesce around a candidate. By the 1970s, the feminist movement had opened more of the careers that lead to politics to women, and women were gaining political skills in grassroots movements for civil rights, anti–Vietnam War, and women's rights. At this point, a small partisan gap opened with more Democratic women elected to the House of Representatives than Republican women.[8] Thus, the 93rd Congress (1973–1974) included 14 Democratic women and only 2 Republican women in the House. With the election of Republican president Ronald Reagan in 1980, more Republican women were elected, and there were largely equal numbers of Republican and Democratic women in Congress.[9]

This trajectory of relatively equal partisan representation of women radically changed after the 1992 elections. Dubbed the "Year of the Woman," the election still embodies the largest increase in women's representation in a single election as the number of women in Congress jumped from 32 to 54. However, most of the growth came on the Democratic side, as the number of Democratic women in Congress increased from 24 to 40 while there were only four new Republican women increasing their representation from 10 to 14.[10]

Since 1992, the number of Democratic women has grown steadily while the representation of Republican women remains stagnant. Even after the 1994 Republican Revolution and the 2010 Tea Party wave elections that propelled Republicans to the majority, representation of Republican women only marginally increased.[11] The anemic growth in Republican women's representation is partially explained by the evolution of the party's electoral coalitions in which the Republican Party has become increasingly conservative with its strongholds in the South and West and a large presence of social conservatives among its base voters and activists. As a result, there is no natural constituency of donors and voters within the Republican Party that is responsive to explicit calls to expand women's representation. Instead, today's Republican women need to be strong conservatives who can appeal to an increasingly conservative primary electorate of social conservatives, Tea Party activists, business conservatives, and libertarians.[12]

WOMEN AND PARTY POLARIZATION

The history of women's incorporation into Congress described above coincided with the polarization of Congress into a more strongly liberal Democratic caucus and a more uniformly conservative Republican caucus. The newly elected Democratic women followed the trend of increased liberalism among Democrats. However, the Republican women in the House were more moderate than their male colleagues through the early 2000s. However, contemporary Republican congresswoman are just as conservative as their male counterparts. By contrast, female Republican senators continue to be more moderate than their male colleagues (for an in-depth discussion on ideological polarization, see chapter 4).

Throughout the 1970s and 1980s, the House and Senate had included a significant number of conservative Democrats hailing from Southern states and moderate Republicans from the Northeast and Midwest. As the South realigned to the Republican Party, Southern Democratic members were defeated and replaced with even more conservative Republicans. In the Northeast, moderate Republicans who were socially moderate and fiscally conservative lost their seats to more uniformly liberal Democrats.[13] Reflecting the polarization of the parties, analyses of congressional voting showed that the policy preferences of members in the two parties were drifting sharply apart. Using a measure that scales all votes cast in a congressional session, Poole and Rosenthal increasingly found that more than

90 percent of voting in Congress can be explained by a single liberal-conservative dimension.[14]

Analyzing the Poole-Rosenthal DW-NOMINATE ideology scores, Frederick found some unique patterns in the evolution of the voting behavior of women in Congress, particularly Republican women.[15] To illustrate the trends in Democratic and Republican women's voting, I plot the mean ideology scores for Democratic and Republican men and women from the 103rd–113th Congresses. The timeline begins with the 103rd Congress, which followed the Year of the Woman election. This election marked the most significant increase in the advancement of women to Congress and initiated the current partisan gap in women's representation. As of this writing, the 113th Congress (2013–2014) is the most recent Congress for which the ideology scores are available. To compare the voting behavior of Democratic and Republican men and women in the House and Senate, I use the DW-NOMINATE Common Space Scores. These scores allow comparisons across both time and chambers of Congress. The scores range from –1, indicating most liberal, to +1, the most conservative.[16] Figure 10.2 shows the ideology scores for the House of Representatives, and Figure 10.3 captures the ideology scores for senators.

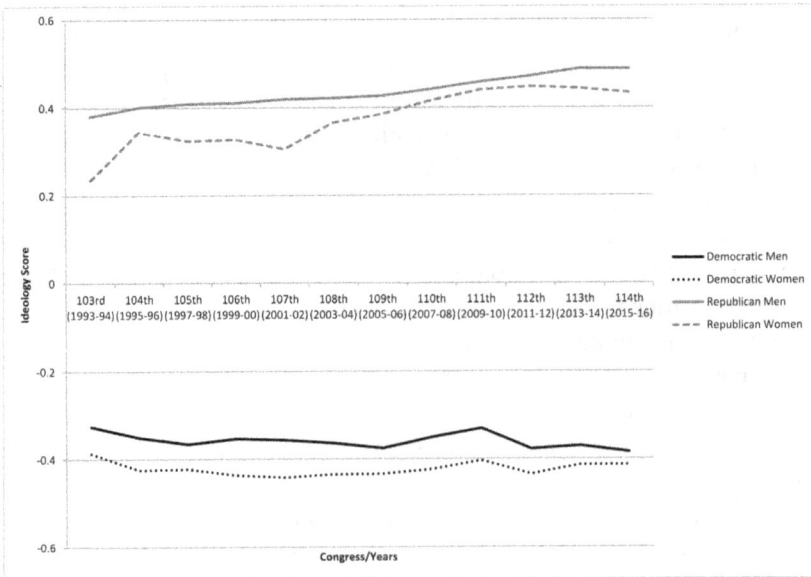

Figure 10.2 House DW-NOMINATE Common Space Ideology Scores by Gender and Party, 1993–2016

Source: "Realtime NOMINATE Ideology and Related Data." https://voteview.com/data.

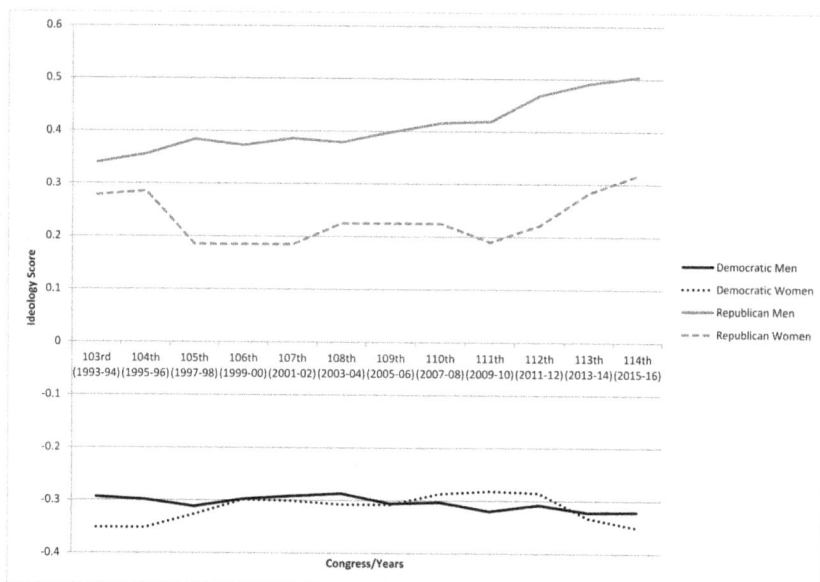

Figure 10.3   Senate DW-NOMINATE Common Space Ideology Scores by Gender and Party, 1993–2016
Source: "Realtime NOMINATE Ideology and Related Data." https://voteview.com/data.

Looking at Democrats, the lines representing male and female Democrats in the Senate largely overlap, indicating that there are no gender differences in the voting behavior of Democratic senators. However, female Democrats in the House are consistently more liberal than their male counterparts. Frederick finds that this is because, on average, female Democrats are elected from more liberal districts than male Democrats.[17] Indeed, many of the women in the current Democratic delegation hail from liberal urban centers in New York and California, and a significant number are African American and Hispanic women elected from majority-minority districts.

While the ideological trends in the voting behavior of Democratic men and women are largely similar, the conservatism of Republican women has lagged that of Republican men. In the House, Frederick found that the small contingent of Republican women of the 1980s and early 1990s consistently voted more moderately than their male counterparts.[18] Indeed Figure 10.2 indicates that in the 103rd Congress (1993–1994), the mean common space ideology score for Republican women was 0.223, while the average ideological score for men was 0.339. The conservatism of Republican women jumped up in the 104th Congress, when the

1994 election known as the Republican Revolution brought Republicans back into the majority for the first time in 40 years and elected a new group of conservative men and women. However, Republican women as a group remained more moderate than Republican men. The voting behavior of Republican men and women finally converged in the 108th Congress (2003–2004), and Republican women in the House are now just as conservative as Republican men. The strength of this conservatism is notable because Republicans as a group are currently more ideologically extreme than Democrats. In the 113th Congress, the average Republican ideology score was 0.435, while the mean Democratic ideology score was –0.307. The current conservatism of Republican women in the House has changed the dynamics of how Republican women approach policy making on women's issues.

In contrast to Republican women in the House, Figure 10.3 shows that the small contingent of Republican women in the Senate remains markedly less conservative than their male counterparts. Since 1993, the number of Republican women in the Senate has remained small, ranging from two Republican women in the 103rd Congress (1993–1994) to a high of six Republican women in the 114th Congress (2015–2016). As in the House, the women who were first elected in the early 1990s, such as Susan Collins (R-ME) and Olympia Snowe (R-ME), are more moderate than more recently elected women. However, even the more conservative women still lag their male counterparts. In the 113th Congress, freshman senator Deb Fischer (R-NE), who was endorsed by the Tea Party and Sarah Palin, is the most conservative female senator. Still, her vote score, 0.378, places her just above the party mean of 0.364.

Although there are still no female equivalents to conservative stalwarts Ted Cruz (R-TX) and Mike Lee (R-UT), we should expect that future female Republican senators will be more conservative. The strongly conservative character of Republican women in the House and the more moderate leanings of female Republican senators have shaped the dynamics of recent policy debates on women's issues, with female House members championing strongly conservative proposals and more moderate female senators crossing the aisle to support Democratic initiatives on women's rights or trying to moderate conservative House bills.

WOMEN'S ISSUES AND THE PARTY WARS

As the parties pulled apart, the rising importance of feminist and pro-choice groups in the Democratic Party and social conservatives in the Republican coalition made women's issues, from equal pay to abortion, a central fault line in the party wars. Democratic women play a key role in advancing women's issues and reaching out to female voters. Meanwhile, the role of Republican women in these party conflicts over women's rights has evolved as more conservative women are elected.

For Democratic women, the alignment of their policy priorities with the electoral interests of the party has made them among the most aggressive advocates for policies related to women, children, and families. In the early 1990s, Democratic women spearheaded efforts to pass the Family and Medical Leave Act (FMLA), open an Office of Women's Health at NIH, increase funding for women's health, and pass a comprehensive bill to combat violence against women. These policies helped define the Democratic Party's reputation as the party of women's rights, and the party utilizes Democratic women to mobilize activists and donors and appeal to women voters, particularly college-educated women, single women, and minority women.[19]

Nancy Pelosi's elevation to Speaker in 2006 highlighted the leadership of women in the Democratic Party. In addition to Pelosi, many of the women who were elected in the early 1990s had earned enough seniority to achieve committee and subcommittee chairmanships in the House and Senate. These women aggressively pursued policies related to women's rights. With the election of Barack Obama as president, Democratic women played key roles in passing the Lilly Ledbetter Fair Pay Act and shaping Obamacare to incorporate women's health concerns, such as inclusion of free contraception and coverage of pregnancy in all basic insurance benefits packages.[20]

While touting the party's commitment to women, Democrats also use Republican efforts to block these initiatives as primary evidence that Republicans threaten the well-being of women and their families. Female Democrats serve as primary spokespersons for these party attacks. In 2012, with Pelosi as minority leader, Debbie Wasserman-Schultz (D-FL) as chair of the Democratic National Committee, and Patty Murray (D-WA) heading the Democratic Senatorial Campaign Committee, the Democrats pushed a message that Republicans were engaged in a "war on women." Democrats highlighted Republican opposition to equal pay legislation and suggested that Republicans would harm women's health by denying women access to contraception through Obamacare. The message contributed to President Obama's reelection victory and the election of more Democratic women to the Senate.[21] Democrats continued to hammer Republican policies and candidates as antiwomen throughout the 2014 midterms and the 2016 presidential election, working to draw a contrast between Hillary Clinton's record on women's rights and Donald Trump's misogynistic behavior. As congressional Republicans work to defund Planned Parenthood and include provisions in their Obamacare repeal that would loosen protections for women's health, Democratic women are among the most vocal opponents of these policies.[22]

REPUBLICAN WOMEN ADAPTING TO THE PARTY CONFLICT ON WOMEN'S ISSUES

Since the 1990s, Democratic women have consistently championed women's issues. Their role in legislating and delivering the party message has grown as more women gain seniority and leadership roles within the committees and the party. By contrast, the positions of Republican women on women's issues and their involvement in party conflicts over these issues continue to evolve as more conservative women are elected and Republican women move between the minority and majority parties.

The election of Bill Clinton in 1992 gave Democrats unified control of the presidency and Congress after 12 years of Republican presidents. As minority party members in a Congress where Democrats had had a lock on the House majority since 1954, moderate Republican women cooperated with Democrats to advance legislation for women's issues. For example, Marge Roukema (R-NJ) was the most prominent Republican supporter of FMLA. She helped forge the compromises necessary to gain some Republican support, including reducing the number of businesses subject to the mandate by exempting those with fewer than 50 employees, rather than 15. She urged the Bush administration to support the legislation and spoke out publicly against President Bush's decision to veto the bill. Roukema's commitment to the legislation stemmed from her experiences as a mother who had left her job to take care of her teenage son, who later died of leukemia.[23] Similarly, Connie Morella (R-MD) was the lead Republican cosponsor of the Violence Against Women Act, a bill designed to reduce sexual assault against women by providing training to law enforcement and services to victims of abuse. The legislation had bipartisan support and originally passed the House with a unanimous vote. Along with Morella, Olympia Snowe (R-ME) and Jan Meyers (R-KS) were among the 8 Republicans who signed on as original cosponsors of the bill, and, ultimately, 7 of the 12 Republican women in the 103rd Congress cosponsored the legislation.[24]

When the 1994 election propelled Republicans to the majority, the political dynamics for Republican women dramatically changed. A new group of first-term women were markedly more conservative than the more senior women. The moderate women now had to balance their views on women's issues with their responsibility as majority party members to support the party. These women also wanted to capitalize on their newfound majority status to advance legislation on a range of issues and thus needed to be careful not to alienate the party leaders and fellow Republicans whose support they would need. Still confronting a Democratic president, Bill Clinton, one of the Republicans most significant initiatives in the 104th Congress was the passage of welfare reform. The bill strengthened work requirements and limited the number of years a person could receive welfare. Democrats objected to how these work requirements might impact the families of single women who did not have adequate child care. The Republican women with seats on the Ways and Means Committee that drafted the bill, Nancy Johnson (R-CT) and Jennifer Dunn (R-WA), convinced Republican leaders to increase child care subsidies, incorporate child support enforcement, and maintain Medicaid coverage for older children and women.[25]

Firmly in control of Congress, the parties also fought over social policy as Republicans pursued legislation to restrict abortion. To push back on these Republican policies, Democrats increasingly deployed their growing contingent of Democratic women. Drawing on their moral authority as women on the House and Senate floors, in press conferences, and media appearances, Democratic women denounced Republican policies as harmful to women and their families.[26]

To counter Democratic criticism, Republicans increasingly turned to their smaller cadre of Republican women. As one Republican staffer explained, Republican leaders will ask women to speak when they know the Democrats will have their women out to demagogue an issue. "By having women speak . . . they get women to put a smiley, soft face on issues and prevent Republicans from looking like mean ogres."[27] Some Republican women embraced the opportunity to defend the party, wanting to improve the party's outreach to women and collect favors that would translate into more power within the party caucus.

Their ability to reach women voters and soften the party's image helped several women earn leadership positions in the party conference, the entity responsible for crafting the party message. In fact, the two women who have served as House Republican Conference chair, Deborah Pryce (R-OH) (2003–2007) and current conference chair Cathy McMorris Rodgers (R-WA) (since 2013), both touted their desire to reach out to women voters and change the tone of the party message as part of the rationale for electing them. Both Pryce and McMorris Rodgers wanted to change the way Republicans talk to women voters, focusing more on personal stories and explaining how Republican policies respond to kitchen table concerns regarding the family budget. Each also sought to place stories about how Republican policies, from health care to taxes, help women voters and their families in women's magazines and on Web sites along with profiles that highlight the accomplishments of Republican women in Congress.[28]

MODERATES AND CONSERVATIVES NAVIGATING THE PARTISAN DIVIDE ON WOMEN'S ISSUES

Outside of leadership, the willingness of Republican women to serve as party spokespersons or to take leadership roles in legislative battles has varied with the ideology of the member and the nature of the issue. Moderate women who disagree with their party's position on abortion or equal pay generally vote their preferences while trying to limit their media profile so they do not hurt the party. Therefore, they do not participate in the media campaigns Democrats pursue against Republicans or speak out against their party on the floor.

Among conservative women, the desire to speak out as women on behalf of the party or to champion conservative positions on various women's issues continues to evolve. Outside of abortion, women's issues are not seen as Republican issues. Indeed, while they may believe that women bring a different perspective to the debate, many conservative Republican women do not embrace the concept of women's issues and prefer to focus on policies that are more central to the Republican brand and important to their constituents, such as cutting taxes and reducing regulations on business. Moreover, women's issues often draw intense scrutiny from activists, and the media focuses even more attention on the stands Republican women take on these issues. Seeing little benefit and potentially negative consequences to their engagement, for these conservative women, it is preferable to stay away from women's issues.[29] Thus, Swers found that, despite entreaties from Senate leadership, to date no Republican women have joined the Judiciary Committee because the committee is dominated by hot button social issues like abortion and is not a good platform for raising campaign money.[30]

While some conservative women do not recognize or prefer to avoid women's issues, there is a growing contingent of socially conservative women with experience pursuing pro-life policies in state legislatures and grassroots movements. The Tea Party wave of 2010 brought more of these women to Congress, particularly in the House. Committed to championing restrictions on abortion, these women are taking a greater leadership role in party conflicts over women's issues by sponsoring bills, headlining press conferences, and speaking out on the floor.

The recent debates over the Lilly Ledbetter Fair Pay Act and the renewal of the Violence Against Women Act illustrate the new dynamics of the party wars over women's rights. By prioritizing policies that expand women's rights, Democrats build enthusiasm with their base of women's groups and abortion rights supporters, expand their appeal to women voters, and undermine Republican support among women. Republicans aggressively pursue abortion restrictions, but they often find themselves playing defense on family planning and other women's rights policies. Moderate Republican women, particularly those in the Senate, try to balance their policy preferences on women's rights with their desire to support or at least avoid hurting the party. Conservative women vote with their party on these issues, and there is a subset of conservative women, largely in the House, who aggressively defend the party and champion socially conservative causes.[31]

Responding to the Supreme Court's 2007 ruling against Lilly Ledbetter's pay discrimination case, Democrats drafted legislation that would make it easier for women to file pay discrimination suits.[32] The issue came to a head during the 2008 presidential primary campaign in which Senators. John McCain (R-AZ), Hillary Clinton (D-NY), and Barack Obama (D-IL) were each pursuing their party's nomination. Controlling the majority in both the House and Senate, Democrats utilized the bill to paint Republicans as opposed to equal pay for women. Republicans and their business allies, such as the Chamber of Commerce, opposed the legislation, fearing that its provisions would subject companies to unlimited lawsuits and leave them open to liability years after alleged discrimination took place. To maximize the electoral impact, Senate Democrats put the bill on the floor on Equal Pay Day, the day marking how much longer women have to work into the next year to catch up to men's wages. Republicans blocked a vote on the substance of the bill by voting against cloture, a procedural vote required to allow debate and passage of legislation. Members are expected to vote with their party on procedural votes; yet, the moderate women, Susan Collins (R-ME) and Olympia Snowe (R-ME), were among six Republicans who voted for cloture. After the procedural vote to allow debate on the bill failed, the legislation became a campaign issue in the 2008 presidential race as Democrats pointed to the bill as evidence of their commitment to women's rights and Republicans' disregard for women's economic well-being.

After Obama won the presidency, the Ledbetter Act was the first bill Democrats brought to the floor. Wanting to avoid being portrayed as opposing equal pay for women, Republican Senate leaders decided to recruit a Republican woman to offer an alternative bill on the floor. Party leaders first turned to Lisa Murkowski (R-AK), who held a seat on the committee with jurisdiction over the bill, the Health, Education, Labor and Pensions Committee. Murkowski refused because she did not want to be associated with a controversial bill as she prepared for a tough reelection fight in 2010. Ultimately, Republican leaders recruited Kay Bailey Hutchison (R-TX) a long-time member of Republican leadership who had served as conference vice chair (2001–2007) and Policy Committee chair (2007–2008). She was also pursuing a primary challenge against the sitting Republican governor of Texas, Rick Perry, and this bill would help shore up her conservative credentials in the primary. Still, Hutchison told party leaders that if the alternative bill failed, she would vote for the Democratic bill because she and the other Republican women did not want to be portrayed as acting against women in the workplace.

Ultimately, only the four Republican women and Arlen Specter (R-PA), who would switch parties to become a Democrat later that year, voted for the Democratic bill. In trying to thread the needle between their policy preferences and party loyalty, Susan Collins, Lisa Murkowski, and Hutchison all voted for both the Republican alternative and the Democratic bill, and Murkowski also cosponsored Hutchison's alternative and spoke in favor of it on the floor.[33]

By contrast, the Republican women in the House steadfastly opposed the Ledbetter bill. Unlike the Senate, the majority party in the House has complete control of what bills are considered on the floor, and the Democrats did not allow Republicans to offer an alternative bill. In both 2007 and 2009, Republicans voted along party lines, with none of the Republican women supporting the legislation. When the bill was first debated in 2007, Republicans called on conservative women to defend the party by reassuring voters that, as women, they understand discrimination, but they oppose the bill because it is not about discrimination but instead would dangerously alter our system of legal liability. Five of the 10 Republicans who spoke on the floor were women, even though women constituted only 10 percent of the Republican caucus in the 110th Congress (2007–2008).[34]

EXTENDING PARTY CONFLICT TO BIPARTISAN ISSUES: THE VIOLENCE AGAINST WOMEN ACT

The increasing ideological polarization of the parties in Congress and the growing status of women's rights as an electoral wedge has expanded the range of party conflict to formerly bipartisan initiatives. For years, issues of violence against women attracted strong bipartisan support. First passed in 1993 as part of the Clinton administration's omnibus crime bill, the Violence Against Women Act improves how the criminal justice system handles domestic violence and sexual assault and provides services for victims. A Republican Congress reauthorized the bill in 2000 at the end of Clinton's term. Connie Morella (R-MD), the moderate Republican who was a key proponent of the legislation when it first passed, sponsored the House bill. The legislation passed with only three dissenting votes. The bill again gained almost unanimous support when it was reauthorized in 2005 under Republican president George W. Bush and a Republican-controlled Congress.[35]

This bipartisan consensus broke down in 2012 when reauthorization of the Violence Against Women Act became ensnared in presidential electoral politics. With a Democratic-controlled Senate, a Republican-controlled House, and President Obama facing a tough reelection race, the policy process was highly polarized. Senate Democrats drafted a bill that included provisions to extend benefits to individuals in same-sex relationships, to expand the number of visas for domestic violence victims who are illegal immigrants, and to address violence against Native American women by giving tribal courts more authority to prosecute non–Native American offenders. Homosexuality, illegal immigration, and the reach of the courts are all issues that inflame various elements of the Republican base. Democrats seized on Republican objections as more evidence of the Republican war on women and highlighted Republican obstruction of the bill in their campaigns.[36]

Concerned about the party's standing with suburban women voters and their presidential candidate Mitt Romney's persistent gender gap in polls, Republican leaders again turned to their female colleagues to defend the party and promote an alternative bill. Reflecting the emerging ideological dynamics among Republican women, a contingent of conservative women in the House vigorously defended the party's position and consistently voted with the party, while the more moderate delegation of female Senators treaded carefully, supporting the party position but ultimately backing the Democratic bill.

In the House, party leaders tapped freshman Sandy Adams (R-FL) to sponsor the Republican bill. Herself a victim of domestic violence and a former deputy sheriff, Adams was a compelling spokesperson on the issue.[37] Eighteen of the 24 Republican women were original cosponsors of the bill, including 7 of the 9 conservative women elected in the Tea Party wave of 2010.[38] With Adams leading Republicans in the floor debate, 7 of the 11 Republican speakers were women. They spoke as women emphasizing the importance of reducing domestic violence, chastising Democrats for politicizing the bill, and explaining how the Republican bill strengthened protections for women.[39]

In the Senate, Republicans also recruited a female senator to offer the Republican alternative. Kay Bailey Hutchison (R-TX) joined with Charles Grassley (R-IA), the ranking member of the Judiciary Committee, which had jurisdiction over the bill. Meanwhile the other four Republican women were among the eight Republican senators who cosponsored the Democratic bill. When Hutchison's amendment failed, she and the other four Republican women all voted for the Democratic bill. Indeed, only Hutchison and Kelly Ayotte (R-N.H) supported the Republican alternative, while the more moderate senators, Olympia Snowe (R-ME), Susan Collins (R-ME), and Lisa Murkowski (R-AK), voted solely for the Democratic bill.[40]

To become law, House Republicans and Senate Democrats needed to agree on a bill. Seeking to deflect Democratic attacks, Republicans led by majority leader Eric Cantor (R-VA) engaged in high-level negotiations with Vice President Joe Biden, a lead author of the first Violence Against Women Act. To pressure Republicans and highlight the party's indifference to the plight of victims of domestic violence, the 12 Democratic women in the Senate penned a letter to the 25 Republican women in the House, asking them to unite as women to convince their leadership to pass the reauthorization: "As mothers, daughters, grandmothers, and women intent on protecting the inclusive and bipartisan history of the Violence Against Women Act (VAWA), we are reaching out to you to ask for your help. . . . With your leadership on this issue we will resolve this matter in a way that puts the safety of all women ahead of partisan politics."[41] Given the strongly conservative stance House Republican women had taken on the issue, compromise was not likely to come from the Republican women.

With a newly reelected President Obama, Democrats made reauthorization of the Violence Against Women Act a top priority. The party also hoped the bill would help them turn out women voters in the upcoming 2014 midterms, when Democratic control of the Senate was at risk. Since Senator Hutchison had retired, Judiciary Committee ranking member Charles Grassley offered the Republican alternative. The newly elected conservative senator from Nebraska, Deb Fischer, was the only female senator to support the alternative. However, she joined the other three Republican women in voting for the Democratic bill, which passed with the support of 23 Republican senators. The strong bipartisan Senate vote pressured House Republicans to bring up the bill.[42]

After Romney's loss and poor showing with women voters, Republicans were eager to move on from the issue. With Adams's defeat in the 2012 elections, Republicans turned to conference chair Cathy McMorris Rodgers (R-WA) to sponsor the Republican alternative, and 7 of the 15 Republican floor speakers were women.[43] When that bill failed, the House voted on the Senate Democrats' bill, allowing the bill to pass with support from Democrats and a minority of Republicans. Republican leaders were so concerned about protecting the party's image with women voters that the Violence against Women Act reauthorization was one of the only nonbudget bills passed that violated the standard practice of only bringing bills to the floor that have support from a majority of Republicans.[44] In the end, the bill passed with 87 Republicans voting with all the Democrats, while 138 Republicans opposed the bill. Taking a closer look at the vote, most of the Republican women supported the McMorris Rodgers substitute. Only three Republican women, Ileana Ros-Lehtinen (R-FL), Candice Miller (R-MI), and Kristi Noem (R-SD), were among the 60 Republicans opposing the substitute. Noem voted against both the McMorris Rodgers and the Democratic bill, a strongly conservative position. The Republican women were split in their support for the Democratic bill that became law. Slightly more than half opposed the bill, while eight (42percent) supported the legislation. Similarly, 37 percent (79) of Republican men voted for the bill.[45]

Clearly, in the contemporary Congress, the Republican women in the House fully support the party's conservative position on a range of women's issues. There is a growing contingent of conservative women who are willing to promote these policies and defend the party against criticism. By contrast, the small group of Republican women in the Senate remain more cautious about navigating party conflicts on women's rights and more reticent to be the public face of the party deflecting Democratic attacks.

ABORTION WARS

Abortion is by far the most debated women's rights issue in Congress. The parties' frequent clashes over abortion highlight the growing polarization of Congress on women's rights and the movement of Republican women from anchoring the moderate middle to leading the conservative charge to limit access to abortion. Using the vote scorecards of the National Right to Life Committee and the annual legislative reviews in the CQ Almanac, I identified major votes on abortion-related proposals between the 104th (1995–1996) and the 114th Congresses (2015–2016).[46] These proposals range from the Partial-Birth Abortion Ban Act, which effectively bans most late-term abortions, to a plethora of funding restrictions to ensure federal money is not spent on abortion. Many of these initiatives are proposed in multiple Congresses, allowing us to compare changing voting patterns on these issues. For example, the partial-birth abortion ban passed the House three times before it became law. Vetoed twice by President Clinton, the legislation finally passed when Republican president George W. Bush held the White House. More recently, House Republicans have passed some version of a 20-week abortion ban three times since 2011, and efforts to defund Planned Parenthood have stalled budget talks, almost precipitated a government shutdown in 2011 and 2015, and continue to roil efforts to repeal and replace Obamacare.

When Republicans won control of Congress in 1994, they then controlled the policy agenda in both houses of Congress for the first time since *Roe v. Wade* was decided. With social conservatives central to the Republican base, many members were eager to pass restrictions. In 1995, more than one-third of the appropriations bills that direct federal spending included some type of abortion restriction.[47] The House and Senate also passed the Partial-Birth Abortion Ban Act. Vetoed by President Clinton, it was the first federal statute to restrict an abortion procedure since the Supreme Court legalized abortion.

During this burst of activism, there were still a significant number of pro-choice Republicans and pro-life Democrats. Indeed, in the 104th Congress, between 35 and 50 Republicans voted against various funding restrictions on abortion and family planning services, and 35–50 Democrats supported them. Republican women were more likely to take pro-choice positions than their male counterparts. For example, 53 percent (9) of Republican women, but only 20 percent (43) of Republican men, voted for an amendment that would restore the requirement that state Medicaid programs pay for abortions in cases of rape and incest.[48] Republicans had inserted a provision in an appropriations bill that would allow states to decide whether they wanted to cover abortions in these cases.

Many of the women who voted for the amendment were moderates from the Northeast, as the nine female Republicans voting for the amendment included Susan Molinari (NY), Sue Kelly (NY), Marge Roukema (NJ), Nancy Johnson (CT), Connie Morella (MD), Deborah Pryce (OH), Tillie Fowler (FL), Jan Meyers (KS), and Jennifer Dunn (WA). Generally, support for pro-choice positions was highest among Republicans on family planning votes and lowest on such votes as the Partial-Birth Abortion Ban Act that focused attention on the fetus or the Child Custody Protection Act that made it a federal crime to take a teenager across state lines to obtain an abortion.

Still, the Republican women who voted with pro-choice forces faced difficult pressures because they were espousing a position that defies the majority of their conference and angers a core set of party activists. In her memoir, Susan Molinari (R-NY) recounts that because of her pro-choice votes as a representative from the heavily Italian and Catholic Staten Island, New York, the Right to Life Party always ran a female candidate against her, and on Saturday afternoons, pro-life activists picketed her district office while "waving photos of aborted fetuses." During her reelection campaigns, protesters screaming "murderer" followed her to fund-raisers and speaking engagements.[49] Moreover, she asserted that Republican women receive more scrutiny of their abortion votes than Democratic men, complaining that when she voted for the partial-birth abortion ban, the pro-choice community singled her out as a traitor, but high-profile Democratic men who voted for the ban, including minority leader Dick Gephardt (D-MO), "got off unscathed."[50]

The pressure was especially intense for women with leadership ambitions, such as Molinari (R-NY), Fowler (R-FL), Pryce (R-OH), and Dunn (R-WA). These women generally had more conservative voting records than the other pro-choice Republican women and closer ties to the leadership. Seeking to bridge their personal and partisan commitments, sometimes they would vote for both the party position and the more pro-choice position. For example, in a debate over international family planning policy during the 104th Congress, Molinari, Pryce, and Dunn all voted for the party amendment sponsored by Chris Smith (R-NJ) that would deny family planning money to international organizations that provide abortions or abortion counseling and would deny funding to the United Nations Fund for Population Activities (UNFPA) until they suspended programs in China.[51] The three also voted in favor of a pro-choice alternative sponsored by Jan Meyers (R-KS) that would delete the Smith provisions regarding family planning funding to nongovernmental organizations (NGOs) and keep the prohibition on funds to the UNFPA.[52]

Occasionally, the congresswomen simply did not vote. Molinari did not vote on a similar international family planning amendment in the 105th Congress,[53] and Pryce did not vote when the amendment was offered again later in the session.[54] Molinari and Pryce also did not vote on an amendment to a defense bill in the 104th Congress that would allow women to pay for abortions with their own money at Defense Department medical facilities abroad.[55] The women had reason to worry because Republicans party leaders had relaxed seniority rules for advancement in committee, preferring to prioritize party loyalty. As a result, in 2001, Marge Roukema (R-NJ), the most senior Republican on the Financial

Services Committee, was denied the chairmanship because she was considered too moderate, bucking party orthodoxy on issues from abortion to gun control.[56]

By the 105th Congress, Republican support for abortion rights was starting to decline. Republican women were still more likely to support reproductive rights than Republican men. For example, 25–35 percent of Republican women generally voted against international family planning and other abortion-funding restrictions, while fewer than 12 percent of Republican men opposed these provisions. As late as the 107th Congress (1999–2000), 28 percent (5) of Republican women, compared to 9 percent (19) of Republican men, opposed a bill prohibiting the government from denying federal funding to health care entities that refuse to provide abortion,[57] and 16 percent (3) of Republican women, but only 5 percent (11) of Republican men, opposed the Child Custody Protection Act that made it a federal crime to take a minor across state lines for an abortion.[58]

When Democrats won control of the House majority in the 2006 elections, they generally sought to keep abortion off the agenda. However, in the 110th and the 111th Congresses, Republicans forced a vote on an amendment to prohibit Planned Parenthood and other providers who perform abortions from receiving federal family planning funds. In the 110th Congress, 29 percent (6) of Republican women opposed the amendment, compared to 8 percent (15) of Republican men.[59] By the 111th Congress, only 2 (12 percent) Republican women and 7 (4 percent) Republican men continued to oppose a similar amendment, and 3 Republican women switched their votes to support the ban.[60]

The trajectory of abortion politics and the role played by Republican women dramatically changed after the Tea Party wave election of 2010. Like in the 104th Congress, House conservatives in the new Republican majority were emboldened to pursue an array of abortion restrictions. With few moderate Republicans or conservative Democrats left in Congress, only a handful of members vote against their party's position on reproductive issues. Whereas votes related to family planning used to draw significant Republican defections, by the 114th Congress, Republican men and women almost universally voted with their party. For example, after a series of videos were released suggesting that Planned Parenthood mishandled the procurement and sale of aborted fetal tissue, Republicans vowed to defund the organization. Democrats and the Obama administration argued that defunding Planned Parenthood would mean that Medicaid recipients who rely on the organization for mammograms and cancer screenings would lose access to these important preventive health services.[61]

But Planned Parenthood was now a partisan football, and Republicans passed three different bills through the House to curb Planned Parenthood funding. The bills included Diane Black's (R-TN) Defund Planned Parenthood Act, which would place a one-year moratorium on federal funds to Planned Parenthood; the Women's Public Health and Safety Act (HR 3495), which would allow states to exclude abortion providers from their Medicaid programs; and a budget reconciliation bill that included a provision to cut most of Planned Parenthood's federal funding for a year. Only between three and nine Republicans voted against any of these bills, and only one Republican woman, Elise Stefanik (R-NY) opposed any of these proposals.[62]

TAKING THE LEAD IN PRO-LIFE POLITICS

In addition to the drastic decline in the number of pro-choice Republicans since the 1990s, the Tea Party wave brought in new and more active socially conservative women who are eager to take leadership roles in the party wars over abortion. Unlike in past years, when major abortion legislation was sponsored by Republican men, Republican women such as Diane Black (R-TN), Renee Ellmers (R-NC), Vicky Hartzler (R-MO), and Marsha Blackburn (R-TN) sponsor legislation and speak out on the floor and in press conferences to champion the pro-life position and vigorously defend the party against Democratic attacks that Republican policies jeopardize women's health. During the fight over Planned Parenthood funding, to counter the Democratic narrative that Republican men want to take away women's health care, House leaders lined up behind the bill by Diane Black (R-TN), described above, that called for a one-year moratorium on funds to Planned Parenthood.[63] Similarly, in the Senate, Majority Leader Mitch McConnell tapped first-term senator Joni Ernst (R-IA) to chair a working group to develop a response to the videos. The Senate then debated Ernst's bill to defund Planned Parenthood and divert the money to community health centers.[64]

In addition to crafting bills and leading party efforts on the floor, conservative Republican women were instrumental in conducting oversight that would keep Planned Parenthood and the issue of fetal tissue procurement for research in the public eye. To underscore the seriousness of the issue, House Speaker John Boehner (R-OH) created a special committee outside of the regular committee oversight process, the Select Investigative Panel on Infant Lives, to investigate Planned Parenthood and the larger industry of fetal tissue procurement. The socially conservative Republican women were eager to take the mantle of leadership on this committee.

Boehner tapped Marsha Blackburn (R-TN), a conservative with Tea Party ties, to chair the committee and appointed equal numbers of Republican men and women to showcases conservative women and insulate Republicans from Democratic attacks that the panel was a partisan witch hunt and part of the Republicans' continuing war on women.[65] Indeed, Minority Leader Nancy Pelosi (D-CA) pointedly renamed the committee the "Select Committee to Attack Women's Health" and appointed five women and one man to represent the party on the committee.[66]

Highlighting the importance of optics in selecting the right members for the committee, Republican leadership consulted with pro-life activists to choose members who were committed to the cause and would send the right public message. Marjorie Dannenfelser, of Susan B. Anthony List, emphasized that it was important for the committee to provide "a platform for women who speak to this issue."[67] In addition to Blackburn, who served as chair and the public face of the committee, Republican leaders also appointed Diane Black (R-TN), Vicky Hartzler (R-MO), and Mia Love (R-UT).[68]

PURSUING PRO-LIFE POLICIES THROUGH A GENDERED LENS

The pivotal role Republican women now play in pro-life politics is highlighted by the fact that achieving policy change requires the buy in of the small contingent of conservative women. When the women do not uniformly support a bill, the Democratic narrative that Republicans are undermining women's health quickly takes hold in the media and can derail the policy. The evolution of the debate over a 20-week abortion ban demonstrates the key importance of Republican women. While federal law bans most abortions after 24 weeks, some states have tried to extend the ban to 20 weeks, arguing that a fetus can feel pain at that stage. Trent Franks (R-AZ), chair of the House Judiciary Committee's Subcommittee on the Constitution, took up the cause at the federal level and drafted the Pain-Capable Unborn Child Protection Act. The first version of the legislation proposed in 2012 would have applied the ban only to the District of Columbia because Congress has jurisdiction over Washington, D.C.[69] By 2013, Franks had expanded the bill to institute a national 20-week ban. In both 2013 and 2015, the bill passed the House, but the Senate has not taken it up.

From the start, Republican women played key roles in the debate over the legislation. In early 2013, the bill did not include exceptions for rape and incest. At committee markup, Franks defended the exclusion by saying that "the incidence of rape resulting in pregnancy is very low." Democrats pounced on the remark, and Republicans, still reeling from rape comments that doomed the electoral fortunes of 2012 Republican Senate candidates in Missouri and Indiana, sought to mitigate the public relations disaster. Leaders added a narrow exception for rape and incest that would only apply if the woman had reported the crime. With no women on the Judiciary Committee, the leaders turned to Marsha Blackburn (R-TN) to manage the floor debate.[70] To demonstrate that Republicans are committed to protecting women, the floor debate included frequent references to Kermit Gosnell, an abortion provider convicted of aborting babies well beyond 24 weeks and harming the women who came to his clinic. Leaders made sure that Republican women delivered this message. Eight of the 11 Republican speakers were Republican women, including Blackburn, Diane Black (R-TN), Michele Bachmann (R-MN), Martha Roby (R-AL), Ann Wagner (R-MO), Vicky Hartzler (R-MO), Kristi Noem (R-SD), and Renee Ellmers (R-NC).[71]

In 2015, Republicans planned to demonstrate their commitment to protecting life by bringing the bill to the floor on the same day as the March for Life, which marks the anniversary of *Roe v. Wade*. In this case, the defection of a small group of Republican women led by Renee Ellmers (R-NC) and Jackie Walorski (R-IN) forced leaders to pull the bill from the floor and created outrage in the pro-life movement. The women opposed the rape and incest exception as too narrow. The exception, which would allow an abortion only if the rape had been reported to police, was part of the bill that passed in 2013. Leaders originally added the exemption to the 2013 bill in the Rules Committee just before it was brought to the floor in an attempt to stem the controversy over sponsor Trent Frank's rape comments. The women objected to the provision then and expected it would not be included in the 2015 bill. At the annual Republican retreat, Ellmers argued that the focus on social issues would alienate millennials and women, two groups the party needed to attract in the coming 2016 presidential election. She also expressed concerns about the rape provision because most rapes go unreported. With leaders still moving forward with the bill, Ellmers, Walorski, and Aaron Schrock (R-IL) took the unusual step of withdrawing their names as cosponsors.[72]

Hoping to avoid the embarrassment of pulling the bill when thousands of pro-life demonstrators were scheduled to march in Washington, D.C., Republican leaders organized meetings with groups of women and moderate members who did not want to take votes on abortion, especially when the bills would be blocked in the Senate or vetoed by President Obama. Even the main Republican cosponsor, Marsha Blackburn (R-TN), was concerned that the bill was becoming one about the definition of rape and not about abortion. The women disagreed on the solution, with some like Ann Wagner (R-MO) believing the rape exception should be dropped and the only exception should be for the life of the mother. Others wanted to drop the reporting requirement to broaden the rape exemption. With the party in disarray, the bill was pulled.[73]

While the conservative women drove the efforts to derail the bill, they were also instrumental in revising the legislation and bringing it back to the floor. Conference chair Cathy McMorris Rodgers (R-WA) handled the delicate outreach with pro-life activists who were angry over the bill's failure and did not want the legislation watered down. Diane Black (R-TN) negotiated the key compromise that replaced the reporting requirement with a 48-hour waiting period in which the rape victim must receive counseling or medical treatment.[74] The final bill still required that minors who were victims of rape or incest must report the incident to law enforcement, and there is no incest exception for adults.[75]

The debate over the 20-week abortion ban demonstrates that conservative women are an emerging force in congressional policy making over women's rights. These women consider themselves strongly pro-life, and their actions are not supported by pro-choice groups or Democratic women. Yet, they do display an additional sensitivity and a distinctive view of women's needs and women's rights that align with their strongly conservative ideology.

LOOKING TO THE FUTURE

Ideological polarization is now an enduring feature of Congress. With women's organizations central to the Democratic coalition and social conservatives a prominent force in Republican politics, the parties will continue to battle over women's rights. Democratic and Republican women will be central players in these fights. As of this writing, Republicans fully control the House, Senate, and the presidency, and they are utilizing their unified control of government to pursue the repeal and replacement of Obamacare and a plethora of initiatives to restrict abortion and reduce funding for family planning services, taking particular aim at Planned Parenthood. Democratic women continue to lead their party's outreach to women voters, denouncing Republican policies as an assault on the well-being of women and their families.

Meanwhile, the role of Republican women continues to develop. With their small numbers in Congress and limited seniority, Republican women still struggle to influence policy deliberations at the highest levels of leadership. However, the Republican women currently entering Congress are more conservative than Republican women who served in the 1990s and early 2000s. There are now a significant number of Republican women, especially in the House of Representatives, that are eager to champion socially conservative policies on women's issues. These women speak with a moral authority as women that helps the party deflect Democratic criticisms. Beyond defending the party, these women are embracing leadership roles in guiding Republican policy decisions, particularly regarding abortion. Their loyalty to the party and outspokenness on women's issues has helped some achieve leadership positions, including Diane Black (R-TN), who chairs the Budget Committee and played an important role in designing and selling the House proposal to replace Obamacare, and Virginia Foxx (R-NC), who chairs the Education and Workforce Committee, which handles issues ranging from sexual assault on campus to workplace regulations that impact women's access to overtime pay and sick leave.[76]

The problem of small numbers remains particularly acute in the Senate where only five Republican women serve in the current 115th Congress (2018–2018). The influence of Republican women is further diluted in the Senate by their ideological diversity, with the more moderate women having more seniority. Indeed, while Republican women in the House generally supported the party's health proposal, moderate Republican women, including Susan Collins (ME), Lisa Murkowski (AK), and Shelly Moore Capito (WV), have objected to the bill's efforts to defund Planned Parenthood and make cuts to the Medicaid program. Yet, these women were excluded from the party's working group to design a Senate health care proposal.[77] Moving forward, conservative women are more likely to win election in today's Republican Party. These conservative women will speak with moral authority as women, providing a conservative perspective on women's needs, and they will continue to play a more central role in crafting policy on women's issues and spearheading party outreach to women voters.

NOTES

1. Sean Sullivan and David Weigel, "GOP Health Care Push Faces New Obstacles as Concerns about Pre-Existing Conditions Grow," *Washington Post*, May 2, 2017, accessed May 2, 2017, https://www.washingtonpost.com/powerpost /gop-health-care-push-faces-new-obstacles-as-concerns-about-preexisting-con ditions-grow/2017/05/02/d25fc760-2f47-11e7-8674 437ddb6e813e_story.html?utm _term=.1b673d6d5c5b; Elise Viebeck, David Weigel, and Sean Sullivan, "Conservatives Endorse Latest Republican Plan to Revise Obamacare," *Washington Post*,

April 26, 2017, accessed April 26, 2017, https://www.washingtonpost.com/powerpost/conservative-pressure-groups-throw-weight-behind-gop-health-care-deal/2017/04/26/918ad730-2a82-11e7-a616-d7c8a68c1a66_story.html?utm_term=.1c2f6825945a.

2. David Weigel, "'I Didn't Come Here to Defend the President Tonight' Republican Who Rescued Health-Care Bill Faces Voters," *Washington Post*, May 10, 2017, accessed May 11, 2017, https://www.washingtonpost.com/news/powerpost/wp/2017/05/10/i-didnt-come-here-to-defend-the-president-tonight-republican-who-rescued-health-care-bill-faces-voters/?utm_term=.793eab1a73cc.

3. Jennifer Haberkorn and Burgess Everett, "White House Pressures Senate to Fix Health Bill's Policy Problems," Politico, May 7, 2017, accessed May 8, 2017, http://www.politico.com/story/2017/05/07/white-house-pressures-senate-to-fix-health-bills-policy-problems-238085.

4. Lauren Fox, Ted Barrett, and Elizabeth Landers, "McConnell Defends Senate Health Care Group That Had No Female Members," CNN, May 9, 2017, accessed May 10, 2017, http://www.cnn.com/2017/05/09/politics/republican-women-health-care-group/index.html.

5. Michele L. Swers, *Women in the Club: Gender and Policy Making in the Senate* (Chicago: University of Chicago Press, 2013).

6. Center for American Women and Politics (CAWP), "History of Women in the U.S. Congress," accessed February 1, 2017, http://www.cawp.rutgers.edu/history-women-us-congress.

7. The proportion of women in the House and Senate party caucuses is calculated using the number of women in Congress reported by the CAWP's "History of Women in the U.S. Congress" and the party divisions reported by the Clerk of the House, accessed May 12, 2017, http://clerk.house.gov/member_info/cong.aspx.

8. Irwin Gertzog, *Congressional Women: Their Recruitment, Integration, and Behavior* (Westport, CT: Praeger Publishers, 1995).

9. CAWP, "History of Women."

10. CAWP, "History of Women."

11. CAWP, "History of Women."

12. Danielle Thomsen and Michele L. Swers, "Which Women Can Run? Gender, Partisanship, and Candidate Donor Networks," *Political Research Quarterly* 70, no. 2 (2017): 449–463; Melody Crowder-Meyer and Rosalyn Cooperman, "Can't Buy Them Love: How Party Culture among Donors Contributes to the Party Gap in Women's Representation," *Journal of Politics* (forthcoming).

13. Davidson, Roger H., Walter J. Oleszek, Frances E. Lee, and Eric Schickler, *Congress and Its Members* (Washington, DC: CQ Press, 2015).

14. Keith T. Poole and Howard Rosenthal, *Ideology & Congress* (New Brunswick, NJ: Transaction Publishers, 2007).

15. Brian Frederick, "Gender and Roll Call Voting Behavior in Congress: A Cross-Chamber Analysis," *American Review of Politics* 34 (2013): 1–20.

16. The Common Space NOMINATE scores can be accessed at http://www.voteview.org/dwnl.htm.

17. Brian Frederick, "Are Female House Members Still More Liberal in a Polarized Era? The Conditional Nature of the Relationship between Descriptive and Substantive Representation," *Congress and the Presidency* 36, no. 2 (2009): 181–202.

18. Frederick, "Are Female House Members."

19. Michele L. Swers, *The Difference Women Make: The Policy Impact of Women in Congress* (Chicago: University of Chicago Press, 2002).

20. Michele L. Swers, "Gender and Party Politics in a Polarized Era," in *Party and Procedure in the United States Congress*, 2nd ed., eds. Jacob R. Straus and Matthew E. Glassman (Lanham, MD: Rowman & Littlefield, 2017), 279–299.

21. Michele L. Swers, *Women in the Club: Gender and Policy Making in the Senate* (Chicago: University of Chicago Press, 2013).

22. Fox, Barrett, and Landers, "McConnell Defends Senate Health Care Group."

23. Swers, *The Difference Women Make*; "Family Leave Waits for Clinton," in *CQ Almanac 1992*, 48th ed. (Washington, DC: Congressional Quarterly, 1993) 353–357, http://library.cqpress.com/cqalmanac/cqal92-1108101.

24. Bill Summary HR 1133, Violence against Women Act of 1993, https://www.congress.gov/bill/103rd-congress/house-bill/1133/all-info.

25. Swers, *The Difference Women Make*.

26. Swers, *Women in the Club*.

27. Swers, *The Difference Women Make*, 25.

28. Michele L. Swers and Carin Larson, "Women and Congress: Do They Act as Advocates for Women's Issues?," in *Women and Elective Office: Past, Present, and Future*, eds. Sue Thomas and Clyde Wilcox (New York: Oxford University Press, 2005), 110-128; Emma Dumain, "McMorris Rodgers Works to Rebuild, Rebrand Party Image, One Republican at a Time," Roll Call, March 6, 2014, accessed March 7, 2014, http://www.rollcall.com/news/home/mcmorris-rodgers-building-new-gop-image.

29. Michele L. Swers, "Pursuing Women's Interests in Partisan Times: Explaining Gender Differences in Legislative Activity on Health, Education, and Women's Health Issues," *Journal of Women Politics and Policy* 37, no. 3 (2016): 249–273.

30. Swers, *Women in the Club*.

31. Swers, *Women in the Club*; Swers and Larson, "Women and Congress."

32. Swers, *Women in the Club*.

33. Swers, *Women in the Club*.

34. Author analysis of floor debate on HR 2831, Lilly Ledbetter Fair Pay Act of 2007, *Congressional Record*, July 30, 2007, H8940–H8950, July 31, 2007, H9219–H9222.

35. Swers, "Gender and Party Politics."

36. Swers, *Women in the Club*; Jennifer Bendery, "Violence against Women Act: House Republican Women Emerge as Key to Possible Action," *Huffington Post*, December 19, 2012, accessed December 20, 2012, http://www.huffingtonpost.com/2012/12/18/violence-against-women-act-house-republican-women_n_2322572.html.

37. Kate Bolduan, "House Passes GOP Version of Violence Against Women Act Renewal," CNN, May 16, 2012, accessed May 17, 2012, http://www.cnn.com/2012/05/16/politics/gop-violence-against-women.

38. Author analysis, Bill Summary HR 4790, Violence Against Women Reauthorization Act of 2012, https://www.congress.gov/bill/112th-congress/house-bill/4970/all-info.

39. Author analysis of floor debate on HR 4790, Violence Against Women Reauthorization Act of 2012, *Congressional Record*, May 16, 2012, H2745–H2780.

40. Swers, *Women in the Club.*

41. Bendery, "Violence Against Women Act."

42. Swers, *Women in the Club.*

43. Author analysis of floor debate on S.47, Violence Against Women Reauthorization Act of 2013, *Congressional Record*, February 28, 2013, H707–H801.

44. Swers, "Gender and Party Politics."

45. S.47 Violence Against Women Reauthorization Act of 2013, House Roll Call 54 H. Amdt. 23, McMorris Rodgers of Washington Substitute Amendment, February 28, 2013, http://clerk.house.gov/evs/2013/roll054.xml, House Roll Call 55 on Passage, February 28, 2013, http://clerk.house.gov/evs/2013/roll055.xml.

46. National Right to Life Committee Vote Scorecards can be found at http://capwiz.com/nrlc/home.

47. "Abortion Foes Press Their Agenda," in *CQ Almanac 1995*, 51st ed. (Washington, DC: Congressional Quarterly, 1996), 7–29, http://library.cqpress.com/cqalmanac/cqal95-1100629.

48. Author analysis of HR 2127, Departments of Labor, Health and Human Services, and Education, and Related Agencies Appropriations Act, 1996 House Roll Call 619 H. Amdt. 727 Kolbe Amendment, August 3, 1995, http://clerk.house.gov/evs/1995/roll619.xml.

49. Swers, *The Difference Women Make*, 113.

50. Susan Molinari with Elinor Burkett, *Representative Mom: Balancing Budgets, Bill, and Baby in the U.S. Congress* (New York: Doubleday, 1998), 143.

51. Author analysis of HR 1868, Foreign Operations, Export Financing, and Related Programs Appropriations Act, 1996 House Roll Call Vote 433 H. Amdt. 477 Smith Amendment, June 28, 1995, http://clerk.house.gov/evs/1995/roll433.xml.

52. Author analysis of HR 1868, Foreign Operations, Export Financing, and Related Programs Appropriations Act, 1996 House Roll Call Vote 432 H. Amdt. 478 Meyers Amendment to H. Amdt. 477 Smith Amendment, June 28, 1995, http://clerk.house.gov/evs/1995/roll432.xml.

53. Author analysis of HR 1757, Foreign Affairs Reform and Restructuring Act of 1998, House Roll Call Vote 194 H. Amdt. 156 Smith Amendment, June 11, 1997, http://clerk.house.gov/evs/1997/roll194.xml.

54. Author analysis of HR 2159, Foreign Operations, Export Financing, and Related Programs Appropriations Act, 1998 House Roll Call Vote 363 H. Amdt. 318 Smith Amendment, September 4, 1997, http://clerk.house.gov/evs/1997/roll363.xml.

55. Author analysis of HR 3230, National Defense Authorization Act for Fiscal Year 1997, House Roll Call Vote 167 H. Amdt. 1054 DeLauro Amendment, May 14, 1996, http://clerk.house.gov/evs/1996/roll167.xml.

56. Swers, *The Difference Women Make*.

57. Author analysis of HR 4691, Abortion Non-Discrimination Act of 2002, House Roll Call Vote 412, September 25, 2002, http://clerk.house.gov/evs/2002/roll412.xml.

58. Author analysis of HR 476, Child Custody Protection Act, House Roll Call Vote 97, April 17, 2002, http://clerk.house.gov/evs/2002/roll097.xml.

59. Author analysis of HR 3043, Departments of Labor, Health and Human Services, and Education, and Related Agencies Appropriations Act, 2008 House Roll Call Vote 684 H. Amdt. 594 Pence Amendment, July 19, 2007, http://clerk.house.gov/evs/2007/roll684.xml.

60. Author analysis of HR 3293, Departments of Labor, Health and Human Services, and Education, and Related Agencies Appropriations Act, 2010 House Roll Call Vote 643H. Amdt. 389 Pence Amendment, July 24, 2009, http://clerk.house.gov/evs/2009/roll643.xml. The three Republican women who changed their positions in the 111th Congress were Shelly Moore-Capito (WV), Ginny Brown-Waite (FL), and Kay Granger (TX).

61. Danielle Paquette, "Here's What Happens if Congress Ends Funding for Planned Parenthood," *Washington Post*, September 24, 2015, accessed September 25, 2015, http://www.washingtonpost.com/news/wonkblog/wp/2015/09/24/defunding-planned-parenthood-would-actually-increase-government-spending.

62. Federal NRLC Scorecard, 114th Congress, Combined Sessions, accessed July 12, 2016, http://capwiz.com/nrlc/scorecard.xc?chamber=H&state=US&session=114&x=13&y=4.

63. Mike Debonis, "GOP Leaders Want Women Leading Anti–Planned Parenthood Efforts," *Washington Post*, July 28, 2015, accessed July 29, 2015, https://www.washingtonpost.com/news/post-politics/wp/2015/07/28/gop-leaders-want-women-leading-anti-planned-parenthood-efforts.

64. Debonis, "GOP Leaders"; Lauren Fox, "Planned Parenthood: Joni Ernst's First Target in the Senate," *The Atlantic*, July 30, 2015, accessed July 31, 2015, http://www.theatlantic.com/politics/archive/2015/07/planned-parenthood-joni-ernsts-first-target-in-the-senate/445854.

65. Cristina Marcos and Sarah Ferris, "Party Leaders Send Women into Committee Brawl over Abortion," *The Hill*, November 7, 2015, accessed November 8, 2015, http://thehill.com/policy/healthcare/259443-party-leaders-send-women-into-committee-brawl-over-abortion.

66. Marcos and Ferris, "Party Leaders."

67. Emma Dumain, "House GOP Looks Outside for Advice on Planned Parenthood Panel," Roll Call, October 7, 2015, accessed October 7, 2015, http://blogs.rollcall.com/218/house-gop-advice-planned-parenthood-panel.

68. Melanie Zanora, "Abortion Opponents Deny Partisan Tilt of New Subcommittee," Roll Call, January 25, 2016, accessed January 26, 2016, http://www

.rollcall.com/news/abortion_opponents_deny_partisan_tilt_of_new_subcom
mittee-244785-1.html.

69. Kate Nocera, "D.C. Abortion Bill Falls Short in House," Politico, July 13, 2012, accessed July 14, 2012, http://www.politico.com/story/2012/07/dc-abortion-bill-falls-short-in-house-079236.

70. Emma Dumain, "Trent Franks Sidelined as Abortion Ban Passes House," Roll Call, June 18, 2013, accessed June 19, 2013, http://www.rollcall.com/news/policy/abortion-ban-passes-house-228-196.

71. Author analysis of floor debate on HR 1797, Pain-Capable Unborn Child Protection Act, Congressional Record, June 18, 2013, H3730–H3743.

72. Daniel Newhauser and Lauren Fox, "GOP Leaders Pull Abortion Bill after Revolt by Women, Moderates," The Atlantic, January 21, 2015, accessed July 22, 2016, http://www.theatlantic.com/politics/archive/2015/01/gop-leaders-pull-abortion-bill-after-revolt-by-women-moderates/446133; Daniel Newhauser and Lauren Fox, "How the House GOP's Abortion Bill Fell Apart," The Atlantic, January 22, 2015, accessed July 22, 2016, http://www.theatlantic.com/politics/archive/2015/01/how-the-house-gops-abortion-bill-fell-apart/445725.

73. Newhauser and Fox, "GOP Leaders Pull"; Newhauser and Fox, "How the House."

74. Daniel Newhauser and Lauren Fox, "How the GOP Fixed the Late-Term Abortion Bill," The Atlantic, May 12, 2015, accessed July 22, 2016, http://www.theatlantic.com/politics/archive/2015/05/how-the-gop-fixed-the-late-term-abortion-bill/445986.

75. Author analysis of Bill Summary HR 36, Pain-Capable Unborn Child Protection Act, https://www.congress.gov/bill/114th-congress/house-bill/36/all-info?resultIndex=1.

76. David Hawkings, "House Republican Women See a Boost in Authority," Roll Call, January 18, 2017, accessed January 18, 2017, http://www.rollcall.com/news/hawkings/house-republican-women.

77. Robert Costa and Sean Sullivan, "Senate Republicans Face Their Own Divisions in Push for Health Care Overhaul," Washington Post, May 9, 2016, accessed May 10, 2016, https://www.washingtonpost.com/powerpost/senate-republicans-face-their-own-divisions-in-push-for-health-care-overhaul/2017/05/09/f9d3558e-34b8-11e7-b412-62beef8121f7_story.html?utm_term=.ce886e794ccc.

CHAPTER 11

Republican Female Lawmakers' Contributions to Legislative Debates in the 113th U.S. Congress

Christina Xydias

Studies of women and politics around the world tell us much more about women in left-leaning parties than women on the right. This is the case for several reasons. Globally, more women are elected from parties on the left, yielding fewer observations of women on the right.[1] Further, women's interests are often defined in feminist terms, leading us to pay less attention to how women on the right frame these interests.[2] One result of this focus on left-leaning women and left-leaning conceptions of women's interests is the general expectation that women (regardless of their party affiliation) will be more likely to advocate for women than their male counterparts. However, the research that does focus on women on the right shows that the intersection between gender/sex and partisanship is more complicated. Women across parties may indeed tend to pay greater attention than men to issues and problems that they identify as disproportionately affecting women, but this does not produce a clear convergence among women on the solutions to these problems.[3]

Republican women in the United States hold office in far fewer numbers than their left-leaning counterparts, mirroring the correspondence between women's numbers and party affiliation that we see elsewhere in the world.[4] The Republican Party itself is not associated with a women's movement, and it has not made advocating for female constituents a priority. Indeed, scholars and pundits alike point to this lack of commitment to women's rights and interests as a central challenge to the Republican Party's vote-getting goals (see several other chapters in this volume).

However, simultaneously—like any U.S. political party—the GOP exercises little party discipline compared to parties in other political systems where electoral and legislative rules incentivize discipline.[5] Without the constraints of party discipline that we see elsewhere in the world, do Republican women diverge from their political party to pay greater attention to women's rights and interests than their party does? Alternatively, do Republican women "stick to the script"?

This chapter addresses these questions specifically in terms of Republican congresswomen's participation in legislative debates, one important form of political representation.[6] Data are drawn from the 113th U.S. Congress (2013–2014), which is widely characterized as a highly partisan environment, which has consequences for the inclusion and representation of women (see Glossary).[7] Republican congresswomen's contributions to House debates in this legislative period are compared with key elements of the Republican "party script" to assess whether and how female speakers diverge from it. For the purposes of this study, this script is derived from the Republican Party's platform for the 2012 congressional elections. It includes the party's language for (1) framing equality (what kinds of equality the platform mentions, and the policies it proposes to enhance equality); (2) framing barriers to equality (what barriers the platform identifies); and (3) addressing women's interests in three categories: family-related interests, political interests, and economic interests. This analysis therefore consists of the extent to which female Republican congress members use this language and the extent to which they diverge to advocate on behalf of women.

The sections of this chapter proceed as follows: First, a review of the literatures on legislative debate, partisanship, and sex/gender establishes expectations for the 113th U.S. Congress. Second, a data and methods section both presents and justifies the process for developing a "party script" as a baseline for comparison and the corpus of legislative debates from the period of study (2013–2014). The third section presents data from the 113th Congress and assesses whether and how female Republican members of the House stick to the script.

LITERATURE REVIEW

This section offers a brief overview of what we know about participation in legislative debate, with particular attention to the intersection between sex/gender and partisanship. Plenary session debates offer voters and constituents a window for viewing their representatives in action. Bernard Manin argues that both the availability of transcripts for these debates as well as opportunities to view televised legislative speech (e.g.,

CSPAN, "parliament TV"), make an "audience democracy" possible, which he views as enhancing participation and accountability.[8] So, who speaks, and what do they say?

Sven-Oliver Proksch and Jonathan Slapin's "theory of parliamentary debate" claims that the factors that shape variation in any individual legislator's participation in debate depend upon the broader political context, that is, they vary cross-nationally. For example, political systems that encourage officeholders to differentiate themselves and develop their public personae individually (e.g., systems such as FPTP that emphasize personal voting over party discipline) are also systems where political parties allow greater latitude for speakers in plenary sessions.[9] Other research shows that legislators' party status as majority or minority plays a role in their likelihood to speak and whether they defect from the party's positions in doing so.[10] In turn, some studies show that representatives' seniority in their legislative body matters (greater seniority allows greater independence), as does the extent to which electoral and legislative rules encourage personalist vote-seeking behavior (more personalist systems allow greater independence).[11]

Specifically, in terms of sex/gender, previous research is divided on the extent to which female legislators' participation in plenary session debates differs from that of their male counterparts. Some of this previous research has analyzed specific issue areas, generally showing that women pay greater or different attention to "women's issues" than men.[12] Other research shows gendered patterns in participation in "harder" (e.g., national security) versus "softer" (e.g., education) topics.[13]

The intersection of sex/gender and partisanship is more complicated. Previous research shows that women across the party spectrum tend to agree on the urgency of issues that are especially important for women (where this importance is measured in various ways, including surveys that show gendered patterns, as well as facts that show women to be more engaged than men in certain occupations, etc.). However, this agreement does not necessarily produce convergence on how government should address these issues, nor even convergence on the idea that government (rather than the private sector) should take this responsibility.[14] More generally, Kira Sanbonmatsu and Kathleen Dolan, for example, find that gendered stereotypes matter differently for Republican and Democratic women.[15] In kind, Tiffany Barnes and Erin Cassese show that partisanship persists even when female Republicans are more moderate than their male Republican counterparts.[16]

In sum, previous research highlights several factors that shape whether an individual legislator will "defect" from her party in legislative speech. In terms of sex/gender, research suggests that women are unlikely to follow *another party's* script, even when they disagree with their male counterparts within their party. When party discipline is low, previous research suggests that female speakers are more likely to diverge from their party's positions. These expectations, however, may be called into question by high levels of overall partisanship.

Do Republican women in the 113th House of Representatives stick to the script?

DATA AND METHODS

Empirically, this chapter focuses on GOP women's participation in House debates in the 113th Congress (2013–2014). Republicans formed the majority party in the 113th Congress's House of Representatives (at the beginning of the term: 233 Republicans, 200 Democrats). In January 2013, 20 of these Republicans were female (8.2% of Republican members of Congress), as compared with 62 female Democrats (29% of Democratic members of Congress).

Transcripts of these congresswomen's debates are part of the Proceedings and Debates of the U.S. Congress.[17] In addition to comments delivered in person, members of Congress may insert written commentary as extensions to the *Congressional Record* ("Extensions of Remarks"). Taken together, these transcripts offer insight into Republican female legislators' priorities and how they choose to appeal to their various audiences and constituencies. They offer an opportunity to assess the extent to which Republican women in the U.S. Congress stick to the "party script," in particular on the matter of the extent and type of advocacy for women. This script is derived from the Republican Party's platform for the 2012 congressional elections, as described below.[18]

The Party Script

Following previous research, the Republican Party's 2012 platform is outlined for key issues and policy positions in three categories: (1) how the platform frames equality (what kinds of equality it mentions, and the policies it proposes to enhance equality); (2) how the platform frames barriers to equality (what barriers the platform identifies); and (3) the spheres of women's interests that the platform identifies (family-related interests, political interests, and economic interests).[19] The first and second categories follow the Comparative Manifesto Project, specifically *Per 503*, a positive reference to social justice, and *Per 706*, a positive reference to assistance for and fair treatment of noneconomic demographic groups.[20] Further justification for these two categories is found in other recent work on the Republican Party, which shows that underlying attitudes toward equality and beliefs about the role of the state in achieving it help explain gendered differences within the party.[21]

Following Xydias (2014), the third category reflects the fact that political parties' attention to different kinds of women's interests varies ideologically. Previous research shows that parties on the right, including the Republican Party, tend to focus on the family and women's role in it rather than on women's interests as individuals separate from the family.[22] A female Republican speaker's divergence from the party script in this category, therefore, would address spheres of women's interests that her party does not address.

This textual analysis of the Republican Party's 2012 platform establishes several quantitative criteria against which GOP women's speeches can be evaluated. Key characteristics of the platform are measured in quantitative terms, including, for example, the ratio between the platform's attention to *freedom* (the relative frequency of free* in the platform's text) and its attention to *equality* (the relative frequency of equal* and equit* in the platform's text).[23] If a speech followed the party script, one indicator would be the extent to which its content mirrors this ratio. As will be discussed in greater detail below, any single speech is relatively short and likely to be focused on one specific topic or policy; therefore, ratios are calculated for all GOP congresswomen's speeches as one corpus (collection of documents) and subsequently for the collection of speeches delivered by each congresswoman, but never for individual speeches.[24]

This textual analysis of the Republican Party's 2012 platform offers few surprises. In the first category—framing of equality—this analysis finds that the Republican 2012 platform refers to equality relatively infrequently, both generally and in terms of women. References to equal opportunities are mentioned exclusively in two senses: economic freedom (in various sections of the document) and primary and secondary education, that is, ensuring children's access to educational opportunity regardless of "address, zip code, or economic status."[25]

Previous research suggests that the concepts of opportunity and equality often overlap. Although the opening passage of the Republican 2012 platform refers to equality of opportunity, the broader document focuses on rejecting the government as a facilitator of this opportunity. This opening passage proceeds as follows: "The pursuit of opportunity has defined American from our very beginning. This is a land of opportunity. The American Dream is a dream of equal opportunity for all. And the Republican Party is the party of opportunity."[26]

Instead of focusing on equality, however, the 2012 Republican platform emphasizes freedom *from* government intervention. Thus, the concept of freedom is framed in terms of barriers to it, and it is primarily discussed with other elements that the platform presents as barriers (below). The platform includes just one mention of gender equality: it states that "sex-selective abortions [are] gender discrimination in its most lethal form."[27] As will be discussed in subsequent sections, as well, abortion is the single inequality/injustice from which the platform states the Republican Party protects women, specifically.

In quantitative terms, the 2012 Republican platform's script in this first category is captured as follows. The platform's emphasis on freedom over equality is captured as the ratio between attention to freedom (the relative frequency of free* in the platform's text, not including words that are unrelated, such as *freezer*) and attention to equality (the relative frequency of equal* added to the relatively frequency of equit* in the platform's text, not including words that are unrelated, such as financial *equity*). Ratios are also calculated between attention to freedom and attention to opportunity (free* : opport*), and in turn between attention to equality and attention to opportunity (equal* + equit* : opport*).

The Republican Party's 2012 platform script in the second category—barriers to equality—is likewise limited. Instead, the party focuses on the government as a source of restrictions on individuals' economic freedom, in particular. For example, the opening line of the platform's first substantive section (*Restoring the American Dream: Rebuilding the Economy and Creating Jobs*) states, "We are the party of maximum economic freedom."[28] Later in the same paragraph, it reads, "Excessive taxation and regulation impede economic development."[29] There is no mention of gendered inequalities and their causes, even to defend gendered outcomes in terms of personal choice (e.g., that women earn smaller paychecks than men due to working fewer hours or working in less lucrative occupations).

In quantitative terms, the 2012 Republican platform's attention to barriers to women's equality is effectively zero, making it unhelpful for generating a positive indicator of the script. Therefore, any mention of gendered challenges in a speech or collection of speeches would indicate that a speaker is going off script.

The platform's script in the third category—spheres of women's interests—follows in kind. The few references to women's rights and interests are almost exclusively framed in terms of protecting women from sources of danger in society, in particular the experience of abortion. The platform reads, "We . . . affirm the dignity of women by protecting the sanctity of human life" in opposing abortion, because "numerous studies have shown that abortion endangers the health and wellbeing of women."[30] This language focuses not on women as autonomous beings but as people who require protection, with particular attention to reproduction.

More generally, discussions of issues that might be expected to include references to women do not do so. Indeed, contrary to the findings of research on right-leaning parties in other advanced industrial democracies,[31] mentions of families and children are not made in connection with women but rather as broader social groups and categories. The platform's references to children and family are made largely in terms of economic deregulation. For instance, there are several references to the need for workplace flexibility as it relates to families. However, women are not mentioned as facing a disproportionate challenge in this regard. Instead, the platform states, "Today's workforce is independent, wants flexibility in working conditions, [and] needs family-friendly options."[32] Similarly, economic liberty is mentioned throughout the document, but (as noted) exclusively in terms of loosening regulations that are argued to restrict that liberty and not in terms of women's economic liberty or lack thereof.

In turn, the platform's discussion of education about sex and reproduction includes no reference to sex or gender. Instead, the platform reads, "We renew our call for replacing 'family planning' programs for teens with abstinence education."[33] Right-leaning parties in other countries often actively advocate for traditional motherhood roles; the 2012 Republican platform is therefore noteworthy in its overall lack of attention.[34] Similar to the previous category (attention to barriers to women's equality), the 2012 Republican platform's attention to spheres of women's interests is very low.

In quantitative terms, the 2012 Republican platform's script in this third category is measured in two ways: (1) attention to women (the relative frequency of wom* in the platform's text, not including the frequently uttered "congresswom*n," "chairwom*n," "spokeswom*n," and "gentlewom*n," because these are used as titles and roles) and (2) the ratio between attention to children (the relative frequency of child* in the platform's text) and attention to women (the relative frequency of wom*, again not including titles and roles).

In sum, Republican women need only refer to women at all to diverge from their party's script. This script is summarized in both qualitative and quantitative terms in Table 11.1. The final column shows key indicators of the script. In subsequent sections of the paper, these indicators are used to measure these elements' presence in GOP congresswomen's speeches. For example, the ratio between references to *freedom* and references to *equality* in the Republican 2012 platform is 6:1. This

Table 11.1   Summing Up the Party Script on Women's Interests: The 2012 Republican Party Platform

Key Issues & Policy Positions	Platform's Emphases	Key Indicators of These Emphases	Values of These Indicators
Equality of opportunity or outcome	Very limited attention to equality of opportunity; equality not otherwise mentioned	Attention† to free*: attention to equal* + equit*	6.077 (free* receives 6.1 × the attention paid to equal* + equit*)
		Attention to free*: attention to opport*	3.695 (free* receives 3.7 × the attention paid to opport*)
		Attention to equal* + equit*: attention to opport*	0.608 (free* receives 0.6 × the attention paid to equal* + equit*)
Characterization of barriers to equality	No mention	X	X
Spheres of women's interests	Very limited attention to economic interests; no other spheres mentioned	Attention to child*: attention to wom*	1.809 (child* receives 1.8 × the attention paid to wom*)

Source: Original chart by author, based on data from the U.S. Congressional Record, 2013–2014.

Note: †Attention to a concept or issue is measured in terms of that concept's relative frequency in the platform (the frequency of that concept's mention/the total number of words).
An asterisk (*) indicates truncation. For example, free captures the word free plus an ending (free, freedom, freeing, etc.). See text for more detailed discussion.

free* : equal* + equit* ratio is calculated for each of the 19 GOP women speakers in the House (2012–2013), and then averaged for an aggregate ratio across the corpus of GOP women's speeches: 2:1. In the aggregate, GOP congresswomen refer to freedom approximately twice as often as they refer to equality. As noted above, the relative frequency of concepts—such as references to freedom—in GOP congresswomen's speeches is calculated by treating each congresswoman's speeches as a single corpus to capture each congresswoman's extent of attention to that concept over the course of the legislative term.

Analysis of *Congressional Record* Items

The *Congressional Record* includes all items submitted to its database for the 20 female Republican members of the House during the 113th U.S. Congress (2013–2014). I refer to these as "items" because they include both speeches delivered to the Congress as well as text submitted for inclusion in the Extensions of Remarks, which are not delivered on the House floor. Republican congresswomen in this legislative term averaged 76 items in the *Congressional Record*, ranging from Rep. Jaime Herrera Beutler with 18 items to Rep. Virginia Foxx with 225 items.[35] This corpus includes a total of 1,445 items, some of which are the declaration of procedural motions (e.g., a motion to adjourn) or announcements about constituents (e.g., wishing a constituent happy birthday). Other, more substantive items engage with policy areas and express the speaker's positions and arguments, offering an opportunity to observe her adherence to or departure from the party script. As noted, these speeches are available on the *Congressional Record*'s Web site. After preprocessing,[36] the speeches were evaluated for the presence of the platform's key indicators, discussed above.

RESULTS AND ANALYSIS

Republican women in the U.S. House of Representatives are relatively few in number. Overall, data from the 113th Congress (2013–2014) show that their participation in legislative debates generally stuck to the script. The caveat is that GOP congresswomen pay considerably more attention to women (measured in terms of their speeches' references to women) than their party's platform. However, ideological elements of the party script, such as those captured by a ratio between *freedom* and *equality*, generally hold among female GOP speakers. The finding that Republican women in the House might refer to women more frequently than their party but nonetheless work within the party's ideological framework resonates with previous research on women in conservative parties. Subsequent sections discuss this finding further.

Figure 11.1 juxtaposes two word clouds to represent the correspondence between the platform and GOP women speakers visually: the first (a) for the Republican 2012 platform and the second (b) for the full corpus of speeches delivered by GOP women. Figure 11.1 contrasts a single

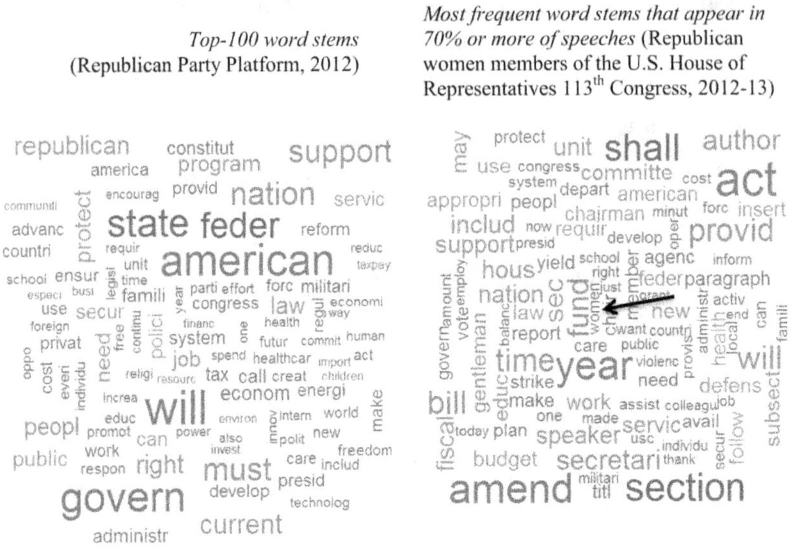

Top-100 word stems
(Republican Party Platform, 2012)

Most frequent word stems that appear in
70% or more of speeches (Republican
women members of the U.S. House of
Representatives 113th Congress, 2012-13)

Figure 11.1   Word Clouds: Visualizing GOP Congresswomen's Adherence to
the Party Script

Source: Original word clouds produced by author, based on data from the U.S. *Congres-*
sional Record, 2013–2014.

document (the party platform) with a collection of documents (*Congres-*
sional Record items). Therefore, it shows the top 100 word stems for the
platform and then the most frequent word stems appearing in 70 percent
or more of GOP women's speeches. The latter measure assures that a few
outlier speeches containing an unusually high frequency of a specific word
will not skew this aggregate picture. This visual summary of the party
script and GOP women's speeches is followed by Table 11.2, which juxtaposes these corpora in quantitative terms.

Figure 11.1 shows that both the 2012 Republican Party platform and
(in the aggregate) female GOP members of the 113th Congress talk a lot
about health care and about the economy. It is far from surprising that
both the platform and congresswomen frequently employ procedural language: system, program, policy, and the like. The exception is that GOP
women refer to women (*wom**) frequently and consistently, while *wom**
is not in the top 100 word stems for the party's platform. Table 11.2 cor-
roborates this finding.

Although GOP women speakers refer to women more frequently
than their party's platform, Table 11.2 shows other indicators of speakers' adherence to the script. Indicators of the first category of the party

Table 11.2   Comparing GOP Women's Speeches (113th Congress, 2013–2014) with Republican Party Platform (2012)

	2012 Republican Party Platform	GOP Women Mean (std. dev.) | Min/Max[◊]
Ratios of Relative Word Frequencies		
free* : equit* + equal*	6.077	1.955 (1.481) | **0.540 / 5.580**
free* : opport*	3.695	0.824 (0.447) | **0.344 / 1.928**
equit* + equal* : opport*	0.608	0.482 (0.177) | **0.268 / 1.094**
child* : wom*	1.809	1.560 (1.443) | **0.309 / 5.6**
Relative Word Frequency		
wom*	0.000658 (0.07% of words in the platform were wom*)	0.00237 (0.00140) | 0.000332 / 0.00519 (0.2% of words in GOP Congresswomen's speeches were wom*)

Source: Original chart by author, based on data from the U.S. *Congressional Record*, 2013–2014.

Note: [◊] Min/Max provide the *lowest* and *highest* values, respectively, for each ratio in the corpora of congresswomen's speeches in this legislative term. For example, in terms of word frequencies, Rep. Herrera Beutler's attention to freedom was 0.540 (54.0%) of her attention to equality, while Rep. Bachmann's attention to freedom was 5.58 times her attention to equality.

* An asterisk (*) indicates truncation.

script—emphasis on equality of opportunity or outcome—include the ratios of *free* : equit* + equal*; free* : opport*;* and *equit* + equal* : opport*.* In this category, GOP women speakers largely stuck to the script, with a focus on the importance of "freedom from" the government. Many of these references took place in speeches in opposition to the Affordable Care Act, with framing that mirrors the platform. Of the 19 speakers, only 5 (Reps. Brooks, Foxx, Herrera Beutler, Noam, and Roby) emphasized *equality* over *freedom*, measured by their word usage. These five congresswomen's ratio of *free* : equit* + equal** was below 1.0 (i.e., the relative frequency of *equit* + equal** was greater than the relative frequency of *free**). The other 14 congresswomen's speeches reflect the platform's greater emphasis on freedom. Further, like their party's platform, GOP congresswomen in the aggregate placed greater emphasis on *opportunity* over *equality*, with an average *equit* + equal* : opport** ratio of 0.482.

Diverging from the party script, GOP women speakers in the aggregate also placed a greater emphasis on *opportunity* over *freedom* (a *free* : opport** ratio of 0.824). Of the 19 speakers, only 4 (Reps. Bachmann, Granger, Ros-Lehtinen, and Wagner) stuck to the script in the sense that they emphasized *freedom* over *opportunity*, measured by their word usage.

As discussed in earlier sections, the 2012 Republican Party platform itself pays little attention to women or to barriers to women's equality. These GOP women speakers do indeed pay greater attention to women, measured by their word usage. However, they do not generally do so to advance women's rights and interests in a manner distinctive from their party's platform. For instance, Table 11.2 shows that these female speakers—like their party's platform—refer to children more than they refer to women. The *child* : wom** ratio for the platform and for the GOP women's speeches in the aggregate is greater than 1.0. Female Republicans may talk about women more than their platform does, but they talk about children to an even greater extent. This attention to children is not necessarily contrary to women's interests, but, as in the party platform, speeches concerned with children are rarely also concerned with women. Many of these speeches are about education. For example, in a speech addressing the establishment of an academic competition, Rep. Miller stated, "We can help America's schools to do more to prepare our children in the STEM fields" (February 26, 2013).

Further, like their party's platform, GOP women speakers' references to women are unlikely to identify barriers to women's equality. Instead, female Republicans appear to include women in statements that otherwise mirror their party script. For example, although Rep. Bachmann mentions women in the speech quoted below, this is while emphasizing the same importance of "freedom from" the government that the platform emphasizes:

> More than anything, I want to say thank you to the Founders of this Nation, who gave us the most incredible ride by believing in us and in our future, by recognizing that these truths are self-evident, that all men and all women are created equal, that we are endowed by our Creator with certain inalienable rights. . . . What that means to me is this: no government gave me rights that only God can give, and no government can take away the rights that only God can give. (December 9, 2014)

These analyses of *Congressional Record* items show evidence that GOP women speakers in the 113th congressional term generally stuck to their party's script. The most notable exception is Republican women's greater likelihood of mentioning women in a speech; however, this attention to women is nested within the ideological frame of their political party. On the one hand, this finding resonates with previous research showing that female legislators in right-leaning parties are unlikely to adopt the ideological frame of another party even when they diverge from their own. On the other hand, this previous research has also found that female legislators on the right have a greater propensity to advocate on behalf of women's rights and interests than their male counterparts. To some extent this advocacy must include recognition of barriers to equality, even if the solutions that these women propose are distinctive from the solutions proposed by their female counterparts on the left. In these terms, the 113th Congress showcases a low level of attention to women's rights and interests by female Republican officeholders. These speakers refer to women, but they do so within narrow ideological parameters.

Second, theories of legislative independence suggest that being in the majority party, especially in a political system with low party discipline, would enable female Republicans to diverge from their party. However, the current partisan contexts of the U.S. Congress, and that of the 113th Congress, seem instead to narrow the range within which legislators— "even" female legislators—can act.

DISCUSSION AND CONCLUSIONS

These analyses show that, in the aggregate, female Republican members of the House (2013–2014) mostly stuck to the script. This result resonates with findings reported in other chapters of this volume, which, taken together, point to the interpretation that the present-day Republican Party has either (a) crowded out potential officeholders in their party who might actively engage in advocacy for women or (b) effectively silenced actual officeholders who would otherwise engage in this advocacy. Whether it is (a) or (b), this winnowing of the Republican Party has occurred *despite* lower levels of party discipline than we see in other countries' legislatures. This suggests that the winnowing does not take place at the time when House members take office and must operate within legislative rules but rather at other stages and locations in the political process.[37]

NOTES

1. Miki Caul, "Women's Representation in Parliament: The Role of Parties," *Party Politics* 5, no. 1 (1999): 79–98; Miki Caul Kittilson, *Challenging Parties, Changing Parliaments* (Columbus: Ohio State University Press, 2006); Andrew Reynolds, "Women in the Legislatures and Executives of the World," *World Politics* 51, no. 4 (1999): 547–72.

2. See discussion in Kathleen Bratton, "Critical Mass Theory Revisited: The Behavior and Success of Token Women in State Legislatures," *Politics and Gender* 1, no. 1 (2005): 97–125.

3. Jennifer M. Piscopo, "Rethinking Descriptive Representation: Rendering Women in Legislative Debates," *Parliamentary Affairs* 64, no. 3 (2011): 448–472; Christina Xydias, "Mapping the Language of Women's Interests: Sex and Party Affiliation in the Bundestag," *Political Studies* 61, no. 2 (2013): 319–340; Christina Xydias, "Women's Rights in Germany: Generations and Gender Quotas," *Politics and Gender* 10, no. 1 (2014): 4–32.

4. See data catalogued by the Center on American Women and Politics (CAWP), http://www.cawp.rutgers.edu/facts/levels_of_office/congress.

5. On cross-national variation in party discipline, see John Carey, "Competing Principals, Political Institutions, and Party Unity in Legislative Voting," *American Journal of Political Science* 51, no. 1 (2007): 92–107; Christopher Kam, *Party Discipline and Parliamentary Politics* (Cambridge, Eng.: Cambridge University Press, 2009); Nolan McCarty, "The Hunt for Party Discipline in Congress," *American Political Science Review* 95, no. 3 (2001): 673–687.

6. Christopher Karpowitz and Tali Mendelberg, *The Silent Sex: Gender, Deliberation, and Institutions* (Princeton, NJ: Princeton University Press, 2014); Sven-Oliver Proksch and Jonathan Slapin, *The Politics of Parliamentary Debate: Parties, Rebels, and Representation* (Cambridge, Eng.: Cambridge University Press, 2014); research specifically on female legislators and debate participation includes, for example, Tracy Osborn and Jeanette Morehouse Mendez, "Speaking as Women: Women and the Use of Floor Speeches in Congress," *Journal of Women, Politics & Policy* 31, no. 1 (2010): 1–21; Piscopo, "Rethinking"; Xydias, "Women's Rights."

7. Danielle Thomsen, "Why So Few (Republican) Women? Explaining the Partisan Imbalance of Women in the U.S. Congress," *Legislative Studies Quarterly* 40, no. 2 (2015): 295–323.

8. Bernard Manin, *The Principles of Representative Government* (Cambridge, UK: Cambridge University Press, 1997), 220.

9. Proksch and Slapin, *The Politics of Parliamentary Debate*, 9; see also John Carey and Matthew Shugart, "Incentives to Cultivate a Personal Vote: A Rank Ordering of Electoral Formulas," *Electoral Studies* 14, no. 4 (1995): 417–439.

10. See Michele Swers, *The Difference Women Make: The Policy Impact of Women in Congress* (Chicago: University of Chicago Press, 2002); Michele Swers, *Women in the Club: Gender and Policy Making in the Senate* (Chicago: University of Chicago Press, 2013).

11. Thorsten Faas, "To Defect or Not to Defect? National, Institutional, and Party Group Pressures on MEPs and Their Consequences for Party Group Cohesion in the European Parliament," *European Journal of Political Research* 42, no. 6 (2003): 841–866; Yael Shomer, "Candidate Selection Procedures, Seniority, and Vote-Seeking Behavior," *Comparative Political Studies* 42, no. 7 (2009): 945–970.

12. Lyn Kathlene, "Power and Influence in State Legislative Policymaking: The Interaction of Gender and Position in Committee Hearing Debates," *American Political Science Review* 88, no. 3 (1994): 560–576; Xydias, "Women's Rights."

13. Hanna Bäck, Marc Debus, and Jochen Müller, "Who Takes the Parliamentary Floor? The Role of Gender in Speech-Making in Swedish *Riksdag*," *Political Research Quarterly* 67, no. 3 (2014): 504–518.

14. Piscopo, "Rethinking"; Ronnee Schreiber, *Righting Women: Conservative Women and American Politics* (New York: Oxford University Press, 2008); Sarah E. Wiliarty, *The CDU and the Politics of Gender in Germany* (Cambridge, Eng.: Cambridge University Press, 2010); Xydias, "Women's Rights."

15. Kira Sanbonmatsu and Kathleen Dolan, "Do Gender Stereotypes Transcend Party?" *Political Research Quarterly* 62, no. 3 (2009): 485–494.

16. Tiffany Barnes and Erin Cassese, "American Party Women: A Look at the Gender Gap within Parties," *Political Research Quarterly* 70, no. 1 (2016): 127–141.

17. These proceedings are catalogued online at https://www.congress.gov /congressional-record, the U.S. *Congressional Record*.

18. For discussions of the extent to which it is appropriate to compare party platforms (which are intended to cover a wide range of issues) with legislative speeches (which are usually focused on a specific issue), see Michael Laver, Kenneth Benoit, and John Garry, "Extracting Policy Positions from Political Texts Using Words as Data," *American Political Science Review* 97, no. 2 (2003): 311–332; Sven-Oliver Proksch and Jonathan B. Slapin, "Position Taking in European Parliament Speeches," *British Journal of Political Science* 40, no. 3 (2009): 587–611; Proksch and Slapin argue that it is preferable to examine the full set of speeches delivered within a given time period so as to avoid the bias inherent in an analysis of speeches that all address the same issue area.

19. See Xydias, "Mapping."

20. Comparative Manifesto Project codebook available online, https://manifes toproject.wzb.eu/down/documentation/codebook_MPDataset_MPDS2015a.pdf.

21. Barnes and Cassese, "American Party Women."

22. Piscopo, "Rethinking"; Xydias, "Mapping."

23. The asterisk indicates truncation, e.g., free* captures both *free* and *freedom*.

24. See Laver et al., "Extracting," and Proksch and Slapin, "Position Taking."

25. *2012 Republican Party Platform*, 36, http://www.gop.com/2012-republican -platform_home.

26. *2012 Republican Party Platform*, i.

27. *2012 Republican Party Platform*, 14.

28. *2012 Republican Party Platform*, 1.

29. *2012 Republican Party Platform*, 1.

30. *2012 Republican Party Platform*, 33.

31. Xydias, "Mapping."

32. Xydias, "Mapping," 7.

33. *2012 Republican Party Platform*, 36.

34. Piscopo, "Rethinking."

35. This total number of female Republican members of the House (20) includes Jo Ann Emerson (Missouri), who resigned at the very beginning of the 113th U.S. Congress, on January 22, 2013, to serve as president and CEO of the National Rural Electric Cooperative Association. The *Congressional Record* contains no speeches delivered or items submitted to the Extensions by Emerson in this legislative term. Because Emerson resigned so early in the term, her zero speeches/items are not included in the calculation of this average of 76. (Emerson's seat was filled by a man.)

36. Here, preprocessing refers to stemming (the deletion of word endings) and the removal of stop words (commonly used words, such as "the"); numbers; and punctuation. This makes it possible to analyze documents without the noise and volume of words with low substantive value, and it makes it more likely that words that should be treated the same (equality and equal, for example) are treated the same.

37. Another work pointing to this hypothesis is Thomsen, "Why So Few?"; Danielle Thomsen, "Ideological Moderates Won't Run: How Party Fit Matters for Partisan Polarization in Congress," *Journal of Politics* 76, no. 3 (2014): 786–797.

PART 5

Conclusion

CHAPTER 12

Republican Party Politics, Women's Electoral Fortunes, and the Myth of Gender Neutrality

Ronnee Schreiber

In 2016, Republicans commissioned the GOP Working Group on Women in the 21st-Century Workforce. Republican congresswoman Martha McSally chaired the group and said of its intent, "I grew up being told you could be whatever you want to be, but the reality is, today, women still face barriers to achieving their full potential simply because of their gender."[1] The current fate of the working group is unknown, but McSally's public declaration suggests that Republicans are eager to tackle gender discrimination. The essays in this volume demonstrate, at least in terms of electoral politics, this has not been the case.

This broad, yet coherent set of articles points to the critical importance of using gender as an analytic category. From these pages, we learn that political parties are gendered institutions, that ideological polarization cannot be fully understood without attention to its gendered effects, and that political opportunity structures are not gender neutral. We also learn that the outcome of these processes means that Republican women's influence, in terms of representation, is muted. We find some threads of hope for GOP women—moments when the Republican Party tries to "feminize" itself and when Tea Party women resist the "good ol' boys,"— but overall, for Republican women, the stories told here demonstrate the climb is steep and uphill.

Kira Sanbonmatsu opens this volume by highlighting the crossroads at which Republican women find themselves—eager to show that their party cares about women, but coming to terms with a Republican president hostile to women's issues and distinctly uninterested in promoting women to leadership positions. Subsequent chapters show that navigating these crossroads requires attention to myriad tensions created when gender, ideology, and partisan politics intersect. As the scholars presented in this collection demonstrate, Republican women, on the basis of their gendered identities, are not exempt from challenges all women face when running for office. However, they also encounter a unique set of expectations and circumstances that differ from Democratic women. Studying these differences highlights the salience of gender in political processes and the importance of considering the fate of all women active in politics. It also confirms that "gender and party categories may each derive their meanings in part from their relationship with the other"[2]—that is, in the context of electoral politics, it is critical to recognize that parties are gendered institutions.

As demonstrated throughout this collection, the relative dearth of GOP women at the state and national levels of electoral politics stems from several interrelated factors: a Republican Party culture that includes a commitment to (alleged) gender neutrality, the Republican Party's inability to cultivate opportunities and resources for women, and increasing ideological polarization among elites and the mass public. These not only shape Republican women's political fortunes, but they have implications for women's representation, widely understood. These factors and suggestions for future research are evaluated below.

REPUBLICAN PARTY CULTURE AND STRUCTURAL CHALLENGES

A consistent finding presented by the research in this volume is that the Republican Party itself hinders women's electoral representation (Cooperman and Crowder-Meyer, Deckman, Elder, Erler, Shames, Wineiger, Xydias, this volume). We learn that not only does the Republicanism of a state have a direct and negative effect on representation of Republican women in office (Erler, Elder, this volume), but the leadership is seen as an impediment. Some, such as the Tea Party activists featured by Deckman, express outright rejection by, or hostility from, the "good ol' boys" who comprise the party elite. Others, like Shames, refer to the party's inhospitable nature as "inattention," and demonstrate how "inattention" really means neglect. Whatever the evaluation, it is clear that the GOP's failure to adequately recruit, coach, and train women is significant. For Democrats, years of feminist advocacy establishing the relevance of gender identity means they have built strong PACs (Cooperman and

Crowder-Meyer, this volume), candidate training programs, and a culture where getting more women elected to office is on the table. Conversely, as several authors show here, Republican opposition to identity politics and anything that smacks of affirmative action has had a negative effect on GOP women's political fortunes (Dittmar, Shames, Xydias, Wineinger, this volume).

What is also evident is that the party's insufficient support is of concern to many Republican women (Deckman, Elder, this volume) and may shape political outcomes and women's general social and political status. For Republican women eager to overcome these hurdles, Erler's analysis is extremely disheartening. In effect, in a number of geographic locations, if Republican women want to win elective office, they must consider moving to a different region (Erler, this volume). Indeed, as she and Elder also show, the stronger the party in a state, the harder it is for Republican women to win seats and be present in positions of electoral power. The absence of pipelines, critical to helping women up and through electoral ranks, is not merely a symptom of women's lack of ambition,[3] or the potency of incumbency (Shames, this volume), but a function of the party's culture, elite behavior, and lack of development of candidates in local and primary elections (Dittmar, Elder, Erler, Shames this volume). There are symbolic attempts at recruitment, as Och documents, but the relative lack of success with efforts to "feminize" the party indicates leaders' unwillingness to address the fundamental challenges to women running for Republican seats.

What is particularly striking is that both moderates and those who are perceived to be especially conservative (e.g., Tea Party women) do not feel that Republican Party leadership takes them seriously (Deckman, this volume). And in some ways, this lack of attention makes sense. After all, it was not necessary for the Republican Party to directly woo women to win the 2016 presidential election—even when the victor was a man who bragged about sexually assaulting women. Trump garnered 53 percent of white women voters, demonstrating that at least among voters in presidential elections, party trumps gender. And with the proliferation of noncompetitive districts, neither party has electoral incentives to woo the other side.

The Republican Party's goal of being "gender neutral" (Och), then, actually results in heightened gendered effects that hinder women's representation. Tea Party women feel alienated on account of their being women (Deckman, this volume); women are not moving through the pipeline (Erler, this volume); and PACs fail to support them (Cooperman and Crowder-Meyer, this volume), demonstrating that institutional gender neutrality is a myth. So, what are Republican women to do? And why do women keep voting for, running as, and supporting Republicans?

To the first question, they should consider working more closely with conservative women's organizations and activists who have been willing to recognize the salience of gender identity in advocating for conservative causes (Deckman, this volume[4]). We know that for many women candidates, support from women's groups helps their candidacies (Cooperman and Crowder-Meyer, this volume[5]). Such groups as the conservative Independent Women's Forum (IWF) criticized the January 2017 women's marches, not because protesters challenged Trump's election, but because they did not represent all women.[6] IWF's message makes it clear that they are primed to make gendered interest claims and thus might be of service to Republican women seeking office. To the second question, Republican women ultimately support their own party because they agree with the issues for which the party advocates. This fact cannot be underestimated. While some women may aim to feminize the party (Och, this volume), many Republican women willingly tolerate sexism and the illusion of gender neutrality in the name of substantive representation.

For those who care about having more Republican women in office, prospects for immediate change are not promising. As shown throughout the narratives presented in this collection, party leaders continue to affirm their aversion to identity politics, hindering any efforts, across all levels and types of offices, to increase Republican women's electoral presence. With Republican women more likely to be challengers (Cooperman and Crowder-Meyer, Thomsen, this volume), PACs usually support Democratic women or Republican men (Cooperman and Crowder-Meyer, this volume), and Republican primary voters are less generous to Republican women (Shames, Thomsen, this volume[7]). Overall, there is a lack of competitive districts, and Republican women face incredible structural hurdles and special challenges in terms of raising money for campaigns or other aspects of being or becoming candidates. In sum, as compared to their Democratic counterparts, GOP women have less power and fewer political opportunities within their own party. These are not outcomes of a gender-neutral process.

IDEOLOGICAL POLARIZATION

By honing in on the gendered nature of partisan electoral politics, this volume highlights how ideological polarization hurts women. Much has been written on political polarization, but rarely have scholars examined its gendered implications.[8] Here we learn that, in terms of ideological polarization, moderate Republican women have become collateral damage. Fueled by siloed media,[9] divisions among elites, activists and partisans,[10] and gerrymandering (Swers, Thomsen, this volume), the election of a moderate Republican to office is becoming a rarity. As noted by several scholars here, since the mid-2000s, elected Republican women have become more conservative and are less likely to collaborate with their Democratic women counterparts (Shames, Swers, Thomsen, this volume). Confounding this, Democratic women are becoming more liberal (Swers, Thomsen, this volume). In these cases, polarization both breeds and reinforces further ideological divides. Less conservative women may not see themselves as a good fit for the Republican Party (Thomsen, this volume), which is reinforced by Republican leaders, voters, and PACs (Elder, Cooperman and Crowder-Meyer, Shames, this volume). Thus, ideological polarization does not merely manifest itself as an increase in the number of people fighting over Facebook or contentious battles over which media sources are legitimate. It obstructs women's progress, especially those who want to build bridges and cross partisan divides. Through their gendered analyses, the authors here show that ideological polarization hinders democratic progress.

What are moderate Republican women to do? Like their more conservative counterparts in the Tea Party, moderate women should form their own organizations at the grassroots and higher levels. They could work with nonpartisan women's organizations such as the League of Women Voters to partake in redistricting efforts and join forces in hospitable cities and states to recruit, train, and support other moderate Republican women (Erler, this volume). They might also consider borrowing from successful candidate-training program models that have helped Democratic women win office, such as Emerge USA.[11] These programs could serve as proxies for a party generally unwilling to promote women and might help counter the negative gendered effects of ideological polarization.

REPRESENTATION

By showing how party culture and electoral processes shape women's political influence, the scholars in this volume also add an important dimension to the study of representation. The predominant scholarship on representation in American politics examines whether elected officials can, should, or do represent their constituents. Although this is an important line of inquiry, it is limited in what it can tell us about political representation more broadly, especially when one goal, increasing women's political presence, conflicts directly with another, opposition to identity politics. A dynamic assessment of representation considers "the multiple possible actors, sites, goals and means that inform processes of substantive representation"[12] and argues for a richer and more nuanced look at the process.[13] To these ends, attention to the context in which women struggle to get elected provides us with rich data about representation and democracy.

Republican women's underrepresentation in office is not merely a numeric problem; it has symbolic and policy implications (Elder, this volume). Myriad scholars have found that increasing the number of women in office is beneficial for the promotion of women's interests. The impetus for this body of work derives from the expectation that elected women will act differently from their male colleagues and assumes that the gender of elected officials will correlate to policy priorities and goals. And many studies of elected women officials support these hypotheses and generally conclude that women can better represent other women.[14] This relationship is based on the assumption that a person who shares a social location with another is more likely to understand and support that person's interests and act accordingly. Scholars have also argued that descriptive representation can give underrepresented groups "de facto legitimacy" by allowing their members to feel as if they themselves are present in the deliberations.[15] Thus, descriptive representation can have symbolic and social implications that are critical in a representative democracy. If the goal of representative democracy is better representation widely conceived, Republican women's lack of electoral progress seriously thwarts this goal.

As found throughout these pages, the Republican Party eschews descriptive representation. Like the Tea Party women featured by Deckman and those who support GROW (Och, this volume), there are some elected women officials and activists who believe that it is important to have conservative women making political claims to give legitimacy to conservative policy goals. And, as Elder notes, Republican women might bring different perspectives to issues than their male counterparts. From a feminist perspective, the relative dearth of Republican women may be a boon for progressive issue representation. For Republicans, however, it may mean conservative women's interests get ignored (Elder, this volume). It also translates into less collaboration among women and fewer opportunities for finding common ground.

If GOP women want to increase their numbers, they must navigate the tension between the party's opposition to identity-based claims and their desire to speak as, and on behalf of, women. To do so requires a reconceptualization of identity politics in ways that might help the Republican

Party. For example, reminding the party's leadership that when women argue against abortion, they could mobilize other women to join and support a broader range of conservative organizations and causes because they are making opposition to abortion a women's issue.[16] In this way, reaching out to conservative women through gendered claims may bridge women to the Republican Party. Some conservative groups intentionally formed as women's organizations to counter feminists and make conservative movements seem more women friendly.[17] The Republican Party should take heed. With Trump's presidency generating regular and visible feminist protests, Republicans may recognize the value of gender identity as they eye the 2018 midterm elections.

CONCLUSIONS AND DIRECTIONS FOR FUTURE RESEARCH

Feminist scholars have long demonstrated that electoral behavior and outcomes cannot adequately be understood without attention to the role of women. This collection of essays goes even further to show that evaluating ideological differences is necessary to fully comprehend the gendered nature of politics. These chapters reflect the challenges Republican women face in overcoming gender biases and structural challenges to increasing their numbers and influence in office. The negative effects that occur when party culture, ideological polarization, and gendered structural opportunities intersect require that we consider Republican women's fate in a rich and multilayered context.

From the perspective of Republican women eager to run for and hold elected offices, the chapters in this volume tell a dismal tale concerning their political fortunes. But in some ways, these outcomes conform to conservative ideology. As noted, many women eschew identity politics, and if the party is focused on ideology (Wineinger, this volume), it should not matter whether women can run and win races. After all, aligning oneself with the Republican Party suggests that endorsing women's electoral success may not be a priority. Thus, to completely comprehend and assess the future of GOP women requires an investigation into why women are drawn to a conservative party that fails to recognize women's distinct needs. Why do women shun feminism or the Democratic Party in favor of Republicanism? As this volume shows, it is imperative that we do not dismiss women who are drawn to conservative politics—doing so means we fail to completely grasp electoral politics and political institutions. Generating a better understanding of right-leaning women's political behavior would reap critical data about why women are willing to focus on partisan goals at the expense of being fully represented. Additionally, while voting behavior among Republicans clearly dampens women's prospects, future research could directly probe the extent to which conservatives, especially women, would like to see more of themselves in the faces of those who speak on their behalf. While party cues trump gender when these women go to the polls, they might prefer voting for a woman if the party can convince them that it matters.

Based on the scholarship presented in this collection, prospects for Republican women are not glowing. From the perspective of a GOP woman, however, there are some avenues of hope. First, some conservative women's organizations and grassroots activists, like those who comprise the Tea Party (Deckman, this volume),[18] value gender identity as it relates to politics. Cooperman and Crowder-Meyer's chapter shows a distinct partisan gap, with Democratic women being more likely than Republican women to report encouragement and support from PACs, but they also demonstrate that some conservative activists and partisan elites recognize the value of having dedicated funding for GOP women candidates. To these ends, another line of inquiry would be to examine what role women's organizations have and could play in supporting Republican women's bids for office or working with Republican elected officials to promote women's issues. Cooperman and Crowder-Meyer show the limitations of these efforts in terms of fund-raising, but there are other strategies that might help Republican women win their bids.

In past elections, conservative women's organizations, such as Smart Girl Politics and Voices of Conservative Women, actively promoted Republican women's bids for office through social media and local organizing. Given that these groups generally represent the ideologically extreme base of the Republican Party and, thanks to polarization, also align with conservative women in office, they may eventually have more influence. Does their work shape how voters think about Republican women candidates, and might this help get them elected? As noted, Republican voters expect women to be more liberal, and conservative women themselves may not feel that their party is a good fit for them. However, as conservative women's groups become more institutionalized and a conservative women's movement grows, this could help shift how voters and the public think about conservative women candidates and thus generate more support for them.

Given that those who identify as Republicans differ among themselves on some policy issues, scholars can also explore whether distinctions among Republican women matter in terms of their viability and success as candidates. The electoral context for Republican women is clearly different from that of their Democratic counterparts. Perhaps those who identify as economic conservatives or libertarians would fare better in certain races than those who prioritize social conservative issues, such as opposition to same-sex marriage or abortion. Broadly, especially in general elections, to attract the widest range of Republican voters, candidates must balance between social and economic conservative values and policy goals. To what extent, then, do women mute ideological splits when they run for office? Might these differences factor more strongly in local or state elections as compared to national races where big tents matter more? Polarization has left moderate Republican women out in the cold, but might some fare better if they focus on, for example, economic conservativism? Or in some campaigns, targeted appeals to social conservatives might prove to be the winning strategy. To address these questions, more research is needed on how ideology, gender, and partisanship factor into local and state races. This collection provides an excellent starting point for these lines of inquiry and also demonstrates the necessity to continue pursuing them.

Another fruitful area of research would be to further assess how Republican women run their campaigns. We know that GOP women are not winning primaries and generally faring worse than Democratic women in state and national races (Dittmar, Elder, Erler, Shames, this volume). More information about how they run for office and address gendered challenges would illuminate how Republican women compensate for (or not) gender discrimination in politics. How do Republican women navigate between primary and general election expectations? Do their tactics differ from their male counterparts? To what extent does ideological polarization factor into their strategies? Do they frame their campaign pitches and ads to take polarization into account? Tea Party women invoke maternal frames; might this tactic work in campaigns, especially if Republican women can link their messages with these conservative grassroots activists? Feminist and conservative women have often referenced their identities as mothers in politics, in part because it gave, and continues to give, women legitimacy to act in the public sphere.[19] Whether this holds true for women running for office is less clear. In the 2010 congressional campaigns, most mothers who ran for office did not articulate that this was relevant to their issue positions. And those who did were more likely to lose their seats.[20] What do more recent campaigns tell us about the relative value of this kind of appeal?

Research could also pursue where feminists stand on increasing Republican women's presence in political institutions. Although feminists have advocated for the need for more women in positions of power, they have not been eager to support conservative women's bids. For example, in 2010, the feminist National Organization for Women PAC reminded its backers that "as feminists, we cannot allow right-wing candidates (not even the "mama grizzlies") to take control of Congress."[21] Given institutionalized feminist opposition, do feminists support nonpartisan efforts to increase more women in elective office? Might they be inclined to help moderate pro-choice Republican women get elected to help tame the growing tide of more right-wing women in Congress? Although feminists have valid reasons to want fewer Republicans in office, there are also good reasons for them to be concerned about men being in power and political institutions creating significant roadblocks for all women, regardless of partisan affiliation.

Finally, what effects will Trump's election and presidency have on Republican women? Will moderate Republicans continue to be marginalized? Will those GOP women who are left out seek collaboration with their Democratic counterparts to counter this administration's extremism? For now, conservative women's groups such as IWF and Concerned Women for America (CWA) are lockstep with Trump's main goals (e.g., opposition to abortion and Obamacare; backing the U.S. Supreme Court nominee Neil Gorsuch; support for a ban on people entering the country from seven predominantly Muslim countries) and thus are speaking out in favor of him. But these are ideologically conservative interest groups who benefit directly from having Republican domination over two branches of government. They work closely with Congress to move their agendas forward. The mass public, however, may not be as willing to overlook Trump's rocky attempts at governing. To this end, scholars could explore where Republican and independent women voters stand in 2018 or 2020. Will increasing partisan polarization generate a backlash from moderates?

Scholars should also follow-up with women in the Tea Party. In her chapter, Deckman tells us that many in the Tea Party did not support Trump. If he is able to enact Tea Party goals, will their views about him become more favorable? Or will his presidency mobilize them to support a different Republican candidate in 2020, or encourage them to become more active in state and local races and possibly urge Tea Party women to run? Given that Trump has sent a message that gender parity in power is not a priority (Dittmar, this volume), will Republican or Tea Party women feel the need to transform the party and its base, or will these candidates and elected officials continue to oblige masculinized behavior and issues to fit in? How Republican women candidates grapple with their own party's continuing sexist image and policy goals will also be something for scholars and activists to watch in the future.

More sanguinely, when Republican women or the Republican Party argue for feminizing the party, it demonstrates that the feminist movement has had success in making gender and women's issues matter politically. When conservatives form women's PACs, even if they are not especially viable, or when the Republican Party convenes a GOP Working Group on Women in the 21st-Century Workforce, or when Sarah Palin fights for her "mama grizzlies," feminists should take heed that they have shaped electoral and interest group politics, even if, ironically, it is in the name of helping Republican women make progress. Thus, studying GOP women reminds us of where feminism has made an impact and where there is still much to be accomplished.

NOTES

1. Alex Gangitano, "Knocking Down Barriers, McSally Style," Roll Call, July 14, 2016, http://www.rollcall.com/news/politics/mcsally-launches-working-group-on-women-in-the-workforce.

2. N. Winter, "Masculine Republicans and Feminine Democrats: Gender and Americans' Explicit and Implicit Images of the Political Parties," *Political Behavior* 32, no. 4 (2010): 587–618, 609.

3. Jennifer Lawless and Richard Fox, *It Still Takes a Candidate* (Cambridge, UK: Cambridge University Press, 2010).

4. Melissa Deckman, *Tea Party Women* (New York: NYU Press, 2016); Ronnee Schreiber, *Righting Feminism: Conservative Women and American Politics* (New York: Oxford University Press, 2012b).

5. Sue J. Carroll and Kira Sanbonmatsu, *More Women Can Run* (Oxford: Oxford University Press, 2013).

6. Carrie L. Lukas, "(Some) Women March on Washington," *Independent Women's Forum*, January 17, 2017, http://www.iwf.org/news/2802602/(Some)-Women-March-on-Washington.

7. D. C. King and R. E. Matland, "Sex and the Grand Old Party: An Experimental Investigation of the Effect of Candidate Sex on Support for a Republican Candidate," *American Politics Research* 31, no. 6 (2003): 595–612.

8. See, for example, J. Evans, "Have Americans' Social Attitudes Become More Polarized?—An Update," *Social Science Quarterly* 84, no. 1 (2003): 71–90; G. C. Jacobson, *Party Polarization in National Politics: The Electoral Connection* (Washington, D.C.: CQ Press, 2000); P. DiMaggio, J. Evans and B. Bryson, "Have Americans Social Attitudes Become More Polarized?," *American Journal of Sociology*, 102, no. 3 (1996): 690–755.

9. M. P. Fiorina, *Culture War? The Myth of a Polarized America* (New York: Pearson Longman, 2005).

10. G. C. Layman, T. M. Carsey, and J. M. Horowitz, "Party Polarization in American Politics: Characteristics, Causes, and Consequences," *Annual Review*

of *Political Science* 9 (2006): 83–110; A. Abramowitz and K. Saunders, "Why Can't We All Just Get Along? The Reality of a Polarized America," *The Forum* 3, no. 2 (2005): 1–22; Evans, "Have Americans' Social Attitudes Become More Polarized?"; Jacobson, *Party Polarization in National Politics*.

11. R. Schreiber, "She Runs, We Win," *Ms. Magazine* (Spring 2017): 28–31; Carroll and Sanbonmatsu, *More Women Can Run*.

12. Karen Celis, Sarah Child, J. Kantola, and Mona Lena Krook, "Rethinking Women's Substantive Representation," *Representation* 44, no. 2 (2008): 99–110.

13. Michael Saward, "The Representative Claim," *Contemporary Political Theory* 5, no. 3 (2006): 297–318.

14. See, for example, S. Angevine, "Representing All Women: An Analysis of Congress, Foreign Policy, and the Boundaries of Women's Surrogate Representation," *Political Research Quarterly* 70, no. 1 (2016): 98–110; D. Dodson, *The Impact of Women in Congress* (London: Oxford University Press, 2006); Michele L. Swers, *The Difference Women Make: The Policy Impact of Women in Congress* (Chicago: University of Chicago Press, 2002).

15. Jane Mansbridge, "Should Blacks Represent Blacks and Women? A Contingent 'Yes,'" *Journal of Politics* 61, no. 3 (1999): 628–657.

16. M. Rose, "Pro-Life, Pro-Women? Frame Extension in the American Anti-abortion Movement," *Journal of Women Politics and Policy* 32, no. 10 (2011): 1–27; R. Schreiber, "Injecting a Woman's Voice: Conservative Women's Organizations, Gender Consciousness, and the Expression of Women's Policy Preferences," *Sex Roles* 47, no. 7 (2002): 331–342.

17. Schreiber, *Righting Feminism*.

18. Schreiber, *Righting Feminism*.

19. Deckman, *Tea Party Women*.

20. R. Schreiber, "Mama Grizzlies Compete for Office," *New Political Science* 34, no. 4 (2012a): 549–563.

21. National Organization for Women Political Action Committee, "VOTE Today for Women's Rights!" November 2, 2010, http://salsa.wiredforchange.com /o/5996/blastContent.jsp?email_blast_KEY=87580.

Glossary of Key Terms

EQUAL RIGHTS AMENDMENT, ERA

In 1923, following the success of the Woman Suffrage campaign to get women the right to vote in the United States, one of the key leaders in that fight, Alice Paul, began the push for adding an Equal Rights Amendment (ERA) to the U.S. Constitution. The right to vote, Paul feared, would not be enough to bring true equality; women would also need equality of other rights under the Constitution. She penned the original in 1923, although it took several decades for it to gain support from the political parties. Finally, it was amended and passed by Congress in 1972. The entire text of the congressionally-approved ERA reads as follows:

Section 1. Equality of rights under the law shall not be denied or abridged by the United States or by any state on account of sex.
Section 2. The Congress shall have the power to enforce, by appropriate legislation, the provisions of this article.
Section 3. This amendment shall take effect two years after the date of ratification.

Despite its apparent simplicity and initial support from both parties, the ERA became deeply controversial by the end of the 1970s, and although it had passed Congress, it narrowly failed to obtain approval by the required three-fourths of the state legislatures. Although there are periodic attempts to get more states to pass it, the ERA has still not been ratified.[1]

FEMINISM, WAVES OF

It is common to speak of U.S. feminism as having happened in "waves," although activists and scholars often disagree on how many waves there have been and when they started and ended. Generally, the first wave is considered to be the Woman Suffrage movement, the inception of which is best marked by the 1848 Seneca Falls Convention, wherein several prominent abolitionists came together for the first major American women's rights meeting. Tying the first wave to the suffrage movement also gives us a clear ending point; this wave mostly ends in 1920 with the passage of the Nineteenth Amendment, granting women the right to vote (although Alice Paul, a first-wave leader, swiftly realigned her troops toward work on the Equal Rights Amendment after this victory). Organized feminism receded over the next several decades, although women were quite active as labor, civil rights, and other movement leaders before the second wave began.

The start date for the second wave is somewhat less clear, although historians mostly agree on a few key events that seem to have kicked off a resurgence of feminism in the United States in the 1960s (or perhaps late 1950s). First was the publication of key feminist books, especially Betty Friedan's *The Feminine Mystique* (1963) but also the translated American version of Simone de Beauvoir's *The Second Sex* (1953). Another critical set of events was the appointment of several prominent women to a President's Commission on the Status of Women (an idea suggested by the U.S. Labor Department Women's Bureau director at the time, Esther Peterson) in 1961. Eleanor Roosevelt chaired the group, and its 1963 report, "American Women," caused a great stir and led to many meetings of state commissions. At a 1966 meeting, commission delegates decided to form "an NAACP for women," leading to the creation of NOW, which became one of the major feminist organizations leading the second wave. Throughout the 1960s, 1970s, and 1980s, the second wave won major legislative and judicial battles for women's rights and brought a large group of women into elective office. Although many of the organizations continued to function into the 1990s, the failure of the ERA in 1982 seemed to signal a decline of the second wave.

The third (and perhaps fourth) wave is by far the most uncertain in terms of timing or goals, not least because many self-proclaimed third-wavers reject the label "feminist" as an identity or ideology. In the mid-1990s, young women (assisted by second-wave feminists) formed the Third Wave Foundation to advance a new form of the movement; this phase of the movement was undergirded by a postcolonial and deconstructionist turn in academic women's studies, leading to an emphasis on the many differences between women (racial, religious, sexual orientation, class, and more) and the difficulties they present for advocacy on behalf of women as a group.

PARENTAL LEAVE, EQUITABLE

Pioneered in Scandinavia, equitable parental leave describes a specific form of leave where both men and women are required to take time off to care for a newborn. For example, in Iceland, paid parental leave is a total of nine months: three months for the mother, three months for the father, and three months for either parent.[2] These rights are nontransferable, which means that the father cannot give his three months of paid parental leave to the mother. If he does not use his three months, the family will lose three months of paid benefits.

The logic behind this type of parental leave is clear: to encourage fathers to take up care responsibilities in the home that traditionally fall on women and to encourage women to return to the workforce after having a child. Together, equitable parental leave not only leads to greater gender equality in the home but also in the workplace because employers can expect both men and women to take time off work to care for children. This in turn makes workplace discrimination against mothers less likely.

PARTY POLARIZATION

If we imagine that political ideology falls along a liberal-conservative scale, the two opposite ends of that scale would be its "poles." In party "polarization," two major things happen: First, the major political parties (in the United States, the Democrats and Republicans) become more cohesive in their ideology, so it is easier to tell what each party believes (that is, there is less overlap on policy positions). Second, the parties move apart from each other, toward the opposite poles, the way that magnets facing the wrong way repel each other.

Since the mid-1990s, the United States has experienced a high degree of party polarization,[3] with the Republican Party becoming more conservative and the Democratic Party more liberal. One way to study this is to assign scores to policy positions, as Danielle Thomsen does in this volume, and calculate an average ideology score for each political candidate for both parties across time. Using this method, Thomsen finds increasing divergence since the 1990s, suggesting the parties are indeed becoming more polarized.

POLITICAL ACTION COMMITTEE (PAC)

PACs are political fund-raising committees that are sometimes organized by individual candidates but more commonly organized by outside groups not associated with any of the campaigns of candidates in a particular race. They can be organized by anyone with an interest in the outcome of the race, and they raise and spend money to either help elect or to help defeat one or more particular candidates. OpenSecrets, a nonprofit organization that tracks PAC spending, reports that "most PACs represent business, labor or ideological interests." The Federal Election Commission (FEC) regulates PAC income and spending, allowing individuals (or other individual PACs or party committees) to donate up to $5,000 each per year. PACs may spend up to $15,000 per election on any individual candidate (or donate such to any national party committee).

PACs are more regulated than "Super PACs," which do not make direct contributions to candidates or parties but instead make "independent expenditures," running ads or otherwise spending money to communicate messages with the goal of electing or defeating a particular candidate but with no connection to that candidate's own campaign. As OpenSecrets notes, as a result of a court decision in *Speechnow v. FEC* in 2010, "There are no limits or restrictions on the sources of funds that may be used for these expenditures." The amount of PAC and Super PAC money in American elections has increased exponentially in the last dozen years.[4]

POPULISM

Populism is a political movement that typically pits ordinary people against the economic or political elite. In general, populism means a return of economic and political power to the people. Populism can emerge both from the left and right. Left populist movements typically center on workers' rights and stress social justice and equality. On the right, populist movements generally focus on national identity and are anti-immigrant or antiforeigners. An example of right-wing populism is the Brexit movement in Great Britain, and Hugo Chavez's rise to power in Venezuela is an example of left-wing populism.

REPRESENTATION OF WOMEN

The idea of representation is fundamental to our modern conception of democracy, but the word can mean different things. Political theorist

Hannah Pitkin has differentiated between three types of representation: descriptive, substantive, and symbolic.[5] *Descriptive representation* refers to a representative who shares some descriptive identity with her constituents, such as gender or race.[6] *Substantive representation* refers to the substantive issues involved in the policy making rather than the people doing the representing. Men, for example, could substantively represent women's issues if they work to make policy that helps women—the research, however, suggests that, on the whole, having more descriptive representation of women also results in greater substantive representation of women. Finally, the *symbolic representation* of women highlights the role model effect of elected women: once women and girls see women as representatives, they might consider running for political office as well and become more interested in politics overall.[7]

SMITH, MARGARET CHASE

Margaret Chase Smith, a Republican from Maine, was an early pioneer and role model for women in office. She was not only the first woman to serve in both the U.S. House and Senate, but she also smashed stereotypes about the issues women could tackle in office and stood up against McCarthyism. Smith began in politics by managing the Washington office of her husband, then a member of the U.S. House, and by working for the Maine GOP party committee. When her husband fell ill in 1940, he persuaded her to run for his seat; she won, and kept on winning, serving that district for three terms. In the House, Smith served on the Armed Services Committee, and she worked to help pass a landmark bill to integrate women into the armed services. In 1948, she won election to the U.S. Senate, where she used her position to take a strong stand against the red-baiting tactics of Sen. Joseph McCarthy in a famous speech called "A Declaration of Conscience."

Throughout her more than two decades of service as a senator, Smith was known as an independent thinker and a supporter of education, civil rights, and military preparedness. In 1964, she became the first woman to seriously vie for the nomination for president by a major political party, and although she did not gather enough delegates to be a competitive candidate, it was a great symbol of women's growing influence in politics.[8]

WOMEN IN POLITICS, WORLDWIDE RANKING

Women's political representation is typically measured by the percentage of seats that women occupy in parliament. The Inter-Parliamentary

Union (IPU) has selected this data since 1997 for national parliaments across the globe. Scholars and practitioners alike consider the number of women in the lower chamber of parliament (if parliament has a dual chambers) as more significant because the lower chamber typically has greater political powers. Nevertheless, the IPU collects the number of women in both chambers across national parliaments and provides regional averages on the subject.[9]

WOMENOMICS

The term *womenomics* was coined by Kathy Matsui of Goldman Sachs, who has long advocated for raising the number of women in the Japanese workforce to address the slow economic decline. *Womenomics* is one of three pillars of Japanese prime minister Abe's economic plan to address such economic woes as a labor shortage and an economic downturn that will grow more severe because fertility rates remain low and people are aging.[10] As a result, Abe has proposed more equitable parental leave, increasing the number of day care spots available to working mothers, and increasing the number of women on corporate boards and in politics. The other two pillars are fiscal spending and radical monetary easing.

WOMEN'S ISSUES

Broadly, women's issues or interests are those that affect women because they are women. We can think of issues relating to child-rearing, such as maternal health, family leave, or education, but also reproductive issues, especially abortion. However, women are not a homogenous mass; not all women share the same interests. For example, Republican women tend to support restrictions on abortion, while Democratic women as a whole oppose restrictions.

Thus, a better way to approach women's issues is to differentiate between gendered and feminist claims.[11] Gendered claims are those that correspond closely to women in their roles as mothers and wives. For example, calls for maternal leave are gendered claims. In contrast, feminist claims refer to demands that are based on women as autonomous individuals (such as demanding equal pay for equal work).

YEAR OF THE WOMAN

In the lead-up to the 1992 congressional elections in the United States, a series of unrelated events combined to make conditions ripe for female candidates running and winning. Although there were other contributing factors, scholars point to three that were key.[12] First, redistricting following the 1990 census resulted in a large number of open seats for Congress. Second, because of the 1991 Clarence Thomas sexual harassment hearings, far more women than usual decided to run for office in 1992. This seems to be in large part because of the skeptical and dismissive way Anita Hill, a black female professor of law, was treated by the white male senators of the Judiciary Committee who questioned her on the matter. Finally, in early 1992, a number of incumbents decided to retire, and many more were tarnished following the House banking scandal (sometimes known as "Rubbergate"), where the public learned that U.S. House members were regularly allowed to overdraw their House "bank" accounts, which raised questions of ethics. Together, these events put the public in a decidedly anti-incumbent mood at the same time that a record number of female candidates were seeking office. The result was a large increase in the number of women elected to both the U.S. House and Senate (see Figure I.1 in the Introduction).

NOTES

1. More information is available from "ERA History," accessed May 30, 2017, http://www.equalrightsamendment.org/history.htm.

2. Guðný Björk Eydal and Ingólfur V. Gíslason, "Equitable Parental Leave, Country Notes," Parental Leave Network, accessed May 17, 2017, http://www.leavenetwork.org/fileadmin/Leavenetwork/Country_notes/2016/Iceland.pdf.

3. Alan Abramowitz, *The Disappearing Center: Cengaged Citizens, Polarization, and American Democracy* (New Haven, CT: Yale University Press, 2010); Sean M. Theirault, *Party Polarization in Congress* (New York: Cambridge University Press, 2008); Gary C. Jacobson, "Party Polarization in National Politics: The Electoral Connection," in *Polarized Politics: Congress and the President in a Partisan Era*, ed. Jon R. Bond and Richard Fleisher (Washington, DC: Congressional Quarterly Press, 2000), 9–30.

4. Open Secrets, "What Is a PAC?" and other pages, Center for Responsive Politics, accessed May 30, 2017. http://www.opensecrets.org.

5. Hanna Pitkin, *The Concept of Representation* (Oakland: University of California Press, 1972).

6. See also Jane Mansbridge, "Should Blacks Represent Blacks and Women Represent Women? A Contingent 'Yes,'" *Journal of Politics* 61, no. 3 (1999): 628–657.

7. See, among others, David E. Campbell and Christina Wolbrecht, "See Jane Run: Women Politicians as Role Models for Adolescents," *Journal of Politics* 68, no. 2 (2006): 233–247; Christina Wolbrecht and David E. Campbell, "Leading by Example: Female Members of Parliaments as Political Role Models," *American Journal of Political Science* 51, no. 4 (2007): 921–939.

8. U.S. House History, "Smith, Margaret Chase," History, Art, and Archives, United States House of Representatives, accessed March 30, 2017, http://history .house.gov/People/Detail/21866.

9. For more information, please visit the Web site for the IPU, accessed June 1, 2017, http://www.ipu.org/wmn-e/arc/classif010117.htm.

10. Otake Tomoko, "'Womenomics' Push Raises Suspicions for Lack of Reality," *Japan Times*, June 15, 2014, accessed May 17, 2017, http://www.japantimes .co.jp/news/2014/06/15/national/womenomics-push-raises-suspicions-lack-real ity/#.VsZmX5MrKRs.

11. Karen Celis and Sarah Childs, *Gender, Conservatism and Political Representation* (Colchester, UK: ECPR Press, 2014).

12. See Elizabeth Adell Cook, Sue Thomas, and Clyde Wilcox, eds., *The Year of the Woman: Myths and Realities* (Boulder, CO: Westview Press, 1994).

About the Editors and Contributors

EDITORS

Malliga Och, PhD, is an assistant professor of international studies at Idaho State University, Pocatello, Idaho. Previously, she was the research director of Political Parity, Hunt Alternatives in Cambridge, Massachusetts. She received her PhD from the University of Denver. She has recently joined the inaugural advisory editorial board of the *European Journal of Politics and Gender* and has published in the Women's Studies International Forum, the Huffington Post, the Conversation, and the Duck of Minerva.

Shauna L. Shames, PhD, is an assistant professor of political science at Rutgers University–Camden. She is the author of *Out of the Running: Why Millennials Reject Political Careers and Why It Matters* (NYU Press, 2017) and has also authored articles, reports, and book chapters on women as candidates, black women in politics, comparative child care policy, work/family conflict, abortion, feminism in the United States and internationally, gay and lesbian rights, and U.S. public opinion. She spent several years working in women's organizations, including the National Organization for Women, the White House Project, and the Political Parity Program of Hunt Alternatives. She received her PhD from Harvard University.

CONTRIBUTORS

Rosalyn Cooperman, PhD, is an associate professor of political science at the University of Mary Washington, Fredericksburg, Virginia. Since 2004, she has served as a principal investigator for the Convention Delegate Study (CDS), a survey of Democratic and Republican Party activists.

In 2012, the CDS research team received the Jack L. Walker Outstanding Article Award from the Political Organizations and Parties Section of the American Political Science Association.

Melody Crowder-Meyer, PhD, is an assistant professor of political science at Davidson College. She is a three-time winner of the Sophonisba Breckinridge Award from the Midwest Political Science Association, and her work has been published in outlets that include *Politics & Gender* and *Research & Politics*.

Melissa Deckman, PhD, is the Louis L. Goldstein Professor of Public Affairs at Washington College, and she chairs the board of the Public Religion Research Institute (PRRI). Her areas of specialty include religion, gender, and conservative political movements in American politics. She is the author or coauthor of more than a dozen scholarly articles and four books; her latest book, *Tea Party Women: Mama Grizzlies, Grassroots Activists, and the Changing Face of the American Right*, was published by NYU Press in 2016. She is also coauthor of *Women and Politics: Paths to Power and Political Influence* (Rowman & Littlefield, 4th ed., 2017) with Julie Dolan and Michele Swers. Her first book, *School Board Battles: The Christian Right in Local Politics*, won the American Political Science Association's Hubert Morken Award for the best work on religion and politics.

Kelly Dittmar, PhD, is an assistant professor of political science at Rutgers University–Camden and a scholar at the Center for American Women and Politics (CAWP) the Eagleton Institute of Politics at Rutgers University–New Brunswick. She is the author of *Navigating Gendered Terrain: Stereotypes and Strategy in Political Campaigns* (2015).

Laurel Elder, PhD, is a professor of political science at Hartwick College, Oneonta, New York. She is the coauthor of *The Politics of Parenthood: Causes and Consequences of the Politicization and Polarization of the American Family*, which explores how and why parenthood and the family have become politicized in contemporary U.S. politics. She is also the author of numerous scholarly articles focused on women's underrepresentation in political office and the coauthor of studies focusing on public opinion toward presidential candidates' spouses.

H. Abbie Erler, PhD, is an associate professor of political science at Kenyon College, where she has taught since 2005. She has written papers on redistricting and women's representation, term limits and fiscal policy and the president's pardon power. Her articles have appeared in such journals as *Presidential Studies Quarterly*, *Public Choice*, and *Poverty & Public Policy*. She received her PhD from Yale University.

Kira Sanbonmatsu, PhD, is a professor of political science and a senior scholar at the Center for American Women and Politics (CAWP) at the Eagleton Institute of Politics at Rutgers University, New Brunswick, New Jersey. Her research interests include gender, race/ethnicity, parties, public opinion, and state politics. Her most recent book (with Susan J. Carroll) is *More Women Can Run: Gender and Pathways to the State Legislatures* (Oxford University Press, 2013). She is the coauthor (with Susan J. Carroll and Debbie Walsh) of the CAWP report *Poised to Run: Women's Pathways to the State Legislatures* (2009). She is also the author of *Where Women Run: Gender and Party in the American States* (University of Michigan Press, 2006) and *Democrats, Republicans, and the Politics of Women's Place* (University of Michigan Press, 2002). Her articles have appeared in such journals as *American Journal of Political Science*, *Politics & Gender*, and *Party Politics*.

Ronnee Schreiber, PhD, is a professor and chair of political science at San Diego State University. She has published widely on conservative women and politics, and her book *Righting Feminism: Conservative Women and American Politics* has been reviewed extensively. Her recent projects include examining how motherhood and ideology intersect in politics, the status of conservative feminism, and how women fare in electoral politics. She received her PhD from Rutgers University.

Michele L. Swers, PhD, is a professor of American government in the Department of Government at Georgetown University. Dr. Swers's research interests include congressional elections and policy making and women and politics. She has written two books examining the policy behavior of women in Congress, *The Difference Women Make: The Policy Impact of Women in Congress* (University of Chicago Press, 2002) and *Women in the Club: Gender and Policy Making in the Senate* (University of Chicago Press, 2013). She is also a coauthor of *Women and Politics: Paths to Power and Political Influence* (Rowman & Littlefield 4th ed., 2017) with Julie Dolan and Melissa Deckman. Dr. Swers has written numerous articles and book chapters on women in Congress and women in elections as candidates and voters.

Danielle M. Thomsen, PhD, is an assistant professor of political science at Syracuse University. She is author of *Opting Out of Congress: Partisan*

Polarization and the Decline of Moderate Candidates. Her research has been published or is forthcoming in the *Journal of Politics, Legislative Studies Quarterly, Political Research Quarterly,* and *State Politics & Policy Quarterly.* She has received financial support from the National Science Foundation, the American Association of University Women, and the Dirksen Congressional Center, and she received the E.E. Schattschneider Award for the best dissertation in American politics in 2015.

Catherine Wineinger is a PhD candidate in political science at Rutgers University–New Brunswick and a graduate research assistant at the Center for American Women and Politics (CAWP). She is a 2017 Woodrow Wilson Women's Studies Fellow and has received research funding from the Dirksen Congressional Center and the Carrie Chapman Catt Center for Women and Politics at Iowa State University.

Christina Xydias, PhD, is an assistant professor of political science at Clarkson University, Potsdam, New York. She has published her work in *Political Research Quarterly* and *Politics & Gender,* among other outlets. She was the recipient of an American Political Science Association small research grant (2014) and a Carrie Chapman Catt Prize for Women and Politics (2015).

Index

The letter *f* following a page number denotes a figure; the letter *t* following a page number denotes a table.

Abe, Shinzo, 4

abortion issue, 206; Affordable Care Act and, 15; Republican lawmakers and, 200, 201, 209–211, 220–222; Republican legislative proposals and, 215–220; Tea Party movement and, 218, 219–220; as women's issue, 264. *See also* Alaska; Born-Alive Abortion Survivors Protection Act; Indiana; Oklahoma; Partial-Birth Abortion Ban Act; platform, Republican (2012); platform, Republican (2016)

Access Hollywood tape, xiii, 64, 137, 138, 141, 142

Adams, Sandy, 213, 215

Affordable Care Act (ACA), 54; abortion and, 15; Cruz, Ted, and, 63; Democratic women and creation of, 200; Medicaid expansion, 171; Republican repeal and replace goal and efforts, 60, 199–201, 216, 222, 223; Republican women critics, 12, 41–42, 56, 239, 256; Tea Party and,

59–60; Trump, Donald, and, 199; women's health and, 200, 207

Akin, Todd, 3, 17

Alabama: Republican women legislators, 143, 163; women as percent of Democrats versus Republicans in state legislature, 161t. *See also* Roby, Martha

Alaska: pro-choice legislation, 171; Republican women legislators, 143, 164–165; women as percent of Democrats versus Republicans in state legislature, 162t. *See also* Millett, Charisse; Murkowski, Lisa; Palin, Sarah

ambition, political, 176–180; discreet, 179; institutional context and, 179; progressive, 179–183; static, 179

American Recovery and Reinvestment Act (ARRA), 54

Angle, Sharron, 64

Arizona: Republican women legislators, 143; 2016 primary, 136; women as percent of Democrats versus Republicans in state

Hasson, Maggie, 140, 141, 142
Hawaii: Republican women legislators,
    143, 164; women as percent of
    Democrats versus Republicans in
    state legislature, 162t
Hayworth, Nan, 13; Project GROW
    and, 11t
Healey, Kerry, 12–13
Herrera Beutler, Jaime, 237
Hill, Anita, 8, 265
Hoeber, Amie, 137
Holding, George, 136
House of Representatives, U.S.:
    Democratic women versus
    Republican women as candidates,
    xviii (f); Democratic women
    versus Republican women as
    percentage of their caucus, xvii (f);
    DW-NOMINATE Common Space
    Ideology scores by gender and party
    1993–2016, 204f; 2016 election,
    131, 134–139, 176. *See also names
    of specific congresswomen*
Hudson, Richard, 133
Hutchison, Kay Bailey, 212, 214

Idaho: Republican women legislators,
    189; women as percent of
    Democrats versus Republicans in
    state legislature, 162t
identity politics, 102, 132, 133, 148,
    150; individualism and rejection
    of, 31–34, 249, 250; need for
    Republican reconceptualization
    of, 252–253; Republican Party
    rejection of, 7, 13, 27, 39, 69,
    102, 132, 148, 249, 250; winning
    elections and, 18. *See also* identity
    politics, Republican women and
identity politics, Republican women
    and: candidate recruitment and,
    33, 249, 250; lawmakers and, xviii,
    32–33, 37, 42; rejection of identity
    politics, 253

ideological polarization: negative
    effects on Republican women, 253.
    See also party polarization
Illinois: 1964 primary, 147; 2016
    general election, 145; 2016
    primary, 137; women as percent
    of Democrats versus Republicans
    in state legislature, 161t. *See also*
    Khouri, Tonia; Mendoza, Susanna;
    Munger, Leslie; Sanguinetti, Evelyn
immigration: Tea Party women and,
    xix, 61–62; Trump, Donald, and,
    52, 60, 69; as women's issue, 40
Independence USA PAC, 142
Independent Women's Forum (IWF),
    57; criticism of January 2017
    women's marches, 250; Trump
    agenda and, 256
Indiana: abortion legislation, 170–171;
    Romney, Mitt, win, 146; Trump,
    Donald, win, 146; 2016 election,
    145, 146; women as percent of
    Democrats versus Republicans
    in state legislature, 161t. *See
    also* Brooks, Susan W.; Crouch,
    Suzanne; McCormick, Jennifer;
    Ritz, Glenda; Walorski, Jackie
individualism, Republican Party and,
    26; rejection of identity politics,
    31–34, 249, 250
Iowa: caucuses, 147, 150; first woman
    U.S. senator, 64; women as percent
    of Democrats versus Republicans
    in state legislature, 161t, 163. *See
    also* Ernst, Joni

Jacobs, Jennifer, 58–59
Jenkins, Lynn, 42
Jindal, Bobby, 16
Johnson, Nancy, 209, 216
Jones, Christine, 136, 137

Kansas: Republican women
    legislators, 143; women as percent

Republican National Committee (RNC): approach to primaries, 10, 12, 18; female candidate mentoring, 10, 248; female candidate recruitment, 9–10, 248; outreach to diverse groups, xiii; Women's Division, 31. *See also* Republican Party

Republican Party: conservative ideology and policy priorities, 27–31; cultural constraints and women lawmakers, 27–36, 248; feminist activists, xvi; gender neutrality and, 248, 249–250; gender-neutral recruitment, 12–13, 14, 18; importance of party loyalty, 37; institutional leadership and top-down structure, 34–36, 248; political culture, 26–27; rejection of identity politics, 7, 13, 27, 39, 69, 102, 132, 148, 249, 250; repeal and replace efforts, 199–201, 223; repeal and replace goal, 60, 199–200, 216, 222; top-down structure, 26, 34–36. *See also* National Republican Congressional Committee (NRCC); Republican National Committee (RNC)

Republican Revolution of 1994, 203, 206

Republican State Leadership Committee (RSLC), 19, 133, 144. *See also* Right Women, Right Now initiative

Republican women, Tea Party women and: differences, 59, 59f, 60, 61f; similarities, 51–52, 55f, 55–56, 59, 64–68

Republican women candidates: political action committees (PACs) and, xix, 7–8, 34, 102, 104, 105, 249, 250; Republican voters and, 254; Tea Party endorsement, 39. *See also names of specific candidates*; Republican women candidates, Democratic women candidates versus

Republican women candidates, Democratic women candidates versus: number of congressional candidates, 78–80, 84, 97–98; number of incumbent congressional candidates, 80–82; primaries, xvii, 98; for U.S. House, xviii (f)

Republican women lawmakers, xiii–xiv, 7, 8, 25, 67–68, 107, 176, 201, 202, 203, 205–206; firsts, 5, 64; fundraising, 7–8, 250; influence of, 87–88; in leadership positions, 25; non–Tea Party percentage, 53f; speaking as and on behalf of women, 39–42, 44; U.S. Senate races, 8–9, 12. *See also names of specific lawmakers*; Republican women lawmakers, Democratic women lawmakers versus

Republican women lawmakers, Democratic women lawmakers versus: career ladders, 87; number of, 95, 97, 229; as percentage of their House caucus, xvii (f); representation, 159–160; reproductive healthcare policy, 86–87

Republican Women's Policy Committee (RWPC), 42–43

Republicans for Choice, 115, 116; campaign finance receipts and expenditures in 2012 and 2014, 119t; endorsement criteria and campaign funding activities in 2012 and 2014, 117t

Rhode Island, women as percent of Democrats versus Republicans in state legislature, 161t

Richards, Cecile, 87

Right Women, Right Now initiative, 18–19, 133

www.ingramcontent.com/pod-product-compliance
Lightning Source LLC
Chambersburg PA
CBHW060149280326
41932CB00012B/1691